Body and Building

Body and Building

Essays on the Changing Relation of Body and Architecture

EDITED BY **GEORGE DODDS** AND **ROBERT TAVERNOR**

The MIT Press
Cambridge, Massachusetts
London, England

First MIT Press paperback edition, 2006
© 2002 Massachusetts Institute of Technology

This book was set in Minion and Scala Sans by Graphic Composition, Inc., Athens, Georgia, and was printed and bound in the United States of America.

The publication of this book has been aided by generous grants from The Graham Foundation for Advanced Studies in the Fine Arts, and from Phyllis Lambert at the Canadian Centre for Architecture.

Library of Congress Cataloging-in-Publication Data

Body and building : essays on the changing relation of body and architecture / edited by George Dodds and Robert Tavernor.
       p.   cm.
    Written for a symposium held at the University of Pennsylvania in March 1996 in honor of Joseph Rykwert.
      Includes bibliographical references and index.
      ISBN 978-0-262-04195-9 (hc. : alk. paper) 978-0-262-54183-1 (pb. : alk. paper)
       1. Architecture—Human factors. I. Dodds, George. II. Tavernor, Robert. III. Rykwert, Joseph, 1926–

NA2542.4 .B618 2001
720—dc21

                                                    2001030604

For Joseph Rykwert on his seventy-fifth birthday

Contents

Preface

Many of the chapters in this book were written for the symposium *Body and Building*, held at the University of Pennsylvania in March 1996. It was held in honor of Joseph Rykwert, whose contribution to architecture—as a theorist, historian, and writer—has had a profound influence on how this art and science is now considered and taught. More specifically, it celebrated a double event: Joseph's seventieth birthday and the publication that spring of his book, *The Dancing Column: On Order in Architecture* (MIT Press), which is now widely acclaimed. An international group of architects, scholars, former students, and friends of Joseph converged on Philadelphia and took part in the three-day symposium. A selection of the papers presented was subsequently developed by their authors, and they have been collected here to represent the broad range of Joseph Rykwert's interests. A few additional chapters have been included to provide continuity across the two and a half millennia of Western architecture being examined. This book does not, of course, represent an exhaustive account of its theme, though many of the authors seek to make sense of the broad perspective being covered through the specific subject they have examined.

The symposium was organized by George Dodds, William Braham, and David Leatherbarrow and took place at the University of Pennsylvania in the Institute for Contemporary Art and the Graduate School of Fine Arts (GSFA). Funding for the symposium was provided by generous contributions from the Samuel H. Kress Foundation; the Canadian Centre for Architecture, Phyllis Lambert, director; the Architectural History Foundation, Victoria Newhouse, director; the GSFA, University of Pennsylvania, Malcolm Campbell, dean; and the Department of Architecture, University of Pennsylvania, David Leatherbarrow, chair. The publication of this book is funded by two grants from the Graham Foundation; the University of Bath Department of Architecture and Civil Engineering; the office of Dean Gary Hack, GSFA, University of Pennsylvania; Phyllis Lambert, the Canadian Centre for Architecture; and the George Howard Bickley Endowment, GSFA, University of Pennsylvania.

We thank Roger Conover of The MIT Press for his support of this project and Anne Engel, whose encouragement and considerable tenacity helped to shape the initial symposium as well as the form of this book.

Body and Building

1

George Baird

Introduction
"A Promise as Well as a Memory":
Toward an Intellectual Biography
of Joseph Rykwert

It is not easy to identify precisely the place of Joseph Rykwert in the international architectural academy. It is difficult even to compare him with such contemporaries and friends as John Hejduk and Colin Rowe (both recently deceased), who have taken up ideological positions in architecture and pedagogical methods in its academy that are sufficiently familiar to be recognizable even in the hands of their many protégés. The analogy that Rykwert made between buildings and the human body, which underpins the chapters in this book, is undoubtedly a powerful one. Nonetheless, one would be hard pressed to identify a Rykwert "school" in contemporary architecture, let alone a Rykwert "style," such as one can do with the approaches to design that have been associated with Rowe and Hejduk at the Cornell University and Cooper Union Schools of Architecture, respectively, over the past two or three decades.

If there is an intellectual method to be characterized as "Rykwertian," it will be one that is neither as definitively articulated nor as readily transmissible as those of such figures as Hejduk and Rowe. It is probably symptomatic of this lack of ready transmissibility of his ideas, moreover, that he has been criticized for intellectual obscurantism. In a 1973 review of *On Adam's House in Paradise*, for example, Kenneth Frampton concluded that the chief problem with the book was the author's "failure to make himself clear."[1] Contemporary architecture students often see him as an esoteric, acquired academic taste: a highly literate and historically knowledgeable figure, but not a promulgator of design ideas that will influence them as Rowe and Hejduk have done.

This view of him is, of course, a popular one, but it seems to me that it is also pragmatically and professionally narrow, not to say intellectually uninquisitive. Even on its own terms, it fails to take account of certain notable manifestations of and responses to the ongoing Rykwert project—for example, how it is that a scholar whose career has been largely

1.1

Charles M. Correa, *Mandala,* 1996.
Ink on hand-made rice paper. Gift
of the architect in honor of Joseph
Rykwert. (Architectural Archives,
University of Pennsylvania)

spent in the field of architecture should be held in such high regard outside that field. The long list of distinguished intellectuals who have followed his career with interest includes the Nobel Prize winner Elias Canetti (an important mentor for the young Rykwert) and the social philosopher and historian of ideas Ivan Illich (a close intellectual collaborator and admirer in recent years).[2]

This popular view also fails to explain how Rykwert should have developed—despite his putative failure to establish an identifiable school in contemporary architecture—a following of students of such variety and intellectual distinction as he has done.[3] Finally, and perhaps most surprising, this sometime "populist" view curiously fails to take account of the long-standing second career of this alleged esotericist as a "reviewer of furniture and fashion" in architectural and other journals. This last failure is perhaps the most curious of all, since Rykwert's second career has involved him in polemical controversy on surprisingly frequent occasions, even with architects, critics, and historians who have also been friends.

An examination of a collection of Rykwert's essays, *The Necessity of Artifice*, makes evident this little-recognized feature of his activities: two of the texts included were rejected by the sponsors who had requested them in the first place! In attempting to get beyond the conventional, esotericist characterization of Rykwert, it will be useful to examine a few of these essays more closely, beginning with the essay from the mid-1950s with which Rykwert chose to open *The Necessity of Artifice*, "Meaning in Building." It was initially commissioned by Eugen Gomringer for an anniversary issue of the *Basler Nachrichten* to commemorate the forty-fifth birthday of the design organization the Schweizer Werkbund. Given that he was unsympathetic to the minimalist, neofunctionalist policy of *Gute Form* that typified both the Werkbund and the new Hochschule für Gestaltung at Ulm at that time, Rykwert was doubtful as to the suitability of his views for such a publication, and said so when Gomringer extended the invitation to him. But Gomringer insisted, and so Rykwert went ahead and prepared his text, attacking what he saw as architects' undue "preoccupation with rational criteria" for the design process. He argued that there was instead an acute need for them to "acknowledge the emotional power of their work," and he insisted that such acknowledgment led to "investigation of a content, even of a referential content in architecture."[4] As Rykwert had suspected, these observations proved too inflammatory to be included in the commemorative publication being planned, and the essay was rejected, seeing publication instead in the Italian journal *Zodiac* in 1957.

Then, some two decades later, there is the essay on a Tate Gallery retrospective of the works of two European artists, Yves Klein and Piero Manzoni: "Two Dimensional Art for Two-Dimensional Man." It was written in 1974 for *Domus*, the Italian magazine to which

Rykwert was a regular contributor for a decade. In this case, one suspects that Rykwert's status as a sort of "London correspondent" for the Italian magazine contributed to the controversy that eventually ensued, given that this status might have led his Milanese editors to fail to anticipate the intensity of what he had to say on this particular topic. Be that as it may, the dismayed editors at *Domus* eventually refused to publish his essay. It appeared only in 1975 in another Italian journal, *Casabella*.

Distancing himself at the outset from the art world phenomenon he characterized as "full-scale canonization," Rykwert launched a comprehensive attack on the exhibition, summing it up as a "sad and squalid affair." Sketching a brief critical account of the careers of the two neo-avant-gardists to whom the show was devoted, Rykwert concluded that when all was said and done, both were only vacuous reprises of the original Duchampian avant-garde of the early twentieth century:

> There are many ways forward from the zero that was reached fifty years ago: the understanding that everything is art is perhaps the most important of them. Klein and Manzoni worked against such an understanding. In the present climate, I cannot accept the operating of the art-market in the interest of exhibitionist personalities, however charismatic, as an entertaining and harmless diversion. It is a camouflage for the sinister forces which degrade the quality of our lives, and to tolerate it means that you accept the alibi of the despoilers of our visual environment.[5]

The editors at *Domus* declined to publish Rykwert's review, even though they had supported him through another polemical controversy only a few months before. This was the occasion of the publication of his review of the Fifteenth Triennale in Milan in January 1974. This text publication embroiled Rykwert in a controversy with two of his Italian friends, the architect Aldo Rossi and the historian Manfredo Tafuri. Rossi responded to Rykwert's challenge with a sardonic reference to "servile academics and reviewers of furniture and fashion." For his part, Tafuri objected to having been quoted by Rykwert second- as opposed to first-hand.

Although it escaped the fate of editorial rejection, this text is surely among the most impassioned polemics that Rykwert ever published. "Like an ageing primadonna," he began, "every time the Triennale reappears, it seems a farewell; every Triennale, we are told by its critics, is so much worse than the others, that it must surely be the last."[6] From this initial assault, he then went on to describe the ongoing deterioration that he saw as having typified a number of recent Triennales. The Thirteenth he saw as problematically cynical, and the Fourteenth, held in 1968, as ending in "the squalor of defeat." But for him, even these, in their respective unsatisfactorinesses, were only precursors of the "waste of talent and resources of a Triennale like the present one," which he could only describe as "unbearable."

The reviewer of furniture and fashion struggled to find some components of the exhibition to admire, including a series of reconstructions of Mackintosh chairs and selections of studio pottery and jewelry. But in between these, and looming over everything else exhibited—at least for Rykwert—was the architectural presentation of the work of the Italian neorationalists or, to use Massimo Scolari's term, the Tendenza. Here I quote Rykwert on the movement in question:

> It has been coming for some time, of course. Its theoretical basis, however, was formulated recently. Manfredo Tafuri, from his splendidly isolated monastery of the Tolentini in Venice, proclaimed the death of architecture. Some time later, he modified his opinion. Aldo Rossi's competition scheme for the cemetery at Modena was another focus: a rigid arrangement of elementary geometries which still dominates the panorama (literally) in this exhibition. The conjunction was not accidental. Rossi, who heads the team which has organized the most important part of this exhibition, that concerned with "rational" architecture and the building and the city, has often and loudly proclaimed the independence, the abstraction of architecture from all ideology, and from any "redemptive" role. His is a "pure" architecture, form without utopia which at best achieves a sublime uselessness. These are Tafuri's words, his apologia for Rossi: "We will always prefer, to any mystifying attempt at decking architecture in ideological dress, the sincerity of him who has the courage to speak of its silent and irrelevant purity."

Responding to Tafuri, Rykwert concluded, "So that's it then. Architecture may stay alive as long as she stays dumb. Dumb and beautiful maybe, but dumb."

Later in the same text, Rykwert returned to Rossi's ideas in an intriguing way, this time attacking his views on the role of function in architecture, particularly in certain ancient Roman buildings. He began by quoting Rossi:

> "Indifference to functional considerations is proper to architecture: the transformation of antique buildings . . . is its sufficient proof. [This indifference] has the force of a law. . . . Transformation of amphitheaters (Arles, Coliseum, Lucca) before the transformation of the (Roman) cities, means that the greatest architectural precision—in this case that of the monument—offers the greatest functional liberty potentially."

To this, Rykwert responded:

Here is as monstrous a *petitio principii* as one could wish to find. Has Aldo Rossi only looked at ancient buildings in Canina's engravings? Has he ever thought how they were used? Or that "the architecture of the Romans was from first to last, an art of shaping space around ritual" (and I quote the most brilliant interpreter of Roman architecture of recent times, Frank E. Brown). Does he not remember from his childhood, the procession of lights and incense at the reading of the gospel? Does he not realize that he was looking at the perpetuation of a Roman civil law-court's ceremonial over 2,500 years, or thereabouts? The buildings of which he speaks, the amphitheaters, theaters, sanctuaries, baths, cannot be understood as "types" in the way he uses the word at all. They are not void forms, repeated in and out of different contexts. They are living forms, elaborated over centuries of use, and polished by it as are the pebbles in a stream.[7]

It seems to me that a few interim conclusions follow reasonably directly from the juxtaposition of these polemical controversies that Rykwert launched. First, it is surely not surprising that both Rossi and Tafuri were taken aback at the intensity of Rykwert's attack on them (even if, for reasons I will demonstrate, it is quite consistent with the basic premises of his moral and intellectual position). Second, this collection of controversies surely makes it just as evident that the familiar characterization of Rykwert as an esotericist and an obscurantist is too easy, based as it is on a reading of his works that both ignores his journalism and fails to see the manifold ways in which his "reviews of furniture and fashion," and the more complex arguments of his books, are in fact conceptually interrelated. Moreover, another conclusion—one that logically precedes the two just cited also follows—is this: a closer examination of the relationship of these three journalistic polemics may enable us to grasp some of these more complex contemporary implications of Rykwert's larger intellectual project.

To start with, we may observe that Rykwert would, in the late 1950s, oppose the "rationalist neofunctionalism" of the Ulm school and the Schweizer Werkbund (this from the perspective of 2001) may not appear surprising, given the current unfashionableness of such ideas. But this observation has to be qualified by an acknowledgment of the widespread acceptance in those years of such ideas and of Rykwert's bravery in declaring his dissent at that time—before the broad-based revival of interests in symbolism and in "referential content" in architecture that he called for did in fact arise a decade later.

By comparison, his 1974 refusal to participate in the art world "canonization" of Yves Klein and Piero Manzoni continues to look somewhat tendentious now, even if these particular artists are not currently seen as among the strongest representatives of neo-avant-gardism, which remains a subject of considerable intellectual interest and admiration. That he would launch such a vigorous attack on neo-avant-gardism only a few years after the one on neofunctionalism is further food for preliminary thought. While it might be thought that his aversion to so many modern architects' "preoccupation with rational criteria" for the design process would make him an ally of artistic neo-avant-gardism, Rykwert rejected both of these tendencies. It seems to me that an awareness of this complex, dual refusal is an early pointer in the direction of a deeper, fuller reading of his oeuvre.

Let us now turn to the most passionate, and (still today) the most controversial of these polemics: that against the Italian Rationalist architectural movement that came to be known as the Tendenza, as it presented itself at the 1974 Milan Triennale. In this case, Rykwert is least in concurrence with contemporary opinion, since the conception of typology that underpinned Rossi's characterization of the antique buildings he cited—particularly his provocative argument for a comprehensive, transhistorical disengagement of function from architectural form—continues to be a central component of the broad antifunctionalist theoretical consensus now widely accepted in advanced architectural circles. Just as Rykwert's early opposition to 1950s "neofunctionalism" does not look at all out of step today, so his opposition to the Tendenza's antifunctionalist conception of typology most assuredly does. Let us take a closer look at what was at stake in this apparently paradoxical dissent.

There are, after all, several premises of the Rationalist and Rykwertian positions in architecture that are held in common. Like the Rationalists, Rykwert has opposed the long trajectory of architectural theory in the twentieth century that has turned old-fashioned, first-generation modernist "functionalism" first into "operations research" and then eventually into the purely economic "cost-benefit analyses" that typify contemporary development pro-formas. He is equally as dismayed as the Rationalists at the powerful, parallel tendency of much architectural production in recent decades to evolve into a widespread system of consumer-oriented imagery that is increasingly difficult to distinguish from that of advertising. Indeed, if we were to add to this list of concurrences the specific subset of the second tendency, which has seen certain formal approaches to architectural design during this same period appropriated by governments and power elites for explicitly political purposes of institutional representation, then I think we could be said to have summarized a number of the key premises of the Tendenza that would have inclined a more sympathetic observer than Rykwert to have endorsed the provocative statement of Tafuri to which he instead took such dramatic exception. After all, would not many of us read Tafuri's objection to "the decking of architecture in ideological dress" and his corresponding argument in favor of its "silent and irrelevant purity" as being cogent consequences of the powerful set of premises I have just summarized? And if this is so, then it means that in attempting to come to a deeper understanding of what was at issue in this particular polemic of Rykwert, we need to move to another plane of the discourse in question.

It seems to me that his key concerns with the project of the Rationalists do not stem so much from their basic intellectual position as from their rhetorical cultural demeanor. For example, Tafuri's inclination to deliver architectural and political edicts clearly irritated Rykwert—hence his aversion to the Italian's putative "splendid isolation" and his "proclamations." Deeper still, Rykwert was obviously unable to accept that the Tendenza's objection to the same dimensions of Enlightenment rationality that troubled him led it to adopt an overall cultural stance of ironical self-reflexivity. He might have been able to go so far as to accept the idea of an architecture that was abstracted from any "redemptive" role, but once it became apparent that one of the consequences of this abstraction was that its purity would be "irrelevant," then Rykwert was bound to object. As troubled by the architectural self-reflexivity of the Tendenza as he was by the artistic one of Klein and Manzoni, Rykwert balked.

It seems to me also that it was this concern that caused him to refuse to accept Rossi's characterization of Roman buildings, notwithstanding the widespread influence that characterization has had. It is surely not insignificant that the authority Rykwert chose to cite to buttress his refutation of Rossi was the "the most brilliant interpreter of Roman architecture of recent times" (the American classical scholar Frank E. Brown) or that the citation in question unequivocally eschewed irony and self-reflexivity, insisting instead that the "architecture of the Romans was from first to last, an art of shaping space around ritual." It is equally interesting in this regard that in pursuing his critique of Rossi's conception of typology, Rykwert went directly on to amplify the conception of ritual he found so important in the writings of Brown—and the absence of which was so troubling for him in the work of the Tendenza. Surely it is in a Brownian perspective that we are meant to read Rykwert's impassioned observation on the long acculturation of form over time that sees buildings being "polished . . . as are the pebbles in a stream." Finally, Rykwert was as troubled by the declamatory representational character of the projects of the Tendenza as he was by the polemical rhetoric of its intellectual promoters—hence, I think, his acute unease with the "rigid arrangement of elementary geometries," which typified the project of Aldo Rossi for the Modena Cemetery, another focus of the exhibition.

If we look again at the emergent set of temperamental and intellectual aversions that appear thus far to typify the stance of the reviewer of furniture and fashion, we can already see that they begin to form a coherent pattern. Provisionally, I summarize them as follows: undoubtedly opposed to the positivist idea of function as a comprehensive measure of the worth of the things of the world, Rykwert is nevertheless troubled by any idea of the ultimate "uselessness" of architecture. Deeply committed to the necessity of "referential content" in architecture and design, he is at the same time wary of modalities of discourse that proceed onward from the idea of "reference" toward ironical self-reflexivity, be those discourses either avant-gardist or "rationalist." Intrigued by the original Duchampian idea that "everything is art," he is prepared to concur that nothing can be ruled out as potential raw material for art, but he is especially engaged by forms of artistic expression that eschew any preoccupation with the individual artistic signature and are instead "elaborated by centuries of use."

A significant clue to the development of this distinctive constellation of convictions can be found in the acknowledgments that appear at the beginning of the 1982 collection of Rykwert's writings, *The Necessity of Artifice*. The "two most important" of the debts that he considered himself to have incurred in his intellectual career up to that point were "to Rudolf Wittkower and Siegfried Giedion, whose wayward pupil I count myself."[8] To begin my account of this biographical trajectory, it is appropriate to ponder the intellectual obligation implied by the term "wayward pupil." There is no doubt that one of the pivotal episodes in Rykwert's intellectual formation occurred during the early 1950s, in connection with a review of Giedion's *Mechanization Takes Command* that he was then preparing for *Burlington Magazine*. That this is so is evident (among other ways) in the fact that when the 1954 review was reprinted in *Rassegna* 25 in 1986, it was accompanied by an introductory commentary by Rykwert himself. A part of it reads as follows:

> When *Mechanization Takes Command* first appeared in 1948/9 copies were hard to come by in post-war Great Britain. Benedict Nicolson, editor of the Burlington Magazine . . . obtained a copy, and knowing of my enthusiasm for Giedion's writing, asked me to review it. . . . I was an untried reviewer, and grateful to Nicolson for the confidence. It seemed to me however, that more than a mere book-review was required: sniping at Giedion had already begun, and hostility to him seemed to me to be based on a misunderstanding of his enterprise. I therefore asked if I could do an assessment of the book in the body of Giedion's work. Nicolson readily assented. Being young and insecure, I even bothered Giedion himself; in the autumn of 1952 I visited him in Doldertal, handed him my article and asked him to read it.[9]

Giedion demurred, and proposed instead that Rykwert read it aloud, to Giedion as well as to his wife, Carola, who had joined them. Rykwert nervously complied and began to read, coming eventually to a paragraph in which he commented on the distinctive intellectual method that he saw Giedion having employed in his earlier book, *Spätbarocker und*

Romantischer Klassisismus (1922). Giedion responded to this part of Rykwert's commentary with particular enthusiasm, since it had the effect, as he remarked at the time, of liberating him from the legacy of his own intellectual mentor, Heinrich Wölfflin. The passage from Rykwert's review that so gratified Giedion reads as follows:

> *Spätbarocker und Romantischer Klassisismus* was written as a doctoral thesis in Wölfflin's school, and in it the method of contrasts and of the autonomy of works of art is used, not for the refinement of connoisseurship, but almost as a weapon against itself. Giedion is concerned to demonstrate that Neoclassicism which had hitherto been considered by historians—if at all—as a style, was actually a blanket term to cover two divergent tendencies: the end of the Baroque era, and the first two decades of the Romantic movement. So that in his first work, by following Wölfflin's method Giedion inverted the achievement of Burckhardt. Where Burckhardt had demonstrated the internal unity of an epoch that had been studied fragmentarily, Giedion demonstrated this internal cleavage in a period which had been accorded an apparent unity.

In amplifying his view of this methodological breakthrough as it appeared in Giedion's *Mechanization,* Rykwert argued that it was

> achieved, not by conjuring up a string of generalizations from the familiar facts out of the usual text-books, but by a method which existed already in a somewhat more primitive form in *Space Time and Architecture;* that of fixing an apparently insignificant section of the field (keys and locks, for instance) and demonstrating in the treatment of an entirely fresh case-history the process which, allowing for differences, operates also in the rest of the field: a method which is as different from the scissors-and-paste kind of historical writing as a Picasso collage is from a Victorian scrapbook.[10]

It would appear evident from Rykwert's depiction of Giedion's method, Giedion's gratified recognition of its identification, and Rykwert's having chosen, some three decades later, to depict in such considerable detail the episode in which this occurred that a key moment in his intellectual formation had occurred.

I have concluded that such an approach is central also to Rykwert's own methodology. Moreover, one can even see encapsulated in his commentary on Giedion how his own early career comprised a series of efforts to develop a method of historical interpretation of the things of the world that would be as compelling and as revelatory as Giedion's had been in its explorations of the "apparently insignificant."

These early encounters with Giedion's thought are later paralleled in a 1967 review Rykwert wrote on Giedion's late, and very controversial, two-volume publication, *The Eternal Present* (1962, 1964). Here again we find Rykwert noting Giedion's preoccupation with the "profound changes that were taking place beneath" the surface of neoclassicism and with "the meanings below the surface ornament." In another passage in the same pair of reviews, we find him focusing on Giedion's method in *Mechanization*. According to Rykwert, Giedion succeeded in conceptualizing a historical account of

the furnishings of a room, the mechanical services of a house, and so on; he even follows the transformation in treating seriously the matter of bathing. But to Giedion the compact bathroom is only the atrophied, individual descendant of a great social institution. The Roman and the Islamic baths are perhaps familiar enough; but Giedion dwells on the function of the bath in societies which are both technically primitive and stuck with unfavourable climates, like the Scandinavian and North Russian peasants. He considers the Medieval bath and its relation to Reformation moralizing, its banishment to the well-provided home, its elaboration within a tiny scale through the development of the American hotel, and finally its part in the prefabricated service core.[11]

Here, surely, we find evidence of an intellectual and methodological lineage that links Rykwert not only to his mentor Giedion, but also to his student Robin Evans. For can we not recognize in Rykwert's characterization of Giedion's account of the "atrophied, individual descendant of a great social institution" a striking precursor of Evans's account of the sad historical emergence of functional zoning and "circulation" in domestic architecture, as he depicted it in his much-admired essay, "Figures, Doors, Passages"—a text viewed until now as an apparently purely Foucauldian one?[12]

Prior to Rykwert's fateful early encounter with Giedion, his long and wide-ranging intellectual search began when, still a secondary school student, he attended lectures by Rudolf Wittkower on "the Classical Tradition." Indeed, Wittkower proved to be a durable interest for Rykwert, for when he made a stormy departure from the Architectural Association in London some years later in 1947, he turned instead to two Wittkower seminars at the Warburg Institute—the first on the topography of Rome and the second on Raphael's *Stanze*. In retrospect, it would appear that Wittkower provided the young Rykwert with an early realization of the renewed intellectual potential of interpretative procedures in architectural history, even prior to the publication of his precedent breaking *Architectural Principles in the Age of Humanism* in 1949.

But such was Rykwert's characteristically restless methodological inquisitiveness that the encounter with Wittkower proved to be only one of an ongoing series. By 1949, for example, Rykwert had already met Giedion and soon complemented Wittkower's distinctive historical approach with Giedion's much more anthropological one. Yet this still does not complete my account of the wide-ranging intellectual search of the young Rykwert. For example, in the years immediately after the end of World War II, he spent considerable time at the Gower Street premises of the Student Christian Movement (SCM), then a center of intellectual activity for young thinkers who saw themselves as on the left politically but wished to dissociate themselves from a communism that increasingly was intellectually discredited. Rykwert met a number of individuals there who became long-standing friends, among them Elias Canetti. Older than Rykwert, Canetti had already published *Auto da Fé* in the late 1930s and was working at the time on *Crowds and Power*. Other strong influences from the SCM period are the philosopher Alasdair MacIntyre,[13] the anthropologist Fritz Steiner, and the psychoanalyst Franz Elkisch. In response to them, Rykwert not only deepened his already established interest in anthropology but also expanded it to take on that precocious modality of contemporary discourse, psychoanalysis.

A last distinct strain of contemporary thought that came to interest Rykwert was phenomenological philosophy. In 1957–1958 he was an academic visitor to the Hochschule für Gestaltung in Ulm. It was there that he wrote the now well-known essay "The Sitting Position: A Question of Method," which launched his modern analogy between buildings and the human body.[14] During his stay in Ulm, Rykwert became friends with the philosopher and sociologist Hanno Kesting (besides himself, the only other "nonrationalist" on the faculty at the time). As a result of Kesting's encouragement, Rykwert extended his reading in this area from Gabriel Marcel and Jean-Paul Sartre, with whose works he already had some familiarity, to Maurice Merleau-Ponty.

As the 1950s were drawing to a close, Rykwert's intellectual formation thus took on the coloration that is now recognizable as definitive. During those key years, an increased unification of his complex set of interests occurred. In a telling comment, Rykwert has observed that he was provoked by Canetti around this time to read Arnold van Gennep's *Rites of Passage*, just as Canetti was himself completing the manuscript of *Crowds and Power*. In a sense both deep and broad, this led Rykwert to understand that the distinctive approach he had been seeking could be to read architecture as a field of meaning.

During this period of his mature formation, Rykwert grew increasingly dissatisfied with the tenor of discussion of architecture then proceeding in London. Particularly disturbing to him was "the Picturesque Tradition," which was being promulgated during those years by a group of writers associated with the *Architectural Review*. Troubled enough by the shallowness of this tendency as it applied to British subject material, Rykwert was more disturbed when its protagonists took on Italian urban form as a topic. By this time he had become a serious Italophile, and his anthropological interests had provoked him to try to understand the ancient origins of Italian urban form. He had been surprised in this regard to discover that the most up-to-date study on the subject remained Fustel de Coulanges's *The Ancient City* from 1864.

In 1963 Rykwert's dissatisfaction with current English discourse coalesced with his growing Italophilia and the maturation of his own intellect. The result was the first version of the now-famous text, "The Idea of a Town," published that year as a special issue of *Forum,* the Dutch architectural magazine edited by Aldo van Eyck.

Continuing the critique of functionalism that had been at the heart of the essay "Meaning in Building," "The Idea of a Town" moved the argument to the plane of urbanism. Opposed to the shallow pictorialism of the picturesque tradition, Rykwert sought to identify the fundamental anthropological and psychological underpinnings of all urban form, ancient and contemporary. He noted in his first paragraph:

> Very occasionally a new town is created. We are then treated to a display of embarrassment on the part of authority and planners who seem incapable of thinking of the new town as a totality, as a pattern which carries a meaning other than commonplaces of zoning . . . or circulation. To consider it, as the ancients did, a symbolic pattern seems utterly alien and pointless. If we think of anything as "symbolic," it is of an object or action that can be taken in at a glance.[15]

Following this polemical opening, Rykwert went on to explore in detail the principles that, as far as he had been able to deduce, had underpinned the overall design of many ancient, and particularly Roman, towns, using as a key part of his evidence documentation from diverse sources on town foundation rituals. Presaging the dispute he was later to have with Tafuri and Rossi, he remarked on the origins of the foundation rite itself:

> I am not at all sure that anything so complex and at the same time so hoary and vigorous can be traced back to two or three clearly identifiable sources; it is surely a syncretic phenomenon, made up of bits originating in different parts of the world,—the whole thing growing through many centuries and altering in flavour and emphasis as the context of religious ideas in general changed and developed.[16]

1.2
Gray Reed, untitled, and undated. Gift of the architect in honor of Joseph Rykwert. (Architectural Archives, University of Pennsylvania)

1.3
Photo of Joseph Rykwert,
by Germano Facetti (c. 1955).
Private collection of J. and A.
Rykwert.

1.4
Photo of Joseph Rykwert
(photographer unknown, c. 1972).
Private collection of J. and A.
Rykwert.

1.5
Photo of Joseph Rykwert, by Anne
Engel (1995). Gift of the
photographer in honor of Joseph
Rykwert. Architectural Archives,
University of Pennsylvania.

The idea of such "a syncretic phenomenon—growing through many centuries and altering in flavour and emphasis" is surely closely related to the image of Roman architecture he framed in 1974 in opposition to Rossi. This conception of the power of cultural forms, so strongly associated with long duration, multiple authorship, and evolutional transformation, had clearly become early on a central part of Rykwert's distinctive historiography.

The editorial sponsor of the original publication of "The Idea of a Town" was Rykwert's friend and ally, van Eyck. One of the key figures in the revisionist modernist architectural movement Team Ten, van Eyck was far and away the most intellectual, the most anthropological, the most poetic member of the group. He was also among the earliest of Rykwert's admirers to sense the potential created by the combination of anthropology and contemporary psychology evinced in his work. Historical anthropology though it may be, "The Idea of a Town" also served as a contemporary rallying cry for van Eyck. In his introduction to the special issue of *Forum*, he noted,

> If we, to-day, are unable to read the entire universe and its meaning off our civic institutions as the Romans did—loss or gain—we still need to be at home in it; to interiorize it, refashion it in our own image—each for himself this time. To discover that we are no longer Romans, and yet Romans still is no small thing![17]

Commenting on Rykwert's conclusion, van Eyck saluted the combination of anthropological and psychoanalytic methods of interpretation that had appealed to him so much, and he pointed directly to Rykwert's recurrent and potent analogy of buildings with persons:

> As we read the closing paragraphs, the "ground of certainty" which our time can still neither find nor face—call it shifting centre or lost home—momentarily reveals its whereabouts. "It is no longer likely that we shall find this ground in the world the cosmologists are continuously reshaping round us, and so we must look for it" Rykwert concludes, "inside ourselves, in the constitution and structure of the human person."[18]

With the publication of "The Idea of a Town," Rykwert launched the mature approach that was to typify his entire oeuvre from then on. Indeed, he recently remarked to me that the argument of his more recent work, *The Dancing Column* (1996), is, among other things, a response to the implicit question about cosmology he had posed to himself at the end of the earlier work.

While I will not discuss that text, in timely celebration of which the festschrift in his honor was convened, I will conclude with a series of observations on the two major texts that Rykwert published in the years between: *On Adam's House in Paradise* (1972) and *The First Moderns* (1980). In doing so, I strive to elucidate the ways they manifest the characteristic historiographical methods I have attributed to him thus far.

On Adam's House in Paradise, like "The Idea of a Town," was first published on mainland Europe rather than in Rykwert's home base, Britain, by a sponsor who was also a personal friend. The place of publication was Milan, and the friend was Roberto Calasso, the editorial director of Adelphi, to whom, together with his wife, *Adam's House* was dedicated. Even as late as 1972, British intellectuals evidently still did not take Rykwert as seriously as continental ones did. Then too, this Milanese episode is a direct extension of his long relationship with Italy. Even his first encounter with Siegfried Giedion in 1949 had an Italian venue, the Eighth Meeting of the International Congress of Modern Architecture, being held in Bergamo. At this same event, he also made the acquaintance of the young Italian architect who was to become a lifelong friend, Vittorio Gregotti.

Rykwert saw the English architectural scene as typically looking to Scandinavia for inspiration. He looked instead to Italy. Having worked for two years in the London offices of Fry Drew and Partners, and Richard Sheppard, he found himself more interested in the work of Persico and Pagano, Figini and Pollini, Gardella, Albini and BBPR, than he was in that of his London employers and their local contemporaries. Together with John Turner (with whom he had traveled to Bergamo in 1949), he even contemplated in those years a joint project to write a book on modern Italian architecture. So admiring was he of Ernesto Rogers that he even hoped to write for Rogers's magazine, *Casabella.* He did, in fact, eventually meet Rogers, but despite his admiration and his own journalistic inclinations, he never struck a chord with Rogers sufficiently strong to be invited to write for him. Unexpectedly, he did strike such a chord with Gio Ponti. As a result, he became the correspondent for *Domus,* where his two controversial texts from 1974 and 1975 were published. Rykwert's interests in Italy and anthropology also led him to spend the summers of 1962 and 1963 working in Rome with Frank E. Brown on his archaeological studies of the Forum. Indeed, it was on one of these trips to Rome that he attended a dinner party that happened to be attended also by Roberto Calasso.

The intellectual bond forged between the revisionist Londoner and the Italian who went on to write *The Ruin of Kasch* (1994) was evidently a powerful one, for clearly, the two shared a number of intellectual inclinations. Among these are a skepticism with regard to the supposed cultural superiority of modernity as a project, as compared with its European historical predecessors, a keen curiosity as to the revelatory potential of comparisons of historical and literary phenomena from non-European cultures, and a disinclination to privilege any one art form—or, for that matter, any one form of knowledge—over any other.

On Adam's House in Paradise begins with a provocative quotation from René Daumal: "In order to return to the source, one is obliged to travel upstream."[19] Faithfully following this injunction, Rykwert took as his theme the curiously insistent and morally compelling idea of the origin of architecture. He explained first the extent to which such an apparently anachronistic idea has preoccupied some of the most notable of twentieth-century architects and then traced the complex lineage of the idea back through the centuries to antiquity.

Documenting the surprising hold this idea has had on such notable figures as Le Corbusier, Adolf Loos, and Frank Lloyd Wright, Rykwert then demonstrated how each had considered the idea within a frame of reference derived (consciously or not) from debates that had taken place among European historians of the preceding generation, including the German historian and theorist Gottfried Semper and his most assiduous critic, Alois Riegl. Working his way back from Riegl and Semper through the writings of Viollet-le-Duc, Pugin, and Quatremère de Quincy, Rykwert proceeded to an account of a controversial figure of the early nineteenth century, Jean-Nicolas-Louis Durand, whose thought, he argued, had been framed in conscious opposition to that of Marc-Antoine Laugier. At the beginning of chapter 5, Rykwert arrived at a point where, in his words, "I cannot avoid a discussion of the text which all the writers I have quoted are forced to allude, and which must be regarded as the source of all the later speculations about the primitive hut: that of Vitruvius on the origins of architecture."[20]

Following an explanation of the influence of Vitruvian thought on fifteenth- and sixteenth-century Italian writers on architecture, especially Alberti, Palladio, and Filarete, Rykwert turned his attention to one of the two profoundly deeply rooted images of the "first building" as it has long been imaged in Western thought. Minimally documented historically but of great importance for cultural thought and religious practice, the "first building" in question was the ancient Temple of Solomon in Jerusalem. Having demonstrated the extraordinary significance of this building for generations of Western clerics, historians, and architects, Rykwert described the intensive efforts made by a group of them between the sixteenth and the eighteenth centuries to devise a convincing reconstruction of the temple, one that would be compelling both as a project of contemporary archaeology as well as of durable religious conviction. Especially notable among those whose efforts are described are the sixteenth-century Jesuit scholar Juan Bautista Villalpando and the eighteenth-century Austrian architect Johann Bernhard Fischer von Erlach.

At the end of his "upstream" historical account, Rykwert turned to more anthropological matters. Chapters entitled "The Rites" and "A House for the Soul" make explicit what had been up to that point in his argument only a subtext: the sheer psychological, not to say ontological, urgency of the origin of architecture in Western European thought. It is no wonder then that Ernst Gombrich saw Rykwert in *On Adam's House in Paradise* as having adopted "the methods of the psychoanalyst."[21] For all this, Rykwert never saw his project as a Platonic or a transcendental conception. Rather, he observed, "An object which has always been lost cannot—in any ordinary sense of the word—be remembered. The memory of which we speak, however, is not quite of an object but of a state—of something that was; and of something that was done, was made: an action. It is a collective memory kept alive within groups by legends and rituals."[22]

If Rykwert's method in *On Adam's House in Paradise* can be seen as a psychoanalytic and diachronic section through history, then that of his next major text was an equally ambitious, complementary one. *The First Moderns* (1980) seeks to isolate a specific, synchronic layer of the history of ideas, this one being the intellectual and psychological prehistory of what we now think of in the broadest sense as "modernism" in architecture.

The period during which this layer is formed is the eighteenth century. Thus, Rykwert's account focuses on arguments put forward by a diverse group of writers stretching from Claude Perrault at the end of the seventeenth century to Jean-Nicolas-Louis Durand at the beginning of the nineteenth. And as his account makes clear, the psychological anxiety about architecture that first manifests itself during those years still marks the substratum of what we think today.

Rykwert returned to a theme Giedion had explored in his *Spätbarocker und Romantischer Klassismus* and began with an etymological account of the differences between the terms *classic* and *neoclassic* in accepted architectural history, quickly making it clear once again how labile the term *neoclassic* really is as a means of description and analysis. Indeed, reading *The First Moderns* as a coded account of the dilemmas concerning thoughtful architects today, in attempting to retheorize their praxis, one cannot help but see it as a Giedionesque effort to bring the unacknowledged subconscious of contemporary theory in architecture directly to the forefront of conscious understanding.

Rykwert used the project of reconstruction of the Temple of Solomon, one of the key themes of *On Adam's House in Paradise,* again in *The First Moderns* to launch a commentary on the complex series of disorienting revisionisms that typify the theory of architecture in the century and a half to follow. He cited the work of Fréart de Chambray, but only to set the stage for the revolutionary ideas of Claude Perrault, who, in his influential translations of Vitruvius of 1674 and 1684 and his *Ordonnance de cinq espèces de colonnes* of 1683, laid down challenges to European architects that haunt them still. Arguing that ancient precedent was no longer a sufficient guide for contemporary practice, Perrault put forward two new categories of "beauty," characterized as "positive" on the one hand and "arbitrary" on the other. Rykwert then used the disorientation caused by Perrault's intervention to characterize the anxious quest for a new ground of architectural certainty by some, and the frivolous but equally anxious play engaged in by others, in a series of episodes of style, theory, and polemic in architecture that typify the century and a half to follow.

The particular, relativist, and playful "orientalist" episode of chinoiserie is tabled, only to be set against an anxious new quest for a so-called universal architecture. But this effort at an ontological reconstruction is challenged in its turn by experiments described under the rubric of the "pleasures of freedom," including work of the painter François Boucher and, especially, the architects Juste-Aurèle Meissonier in France and Vanbrugh and Hawksmoor in England. Finally, the last stage of these parallel eighteenth-century trajectories is what Rykwert calls a "return to earnestness," typified in France by Servandoni's project for St. Sulpice and in Britain by the later eighteenth-century work of the new "Palladians," Colen Campbell and William Kent.

And if this oscillation is not disorienting enough, it is followed by a pragmatic new philistinism at the beginning of the nineteenth century in the vastly influential work of Durand. Although Rykwert shows this to be a decisive conclusion to the vast synchronic portrayal of anxiety of the eighteenth century, Durand's new instrumentality is nonetheless not permitted to have the last word. In his conclusion, Rykwert takes considerable pains to refute it:

> Seen from the vantage point of the 1970's and 1980's, Durand's positive dismissal of the problems which engaged and worried seventeenth- and eighteenth-century architects does not seem quite final. The nature of our responses to the world of artifacts, the way in which groups and communities appropriate space, occupies sociologists and anthropologists, and we acknowledge these human scientists as important and wholly serious people. Yet their studies are, in the last reduction, almost inevitably about problems of form. . . .
>
> Perhaps, if there is a place for the architect's work within a future social fabric, he will have to learn how to deal with such problems again.[23]

I will not here propose any analysis of *The Dancing Column,* but will instead essay a few provisional conclusions with respect to the intellectual influences that I see as contributing seminally to his intellectual formation, as well as to the structure of his typical methods, as I have been able to identify them.

Rykwert began with an intense interest in the new potentials of historical analysis in architecture as they were pioneered by Rudolf Wittkower in the late 1940s, and then went on to complement this interest with equally intense ones in the potentials of anthropology, archaeology, psychoanalysis, and phenomenological philosophy. It seems to me that it is in a complex hybrid of archaeology and psychoanalysis that we can delineate most aptly an image of the method that he was eventually able to formulate for himself, on the model of the one of Siegfried Giedion that he admired. These two disciplines have in common a method that always looks below the ostensible surface of things in an attempt to derive significance from that which lies beneath. What is more, both archaeology and psychoanalysis share with anthropology a manifest interest only in an indirect relationship of cultural production to individual authorship.

It may by now go without saying that Rykwert shares in a generally understood episteme of our era that I call Foucauldian. That is, like most of his contemporaries, he has lost confidence in the efficacy or legitimacy of grand intellectual systems or systematic social or historical projects. By the same token, he is of a generation that abandoned teleological notions of progress in history and has particularly eschewed any interest in the once apparently potent forms of instrumentality in human affairs.

All this having been said, Rykwert's oeuvre, given the formulation of his characteristic method described above, has nevertheless been deeply marked by his conviction as to the power of the subconscious in history—in some respects, even of a subconscious that in some sense is collective. What is more, there is no doubt that he is also convinced of the powerful cause-and-effect relationship produced by that subconscious in the broad playing out of human events across time.

Thus, although his view of the sheer stuff of history is neither teleological nor deterministic, I think he sees it as possessing an apparently intractable density and thickness that commands the sustained attention and curiosity of the engaged intellectual. Indeed, I would be inclined to argue that it has been his lifelong intellectual project to employ the distinctive analytic methods he has devised, to bring to the conscious awareness of his contemporaries, the implications and potential consequences of the assumptions lying within the beliefs, social forms, and artifacts that form their horizon of existence, however individualized or however collective those forms may at first seem to be.

What is more, it seems to me clear that he sees those beliefs and forms as themselves being the product of a complex formation, as he put it, "altering in flavour and emphasis as the context of . . . ideas changed" and "polished by [centuries of use] as [are] the pebbles in a stream." Given this, and given the relatively modest roles particular individuals in history will have been able to play in their evolution, we may understand that the techniques of interpretation required to elucidate their significance will require a Rykwertian ellipsis. But this having been said, it will also be true that while not straightforward, such techniques will surely also be neither self-reflexive nor ironical.

Notwithstanding the difficulties of the tasks his methods have been formulated to address, it surely remains a matter for admiration that Rykwert continues to hold such high hopes for the project of architectural design in human affairs, Indeed, it can be said that he sees the relationship of interpreting to designing to be not only possible but even ontologically urgent. If, for Rykwert, it remains as true as it ever was that the project of architecture is to create a "house for the soul," then his intriguingly McLuanesque sympathy for the avant-garde conviction that "everything is art" (for him, it is admittedly only potentially so) comes to be understandable. For, in these terms, it is surely impossible ever to be able to determine in advance what the limits of any tectonic accommodation of the "soul" might be. Hence his keen curiosity in regard to the range of manifestations of creative activity extant in the world, furniture and fashion among them.

If this effort at a provisional delineation of Rykwert's historiography has succeeded in some measure, then it seems to me also that it can explain the absence of an obviously Rykwertian school in contemporary architecture or history. After all, the central analytic focus of his research is (speaking almost archaeologically) several levels below the operative layer within which most cultural and, even more particularly, design praxes have been promulgated by such contemporaries as Hejduk and Rowe. Indeed, Rykwert's distinct, intense, long-standing engagement with the long acculturation of architectural forms, coupled with his decidedly lesser curiosity with respect to the signature of the individual designer, make it clear that such readily visible praxes would not have been an appropriate result of his methodology in any event.[24] It seems to me instead that the Rykwertian school will surely lie for some indeterminate period of time largely operationally invisible, obscured in that very phenomenological thickness of history that I have called the central focus of his personal historiographical project. Only at some future historical moment will its effects be able to be clearly discerned.

In the end, it is for me the intensity of Rykwert's engagement with the sheer phenomenological thickness and historical embeddedness of reality that is so exhilarating. How astute it is of his Italian colleague Gregotti, at the end of this book, to label him "an anthropologist of architectural history." There is no doubt that Rykwert's own oeuvre, like so many of the complex historical phenomena that have been the subject of his interpretative projects over the years, indeed constitutes "a promise as well as a memory."

Introduction to the Chapters

The chapters in this book, written and compiled in honor of Rykwert, can be organized into three broad groups. The first three focus on embodiment and on revisionist readings of architectural and other artifacts from the ancient world. These are followed by a group that looks at a series of cultural products across Europe between the fifteenth and the eighteenth centuries: paintings, buildings, sculpture, fortifications, and texts. The last group studies a wide series of contemporary phenomena, both social and cultural.

In "The Architectonics of Embodiment," Dalibor Vesely reviews concepts of the body in pre-Platonic philosophy, before giving an account of that philosopher's own reading as a "process of ordering." He demurs at Vitruvius's characterization, arguing that the primary tradition of the body (and for that matter of "embodiment" itself) has not been a Vitruvian one. This leads him to a phenomenological and a hermeneutic characterization: "Together they suggest a fusion of horizons in which the nature of the human body, and its relation to architecture and to the rest of reality, changes into one of embodiment and its structure." Reviewing a series of interpretations of both the body and proportion, Vesely argues that even proportion must be seen as a "deeper level of articulation of the world as a whole."

In "Greek Temple and Greek Brain," John Onians develops a hypothesis regarding the manner of looking at temples, which for him must have been operative in the ancient world. Developing his argument in considerable detail, Onians makes a case that contemporaries would have been likely to see Greek temples as, among other things, phalanxes of warriors. Pursuing his hypothesis, he argues that the Doric temple would be read as a phalanx of land-based warriors and the Ionic as a naval one.

Mark Wilson Jones begins "Doric Figuration" by citing a turn-of-the-century observation of Otto Wagner to the effect that architectural forms always arise from constructional considerations. He then seeks to refute this claim definitively in arguing that ritual, as formulated by Rykwert, is actually a far more powerful generator of form than construction. To demonstrate this, Wilson Jones pursues an argument regarding the characteristic triglyph of the frieze of the Doric temple. Downplaying other scholars' "constructional" readings of its formation, Wilson Jones proposes instead that it can be seen as derived from the form of the tripod cauldron, so central to many ancient religious rituals.

In the first of the second group of essays, Robert Tavernor undertakes a close reading of Piero della Francesca's painting *The Flagellation of Christ*. Arguing for its status as a definitive representation of bodily perfection, he explains how the construction of the space of the painting is a complex hybrid of emergent systems of proportion and perspective. He concludes that Piero's methods have the effect of creating a figure equally Christian and

Vitruvian. In her "Figural Ornament in Italian Renaissance Architecture," Alina Payne begins by speculating on the surprising fact that the sculptural program of architecture in Renaissance Italy is nowhere theorized in contemporary treatises. Nor, she observes, is it much interpreted in modern scholarship. Attributing this last fact to modernist art historical biases against ornament, she then sets herself the task of retrospectively theorizing this extensive Renaissance practice. Simon Pepper follows Payne with an account of a series of commentaries on fortifications and the treatises to which they relate, from Francesco di Giorgio Martini to Filarete. Showing how the image of the human body suffused even the most militaristic of architectural and urban forms during this period, Pepper accounts for a range of examples throughout the Mediterranean, including the Ottoman Empire.

Harry Mallgrave and then Vaughan Hart move the discussion from southern to northern Europe and Britain. Tracing the gradual influence of Italian precedent through Germany and the Low Countries, Mallgrave shows how the strong, extant cultural context of the Gothic in which artists like Vredeman de Vries, Dietterlin, and even Rubens were working, together with the significantly lesser commitment to fastidious correctness operative in northern Europe, led to a robust corporeality in their paintings, engravings, and buildings that often surpasses the work of the southerners they ostensibly emulate. Hart takes up the topic of the "Stuart Legal Body," in Britain in the seventeenth century, showing how, in Inigo Jones's Banqueting Hall, a quite explicit analogy was drawn between the "column" and the perfect body of the king. Hart proposes that one of the purposes of this corporealism was to reinforce royal power in a period of political instability.

Karsten Harries then contemplates a theme prompted by his personal experience of the Roman Pantheon. He begins by citing observations of Vitruvius that associate human verticality with the "starry firmament"—and, by implication, horizontality with sleep or death. Harries states, "The Roman Pantheon, whose one great eye opens its body to the starry firmament, invites interpretation as an attempt to raise this Vitruvian insight into the verticality of human beings to the level of great architecture." He qualifies the status of "sublime" verticality in a commentary on a series of later projects. First is a group of directly related utopian proposals by Ledoux, Vaudoyer, and Boullée. A more elliptically related group includes ones by van Doesburg and Le Corbusier. In all of these cases, he sees the ambition of the designers to deny gravity, and thus to privilege the sublime over more intimate, corporeal human considerations. In the end, Harries argues the necessity to join the vertical—the sublime—with the horizontal—the earthbound.

In the concluding essay in this section, Alberto Pérez-Gómez takes up the topic of Charles-Etienne Briseux, the late eighteenth-century architectural theorist who sought to employ the musical theories of his contemporary and friend Jean-Philippe Rameau to refute the influential arguments of Claude Perrault. Pérez-Gómez makes the argument that in seeking to refute the problematic relativism of Perrault's construction of "positive" and "arbitrary" beauty in architecture, Briseux nonetheless participates in a further instrumentalization of architectural theory.

The final series of chapters deals with a broad range of contemporary topics. Richard Sennett's "The Foreigner" begins with a short account of the poles of home and exile in Oedipus Rex and of the two "scars" that make up Oedipus's psyche. Having set the stage, Sennett gives an account of the rise of nativism as a newly aggressive self-declaration on the part of numerous social groups in the romantic era in Europe, after 1848. He concludes by radically qualifying the claims of nativism, using as his exemplars the two nineteenth-century figures of Edouard Manet, the painter, and Alexander Herzen, the writer. He ascribes to them both a subtle dialectical stance that balances exile carefully against the freedom that is its unanticipated reward.

Neil Leach follows Sennett with a companion argument to Tavernor's. Here, instead of the conflation of Vitruvian and Christian motifs in painting, we see the appropriation of the image of the ideal Vitruvian man into that of Christ crucified. Leach extends the theoretical reach of his text to explore a post-Freudian, and then a poststructuralist, set of themes focusing on the death instinct. Offering a culturally affirmative reading of the myth of Narcissus, Leach suggests that even narcissism can in part be read as a process of identification with the other that leads to the creation of beauty. In her chapter on the insufficiently discussed Bauhaus teacher Oskar Schlemmer, Marcia F. Feuerstein takes up Rykwert's famous characterization of the "dark side" of that now canonical institution. Opposing Schlemmer both to Walter Gropius's and Herbert Bayer's "rationalism" and to Johannes Itten's "mysticism," Feuerstein makes a case for the cogency of Schlemmer's distinctive hybrid of costume theory and body type. She argues that his position was a bold plea for "openness, incompleteness and playfulness."

George Dodds undertakes a very close reading of Carlo Scarpa's Brion Cemetery to make manifest two themes in that project. First is what he sees as a powerful corporeality, especially as focused on the female body, and second is a structured orchestration of visibility of particular long landscape views. Both these themes, Dodds argues, can be tracked in Scarpa's own sustained personal interpretation of paintings of the school of Venice over several centuries. Marco Frascari follows Dodds with an account of the employment of the body image in the design method of the Italian architect Valeriano Pastor, a student and protégé of Scarpa. Employing a series of Pastor's own architectural drawings, Frascari argues the possibility of demonstrating a transmissible method for the incorporation of the body image in contemporary architectural projects.

David Leatherbarrow begins his account, "Sitting in the City, or The Body in the World," with a critical comparison of Frank Lloyd Wright's and Adolf Loos's respective ideas of the appropriate role of the domestic interior in architecture. Having readily set Loos's well-known critique of the *Gesamtkunstwerk*—the total artwork—against Wright's more favorable position, Leatherbarrow explores the ideas of two less well-known polemicists on this topic, Josef Frank and Rudolf Schindler, an exploration rendered more intriguing still by the facts of Schindler's own Viennese background, as well as his early collaborations with Wright himself. In his account of Frank's and Schindler's subtly modulated contributions to this discourse, Leatherbarrow amplifies an unexpected perspective of the body in the world.

William Braham and Paul Emmons address the topic of posture in relation to two highly rhetorical examples of gymnasia: John Russell Pope's 1932 Payne Whitney Gymnasium at Yale University and the ubiquitous contemporary phenomenon of the Bally Fitness Centre. They set their argument in a sharply contemporary context by juxtaposing it to the ambition manifested by such contemporary figures as Greg Lynn to use the computer literally to "animate" an architecture bodily in a fashion not hitherto possible. Kenneth Frampton concludes this group of chapters with an account of the theme of corporeality in the work of Tadao Ando. Frampton notes the extent to which Ando attempts to emphasize bodily, as opposed to semantic meanings in architecture, as well as the extent to which the Corbusian *promenade architecturale* is reinterpreted as ritual in that work. Finally, Frampton strongly endorses Ando's expressed conviction that architecture today needs to be appropriated in a less visual and much more tactile manner.

The book concludes with a tribute to Rykwert by his colleague of long standing, Vittorio Gregotti, who so insightfully named the figure in whose honor these essays have been prepared "an anthropologist of architectural history." I think it is clear from my account of Rykwert's intellectual formation how widely beyond architecture his own intellectual interests have ranged. It is a fitting form of tribute back to him, that his influence and inspiration have provoked such a diverse range of intellectual explorations as the chapters in this book.

2

Dalibor Vesely

The Architectonics of Embodiment

The relation of the body to architecture and the complex phenomenon of corporeality has always had a privileged position within the history of European culture. This is particularly true of the tradition springing from Vitruvius, who compares the human body directly to the body of a building (in book III, chapter 1 of *De architectura*), and then makes a sequence of claims for this analogy that far transcend the need to explain the meaning of proportion, symmetry, and harmony in architecture. Although this highly provocative subject has been treated with great attention and subtlety by critics, it remains nonetheless poorly understood.

The Notion of Body

The most critical aspect of the role of the body in understanding reality is the relation between the body and that which truly exists. It was raised originally by the Eleatics (Parmenides and Melissos), who sought to define that which must be homogeneous, and therefore exists without a body. Their definitions led to a reaction by such fifth-century thinkers as Gorgias of Leontini,[1] the Atomists (Leukippos and Demokritos),[2] and the Pythagoreans (such as Ekphantus).[3] Thereafter, the body is used to designate not only conceptual but also material reality. Plato, followed by Aristotle, took the decisive step toward a coherent understanding of corporeality. The body for Plato is not a given or something that can be isolated or defined as an entity; rather, it is part of a process of ordering within the domain of necessity. This process is never complete and is always open to further improvement through the continuous reciprocity of necessity and reason.[4] As a result, the body appears as a relatively stable structure ordered in the context of reality as a whole (*cosmos*). The openness of the ordering process speaks not only about the contingency of the world but also about the contingent nature of the body. Contingency in this case stems from the tension between the conditions and possibilities of what is perceived as the cosmological process itself.[5]

Aristotle's contribution to the understanding of corporeality has much to do with his emphasis on the individualization of *eidos*, on the particularity of the essential structure of things or bodies and their substance, *ousia*. That only particular substances are self-subsistent does not mean, of course, that they are the only substances that exist. Aristotle insists that there can be no action without contact, and from that he deduced not only the importance of contact but also of position, existence in place, lightness, and weight.[6] This brought his vision of corporeality dangerously close to the later Stoic doctrine in which everything that either acts or is acted upon is a body; in other words, the only things that truly exist are material bodies. Aristotle himself had feared that if the existence of immaterial substances ever came to be doubted, physics, and not metaphysics, would be considered the first science. In the Stoic manner of thought, this is exactly what has happened: the notion of material body extended not only to the human body but also to the human soul, *pneuma*. The Stoics believed that "nothing can act or be acted upon without body nor can anything create space except the void and emptiness. Therefore beside void and bodies there can be no third nature of itself in the sum of things."[7] This led inevitably to the conclusion that even the soul and the divine are corporeal.[8] On this basis it became possible to read the meanings traditionally associated with the incorporeal nature of the soul directly into the visible manifestation of the body. It was under the influence of this radicalized, and in a certain sense distorted, Aristotelian understanding of corporeality that the Vitruvian doctrine of the body came into existence. In the Vitruvian understanding of corporeality, which was strongly influenced by Stoic philosophy (Posidonios), the relation of body and soul was no longer clear.

The Vitruvian tradition was strongly influenced by the general reification of the inherited classical culture as manifested in eclectic commentaries and encyclopedic treatises during the first century B.C. The consequences of this influence are evident in the need for elaborate commentaries on Vitruvius after he was "rediscovered" in the fifteenth century and in the inconclusive attempts to understand areas of implied or potential meaning that nonetheless remained enigmatic. It was difficult to understand the meaning of the text as long as its reading followed the same assumptions on which the original text itself was based. An additional reason for the difficulty in seeing the problematic and derivative nature of Vitruvianism was the uncritical acceptance of the ancient authority of the text, combined with a concern to support the new author's own position.[9]

There is good reason to believe that creative architectural thinking is possible only in collaboration with other disciplines, such as philosophy, astronomy, music, geometry, and rhetoric. Otherwise the difficult formulations that we find so often in architectural treatises remain enigmatic and often controversial. The exceptions are those commentaries that broke the orthodoxy of dogmatic thinking by moving into more distant areas of culture. A good example is Guarino Guarini's *Architettura Civile,* which, without his *Placita Philosophica* and other philosophical and scientific writings, would be regarded as no more than a dogmatic technical treatise that is difficult to comprehend. It seems appropriate, therefore, to view Vitruvianism as a secondary tradition—one that is not only derivative but also has a tendency to dogmatism that obscures the "primary tradition," alive until recently in a more or less uninterrupted continuity.

Body and Microcosm

In the primary tradition that goes back to Plato and Aristotle, and remained alive until recent times, the body is always seen as linked with the soul, which in turn is related to the animated structure of reality as a whole. In a discussion of the "generation of bodies" in *Timaeus,* Plato explains:

> The revolutions which are two and are bound within a sphere, shaping body in imitation of the spherical form of the all, which body we now call head, it being the most divine part and reigning over all the parts within us. To it the gods delivered over the whole of the body, which they had assembled to be its servant, having formed the notion that it should partake in all the motions which were to be.[10]

In his interpretation of a living body and its relation to cosmic movement, Aristotle argues:

> If a living body or thing is ever absolutely at rest, we shall have a motionless thing in which motion is originated by the thing itself and not from without. If this can happen to a living thing, why not to the universe? And if in a smaller cosmos [*microcosmos*], why not with the larger cosmos [*megalocosmos*].[11]

This is probably the first consistent formulation of a relationship between the human body and the rest of reality, which is better known as microcosm, and is later referred to in the Middle Ages as *minor mundus.* This issue dominated the nature of European cosmology and anthropology until the eighteenth century. In fact, the shadow of this tradition still appears in Humboldt, Lotz, and Fechner. In this, the primary tradition, the problem of human existence is seen as a drama played out on a cosmic stage, and the vision of human existence is, more often than not, identified with the human body, where there is a close affinity between human, corporeal, and sensible realities (see figure 2.1). Under these conditions the human body becomes a manifestation or exemplum of reality as a whole, encapsulated in the Middle Ages in the formula *mundus minor exemplum est–maiores mundi ordine.*[12] In his *Hexaemeron* St. Ambrose speaks about the nature of the world

2.1
Microcosmos. MS. Cod. 126000,
f. 29r., N.B. Vienna, twelfth century.

(*mundus*) as being "framed like man's body and as in man the head, so in the world the sky is the most excellent member, and as the eyes in man so are the sun and moon in the world."[13] In his influential commentary on Plato's *Timaeus*, Chalcidius speaks summarily about man as *mundus brevis*—man as the abbreviation of the world.[14]

There is little doubt that the phenomenon of microcosm poses serious difficulties to modern thinking. Yet if we ignore the problematic speculations, the excessive level of mysticism, and the excessive physical or naturalistic analogies (such as "man's hair is like a grass, his veins and arteries like rivers and canals and his bones like mountains"),[15] then we are likely to be rewarded by a surprising richness and depth of understanding of the relation between the human body and the world—their common corporeality and meaning. This coincides, to a great extent, with current views of philosophical anthropology, the phenomenological understanding of corporeality, the world structure of human existence, and the communicative nature of the world as understood in current hermeneutics. Together they suggest a fusion of horizons in which the nature of the human body and its relation to architecture and the rest of reality changes into one of embodiment. This is inevitable because the reality of the world is not structured around identifiable independent entities such as isolated human bodies or isolated architectural elements and their corresponding meanings. Rather, it is structured through degrees of embodiment, which represent a continuum of mediation between the human and divine, terrestrial and celestial, sensible and intelligible levels of reality.

To appreciate the real meaning of microcosm and its contemporary relevance, we should look more closely at the deep reciprocity that exists between the human body and the world and, by implication, between the human body and architecture (figure 2.2). In the Aristotelian tradition, the body is always seen as engaged with its place and ultimately with the hierarchy of places (topology) within a unified cosmic framework. Aristotle explains, "If a thing [body] is not separated from its embracing environment, but is undifferentiated from it, it is indeed 'included in' it—not however as in its place, but only in the sense in which a part is said to be 'included in' its whole."[16]

If the notion of reciprocity between places and bodies is taken one step further, then it is clear that places must be contained and situated in the same way as things or bodies are. Moreover, they constitute the same hierarchy, culminating in the same unifying cosmic place. Aristotle explains the nature of the hierarchy in the following statement: "The earth as the centre of the universe and the inner surface of the revolving heavens constitute the supreme 'below' and the supreme 'above;' the former being absolutely stable and the latter constant in its position as a whole."[17] When considering the human body, the hierarchically structured space in which all bodies have their place (*topos*) must be further qualified with respect to its animation by the soul.[18]

Schema prædictæ diuisionis.

2.2
Macrocosmos. From the
Cosmographia of Peter Apian,
1584.

It is a serious mistake to see the human body as isolated from the soul and to discuss the problem of order and harmony as a direct manifestation of the invisible principles in the visible appearance of bodies. Such a simplified and distorted understanding can be found in many Renaissance architectural treatises and modern commentaries (figure 2.3).

The following statement illustrates very well my point: "The man-created forms in the corporeal world were the visible materialisations of the intelligible mathematical symbols, and the relationship between the pure forms of absolute mathematics and the visible forms of applied mathematics were immediately and intuitively perceptible."[19]

It is appropriate to speak here about a general tendency that coincides with the development of modern perspective. Its main characteristic is the confusion of the distinction between sense and intellect and a naive belief in the ability of sight to see intelligible reality

PORTICVS PERSICA INSIGNE VIRTVTIS CONSTITVTA CAPTIVORVM
PLATEENSIV SIMVLACRA PRO COLVMNIS TECTA SVSTINETIA .
PAVSANIÆ . LACONVM
DVCIS GLORIA .

2.3
Cesare Cesariano, the Persian
Portico. From his translation
and commentary on the
De Architectura of Vitruvius,
Liber Primus, VIII, Como, 1521.

directly, without any mediation with sensible reality. In his *Questiones Perspectivae,* Biagio di Parma (Pelacani) speaks about the judgment of sense (*Iudicium sensus*) and the ability of sight to grasp things in the same manner as intellect does or can.[20] This immanentization of the soul, the reduction of its higher capacities to corporeal form, makes it almost identical with the body. The body is still animated, but in our modern way of thinking, the cryptic presence of the soul cannot be easily detected. For evidence of the presence of the soul, we have to turn to more explicit examples. In his *Idea del Tempio della Pittura,* Lomazzo describes the axis of a figure as its anima or soul: "It is necessary that painters and sculptors know what the soul is, that which descends from the head to the bottom of the foot through the middle and equally from one extended hand to the other. See the figures drawn in the *Simmetria* of Dürer which have a line which passes through the centre of the figure which is its soul."[21]

The identification of the soul with the axis of the body or with the body's center of gravity (for example, in Alberti's *De statua* or Francesco di Giorgio's *Trattati di Architettura*) has its origin in the Aristotelian tradition where the notion of animation is seen as a dialectic of movement and its source (figure 2.4). Speaking about the place of the soul in the human organism, Aristotle says, "Since the left and the right sides are symmetrical and these opposites are moved simultaneously, it cannot be that the left is moved by the right when it remains stationary, nor vice versa; the origin of movement must always be in what lies above both. Therefore the original seat of the moving soul must be in that which lies in the middle."[22]

In a complementary statement, critical to my subsequent argument, Aristotle describes the role of the soul in the following manner: "The soul does not have to be in each part of the body, but she resides in a kind of central governing place of the body and the remaining parts live by the continuity of natural structure, and play the parts nature would have them play."[23] The notion of "the continuity of natural structure," which gives life to the remaining parts of the human body, is very close to the contemporary phenomenological understanding of the same problem, most notably to the position of Merleau-Ponty when he says that "there are several ways for the body to be a body and several ways for consciousness to be consciousness."[24] In both cases the conventional vision of the body—distinct from the soul—appears as an abstraction that obscures the traditional notion of corporeality manifested as embodiment and animation.

The analogy of body and architecture, or body and cosmos, would be incomprehensible without a mediating link or structure between such ontologically different realities. It is all too easy to say that cosmic order is reflected in the human body, or that the proportions and configuration of architectural elements can be derived from the human body. How is it possible, therefore, and what are the conditions under which such claims can be turned into a meaningful and convincing understanding? These questions are usually left unanswered. The role of the human body in the process of embodiment in which architectural and cosmic order become apparent is comprehensible only in the context of the primary reality. This is a reality of our natural world where all relationships and references are constituted in the spontaneity of our continuous encounter with the conditions of our existence. In the context of the natural world, it is as futile to speak about anthropomorphism as it would be to speak about cosmomorphism. Both represent given conditions that we cannot escape. We can only isolate ourselves from them, or suppress them, and pretend that our own vision of reality is neutral and self-sufficient. It is quite obvious that upholding such a vision requires a considerable effort and a high integrity of representation, which by definition is derivative and secondary. And yet it is the secondary representation that we usually encounter first. The analogy on which secondary representations are based is a

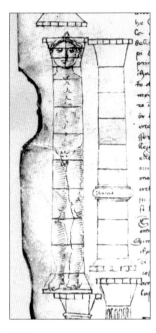

2.4

Francesco di Giorgio, detail from marginal drawings of columns, capitals, and pilasters. From the Ashburnham Codex, Florence, Bibliotheca Mediceo-Laurenziana, 361, f.13v, late fifteenth century.

symbolic structure that links together similar yet heterogeneous phenomena through participation in the articulated continuum of our natural world.

Most decisive for the nature of analogy and its historical development is the breakdown of the symbolic structure that had sustained its meaning and authenticity. Its dissolution led to the transformation of direct symbolic relations into distant abstract concepts, or into a continuous metaphor, culminating in speculative and far-fetched allegory. Abstraction is characteristic of the transformation that led to determinism and the calculated appropriation of reality. Metaphor conversely leads to numerology and the comparative "anatomy" of the human body to elements of architecture and certain themes in astrology. The attempt to establish a precise relation between zodiacal phenomena and zones of the human body, for example, is frequently discussed and illustrated in the naturalistic microcosmic texts.[25] To assess the plausibility of a particular text requires a certain level of historical imagination and interpretative skill, but in many cases, certain analogies remain problematic and unproductive, as they may have been in their own time.

The tendency to reduce the continuum of transcendental relationships to purely corporeal analogies undermines not only the relevance of microcosmic speculations but also the relevance of analogy itself. Already in the fifteenth and sixteenth centuries, many intelligent minds struggled with the question of whether the body was a literal or figurative microcosm. The following passage is a good illustration of the dilemma:

> The body also, as far as it was possible, carries the image of God not in figure as the anthropomorphites have foolishly dreamed . . . , but because the admirable structure and accomplished perfection of the body carries in it a representation of all the most glorious and perfect works of God as being an epitome or compendium of the whole creation, by which he is rather signified than expressed. And hence it is that man is called a microcosm or little world. The divines call him *omnem creaturam*, every creature, because he is in a manner of things; not for matter and substance as Empedocles would have it but analogically by participation or reception of the several species or kinds of things.[26]

Participation and reception refer to the most important aspect of analogy: its symbolic nature. In the process of symbolization, analogy articulates the relationship between soul and body, between the intelligible order of reality and its visible corporeal manifestations. The process of symbolization belongs to the vertical organization of our culture, where the high and low, divine and human, were related and mediated by a sequence of stages, better known as the Chain of Being (*Catena Rerum*). It is against this background that the meaning of the relationship between the individual parts of the body or a building may be understood. The relationship would be empty and meaningless without such a background.

The same is true for some of the more significant concepts that shaped the history of European architecture, such as order, proportion, and harmony (figure 2.5). Proportion, the most important in this sequence, is a key to the process of mediation. Before it is a relationship that can be represented numerically, proportion is, as the original Greek term *analogia* indicates, an analogy.

Metaphor, Analogy, and Proportion

In the primary tradition *analogia* is a symbolic structure that has nothing directly to do with numbers. It depends on resemblances, similarities, and eventually a balanced tension of sameness and difference when related to various phenomena. Thus, the origin of proportion is not in mathematics, understood in the conventional sense, but in language, and even when it is expressed numerically, it still depends for its meaning on language.[27] In order to appreciate the close link that exists between language and mathematics, we need only remember the role that geometrical demonstration played in the formation of syllogistic reasoning.[28] The representation of proportion as number derives from the original form of analogy, and more specifically the tension between "the one and many" (identity and difference), which is the essence of metaphor.[29] It is perhaps no coincidence that the geometrical proportion that is a paradigm of all other proportions reflects the structure of metaphorical analogy (A is to B, as C is to D).[30] The principle of "the one and many" is preserved in the original understanding of number as "how many," whereas modern number is a pure concept.

The system of proportions that dominated architectural thinking for almost two millennia has its origin in the Pythagorean-Platonic tradition, in which number was known as *arithmos*. Apart from its prosaic meaning as a sum of numbers for counting, *arithmos* has a more elevated meaning as a paradigm of unity in multiplicity. Each sum contains "many" units and yet is always "one." This rather mysterious character of *arithmos* is well described as the "*arithmos* structure of *logos*."[31] It reveals the deep structure of our experience, the metaphorical articulation of analogies, and dialectical reasoning: "Precisely for that reason the sum number (*arithmos*) proffers itself as a prototype of the order of Being and the ideas. And it claims nothing more for itself than to be such a prototype."[32] The metaphorical nature of analogy, represented numerically as a form of proportion (similar to the nature of syntax or grammar in language), suggests that underlying proportion (and other summary

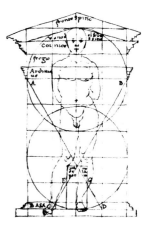

2.5
Francesco di Giorgio, youth measured to temple elevation. From the Ashburnham Codex, Florence, Biblioteca Mediceo-Laurenziana (f. 38v, tav. 228), late fifteenth century.

2.6

Robert Fludd, *The Temple of Music*. From his *Utriusque Cosmi . . . Historia*, I, b: *Tractatus Secundus De Natura Simia Seu Technica macrocosmi . . .* ; Oppenheim 1618 and Frankfurt, 1624; pp. 160–161.

notions such as universal beauty, order, and harmony) there is always present a deeper level of articulation, coextensive with the articulation of the world as a whole.

Scrutinizing the ontological foundations of proportion reveals its equivalence to embodiment: that which manifests itself as a proportionality or analogy of the visible and invisible, sensible and intelligible levels of reality. This revelation challenges the conventional understanding of proportion as a static harmony of different elements and supplies a more authentic understanding, where proportion is an open and dynamic paradigm of mediation and participation of the visible phenomena in the unity of the world, in the one (*hen*) and the good (*agathon*). Proportion tends toward mediation, but this can never be fully achieved. Proportion nonetheless remains a tool with which it is possible to approximate the process and its goal. Plato speaks in this context about *hypothesis,* as something we humans can achieve in order to anticipate the essential nature of reality.[33] Through *hypothesis,* numbers and proportions serve as a model, or *propaedeutics,* to a full representation of reality through dialectics. In that role they "facilitate the apprehension of the idea of good . . . and force the soul to turn its vision round to the region where dwells the most blessed part of reality."[34] Numerical proportions share the advantages but also the limits of mathematical disciplines, which, like "geometry and the studies which accompany it are, as we see, dreaming about being, but the clear, waking vision of it is not possible for them as long as they leave the assumptions which they employ undisturbed and cannot give any account of them."[35]

Returning to the problem of proportion in architecture, there is very little dialectical thinking in Renaissance architectural treatises and, regrettably, even less in modern commentaries. We hear about basic harmonies of the universe, universally valid ratios and proportions, about the parallelism of musical and visual harmonies, but it is far from clear how these ambitious statements relate to reality or under what conditions they can be sustained or justified. In a memorandum written in 1567, Palladio goes one step further than most other architect-theorists when he writes, "The proportions of the voices are harmonies for the ears; those of the measurements are harmonies for the eyes. Such harmonies usually please very much without anyone knowing why, excepting the student of the causality of things."[36]

The knowledge of the "causality of things" is not a reference to musical theory or the study of analogies but to demonstrative thinking. There is no evidence that Palladio himself was at home in this field. But some of his friends were, particularly Daniele Barbaro, whose knowledge of philosophy, mathematics, and music was exceptional and who was in close contact with scholars such as F. Barozzi, the translator of Proclus's commentary on Euclid, an exemplary introductory text to Platonic dialectics. In his commentary on Vitruvius, Barbaro speaks about "certain knowledge," "true architecture," and the knowledge of how to "conclude many things from the right principles (*scire per causas*)." Early in his introduction, he states that "truly divine is the desire of those, who raising their minds to consider things, search for the reasons behind them" (figure 2.6).[37]

In the musical section of the commentary, Barbaro raises questions about too simplistic a reliance on musical analogies: "Many think that with the diatonic genus they can satisfy every quality of things. I wish this were the place to explain the ideas and colours suitable to every quality of thing according to their genera, because with the living experience of their ears confirmed by invincible reasoning—I would make them confess their errors."[38]

The example of Barbaro illustrates the extent to which the meaning of architectural proportions depends on a broader milieu of discourse. Moreover, it demonstrates the necessity of being situated in a culture where communication between the different arts and disciplines still plays an important role. This was openly recognized by a number of authors, including Leon Battista Alberti, who referred to philosophers and mathematicians to substantiate his statements. We know that among those very close to him were Nicolas Cusanus (and possibly Paolo Toscanelli and Marsilio Ficino), scholars with a deep understanding of Platonic dialectics and the ontology of proportions. In view of the presentation of the same issues in architectural discourse, however, it is not easy to see how their position influenced contemporary architectural thinking. The difference between philosophical and artistic interpretations can be explained as a tendency in art to treat the tradition of transcendental dialectical understanding of proportion and harmony as an immanent problem. This is clearly illustrated in Alberti's own words: "The very same numbers that cause sounds to have that *concinnitas,* pleasing to the ears, can also fill the ideas and mind with wondrous delight." As a result "we define harmony as that consonance of sounds which is pleasant to the ears."[39]

The audible musical consonants accepted as a paradigm of universal harmony became a foundation of architectural thinking in the early fifteenth century, and their role was not seriously questioned for almost three hundred years. The primary consonances and their legitimacy were derived from the description of the structure of the soul in Plato's *Timaeus,* which has nothing directly to do with music. It is surprising that Renaissance authors and most modern commentators have not commented on this. The *Tetraktys,* which Plato chose as a point of departure, includes musical ratios, but its primary meaning is elsewhere. It is a progression of the first four numbers generating the perfect number 10 (*decad*), which "completes the series of numbers, containing in itself the nature of both even and odd and of that which is in motion and that which is still."[40] *Tetraktys* is used primarily as

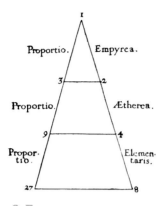

2.7

Robert Fludd, the Platonic lambda (tetraktys) as structure for the three levels of creation. From his *Utriusque Cosmi . . . Historia*, I, a; Oppenheim 1618, p. 164.

a key to dialectical reasoning. In the creation of the body of the world that the soul is supposed to animate, the process that Plato described begins with the making of fire and earth, representing the visible and tangible characteristics of corporeality, and also the highest and lowest elements in the vertical structure of the world. They are linked together by two means, air and water, in "a continued geometrical proportion to effect this most perfectly."[41] Continuous proportion is used for reasons of mediation and unity, as a vehicle in the formation of the soul. The progression from one to solid numbers represents the process of participation (*methexis*) in which the corporeal phenomena are related through a continuous sequence with the source of their potential unity (one).[42]

The meaning of the process of participation is ontological and not musical.[43] Music plays only an intermediate role in the generation of proportional ratios, as is illustrated in the following commentary:

Seeing, then, that the *Tetraktys* supplies the proportion of the symphonies mentioned, and the symphonies serve to make up the perfect harmony, and according to the perfect harmony all things are arranged, on this account they have described it as "the fount containing the roots of Nature ever-enduring". Again, they argue that it is according to the ratios of these four numbers that both body and the incorporeal, from which come all things, are conceived—for it is by the flow of a point that we form a notion of a line, which is length without breadth, and by the flow of a line we construct breadth, which is surface without depth, and by the flow of surface solid body is produced. . . . Thus it is reasonable to hold that the *Tetraktys* is the fount of universal Nature. [See figure 2.7.][44]

The ontological meaning of embodiment is closely linked with the phenomena of proportion, in the sense that one speaks for the other. In the primary tradition in which proportion is understood dialectically, the relationship between different levels of reality coincides with the degree of their embodiment. This was most clearly expressed in the late medieval philosophy of light: "It is clear that light through the infinite multiplication of itself extends matter into finite dimensions that are smaller and larger according to certain proportions that they have to one another and thus light proceeds according to numerical and non-numerical proportions."[45]

The philosophy of light was incorporated into architectural thinking and found its expression in the overall vertical organization of the architectural body. The paradigm of such an organization was the structure of the spire or pinnacle that can be seen as a pyramid of light articulated by a continuous proportion. In Albertus Magnus's interpretation, the creator is a source and point of light (*punctus lucis*) that radiates layers of light in the form of an infinite pyramid toward its base, which becomes in the shadowy domain of the material region darker and darker. All the strata of the cosmos have their origin in this first principle of light, which radiates light as a form (species) of all created things in a pyramid, that is, in accordance with the laws of light geometry. The pyramidal shape of the spire or pinnacle is the symbolic representation of the process of creation and, in another sense, of a participation in the unity of being and in the good. Things are beautiful only to the degree to which they participate in the good.[46] In the introductory section of his *Fialenbüchlein*, M. Roriczer speaks about the correct proportion of the pinnacle: "Since each art has its own matter, form and measure I have tried with the help of God to make clear this aforesaid art of geometry and for the first time to explain the beginning of drawn-out stonework, how and in what measure it rises out of the fundamentals of geometry through manipulation of the dividers and how it should be brought into the correct proportions (*rechten Masse*)." [See figure 2.8.][47]

If we accept that the hierarchy of reality is articulated in a precise proportional manner as a world, then we may be able to describe the process as the architectonics of embodiment in which architecture itself plays a very important role. Architecture represents the most elementary mode of embodiment that enables the more articulated levels of culture, including numbers and ideas, to be situated in reality as a whole. The distance that separates architecture from ideas or numbers cannot be bridged directly and in a simple way. The task is open to mediation, but this is never a perfect or complete process because human understanding and modes of representation limit it. Representation is mediated through culture, and thus primarily through philosophy, science, literature, music, painting, sculpture, and architecture. In a hierarchically differentiated way, each area represents a particular mode of articulation with a corresponding mode of embodiment. The continuity of embodiment that penetrates and unites them all is only a different term for the architectonics of embodiment mentioned earlier.

The way in which the primary structure of architecture (architectonics) determines the structure of sculpture, painting, language, and eventually the structure of ideas cannot be discussed here in further detail. Suffice it to say that what a book is to literacy, architecture is to culture as a whole.

It can be concluded that the architectonics of embodiment reveals the most essential characteristics of proportion as they were understood in the primary tradition. In that tradition, as we have seen, things are proportioned with respect to a unifying whole, as an open dialectical structure, and not for themselves as a visible unity or closed system of proportions. This difference is a sure guide to a better understanding of the much quoted commonplace about the nature of cosmos—that it is arranged by measure, number, and weight.[48] It is the credo of so many discussions about proportion, yet this phrase is

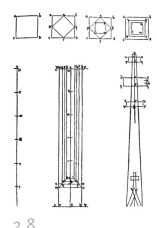

2.8

Matthew Roriczer, generational square and elevation of a pinnacle. From his *Das Büchlein von der Fialen Gerechtigheit,* late fifteenth century.

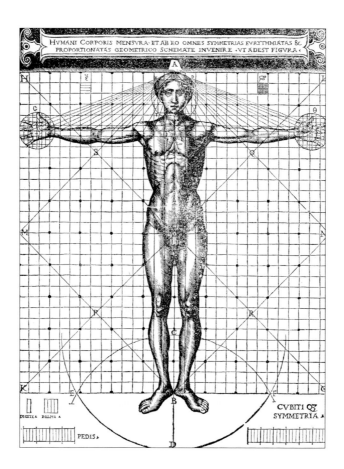

HVMANI CORPORIS MENSVRA· ET AB EO OMNES SYMMETRIAS EVRYTHMIATAS &
PROPORTIONATAS GEOMETRICO SCHEMATE INVENIRE ·VT ADEST FIGVRA·

DIGITA PALMI
PEDIS

CVBITI Q̃
SYMMETRIA

2.9
Vitruvian man within a square, after
Cesare Cesariano, *De architectura*,
Como, 1521.

interpreted, almost without exception, as a confirmation of the mathematical (numerical)
structure of reality, while the original meaning, clearly grasped until modern times, was
fundamentally different. In many earlier texts, we find a definition like that formed by
Bonaventura:

> In the first way of seeing the observer considers things in themselves and sees in them
> weight, number and measure; weighted with respect to the place towards which things
> incline; numbers by which things are distinguished and measure by which things are
> determined. Hence he sees in them their mode, species and order, as well as substance,
> power and activity. From all these considerations the observer can rise, as from a vestige
> to the knowledge of the immense power, wisdom and goodness of the creator.[49]

Modus, species, and order "are in fact various modalities of proportion."[50] Together they represent the qualitative criteria of harmony, the beautiful, and the good.[51]

This brings us to the last point: the nature and use of a module by which the nature of proportion is probably most clearly revealed. In conventional interpretations, the module is seen as a vehicle for a clearer and more efficient execution of a building, or simply as a unit of commensurability (figure 2.9). If, however, we take into account the importance of the concept of identity and the good or the unity of being in the understanding of harmony, then the module is something quite different. It appears as a visible manifestation of identity and as an embodiment of our efforts to grasp the moments of sameness in the hierarchical order of things.[52] The numerical representation of the module is a visible entry into a world structured by analogy and proportion. In relation to that world, it is the most tangible embodiment and paradigm of proportion in the primary tradition. The meaning of the module and its role in proportioning architectural elements or the human body depend entirely on the presence of an articulated world in which the body is connected with embodiment and proportion with architectonics. The presence of an articulated world and "primary tradition" determined architectural thinking and practice in the past. I believe it should continue to determine the relevance of our interpretations today.

3

John Onians

Greek Temple and Greek Brain

We all know that when we look at a building with our eyes, we are also seeing it with our heads. This is why when we look at a Greek temple, we cannot do so without seeing it in terms of our preexisting knowledge of its conventional attributes. These include its underlying schemata, as represented by its proportions and measurements; its embedded history, as represented by the wooden origins of the Doric order; its construction out of a collection of elements, such as base, column, and capital, or echinus, dentil, and torus; and even the analogies with which it is associated, such as that between the column and the human form. Confronted with a Greek temple, we see it in terms of numbers and origins, names and correspondences. Most of these have entered our heads from books, typically in the form of words.

This situation is not surprising. We are used to believing that most—and certainly the best—knowledge is formulated and transferred in verbal form, and we are used to thinking of our heads as large libraries full of information stored in booklike repositories. Of course, we all realize that our heads are also filled with visual information, but this we also imagine typically as illustrative material accompanying the booklike compendia of information. This is why even visual knowledge is organized verbally. When we think of buildings, we think of names, places, and dates, to which are attached ground plans, facades, and interiors, to which are attached in turn such labels as capital, volute, cyma recta, and so on. We represent such knowledge verbally for good reasons. The founders of our mental tradition, the ancient Greeks, used the term for *word, logos,* for thought too. Since the ancient Greeks, we are accordingly all predisposed to believe that we think best when we think in words. Numbers, of course, and diagrams are also allowed, but these are only respectable because, like words, they constitute a mutually agreed recordable schematization of experience. Words, numbers, and diagrams are what we have in our heads. We think in these terms, and when we think about a Greek artifact, such as a temple, it is also in these terms. We are even proud of doing so, because we believe that we are then most in tune with the most famous Greek artifact, the Greek mind. This pride is appropriate, but only when *thinking* of a Greek temple is concerned. Where we go wrong is in *looking* at Greek temples in the same terms. When we look, we would be wise to try to look not with a Greek mind but with a Greek brain.

To think of looking in terms not of the mind but of the brain has several advantages. The most obvious is the prima facie one: that it brings us closer to the specifics of real experience. When we talk of the mind, we are necessarily talking in terms of the conventions of a long tradition. When we talk of the brain today, we are able to talk in terms not just of conventions and assumptions, but of the functioning of neural mechanisms. It is in these terms that this chapter will operate. The basis of its argument is that any study of the human mind and its activities that is undertaken now should move beyond the conventional language used to describe mental activities to take account of what has recently become known about the detailed workings of the brain. If we take advantage of that knowledge, it should be possible to develop new hypotheses that are more precise and more testable than any obtained earlier.

The knowledge I am referring to is that obtained by neurologists, neurobiologists, and neuropsychologists using techniques of experiment and observation available only recently. Among the most important of these techniques are those involving the implanting of electrodes into the neural networks of animals and the scanning of the human brain to observe the differential absorption of oxygen. These techniques have allowed the identification of the functions of particular neurons and groups of neurons and an understanding of the laws governing their growth and decline. Techniques such as these have made it possible to establish, for example, that the brain is only about 50 percent formed at birth, its subsequent development being fundamentally shaped by postnatal experience. Although the genes already determine much of the brain's structure, especially that of the stem, that of the cortex will be determined largely by subsequent interaction with the environment. The use of particular motor or sensory organs will stimulate the growth and interconnection of particular neural networks in particular ways. Often there is a latent propensity that must await precise activation after birth. An obvious example is the propensity to learn what is desirable and undesirable. The brain has lower areas such as the parietal lobes and amygdala that are solely concerned with helping us to have a positive response to some things and a negative response to others.[1] What these things are has to be determined by other upper and outer areas concerned with cognition. Some responses, such as the taste for sweet things or attraction to the opposite sex, are largely genetically prescribed, but others are not, such as the determination of which humans or other large animals might be friendly or dangerous, which plants might be nutritious and which poisonous, which raw materials useful and which not, and even which tool shapes are more effective and which less.

Equally familiar is the way we acquire speech. The tendency to babble is genetic, but the languages we learn will be determined by early experience. That we learn languages most easily when we are young is a clear indication that such learning is made possible by associated neural development. Just as significant, though much less obvious, is the fact that in other fields, such as looking, our brains are predisposed at birth to develop neural structures in a process of often passive interaction with our environment.[2] This means that such apparently inconsequentially variable aspects of our environment as climate, landscape, flora, and fauna will critically influence the formation of our brains. Depending on whether we live in a desert or a snowfield, a tropical jungle or a temperate city, on a small stream or the sea, our neural networks will be different to some extent. In the case of the visual cortex, the neurons that deal with the analysis of such separate elements as color or line, or with the convergences of feature recognition and categorization, will be stimulated in total different ways and consequently will grow and connect in totally different patterns, with the result that our basic sensory discriminations and the knowledge on which they are based will be equally differentiated. At the same time this passive process is powerfully influenced by much better understood factors such as language, social habit, and training. Finally, while many of these tendencies lead to members of the same group having similarly formed brains, others, such as the brain's tendency to be affected by intimate emotional relations, ensure that each person's neural development is also profoundly influenced by experiences that are specific to the individual.

The fundamental point that emerges from all this is that some aspects of our brain are shared with all other humans; some are shared with all who live in a similar place at a particular time, or by all who share an instrument of social formation such as a language, religion, or family; and some are unique to ourselves. This is true of both the structure of the brain and the information it contains, since the latter is directly influenced by the former. This is why, if we are going to understand what goes on inside our heads, we have to know what goes on inside our brains, and if we are to understand the role of the brain in the control of behavior, we have both to understand our genetically determined drives and to familiarize ourselves with each individual's or group's social and natural environment. Understanding such differences enables us to understand why the temples in our brains are different from those in the brains of ancient Greeks.

What then were they like, the temples in the brains of those who built them? I argued some time ago that if they were like anything, they were like phalanxes, that is, rectangular formations of armed warriors, and I am now prepared to refine this hypothesis by drawing on the new knowledge of the brain's role in perception.[3] It follows from what has been argued above that if we are to understand what the Greeks saw in temples, we have to ask what they saw in general, that is, what they perceived and how it engaged them. Before proposing answers to these questions, we should remind ourselves of the ground rules we need to observe and of their consequences.

We have to start by rebuilding our assumptions about the Greeks. The first step is to abandon a notion, implicit in the term *Greek* itself, that the principal mental community of the people who built these temples was linguistic. They did share a language, but language was only one of the things they shared. They also shared physical activities, rituals such as the Olympic Games, and other social activities, such as drinking. Most important, they shared the experience of a similar geography—the land, sea, and sky and all that was in them. In particular, associated with their shared experience of geography was a shared experience of raw materials—of stone, clay, metals, and wood—to which the biochemistry of their brain stems ensured that they paid particular attention because they were vital to their survival. The Greeks shared a language, but they also shared an experience of the natural and social environment, of the body and of society, of activities and of materials.

Language had a much less important role in their mental formation than we, who know them best by their books, are apt to think. Much more important would have been other shared experiences. These could be natural: a landscape of fertile river valleys flanked by rocky mountains; a surrounding that was alternately life sustaining when it allowed fishing or trade and life threatening when it brought an enemy fleet or storms; a climate that brought a series of changing temperatures and humidities and alternating waves of sun and rain that could be either beneficial or destructive. They could also be man-made, especially those man-made things that gave them pleasure when they were their own and pain when they were their enemies'. These included such essential elements of the food supply as cornfields, vineyards, and olive groves; such essential elements of the craft system as potters' wheels and pots, forges and metalwork; such essential elements of the trade system as the appurtenances of shipping, ropes, sails, and planks; such essential elements of the defense system as soldiers and ships, especially when arranged in formations as armies and fleets; and such essential elements of city life as walls, streets, agoras, and temples. These were the things that most engaged the Greeks visually, and so it was these that were likely to have an important place in their brains.

It is necessary to say "likely" because we must remember that depending on habitat or activity, each Greek would have his or her own preoccupations. For each tradesman, for example, some things would have a greater importance than others. A farmer, potter, smith, or sailor would each have a greater concern with the forms and materials on which their livelihood depended. Equally, communities that consisted more of potters or sailors would each share diverse preoccupations. The same would be true of communities living in different natural environments—in the mountains, on a plain, on the coast, or on an island. In each case the preoccupations would actually affect the formation of the brain. Thinking of the Greeks as similar because they shared a language through space and time leads us to forget the extent to which the experiences they had were different depending on place and period. Although the part of the brain concerned with language, and especially grammar, would have a similar formation through time and space, other areas would be much more highly differentiated.

This is not to deny the role of language in the formation of Greek culture, only to redefine it so as to make clear that one of its original and principal functions was precisely to facilitate the sharing of mental experiences that were preexistent and neurally constituted. Thus, the myth about the Greeks descending from a race born from the stones thrown over their shoulders by Deucalion and Pyrrha was invented and accepted only because of the prominence of stone in the Greek landscape, which is such that those who lived there acquired a natural empathy with it. Other myths result from the correspondence between critical experiences in different fields. Thus, the myth that the Thebans descended from men who grew from sown dragons' teeth was possible only because the Greeks were used to giving particular attention to three similar phenomena that were particularly life saving or life threatening: the sight of men lined up in rows for warfare and military training, the sight of rows of corn grown from rows of seed, and the sight of the most deadly threat in the animal world of the Greeks, the rows of teeth in a snake's mouth. It was the brain's genetically driven predisposition to pay attention to things that secured or threatened its survival and its tendency to form neural networks specializing in phenomena in this area that led to the development of a tendency to see convergences in the appearances of these very different sets of objects. It was a series of linkages between the neurons in the visual cortex and other areas essential for cognition that put them together. All that the inventor of the story did was render the convergence visible. All that his words did for his listeners was to make a shared unconscious mental experience conscious.

While the creators of myths help to shape communal culture, other users of language give more objective and private views of it in operation. Thus, the clearest statement on the linkages between the Greek brain and the Greek eye around 600 B.C., when the Greek stone temple became established as a type, is provided by someone who was a clever psychologist, if not a neuropsychologist, Sappho. In a poem celebrating the simple power of sexual love, she mockingly reminds her contemporaries how distorted their visual interests have become: "Some say the most beautiful thing in the world is an army of horsemen, some say

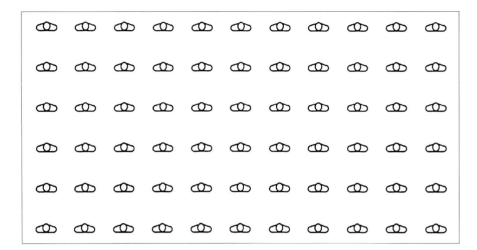

an army of foot soldiers, some a fleet of warships . . . but I say it is one's beloved."[4] Without understanding the mechanisms that underlie the phenomenon she is observing, she is able to point out how the Greek brain has been so modified by experience that the neural connections between the eye and the base of the brain, which normally function to focus our attention on the object of sexual desire, have become so modified that the object of supreme desire is not a human individual but a formation of cavalry, infantry, or ships. In noting "some say this" and "some say that," she may even suggest a realization that the different abnormal preferences she notes relate directly to the critical experience of particular groups. Those, like the aristocracy, who relied more on horses, might most desire to see cavalry; those, such as the newly important middle classes whose critical role was as hoplites or foot soldiers, infantry; and those, such as traders and sailors, who depended more on ships, the fleet. She is certainly likely to have known that, increasingly, the most important common element of the defense system of all Greek states was the infantry, more particularly the phalanx, whose sexual desirability is shown by its illustration on a vessel such as the Macmillan aryballos, used to contain the perfumed oil with which young men anointed themselves after exercise. This indeed we might have predicted on the basis of the laws of neurology. Since the thing, the sight of which brought most pleasure deep in the center of the brain of most Greeks, was the infantry formation or phalanx (figure 3.1), it was this that becomes an object of almost sexual fixation.

At this point we have to remember exactly what sight involves. The eye does not, of course, see either soldiers or a phalanx. What it does is feed signals to networks of neurons in the brain, each specialized in its own task of feature detection, pattern recognition, or the response to such separable elements as vertical lines, horizontal lines, color, the face, the body, an emotional expression. These neurons are connected to others involved with classification and other cognitive activities, and these are in constant contact with the base of the brain. If classified as beneficial, they provoke a positive, if as dangerous, a negative, response. It is in the nature of vision that anything that generates signals that are sufficiently similar to those that would be generated by something genuinely dangerous or attractive is likely to generate the same cognitive response in the cortex and chemical reaction in the base of the brain as the real thing. Something that has sufficient visual properties in common with something desired or feared may elicit a similar response. The best examples of this phenomenon are the responses evoked in the human being by highly reduced representations. Dolls, for example, can give almost the same pleasure as babies, and pin-ups can give almost the same pleasure as real members of the desired sex. Indeed any painted and sculpted representation may evoke almost the same positive or negative response as the thing represented. Less known, though frequently exploited, are the responses evoked only subconsciously by a vast number of other objects in the human environment, of which the car as woman and the car as animal are among the most familiar, having long been exploited by designers. More significantly in the present context, the same phenomenon also lies, I would argue, behind the development of the Greek temple.

My core argument is this: that when the Greeks began to build temples to their protective deities, because they looked to them for defensive properties that they believed were secured by the phalanx, they tended to strengthen in them those phalanx-like attributes that were already emergent, because that made them feel good. For the citizens of the valley towns of Greece, to whom the need for military training was increasingly apparent, it would have been easy to see a rectangular house as having a similar configuration to a rectangular phalanx and a post or column a similar configuration to a standing warrior. The more the temple was lengthened and the more it was surrounded by aligned identical supports, the more of a positive phalanx-like reassurance it would have produced. These first temples with their brick walls and wooden posts were built in the eighth and seventh centuries B.C., at the same time that the phalanx was beginning its development. Moreover, in the eighth-century B.C. text of Homer, not only is there a celebration of the phalanx in which the front rank is compared to a fence, with "shield against shield, helmet against helmet and man against man,"[5] but Pirithous and Leonteus are described as "tall oaks" standing before the gates of the Greek camp,[6] and Asius, as he dies, is compared to a felled oak, poplar, or pine.[7] Since the phalanx in question is made up of Greeks, and Greek too are Pirithous, Leonteus, and Asius, there is a clear sense that Greek soldiers could be thought of as vertical tree trunks, making it easy to see how a row of tree trunks or posts could be

seen as having the reassuring properties of Greek soldiers. When they saw a soldier, they desired to see him as a tree, and when they saw a post, they saw something that embodied those properties. As a result, putting up posts in front of the deity's house gave a feeling of reassurance. Putting up a larger number increased that feeling. Posts all-round produced maximum reassurance.

Homer also compared the members of the phalanx to stones in a wall, and around 600 B.C. the wooden posts become stone columns. This change of material had advantages in terms of durability, but it too is likely to have been encouraged by preexisting neural conditioning. Given the way the Greek experience of their environment led to the formulation of the myths of Deucalion and Pyrra and of the Theban Spartoi in which they identified themselves with stones and regular hard objects such as snakes' teeth, the change from timber post to stone column had obvious advantages, improving as it did the match between what was seen with the eyes and what was desired or imagined in the brain. The new stone colonnades also evoked even better an imagined phalanx. The demands of stone cutting ensured that the buildings were now in themselves more disciplined in their geometry, the forms more standardized, and the edges of the blocks harder and sharper. For the generations after Sappho, obsessed with phalanxes in the same way that people in other places and periods were obsessed with sex, the tendency to increase their visual pleasure by increasing the correspondence was unconscious but remorseless.

This was especially true of the forms we now call Doric. The alignments became more rigorous, the disciplined uniformity of column and capital more insistent and precise, and the arrises between the flutes acquired more and more the look of the hollow ground blades of spear and sword (figure 3.2). The correspondence even affected the sculptural decoration. Homer compared warriors to lions, and those who noted the water gurgling out of the gutters, even as they looked in the temple for signs that they might protect them, easily imagined roaring. It was a small step for those who were also sculptors to turn the outlets into lions' heads. In the Olympieum at Acragas in Sicily, the assimilation between column and warrior was directly materialized in the alternation of half-columns and naked males. The Olympieum was erected to commemorate a military victory over the Carthaginians in the same way that the Temple of Zeus at Olympia and the Parthenon were erected to commemorate victories over the Persians. It is not surprising if these fifth-century B.C. buildings, which were erected to call to mind military successes, embody even more effectively the qualities on which victory was founded. Sparer, harder forms evoked the aesthetic of the armourer. In the Parthenon this was particularly emphasized by the introduction of marble as a new high-technology building material. Also in the Parthenon, the elaborate geometries of curving stylobates and converging columns recall the refinements of a parade ground performance such as might have been staged to commemorate and keep alive the uniquely disciplined flexibility of the Athenian phalanx, which had almost single-handedly defeated the Persian masses at Marathon. Paid for out of the defense budget of the Delian League, commissioned by Pericles, the general who was head of the militarized Athenian state, home of the warrior goddess and decorated throughout with martial scenes, the Parthenon was a structure designed to fulfill the deepest dream of citizens pre-occupied with military success.

The extent to which the images in the Greek brain now affected Greek vision is illustrated by Euripides in his *Iphigenia in Tauris,* performed below the Parthenon fifteen or twenty years after its completion in 431 B.C. In her nightmare, Iphigenia sees her ancestral house collapsing: "One column alone was left. . . . From its capital streamed golden hair and it took on a human voice' that of her brother Orestes . . . for the columns of a house are sons."[8] Euripides, like Sappho, knew how desire could distort perception. Just how deep

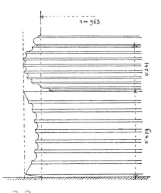

3.3
Temple of Hera at Samos,
late sixth century B.C., column base.
After Dinsmoor.

were the implications of the tendency to imagine people as columns and columns as people is apparent in the female figures who carry the porch of the Erectheum (421–405 B.C.) (figure 3.6) , a building even closer in date than the Parthenon to *Iphigenia*. It has long been recognized that the flutes of the girls' dresses recall those of the adjoining Ionic columns, and we now know why. The Greeks in a sense actually desired their sons and daughters to be like columns. They were even capable of seeing them as columns when they looked at them. By the late fifth century B.C., an Athenian was likely to see as a column any man or woman on whom he or she depended and could not look at a column without experiencing this vital assimilation. The extent to which this had all become a normative experience is documented by the Vitruvian story that the Doric and Ionic columns were derived from male and female figures. Although the underlying association may relate to a correspondence recognized earlier, the story itself is likely to be the product of a specific mental climate in fifth-century B.C. Athens, when anxieties led people to see the rising generations as columnar supports.

So far I have argued that all Greek temples have properties in common with the phalanx and that this is especially true of Doric forms. What, then, was it in the Greek brain that led to the emergence of the other set of forms, those now known as Ionic? We may remember that Sappho, writing just before Doric and Ionic became established, talked of people finding beauty in either a land army or the fleet, and it happens that the area where Ionic is most popular is one as much united by sea as the Doric area was by the land. Moreoever, Samos, the site of the first great Ionic building, was in the sixth century the greatest naval power in the Aegean. It cannot be claimed that the correspondence between temple and ship is as close as that between temple and phalanx, but there are clear similarities in the general configurations of a ship with its multiple rows of oars and a temple with multiple rows of columns. A subliminal association with a trireme might thus help to explain the otherwise puzzling Ionic preference for temples, which, more clearly than Doric ones, possess clear front and rear facades, the latter often with a central column. The single column at the rear, as in the earliest temple at Samos with its row of posts down the center, gave the temple plan an axis much as the keel and stern did a ship. Moreover, if the assimilation of Doric temple and phalanx explains why there are large steps all around, as if waiting for the columns to move in any direction, the placing of steps at one end on the Ionic suggests that it, like a ship, has only one "business" end. The beak on a Greek war vessel occupied a similar position in the ship's silhouette to the steps on the Ionic temple.

So much for the general configuration. What of the details? The principal element that is absent in Doric and present in Ionic is the base. The origin of the element in the architecture of the Near East is beyond question, but the particular form is totally new. The simple round molding of the torus, like the concave scotia or trochilus flanked by rectan-

gular fillets, are all plain moldings without ornaments. What did the Ionian brain see in such forms to get a positive feeling from them? The answer is probably pulleys and ropes. This is supported by the names of the moldings themselves. *Torus* regularly means knot, and *trochilus* is the Greek word for pulley (from *trechein*, a place for a rope to run in). No Ionic bases are more like pulleys than the earliest ones from Samos circa 560 B.C., with their convex and concave profiles marked by hollows that seem only to await the rope (see figure 3.3). The Samos bases were turned on a lathe, a giant version of the instrument that would have been used also to produce the best pulleys. Even the so-called Attic base with its splayed form running down to a fillet looks like one-half of a pulley or the flanged end of a drum, such as would be used to wind the ropes of rigging and anchor. Most torus moldings were smooth, but one form was decorated with a guilloche, a pattern deriving from the twining of fibers, one that could be a natural allusion to the surface of a rope.

As with the base, there is no doubting the origin of the Ionic capital in oriental leaf forms, and, indeed, in the Aeolic capital we have examples of the oriental form in a Greek context at the end of the seventh century B.C. What then is the basis for the transformation of the downturned leaves into the Ionic bolster, narrowing in the center and broadening at the ends, where tight spirals are seen on the faces (figure 3.4)? Something that possessed many of the same properties was a sail. Strengthened at the edges by a cord, it too when rolled up would be narrow in the center and fatter on the ends, and the ends themselves would present the appearance of a tightly rolled spiral. The round molding on the spiral would recall the cord on the end of the sail, and the similar rounded moldings, which are spaced regularly across the bolster, would recall similar cord reinforcements across the sail

3.5
Detail of ship from the scene of
Odysseus passing the Straits
of Messina, red figure vase, fifth
century B.C. (After Pfuhl)

(figure 3.5). It is interesting that at Ephesus, where the earliest capitals survive from around 560–550 B.C., the moldings on the bolsters correspond exactly with the molding on the lower section of the base, and it is easy to see how a drum with ropes around it and a sail with ropes sewn in might present similar appearances.

The surprising tendency to transform a leaf pattern into something resembling a sail must have been greatly encouraged by the form's position at the top of a vertical element. The column has much in common with a ship's mast, and before the wooden form was turned to stone, the resemblance would have been all the greater. Indeed the sailors of Samos, who would have been more used to masts than to the palm trees from which the oriental capital form derived, might naturally have tended to see the leaves as sails and to give them saillike forms. There is no trace of the sail origin in the terminology describing the Ionic capital, but the Vitruvian *pulvinus*, "cushion," like the "bolster," which is its English translation, indicates that the form presented the appearance of a filled textile, and a rolled sail could be described as just that.

The argument advanced here about the origins of Ionic forms is not supported by any text, nor should one expect it to be. It is, however, either a happy chance or a silent confirmation that the first use by the Athenians of the Ionic form is in the stoa that they erected at Delphi to house and display the ropes and other ornaments taken from the Persian ships after the defeat of the Persians at Salamis in 480. The ropes, which perhaps lay behind the columns, might have related suggestively to the flangelike bases close by, and the lighter tackle is likely to have been stored in tight coils resembling the volutes. Forms, which had previously only been juxtaposed in the brains of the Ionian population, now lay beside each other on the stone platform.

The other main difference between the columnar elements of Doric and Ionic is in the flutes. As I already suggested, the Doric shallow flute and its sharp arris acquired its classic form because it recalled in a satisfying manner the hollow grinding that was necessary to make the sharpest spear or sword blade, the essential offensive instrument of the member of the phalanx. The mental pleasure that explains the popularity of the deeper rounded flutes of Ionic separated from each other by flat bands must have a different origin. The similarity of the flutes of the columns from the earliest temple at Ephesus to the moldings of base and capital suggest that all were felt to come from the same world, and the easiest explanation of the similarity would be that the flute recalls the negative images of ropes. Then, as now, drums may have been deliberately grooved to encourage the alignment of coils, and elsewhere on a ship, rounded grooves would have emerged anywhere where ropes ran repeatedly over wood. The sight of a flute that evoked the negative image of a rope, such a vital piece of equipment in a maritime community, would always have given the brain pleasure.

In stressing that the Doric order was developed by people for whom the phalanx was the most important element of the war machine and Ionic by people for whom it was the trireme, I do not intend to suggest that these are exclusive cerebral obsessions. The common preoccupation with warfare was of universal and overriding importance, as is suggested by the detailed forms of both building types and the names by which they were identified. Typical is the echinus, the element at the top of the Doric shaft. This word is originally the designation of the hedgehog or sea urchin, and given its shape, it is probably a correspondence to the latter that is suggested. Whichever it is, the common element is that both animals are equipped with a spiny protective mechanism, which would fit well with a desire to see in the building to which it was attached a defensive function. The use of the term *dentils,* or little teeth for the beam ends of Ionic, would carry exactly the same implication. A more modern name for an Ionic detail and one that brings us even closer to the phalanx is the *egg and dart.* The word *dart* refers to a pointed element that by the Roman period does indeed take on the shape of an arrow or spear. This, however, is only the final stage of a series of transformations that go back to a molding that was originally a series of downturned leaves. The process by which the downturned leaves were slowly transformed by generations of sculptors is a perfect example of the way that what people have in their brain affects both what they see and what they make. Already during the sixth century, the pointed shoots have acquired ridges and a curved profile that gives them a threatening sharpness, and the soft leaves have hardened into convex rounded forms with metallic borders and this tendency continues in the fifth.

The most likely explanation for the transformation of innocent vegetation is that people who saw the leaves were in fact, as Sappho tells us, dreaming of phalanxes and saw in the pattern something like the series of shields and spears that Homer described. Unconsciously the carvers, who were also trained as soldiers in the phalanx, modified the leaves so that they looked enough like a row of spears and shields that they gave them the same pleasure. In some places, there was also a tendency to make the sharp elements look more like lions' claws, and this should not disturb us. Because when the Greeks looked at warriors, they desired them to be lions, there was no conflict between making the same element look both more like a row of spears and a row of claws. Both tendencies worked simultaneously to create the form we see on buildings like the Siphnian Treasury at Delphi, and, curiously enough, the molding there finds itself juxtaposed both with one of the best portrayals of a phalanx front with its alternation of spears and shields and with a marvelous celebration of the destructive power of the lion's claw. Subsequently, as the lion lost its authority and weapons gained in theirs, the molding came to look more like a sequence of spears and shields, until in the Roman period this is what it could become. Even when the shield is not a full shield, the intermediate spike does acquire the barbs of a killing weapon, but there are cases when the shield too is fully represented. An assimilation, which had been subliminal for hundreds of years, at last became explicit. A continuous pressure in the imaginative faculty slowly turned soft leaves into the hard tools of war.

Why, if the assimilation had always been hinted at, was it never fully expressed until the Roman period, and then only once or twice? Probably the answer lies once again in the nature of the neuropsychological response. For a form to have enough elements to lead the feature detectors in the brain to recognize it as shield- and spearlike and so trigger the feel-good response at the brain's base was one thing. For it to constitute a representation of those things was something else. An actual row of spears and shields would have been frightening rather than reassuring. The phenomenon is familiar in such banal areas as women's dress. For a girl to wear a blouse with a leopard-skin pattern and to display long nails is effective; for her to have a hat in the shape of a leopard's mask or nails sharpened to become real claws would be counterproductive. The same factors apply to all the other assimilations proposed. Forms that have enough properties in common with desirable phenomena to trigger positive responses are one thing. Forms that look like those phenomena are something else. Columns that actually looked like warriors, or moldings that really looked like sea urchins or teeth, would be off-putting. Only if we analyze visual perception into its neural and chemical elements can we understand how forms are pulled in a particular direction by a desired assimilation but never need to be fully transformed.

I previously played down the importance of words for the formation of culture, especially of Greek architectural culture, but the importance of words cannot be denied. The texts referred to—the myths, the epics of Homer, the lyrics of Sappho, the drama of Euripides—were not just passive reflectors of neural activity. They also influenced it, and by the time of fifth-century B.C. Athens, especially during the Peloponnesian War, when citizens were often shut up behind walls, words must have taken on a new importance. Like the radio broadcasts of World War II, the plays the Athenians saw, the poems they read, and the myths they told must have filled that part of the brain we call the imagination (and the Greeks called the *phantasia*) with a wealth of vivid imagery. The functioning of this part of the brain was essential to many of the experiences that have already been discussed. Our survival depends on the brain's ability to store images of those things it most desires, whether those desires are genetically formed, as in the case of mates, relatives, and friends, or environmentally formed, as in the case of phalanx and trireme. However, as is so often the case with the human brain, a facility that exists for one reason can be activated in quite other contexts. Our ancestors discovered long ago that it was possible to activate the visual imagination not by a visual memory but by verbal storytelling, and in fifth-century B.C. Athens, where Homer's plays were performed at the Panathenaia and myths were presented as dramas in front of large sections of the population, people must have shared a large common world of the imagination. This was the world in which the heroes of Greek mythology once again came to life, and buildings such as the ancestral home of Iphigenia, the palace of Mycenae, imaged in Euripides' dream, rose once again in the minds of the play's spectators. Such buildings existed only in the electrochemistry of the brain's neural networks, but there they had much the same power as real structures, which is why Iphigenia's speech must have been so compelling. But perhaps an even better demonstration of their power is a building that is unlike all others in the history of Greek architecture, the Erectheum, which was being built on the Acropolis as Iphigenia spoke her lines (figure 3.6).

Two principal features of this structure are the flat roof and the row of disks on the frieze. The two elements are almost certainly connected, the disks being understood as the vestiges of the ends of round beams laid horizontally to support a flat roof, or rather of the metal ornaments that covered their ends. If we ask where this idea comes from, the best answer is the Lion Gate at Mycenae (figure 3.7). There in the triangular tympanum stands a single column. This carries an architrave with, above it, a row of cylindrical shapes, which must be intended as the representation of beams designed to support a flat roof. It is hard to avoid the conclusion that the designer of the Erechtheum intended the porch to be a reconstruction of just such an architectural system as exists here. The main difference is that while in the one case we have a carved representation of real timber architecture, in the other we have a real stone architecture whose forms allude to its timber origins. Confirmation that the porch of the maidens is a conscious reconstruction of an explicitly flat-roofed architecture is found in another detail of the entablature. Dentils, which are omitted from all the other parts of the building with sloping roofs, are introduced here as if they are the ends of rectangular horizontal beams. Explaining this imitation of Mycenaean style in a classical building gives further insight into the Athenian brain. Many visitors must have visited the ruins of Mycenae, the capital of Homeric Greece. To study the architecture of the Lion Gate, its grandest relic, with a view to reconstructing it must, however, have been exceptional. The reason that the architect of the Erectheum did so is almost certainly because he wanted to build a structure that would recall the great palace of the Bronze Age rulers of Athens. The remains of the foundations of the legendary residence were always visible on

the rock, and they took on a new significance when the Peloponnesian war forced the Athenians to find or invent evidence of ties with their Ionian allies, as Euripides did around 415 B.C. in his *Ion*, which made the founder of the Ionian race a grandson of Erechtheus. The decision to rebuild the temple of Athena Polias using Ionic forms and to give a new prominence to Erechtheus in its dedication had been a move in the same direction a few years before. The Athenians who knew that they had once had a palace on their Acropolis would have loved to be able to show their Ionian allies the home of their common ancestor. Given that their other principal allies were the Argives, whose ancestral royal family lived at Mycenae, it was particularly appropriate to take from that site the model for their reconstruction. Restoring on the Acropolis the carved architecture of the Lion Gate allowed them to materialize their dream of a lost past. It also helped them in identifying their enemies as Dorian invaders, destroyers of a great civilization.

3.7
Lion Gate, Mycenae.
(Photo: Alison Frantz)

The need to evoke Erechtheus's palace would explain why what was originally the reconstruction of a temple of Athena Polias came to be called the Erechtheum, as it is identified by Pausanias. It also explains many of the Erechtheum's unparalleled features. Principal among these is its extraordinary asymmetry and its row of windows framed by engaged columns, both more appropriate in domestic than sacred architecture. But no feature is more remarkable than the porch of the maidens. This is probably the part of the building most closely identified with the palace, since the two symmetrical groups of three maidens to the left and right are best understood as representations of Erechtheus's three daughters. It might be asked where the Athenian architect got the idea of turning princesses into columnar statues. The answer is most likely again the Lion Gate. Mycenae was the ancestral house of Iphigenia, and it is natural to find the inspiration of her dream in a tourist's experience of the lone column above the gateway, which was indeed all that was left of the palace. A visiting Athenian, who was already predisposed by his neural networks to see men as columns and columns as men and who might have come to Mycenae looking for the spirit of Orestes, would not have found it difficult to see in the isolated column the lone protector of the family's honor. He could equally easily have imagined golden hair streaming from the capital and even a voice as well. Once the assimilation between column and Bronze Age prince had been made, it was no great step to introduce Bronze Age princesses in the reconstruction of the Athenian palace.

The Erechtheum reveals much about the Greek brain. It shows that Iphigenia's dream was an experience that someone really had. It shows that Athenians were able to imagine an invisible building. Perhaps most interesting for the history of architecture, it shows that Athenian architects could look at an ancient monument, recognize it as a representation of a timber structure, and when reconstructing it set out not to copy it but to show by the details of a modern building its dependence on the earlier one's timber forms. It is thus likely that the experience of the Lion Gate inspired the theory of the wooden origins of Greek temple architecture found in Vitruvius. Once they had discovered that the earliest Greek architecture was timber, they looked anew at all their own buildings and saw in them proof of their wooden origins. They could see this only because even as they looked with their eyes at stone buildings, their brains could imagine them as wood.

If this chapter has worked, the temples in the reader's brain will now be different from those that filled them before. Instead of thinking of ratios and measurements, ground plans and elevations, labels and structural origins, you will now imagine phalanxes and triremes, spears and shields, ropes and pulleys, sails and masts. This does not mean that when you look at Greek temples themselves you will also see them in those terms, because while the Greek brain had feature detectors for these objects in the cortex, linked directly to pleasure centers lower down, you do not.

Our neural networks are differently configured because our environment is different, and so is our emotional attachment to objects within it, which is why it is these we have to understand if we are to write the history of modern architecture. After all, similar mechanisms to those described here have necessarily influenced design processes over the past century too. It is thus no accident that the businessmen who commissioned the grids of the Lever and Seagram buildings had neural networks adapted to working with the apparatus of modern commerce, from cash registers to profit graphs. Even more intriguing is the link between the histories of modern and ancient architecture through the general type of the tall American building. Before the term *skyscraper* was applied to a structure on land, it was the name of the topsail of a great sailing ship. For the inhabitants of the port cities of New York and Chicago a hundred years ago, tall ships were more important than tall buildings, and the pleasure in making tall and tower-like edifices came partly at least from their evocation of the great four- and five-masters. The neural networks of the inhabitants of Manhattan in the late nineteenth century A.D. had surprising convergences with those of the islanders of Samos twenty-five hundred years before.

4

Mark Wilson Jones

Doric Figuration

"EVERY ARCHITECTURAL FORM HAS ARISEN IN CONSTRUC-
TION AND HAS SUCCESSIVELY BECOME AN ARTFORM"[1] So
Otto Wagner, in the chapter on construction in his work
Modern Architecture, used uppercase fonts to score the point. Writing around 1900, his convictions reflected the evolutionary concerns of the nineteenth century—the century of
Darwin, Viollet-le-Duc, and Semper—while at the same time setting the tone for modernist theory in the twentieth century. The idea that art is born of necessity was not new, of
course, beginning in antiquity with the Stoic philosophers and later Roman writers. The
primary difference lay in the degree of autonomy and authority that the "art forms" acquire
once established by custom, the latter being paramount in Cicero's view:

> It was certainly not the search for beauty, but necessity, that has fashioned the celebrated
> pediment of our Capitol and other religious edifices. But to tell the truth, once the prin-
> ciple had been established of collecting the water on either side of the roof, dignity came
> to be added to the utility of the pediment, so much so that even if the Capitol were to be
> set up in the heavens, where it should not rain, it could hardly have any dignity without
> its double pitch roof.[2]

The formation of the Doric order is the archetypal example of both the passage from
construction to art and the doctrine of petrification, by which the formal characteristics of
a timber system are canonized in stone. A half-generation or so after Cicero, Vitruvius described the developmental phases in a famous passage in his fourth book, telling how ancient carpenters employed tie beams projecting beyond the main walls, later cutting them
off flush, and "as this had an ugly look," subsequently covering them with boards "shaped
as triglyphs are now made." Similarly, the mutules in the geison or cornice capping the

frieze were "devised from the projections of the principal rafters."[3] Meanwhile, the Ciceronian triumph of custom is illustrated by countless versions of the Doric order down the centuries that have been treated in ways that have little or nothing to do with the tectonic context. From this arises the contradictory modern reception of Doric. It is both a paradigm of the constructive origin of form and as independent of constructional "truth" as any part of the classical lexicon.

The Vitruvian thesis is sustained by clear cases of petrification in disparate architectural traditions, particularly those of China, India, and ancient Lycia, where there are many surviving substantial stone sepulchral monuments, both free-standing and rock cut, that celebrate an elaborate timber language of beam, joist, log, mortise, and tenon. Vitruvius's version of events sounds so reasonable, at least in general terms, that from the time of Raphael, artists, architects, and archaeologists have delighted in speculating about the possible primitive, timber form of the proto-Doric temple. For a century or so after 1750, propelled on the one hand by the success of the Greek Revival and on the other by Abbot Laugier's discourse on the primitive hut, the theme became a staple of architectural theorizing, and the literature on Greek architecture contains dozens of variations on the theme.[4]

As a unique ancient witness, Vitruvius can hardly be dismissed out of hand, yet reams of accumulated criticism refute his interpretation.[5] Since the sources on which he relied date from the fourth to the second centuries B.C., well after the rise of Doric in the seventh century B.C., it would not be surprising if Vitruvius had enlarged on a kernel of truth to create a comprehensive theory, and it is the equation of triglyph to beam end that smacks the most of postrationalization. Indeed, the physical configuration of the triglyph frieze positively contradicts a timber origin on several counts. Here I highlight the most frequent objections: that triglyphs run around both ends and flanks of rectangular buildings, whereas constructional logic anticipates them only on one or the other; that triglyphs are far too big and too frequently spaced to mimic beam ends;[6] that early peristyles were only so wide as to require inclined rafters/mutules rather than cross-beams; that the timberwork of Greek temples typically lay not at the level of the frieze but above it.[7] The detailed resolution of the triglyph, with the canonic three chamfered verticals and horizontal capping piece, is also something of a puzzle. Some have been tempted to see here the legacy of the joints between three slim beams,[8] but I find it hard to believe that the early Greeks had stumbled on the structural advantages of composite deep beams only to forget them as technology otherwise improved. These and other doubts about the beam-end theory have prompted many attempts to trace the origin of the triglyph by applying the concept of evolution and petrification in other ways. Inspired by potential parallels in various vernacular traditions, putative ancestors include windows or window bars (a theory that Vitruvius explicitly refuted),[9] structural stub-piers,[10] and colonnettes associated with a clerestory system or even a second story.[11] It cannot be denied that such exercises have a certain fascination, nor that vernacular construction down the ages offers important insights, but great caution is needed if we are not to force evidence to fit our preconceptions.

Theories like those just mentioned all envisage an evolutionary process by which older constructional forms were progressively transformed or atrophied, just as horses' hooves developed from claws, or penguins' flippers from what were once fully functioning wings. But in the run-up to the seventh century B.C., there simply did not exist the social and economic framework capable of sustaining an extended evolution. Terra-cotta models of Dark Age buildings with their steep thatched roofs give no hint of proto-Doric. As J. J. Coulton observes, when they do arrive, "the forms making up the Doric order appear ready developed."[12] So there is growing support for the theory that Doric was invented around the third quarter of the seventh century B.C.,[13] probably in the Peloponnese, although possibly in Corinth[14] or Argos.[15] The remaining challenge is how to explain the "ready developed" forms. One line of thought presumes that early Greek architects borrowed from Mycenae, the Near East, or Egypt, where there are forerunners to be found for the fluting of shafts, Doric capitals,[16] decorative motifs like the palmette,[17] and figural fabulations such as gorgons and griffins (which the Greeks used for acroteria, antefixes, and metopes). Once again the triglyph frieze eludes a sure ancestry. The most plausible pre-Greek source is the Mycenaean split-rosette frieze, the rosettes often being "split" by tripartite motifs;[18] alternatively, the inspiration might lie with the characteristic alternation on Geometric vases of decorative fields and groups of vertical stripes,[19] if not with the practical and aesthetic logic of working stone from the outset.[20] Nonetheless, there is nothing here to tell us why triglyphs have only a horizontal capping piece at the top, why the uprights have chamfered facets, nor why these are linked by arches.

The weaknesses of theories to do with constructive logic, evolutionary development, and external influence open the door to other kinds of interpretations. Modern perceptions of ancient theory have been overly conditioned by the much repeated Vitruvian triad: *firmitas, commoditas,* and *venustas* (firmness or durability, commodity or utility, and delight or beauty).[21] This tripolar model should rather be seen in context—that is, Vitruvius's desire to devise a conceptual scheme for architecture comparable with the triads that Greek philosophers applied to other disciplines. In reality there is nothing inevitable about these three materialist or gratificational poles; elsewhere Vitruvius brought together *venustas, firmitas,* and *decor,*[22] *decor* having little to do with mere decoration, but rather with propriety and meaning—with what is programmatically appropriate, subject to social

4.1

Panathenaic amphora showing
Athena striding between two
timber columns crowned with cocks
(ca. 530 B.C.). The tripod was a
common shield device. (Rome,
Museo Nazionale Etrusco di Villa
Giulia, inv. no. 74957. Photo:
Soprintendenza Archeologica per
l'Etruria Meridionale, neg. no. 22965)

hierarchies sanctioned by custom. If we must reduce ancient architecture to root principles, it seems to me impossible to do so without at least four: the realms of abstract theory, visual beauty, practicality, and communication of content.[23]

From this point of view, it is likely that the architectural orders were more than the fruit of constructional logic mediated by aesthetic experience. In recent years we have learned from George Hersey, John Onians, and Joseph Rykwert that the orders can sustain multivalent layers of meaning founded on ritual acts and responses to the human organization of space and material that often refer back to the body itself. Yet while there is much to appreciate in these writers' reflections on the nature of the Doric order, they have relatively little to say on the old problem of the frieze itself. Onians pursues a masculine and military analogy for the Doric colonnade as a whole, seeing in its strength, erectness, and disciplined regularity the qualities most prized in the phalanx of a hoplite army.[24] In chapter 3, he presents a compelling clue to the distributive qualities of Doric temples—their compact and relentless repetition of standard elements, their competitive, bristly character—but he leaves the frieze out of account. At the danger of taking this idea too literally, might we not expect forms recalling a run of hoplite shields, such as a pattern of overlapping circles? Rykwert too is concerned with the anthropomorphic component of classical architecture, but regarding the triglyph he is persuaded by Vitruvius's constructional explanation.[25] Hersey alone embraces this element within his etymologically driven interpretation of the orders as assemblages of sacrificial victims and related paraphernalia. Aware that thigh bones figure prominently in Homeric accounts of sacrifice as the gods' portion,[26] Hersey reads the uprights of the triglyph, which Vitruvius says the Greeks called *meroi* or thighs, as the thigh bones of goats and oxen, or rather thrice-cloven thigh bones since *triglyphos* can mean thrice recessed, thrice sculpted, thrice cut.[27] But such a notion is hard to sustain without some ancient image of triglyph-like thigh bones. And might not a triglyph better be read as something with three *meroi,* three thighs, or perhaps three legs? In fact, a three-legged object was of considerable importance in early Greek social and religious ritual and is referred to more times in Homer than sacrificial thigh bones: the tripod cauldron. It might seem that any thesis claiming an important role for an object (man-made or not) stands in opposition to analogies with human and animal figuration of the kind just mentioned. Yet the tripod can in fact be seen to reinforce certain aspects of the theme of body and building.

Intriguingly, several Greek vases depict preparations for sacrifice in front of or beside a tripod-topped Doric column (see figure 4.4e).[28] Since images such as this tend not to date much before the mid-fifth century B.C., they might only reflect a fashion for this kind of monument in the sanctuaries of the classical period. The symbolic character of tripod representations, however, is evident from other types of images which were popular in earlier periods. From around the second quarter of the sixth century, tripods were frequently used as talismanic devices on the shields of both mortal warriors and the goddess Athena (figure 4.1).[29] Representations of single stylized tripods were often framed in an heraldic manner by two opposing horses as early as the eighth century B.C. Significantly, architectural elements were used likewise.

During the seventh and early sixth centuries B.C.—around the time of the invention or consolidation of the Doric order—there are considerable formal parallels between triglyphs, tripods, and representations of tripods.[30] As in the case of triglyphs, representations of tripods invariably show one leg on the central axis, with the other two disposed symmetrically either side, with a horizontal piece on the top alone. Triglyphs are mostly

straight and vertical, but a minority have the side legs inclined inward; on occasion they are
bowed.[31] The same can be true of tripods and trident heads, but there are further telling
parallels regarding tripods. Solid-core bronze tripod legs tend to have a roughly hexagonal
cross-section, a form that presents to the viewer one front face and two chamfers on either
side. The tripod over which Apollo and Hercules wrestle on the Siphnian treasury pediment has regularly spaced chamfered legs of equal width all in one plane, as in the case of
triglyphs. In some tripod images, the legs are joined at the top by pronounced curves or
arches, the forms of which (semicircular, pointed, and ogive) find counterparts on early
forms of triglyph. A few noncanonic archaic triglyphs display features found on bronze
tripod legs, including facets with a slight concavity and frontal ones enriched by a slim
central rib.[32] Equally significant is the existence of a genre of late Geometric pottery friezes
with tripod representations used to divide, frame, or punctuate decorative scenes, as
do triglyphs and metopes. A three-legged vessel from Thasos—an *exaleiptron* or tripod
kothon (figure 4.2)—is an unusual variant on the theme in the form of three stylized
tripods introduced between the standard main supports.[33] The character of the fantastical
creatures framed by the tripods—sphinx, triton, and hippocampus—recalls the gorgon
on one of the famous late seventh-century B.C. painted panels (*pinakes*) from the Temple
of Apollo at Thermon, as well as a slightly later bronze relief of griffin and young from the
Heraion at Olympia. Both panels may have accompanied triglyphs or proto-triglyphs.[34]
It is true that tripod representations like those on the Thasos kothon typically have ring
handles on top as well as gaps between the individual legs, whereas triglyphs do not;
nonetheless this absence might be attributed to the transformations that seventh-century
B.C. designers judged necessary in an architectural context due to either the physical or perceptual need for tripod/triglyphs to carry a load.

Without sight of other illustrations to back up these assertions, I can only invite readers to
suspend disbelief temporarily and participate in a series of reflections aimed at understanding why tripod imagery might have been adopted for temple exteriors. Talking of the
sanctuary of Apollo at Delphi, Rykwert notes:

Tripods of various sizes proliferated in the sanctuary. By far the most important of them was the golden tripod inside the temple on which the Sybil sat for the god to possess her when she prophesied. . . . Display and ritual tripods were *apuroi*, "not meant for the fire" or cooking, much as modern athletic trophy cups are not really meant for drinking. . . . In Greek ritual usage, the tripod proper had assumed a curious role: in its votive form it was bullion, and such bronze, electrum, gilt and even golden tripods crowned temple treasuries . . . or stood on stone stands at temple approaches, as many did at Delphi. Tripods were also tokens of power in diplomatic exchange. They could be used as trophies as well as ritual instruments.

Rykwert suggests that a link between the tripod and the Corinthian order then proceeded via connections with Medea, rejuvenation, acanthus, and monuments such as the extraordinary acanthus or dancers' column at Delphi (figure 4.3). Perhaps such cross-fertilization could have taken place as early as the seventh century B.C. It then follows that the order most affected by this was the oldest, the Doric.

To amplify Rykwert's summary, it may be helpful to remember that the root function of tripods was domestic, as mortars or cooking receptacles. Unlike ones with a single central pillar or four legs, three-legged vessels are stable on uneven surfaces. Is it possible that tripod imagery on a building may have conveyed a sense of stability, of unshakability?

Homer cites tripod-supported cauldrons for heating bath water for Achilles, Hektor, and Odysseus[35] and for washing Patroclos's corpse.[36] But already in the Bronze Age a proportion of tripods began to transcend utilitarian roles, made out of bronze or other metals for ceremonial or ritual functions and display. For this purpose, the preferred form of tripod shifted from three-legged stands and removable cauldrons to the so-called tripod-cauldron, in which the legs were integral with a relatively shallow vessel akin to a brazier.[37]

The Homeric epics underscore the aspect of ritual; tripods are cited as princely gifts and tokens of honor and respect,[38] as appeasement,[39] and as ransom payment.[40] On several occasions Homer tells of tripods offered as prizes for the winners of athletic, equestrian, or martial competition in which the donor and the contestants include major protagonists in the Trojan wars (Achilles, Aias, Idomeneus, Odysseus).[41] The same themes find correspondence in visual art,[42] earlier in formulaic vignettes, as when a tripod prize is flanked by two horses, and later as part of more realistic scenes, sometimes with a narrative content. Chariot races, for example, either pass in front of or terminate at one, two, three, or five tripod prizes (figure 4.4a), and rivals are shown grappling with a tripod, a theme played out on a divine plane in the struggle between Apollo and Hercules for the Delphic tripod (figure

4.3
So-called dancers' or acanthus column, a votive monument from Delphi with the shaft punctuated by tiers of acanthus leaves and a capital-cum-colonette in the form of three dancers with acanthus leaves, which together originally supported a bronze tripod. (Delphi, Archaeological Museum; Photo: Ecole Française d'Athènes, neg. no. 2.266)

4.4a–e

Selection of red figure vase paintings. (Drawings by author.)

a. Chariot race at the funeral games for Pelias. (Berlin, Antikensammlung F 1655— so-called Amphairaos Vase, now lost; drawing after Adolf Furtwängler and Karl Reichold, *Griechische Vasenmalerei,* Munich, 1904–, hereafter *FRGV,* pl. 121.)

b. Struggle for the Delphic tripod between Hercules and Apollo. (Tarquinia, Archaeological Museum, inv. no. RC 6843; drawing after *FRGV,* pl. 91)

c. Apollo seated on a winged tripod, with allusion to his voyage over the sea from Delos to Delphi. (Vatican, Museo Gregoriano Etrusco inv. no. 16568; drawing after *FRGV,* pl. 144, and Louise Bruit Zaidman and Pauline Schmitt Pantel, *Religion in the Ancient Greek City,* Cambridge 1992, fig. 16 by F. Lissarrague)

d. A *Nike* and woman prepare a bull for a sacrifice associated with the consecration of a tripod. (Munich, Antikensammlung, inv. no. 2412; drawing after *FRGV,* pl. 19)

e. Laurel-wreathed man and assistant about to decorate a bull prior to sacrifice in the sanctuary of Apollo at Delphi, which is symbolized by the presence of a tripod-topped column and the acanthus/dancers' column in the background (see figure 4.3). (Leningrad, National Museum, 33; drawing after *FRGV,* and Jean-Louis Durand, *Sacrifice et labour en Grèce ancienne. Essai d'anthropologie religieuse,* Paris, 1986, fig. 44 by F. Lissarrague)

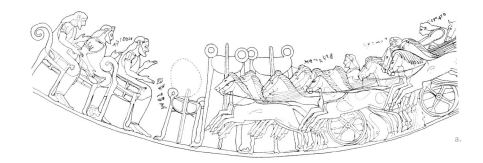

a.

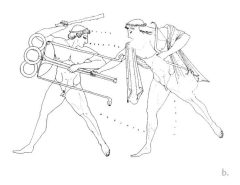

b.

c.

e.

4.4b).[43] Other scenes concern the events following victory, as when athletes or their stewards are shown carrying off tripod prizes (figure 4.5).[44] Another type of image (figures 4.4d and 4.4e) depicts ritual preparatory to the animal sacrifice accompanying the consecration of tripods to the gods in their sanctuaries.

There is abundant complementary archaeological evidence at Olympia, Delphi, and other sites where games were celebrated and tripods were won or dedicated. Susan Langdon explains that at sites like Olympia, "bronze tripods bridge the two worlds of Homeric poetry and archaeological reality."[45] Apart from the agonistic aspect, at Delphi there was an Apolline and oracular resonance to tripod dedications. In vase paintings, tripods often alluded to one or both. A curious example is the depiction of a young Apollo sitting on a winged tripod (figure 4.4c). Tripods were associated with non-Apolline oracles as well—notably that of Zeus at Dodona. This similarly helps account for the quantities of tripods found at this remote yet venerable sanctuary.

Tripods were also offered as prizes for musical, choregic, poetry, and theatrical competitions. Hesiod makes proud mention of the time he won a tripod at Chalcis and then dedicated it at the sanctuary of the Muses at Helicon.[46] The monumental tripod dedications in Athens that led to Dionysios's sanctuary became so numerous that they created the "Street of Tripods." The choregic Monument of Lysicrates, built to support a bronze tripod on the crowning finial, is only the most imposing survivor of what must have been a spectacular accumulation. The architect made a further reference to tripods in a frieze of stylized tripods in between the Corinthian capitals. Could a similar impulse some three centuries earlier have affected the design of the Doric entablature?

By virtue of their cost and long-standing associations with value, metal tripods were frequently the vehicle that civic and military authority leaders chose for absorbing the gods' "10 percent" (the tithe due to them following a victory in war or when some other prayer was answered).[47] After defeating the Persians at Plataea, the Greeks elected to show their gratitude with an extraordinary gold or gilded tripod supported by three bronze serpents twisted into a tall column.[48] It is therefore with good reason that the tripod has been called the Greeks' dedication par excellence.[49]

Finally, tripods were loosely identified with the divine lifestyle. Homer describes a visit to Hephaistos's palace that happens to catch him in the process of fabricating twenty bronze tripods to line the hall.[50] According to one of the Homeric hymns, there were tripods "all around the house" of the goddess Leto.[51] Attic vase painters of the classical period showed tripods on columns to indicate sacred space in views of sanctuaries (figure 4.4e) or in the company of a god (often, but not always, Apollo). Tripods on columns also appear in the background of scenes with multiple divinities, a probable symbol of their home or environment whether it was Mount Olympos or the depths of the sea in the case of Poseidon and Amphitrite.[52]

Having thus reviewed the roles played by the tripod in Greek ritual and religion, the goal is to understand how this might have influenced temple design in the seventh century B.C. First and foremost, temples were the conceptual house of a divinity and the real house of his or her cult statue.[53] Significantly, tripods were fixtures of the gods' ex-terrestrial homes. We might even intuit an analogy between the triglyphs of a temple and the tripods that Hephaistos made to line the hall of his house or those that stood "all around" Leto's house.

Temples and tripods were both made and set up for display. The tripod was a symbol of competitive excellence, and the *poleis* competed with each other to build magnificent temples. Just as the god's tithe of war booty could take the form of tripods, temples were similarly the fruit of war. Kendrick-Pritchett may go too far when he declared that "without wars, few of the temples and other sacred buildings of Greece would have been built,"[54] but he certainly has a point.

Treasuries were introduced in the first half of the sixth century B.C. at sanctuaries to protect the most valuable votives, including tripods. Until this time, and often later too, this function was served by temples. Alexandre Mazarakis-Ainan stresses the importance that this aspect had for the emergence of autonomous temples.[55] Tripod imagery therefore could have signaled this purpose too.

Over and above the various functions cited, Walter Burkert argues that when all is said and done, temples were dedications to the gods; they were the most visible and expensive offerings made by the Greeks.[56] And since the tripod was their most time-honored votive—one that was already present in both large sizes and large numbers in sanctuaries *before* the creation of the Doric temple—here is perhaps the most conclusive possible motivation for the adaption of tripod iconography to the dressing of temples.

The possibility that the Doric frieze initially conveyed an intelligible and appropriate message might answer two longstanding puzzles: the remarkably rapid diffusion of the triglyph frieze and the consistency of the triglyphs themselves. Neither follows directly from the logic of constructional evolution and petrification, although it is possible to supplement this with the quasi-Ciceronian hypothesis that once a timber system happened to become sanctioned in a stone temple of great renown, such renown would then have been enough to authorize later copies. Vitruvius himself gives some credence to this scenario with his statement that Doros, the mythical progenitor of the Dorians, "chanced" to use what was later called the Doric order at Hera's temple in her sanctuary near Argos, and then in other temples in Achaea.[57] The tripod-triglyph connection resolves the arbitrariness Vitruvius describes, giving us the reason for Doros's choice of architectural language over rival candidates.

The proposed tripodaic connotations of the Doric frieze meshes intriguingly with other Vitruvian notions. He famously promulgated a gender hierarchy for the orders, likening the Doric column to the upright body of a man, the Ionic column to that of a woman, the Corinthian to that of a maid or virgin. This was a fundamental theme, although it is unlikely that earlier associations and nuances were harnessed into a clear system until after the appearance of Corinthian in the fifth century. Aside from military and sexual attributes, there could hardly be a more male symbol than the tripod: a status gift for Homeric heroes and princes, a prize for male agonistic events, a symbol of victory in either a competitive or military context. Thus, the masculine overtones of the tripod seem to complement well both Vitruvius's gender theme and Onians's emphasis on its military component. The only female figures that regularly accompany tripods are personifications, especially Victories (*Nikai*) (figure 4.4d). The great majority of Greek personifications were in any event female, despite the masculine character of the values for which they stood. The few male personifications that appear with any frequency in figural art are Eros, Ploutos (Wealth), Hypnos (Sleep) and Thanatos (Death). There was no particular reason for any of these to be associated with tripods, save for Ploutos, because tripods were commonly costly status symbols.[58] The masculine associations of the tripod were certainly overwhelming in the seventh century B.C., although later, specifically at Delphi, feminine aspects arrive in the guise of Apollo's medium Themis, the Sybil, and architecturally as caryatids, paving the way for the combination of tripod and female dancers/caryatids on the Delphic acanthus column. Originally the bronze tripod was either supported on the three dancers' outstretched hands (figure 4.3), or they supported the cauldron itself, with the legs coming down in front of them to rest on the upper tier of acanthus. Unfortunately, the top of the monument is missing from the fragment illustrated here (figure 4.4e).

The very existence of caryatids sustains the analogy between body and column. But what do they carry apart from beams? Once again the tripod insinuates itself into speculations of this kind. There is, for example, a kind of parallel between paintings on vases depicting tripod-bearing columns (figure 4.4e) and tripod-bearing men. The latter are admittedly rather enigmatic, as it is often difficult for scholars to distinguish between real events and mythic allusions. The amphora at Villa Giulia in Rome (figure 4.5) shows a beefy nude athlete presenting his crowns of victory to a seated figure (patron? peer? spectator?). The two tripod-bearing men could be the victor's attendants, while the tripods

themselves are either prizes like the crowns or the dedications that victor or patron conse-crate as thanksgiving.[59] If such a scene describes a specific event, this is not the case for an unusual *loutrophon* from Kerameikos. It consists of two tiers of multiple tripod bearers treated in almost friezelike manner (figure 4.6). The necropolis context and the type of vase signify that it was commissioned to commemorate a funeral. Yet the economic stand-ing of the defunct cannot be remotely commensurate with the level of wealth implied by the display of so many valuable tripods. The vase therefore harks back to a mythical heroic funerary procession, one in which the tripods were paraded as evidence of the wealth and *aretē* (excellence) of the dead man, or perhaps as prizes awarded at the funeral games.[60] Sometimes tripod bearers carry their load with nonchalance, as though they were almost featherweight; at other times they struggle and strain. A vase in Munich shows Hercules at-tempting to stagger off with a tripod that is much bigger than he is. The legs of the tripod still touch the ground. The hero fits roughly into the space defined by the legs and bears the cauldron on his bowed shoulders.[61] It is also interesting to ponder on the spatial implica-tions of the Kerameikos *loutrophon*. Can we liken the rhythmical procession of tripods on bodies to a linear file of columns or a circuit of them—a kind of living *tholos*?

The outstanding question concerns the Dorian connection. It remains possible that the Doric was named by virtue of its being Doros's choice. Yet as has often been noted, there seems to be at least a loose match between the diffusion of the Doric order and the Dori-ans' sphere of dominance, primarily central Greece and the Peloponnese. This is where the greatest concentration of tripods has been found, most notably at the sanctuaries of Olympia and at Dodona, Delphi, Ptoion (a Boetian sanctuary), Sparta, and Thebes. Tripods may well have been prominent in Apollo's sanctuary at Corinth, the city that was not only in the vanguard of Greek architecture in the seventh century B.C. but also the leader in bronze production. There is evidence of tripods in the sanctuaries of Athena on the Athenian acropolis, and Hera in the Argive plain and on Samos, but in fewer numbers than those found at Olympia and Delphi. Samos aside, tripods did not enjoy such a prominent role in other Ionian-Ionic strongholds like Miletos, Ephesos, or Naxos—or for that matter anywhere else in Ionia.

So the circle closes. According to this interpretation, a single clue may clarify an extraordinary web of trends, values, and meanings. Male and Dorian, the tripod could symbolize competition, excellence, victory, oracles, gifts to the gods, and even their divine realm. So many are the possibilities that it is probably futile to try to isolate the particular influences that could have created the first Doric temple. At some point the architect of a prestigious temple in the Peloponnese realized just how appropriate would be a tripod frieze (the frieze always being a prime locus for display), and so was born the progenitor of all later Doric temples. It is not possible, however, to know how different were the first triglyphs or proto-triglyphs from the definitive solution; nor is it possible to know with any certainty whether the frieze was generated *ex novo* or was applied to a preexisting timber structural element, as Vitruvius relates. A constructional influence cannot after all be ruled out altogether; by virtue of their rhythm, shape, and inclination, it is reasonable to interpret mutules as rafter ends, and guttae may well hark back to some system of pegs or dowels. The details of the synthesis will no doubt always elude us. This much, however, is clear: Wagner's assertion quoted at the beginning is a statement of conviction and not a historical fact. It fails to acknowledge the rich potential of architecture for content, allusion, and communication. The Doric order, in origin, had meaning.

4.6
Funerary procession with two tiers of men carrying tripod prizes on their shoulders, perhaps to present to the clothed man visible on the left side of the upper tier. Black figure Loutrophon by the circle of Pan Exekias from Kerameikos (ca. 540 B.C.). (Athens, Kerameikos inv. no. 1682; photo: Deutschen Archäologischen Institut, Athens, neg. KER 6138)

5

Robert Tavernor

Contemplating Perfection
through Piero's Eyes

Modern science and technology have made Western society materially rich. We may wish it could make us happier too. But emotional and spiritual well-being and the framing of morality in an all-embracing belief system or faith is the realm of religion, not science. These two systems have been in conflict since the seventeenth century. This is because religion demands acceptance of and obedience to a nonrational and unseen controlling power, while, antithetically, modern science is determined by rationality, objectivity, and proof.

Sir Isaac Newton, the Father of Modern Science, wrestled with this conflict three hundred years ago without losing his belief in God. In the *Optics* he pointed to the evidence for God, a "Being, living, intelligent and omnipresent," in the phenomena of nature.[1] As he made clear in the second edition of his *Principia*, however, this Being differed from the Christian God who had dominated Western thought for centuries. Newton's modern God is "utterly devoid of all body and bodily figure, and can therefore neither be seen, nor heard, nor touched; nor ought he to be worshipped under the representation of any corporeal thing."[2] Thus, Newton challenged a tradition that had endured for sixteen hundred years that identifies Christ as the son of God, who was formed in his image. As Joseph Rykwert outlined in *The Dancing Column*, the substance of this tradition actually precedes Christianity—its roots firmly established in classical definitions of corporeal perfection. These had been formalized through idealized proportions of the male figure, which expressed the equilibrium that bound the ordered universe into a unity. This order was demonstrated by the ancients in perfect relationships of the parts of the body to its whole form, in figural sculpture and reliefs, and as a written canon.[3]

Both strands of this tradition, pagan and Christian, were reexamined, conflated, and absorbed into the art and architecture of Renaissance Italy. I contend that one of the most enigmatic paintings of the late fifteenth century, *The Flagellation of Christ* by Piero della Francesca, can be more fully comprehended through this conflated tradition. Moreover, the depiction of Christ in this painting is, as a microcosm of universal perfection, reflected in the entire architectural composition of the painting. In the *Flagellation*, body and architecture are—*convenerunt in unum*—unified physically, spatially, and spiritually.[4]

Defining the Perfect Body

Vitruvius opened book 3 of *De architectura*, with a list of numbers that comprise the "symmetrical proportions" of the ideal body. He combined these with the pure geometry of square and circle to generate the image of geometrical and corporeal unity now inseparable from Leonardo da Vinci's famous drawing of the ideal human figure.[5] Embodied in Vitruvius's ideal body are three numbers, fundamental to architectural design—6, 10, and 16—that ancient philosophers and mathematicians had identified as signifiers of perfection.[6] According to Vitruvius, these numbers were used by the ancients (the ancient Greeks) to structure the measuring standards used in the design of buildings. Consequently, bodily perfection was expressed in the symmetry of the most perfect architectural expressions of antiquity, especially the temple: "It was from the members of the body that [the ancients] derived the fundamental ideas of the measures which are obviously necessary in all works, as the finger, palm, foot and cubit."[7]

Belief in this particular anthropomorphic tradition survived the religious conversion of the Roman world to Christianity, and four centuries after Vitruvius, the early Christian church father St. Augustine remarked that the "harmonious congruence" between the parts of the body, "a beauty in their equality and correspondence," would be "more apparent to us if we were aware of the precise proportions in which the components are combined and fitted together."[8] Augustine's authority was the Bible, in which Christ is presented as the model of sacred and corporeal perfection, as "the mediator between God and men."[9] His body was a microcosm of heavenly perfection. God had provided it for human salvation as he had Noah's ark for the Flood that symbolized and the design of which was based on the overall proportions of the human body.[10]

This tradition was still intact a millennium later when Alberti synthesized pagan and Christian attitudes toward the sacred body by relating the thinking of Vitruvius and Augustine. Introducing the main column types in his treatise on architecture, *De re aedificatoria*, Alberti considers that "the shapes and sizes for the setting out of columns, of which the ancients distinguished three kinds according to the variations of the human body, are well worth understanding. When they considered man's body, they decided to make columns after its image." By relaying the key proportions of the body, he concludes, after Augustine, that "the ark built for the Flood was based on the human figure."[11]

There can be little doubt that the analogy of sacred body and architecture that Alberti promoted was well accepted in the dominant circle of Florentine artists, architects, poets, and philosophers for whom Lorenzo de' Medici (Lorenzo the Magnificent) was the foremost patron. Marsilio Ficino, the leading philosopher of the Florentine Platonic Academy that Lorenzo funded, took up the same theme in his *De vita coelitus comparanda* (*On Life Connected with the Heavens,* 1489).[12] Ficino argues that Christ is the *primum* of the genus *Humanitas* and the universal symbol of human civilization and culture. As Christ is both sacred and human, he is understood to mediate between God and humanity, and he is also present in baptized Christians. As embodiments of Christ, Christians are able to reflect universal harmony in their own creations and consequently make works of beauty. This is stated explicitly by Ficino in his early commentary on Plato's *Symposium* (1469), where beauty is described as the divine splendor of the world and art as a demonstration of the equivalence of human artifice to the acts of the divine creator. This commentary, coupled with documentary evidence connecting him to the program of Sandro Botticelli's *Primavera* (c. 1478), encouraged Gombrich to interpret the depiction of Venus in that painting as a symbol of virtue and "humanitas."[13] While this reading has since been disputed, the *Primavera* is generally accepted as a prime manifestation of the culture promoted by Lorenzo de' Medici. It is also regarded as a mature response to Alberti's earlier treatise on painting, *De pictura* (1435), and his mention there of the trio of figures—the Three Graces—who were to provide the focus for the composition of the *Primavera*.[14]

Cosimo de' Medici, on whose inheritance Lorenzo had built, had supported a circle of Florentine artists in the early part of that century who provided the foundations for its subsequent refinement. Filippo Brunelleschi, the sculptor and architect who was prominent among them, created a life-sized sculpture of Christ, *Christ Crucified* (c.1410–1415), now in Santa Maria Novella in Florence, which has dimensions and proportions similar to those of Vitruvius's *Homo quadratum* (figure 5.1). The ancient notion of beauty is unified in its form with the perfect sacred body of Christianity. The sculpture was shocking in its naturalism, even causing Donatello (as Vasari relates the story) to drop his basket of eggs in astonishment when first encountering it.[15]

Alberti had written *De pictura* within a year of meeting Brunelleschi and his artistic contemporaries in Florence. Their approach to nature, and their ability to recreate the human form accurately in sculptures and paintings, undoubtedly impressed him. In *De pictura* (and the subsequent vernacular edition, *Della pittura,* dedicated to Brunelleschi in 1436), Alberti described painting as a cultural endeavor, for he believed (as Ficino was to reiterate) that the arts were an essential part of a civilized and humanist society. Consequently, he framed his account of the technique that Brunelleschi and his contemporaries developed with a theory of the art of painting, derived mainly from classical authors. It was not

directed at the artists who wished to learn the new techniques, but at the patrons who shaped society. The most useful text for established and would-be artists, and which presents in detail the most important technique that Brunelleschi had developed, that of perspective, was written by Piero della Francesca about a decade later in *De prospectiva pingendi* (*On Perspective for Painting,* c. 1450s). Although as Piero makes clear in his introduction, instead of *perspective,* he prefers the term *proportion:*

Drawing we understand as meaning outlines and contours contained in things. Proportion we say is these outlines and contours positioned in proportion in their places. . . . I intend to deal only with proportion, which we call perspective, . . . and we shall deal with that part which can be shown by means of lines, angles and proportions, speaking of points, lines, surfaces and bodies.[16]

The treatise is arranged into three books. Piero demonstrates in the first, through theorems, propositions, and proofs (derived from Euclidean optics), how apprentice painters can produce drawings that appear three-dimensional. He commences with plans and elevations of forms, such that their planes converge on a single point. Although it is left unnamed by Piero, Alberti defined it as the "centric point" and later still it became known as the "vanishing point." In the second book he is mainly concerned with the perspectival presentation of pure and combined prisms. As in the first book, he draws plans and elevations of the prism before projecting them. In the third book, he describes complex shapes, such as capitals of columns and the human head, for which he uses what Robin Evans has identified as the "other method," one that effectively separates "the form of the object from the form of its projection."[17]

This "other method" demands that plans and elevations are drawn of the object to be painted, though when its profile is particularly sinuous and three-dimensionally complex, as with the human head, contours are also plotted. Thus, a head is "cut" into eight horizontal slices, and vertically by sixteen points that radiate at 22 ½ degree intervals from the top and center of the head: two additional points are used to outline the nose (figure 5.2). Although Piero does not describe how the artist is to find these points, presumably he would have had to use a device similar to the *finitorium* devised and described in detail by Alberti in his treatise on sculpture, *De statua* (c. 1443–1452). Alberti used the *finitorium* to measure the proportions of three-dimensional figures and, most significantly, those of the ideal human figure, that he recorded in an appendix, "Tabulae dimensionorum hominis," attached to his treatise.[18]

According to Alberti, the sculptor's *finitorium* is a disc that has six equal divisions, called degrees, marked around its circumference, with each degree subdivided into 6 minutes (a total of 36 minutes for the circumference). A movable *radium* rotates from the center of the disc and has a radius 3 feet long, the same as the disc's diameter, and so protrudes well beyond the edge of the disc (figure 5.3). The length of the radius is divided into degrees and minutes and has a vertical plumb line hanging from its protruding tip, so that when this assembly is placed above the central axis of the subject, the main parts of the body can be measured in relation to the plumb line and the radius relative to the disc.[19]

A related tool, a rod Alberti calls the *exempeda*, is used to measure specific lengths. This is calibrated by the perfect numbers 6 and 10 that Vitruvius had described. It is actually a

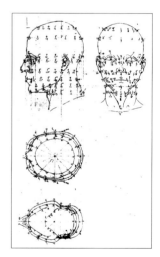

5.2
Piero della Francesca, *De prospectiva pingendi*, fig. lxiv. A head is "cut" into eight horizontal slices, and vertically by sixteen points that radiate at 22½ degree intervals from the top and center of the head.

5.3
Leon Battista Alberti,
De statua (c. 1443–1452).
The illustration (from the Paris
edition, 1651) depicts the
sculptor's *finitorium* placed on
the head of a sculpture. The
exempeda is propped against
the furniture to the left.

scale that is adjusted to the height of the figure being measured. Thus the *exempeda* is always 6 "feet" (*pedes*) long, and 1 "foot" (*pes*) is always one-sixth of the height of the individual being measured.[20] As the *exempeda* is a relative measure, it records the relationship between the parts of the body as proportions, making possible a direct comparison of bodies of varying heights. Each "foot" of the *exempeda* is divided into 10 inches (also referred to as "degrees" in the *Tabulae*), and each inch into 10 minutes: 60 inches and 100 minutes for its entire length. Alberti clearly conceived this tool so that it could be used to reveal the actual proportions of the body and in relation to the ancient notion of perfection expressed numerically.[21]

Piero's expression of perfect head types in his paintings parallels Alberti's search for ideal bodily proportions in *De statua*. Piero uses a limited number of head types that are rotated for the different figures that populate a composition. Consequently, although he would paint an accurate likeness of a patron, associated figures replicate one of several types. Only their separate gestures, poses, hairstyles, coloration, and garments differentiate them.[22] It is as if Piero conceived of heads as Alberti had described the principal ornaments used in architecture, the Doric, Ionic, Corinthian, and the Composite—or "Italic"—column types: each has its own distinctive characteristics, proportions, and specific gender.

Piero was familiar with the concept of Christ as microcosm of universal harmony. Evidence for this comes from his sometime collaborator, the mathematician Luca Pacioli, who came from Piero's native Borgo Sansepolcro, near Arezzo. In his *De divina proportione* Pacioli explained, "From the human body derive all measures and their denominations

and in it is to be found all and every ratio and proportion by which God reveals the innermost secrets of nature."[23] Their thinking clearly interweaves, and Pacioli's *De divina proportione* is either a close adaptation or a plagiarized version of Piero's *De quinque corporibus regularibus* (c. 1480s), an account, after Euclid, of the geometry of the five regular solids.[24]

Body, geometry, and architecture unite in Piero della Francesca's painting of the *Flagellation* (figure 5.4a). Since Rudolf Wittkower and B. A. R. Carter first reconstructed the composition of this painting in plan, section, and elevation (using Piero's declared methods), it has been acknowledged that a single module was used throughout its design. They also identified that Christ's height is "a unit of measurement which appears to have played an important part in the [painting's] surface organization."[25] More recently, Carlo Ginzburg has drawn attention to the measurable height of Christ in the painting (figure 5.4a). He has compared this height to the column that has traditionally been held to represent the measure of Christ—the "mensura Christi"—in St. John Lateran on the edge of Rome. This column was brought to the site of the Lateran as an object for veneration by Emperor Constantine's mother, Helen, and is now in the Triclinium of Pope Leo II. It measures 1.78

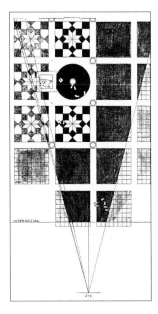

5.5a

Plan of the *Flagellation* as reconstructed by Wittkower and Carter (1953, 44).

meters or 6 *pedes* (Roman feet) tall, and other "mensura Christi" have been identified of a similar height (usually between 1.7 and 1.8 meters tall).[26] Ginzburg measured the height of Christ on the surface of the painting and found him to be 17.8 centimeters tall, or exactly one-tenth the height of the Lateran "mensura Christi."[27]

Ginzburg did not relate his discovery to the kind of reconstruction and analysis of the painting that Wittkower and Carter had made. Had he done so, I believe he would have been able to demonstrate that Christ's height is more than "a unit of measurement which appears to have played an important part in the [painting's] surface organization." I believe that the figure of Christ in the painting is the key to understanding the theme of perfect proportion that underpins the painting's composition. Christ's perfect measures determine the spatial and physical structure of the architecture in the painting and the positions of the bodies being portrayed, relative to the body of Christ.

There are two main ways of presenting the evidence for this: by reconstructing Piero's methods of perspectival composition (as Wittkower and Carter have done) or by meditating on the figure of Christ as the corporeal symbol of perfection, something that I believe an informed quattrocento observer would have been inclined to do. Both routes are revealing.

The Architecture of the *Flagellation*

By accurately reconstructing the painting's perspectival construction, Wittkower and Carter were able to locate exactly the positions of objects within the painting (figure 5.5a). They found that the bays of the finely ornamented loggia, identified as the biblical Praetorium attached to the house of Pontius Pilate, are 19 modules wide, where 1 module equals half the width of a terra-cotta tile in the floor of the piazza. The column and statue to which Christ is bound is also 19 modules high according to their measurement.[28]

Once it is understood that Christ is 6 Roman feet tall, however, these modules can be reread as dimensions in Roman feet. For instance, using Christ as a scale, the column and statue measures 10 feet tall, such that the perfect numbers 6 (Christ's height) and 10 (column and statue height) are literally combined.[29] By direct substitution of Wittkower and Carter's modules for feet (where 19 modules equals 10 feet), it is evident that the Praetorium is located on a 10-foot-square grid; intervals of 10 feet separate the painter's eye from the foreground trio of figures, which is placed midway between the "eye" and the turbaned figure facing Christ. Christ and Pilate are at a distance 50 feet from the "eye." Intervals of 15 feet unify the scene separating the foreground figures from the first column, this column from Christ, and Christ from the back wall of the Praetorium.[30]

An alternative way of presenting the structure of the painting is to remove the perspective and describe the composition in plan, with the body of Christ—and more specifically the column to which he is tied—located at the center of the painting's organization. Christ as the immutable, immobile "center" of the scene is the source of the painting's composition. Christ is viewed through the frame of the Praetorium and highlighted by an unseen light source brightly illuminating the bay overhead, as if light is emanating from his body.[31] (The lighting in the painting was recently reconstructed on a computer model. That model is represented here as a line drawing, for comparison with the original painting and Wittkower and Carter's reconstruction in plan.)[32] (See figures 5.5a, 5.5b, and 5.5c.) From this

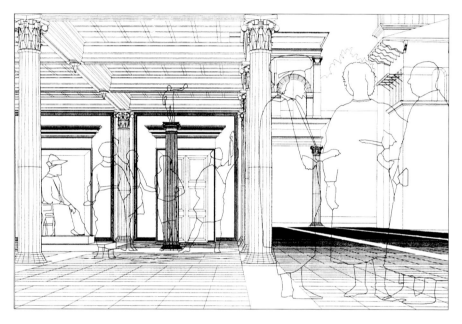

5.5b
Three-dimensional computer model of the *Flagellation* viewed from the same position as the original painting. (Computer drawing: Olivetti/The Alberti Group)

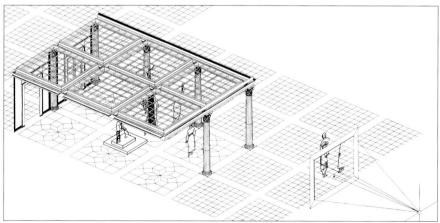

5.5c
Three-dimensional computer model of the *Flagellation* viewed from above. The "eye" and picture frame as Piero describes the composition can be seen to the right. (Computer drawing: Olivetti/The Alberti Group)

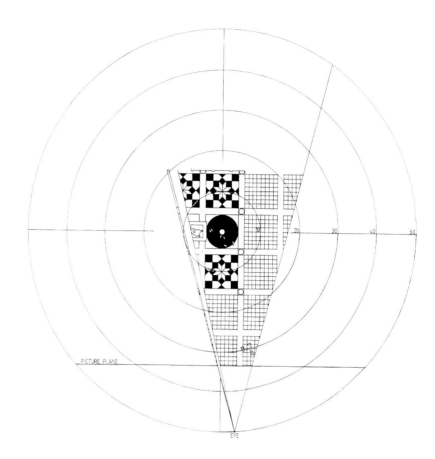

5.6

Plan of the *Flagellation* scene, as constructed by Wittkower and Carter (1953) and incorporated within a graduated disc, or "horizon," by the author. The column of Christ is located at the center of the "horizon," and concentric rings of radius 10, 20, 30, 40, and 50 feet (a 100-foot total diameter) mark the positions of the groups and individuals in the composition (marked by their footprints), and the "eye" from which the perspectival scene is viewed. (Drawing: Author)

sacred place, a divine light and perfect numbers emanate as a series of concentric circles. The viewer is invited to focus on Christ's form from the perimeter edge of the outermost circle that has a diameter of 100 feet—the square of the perfect number 10 (figure 5.6).

There are some obvious parallels to this reading. The earth as macrocosm was perceived, pre-Copernicus, as the only fixed planet and as the anchor and soul of the universe surrounded by whorls of change. This notion of centrality had its counterpart in idealized views of established cities as well as urban planning. In his *Laudatio*, Leonardo Bruni had envisaged the city center of Florence as the first or most central of five concentric circles. At the very center was the Palazzo della Signoria (Palazzo Vecchio), the political and physical heart of that city's organization.[33] Alberti's physical survey of the city of Rome in his *Descriptio urbis Romae* (c. 1444) is predicated on similar principles. The Capitol of Rome, the traditional and historic governmental seat of the city, from which "order" radiates, was marked at the center of his surveying disc, which Alberti calls the *orizon*. Every other feature of the city is made to refer to this central point, including the Vatican and St. Peter's.[34] The horizon is defined as a disc having a diameter of 10 feet and a radius divided into 50 parts, such that its diameter is subdivided into 100 units (figure 5.7).[35] It resembles Alberti's earlier design for the *finitorium* in *De statua*.

As Alberti's horizon is 10 feet wide, it is exactly one five-millionth of the diameter of the earth using Nicholas of Cusa's version of Pi.[36] Also, as the *finitorium* in *De statua* is 3 feet—half the height and span of the ideal man 6 feet tall—there is an implicit size relationship in the tools that Alberti devised, which unite the measure of man, city, and earth.

This micro- to macrocosmic relationship is also suggested in Piero's *Flagellation* in the relationship of the 6-foot-tall Christ and the 10-foot column and statue to which he is tied. Overtly, this may be taken to imply spiritual and physical unity, where Christ is bound to the perfected artifice of man. But more profound, Carlo Bertelli has linked the inclusion of the column in this scene depicting Christ's flagellation to the *Helia Capitolina* of Jerusalem. The *Helia Capitolina* was so-called because emperor Hadrian (*Aelius Hadrianus*) rebuilt Jerusalem after Titus had had it destroyed and gave the city the name *Colonia Aelia Capitolina*. A single column became the city's symbol. Bertelli argues that in the absence of the wooden cross, the *Helia Capitolina* "has become the column of the flagellation."[37] And as a symbol of microcosm, the single column of Jerusalem was identified by Bede in the eighth century with the "center of the earth" and by others as the "umbilicus of the world."[38] It cannot be a coincidence that in this context, the groups of figures in Piero's painting are positioned astride five concentric circles, each 10 feet apart and the largest having an overall diameter of 100 feet. As Christ is scaled in the painting to one-tenth of life size, so this diameter of 100 feet is equivalent to 10 feet, the diameter of Alberti's horizon, itself a symbol of the earth that it is used to survey (figure 5.6).

Surveying the Scene

Piero surely benefited from Alberti's intellectual approach, methods, and special tools for artists. A combination of Alberti's measuring discs would have made a useful tool for setting out the object relationships in this particular painting. By translating the three-dimensional architectural scene into a circular plan and making use of a measuring disc, like Alberti's horizon, with its rotating *radium* or pointer centered on Christ's column, then from any viewpoint, the resulting arrangement would have a perfect order relative to Christ, who provides the measure for the entire composition. Thus, the principal architectural and figural elements are multiples of 10 feet, and the picture plane of the *Flagellation*

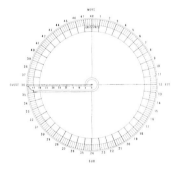

5.7
Reconstruction of the surveyor's "horizon" as described by Leon Battista Alberti in his *Descriptio urbis Romae* (c. 1444). It is defined as a disc having a diameter of 10 feet and a radius divided into 50 parts, such that its diameter is subdivided into 100 units.

makes an imaginary line at one-third of the distance from the painter's eye to Christ, a distance of 16⅔ "feet," or one-sixth of the 100-foot diameter that encompasses the entire composition.[39] Piero provides the figures in the painting with a measured relationship to one another using the perfect ratio. The three foreground figures are placed at the edge of a circle 60 "feet" in diameter, which, relative to the overall diameter of 100, is 6:10, the same ratio that describes Christ's height to that of the column and statue to which he is joined.[40]

We know that Piero's perspective methods required plans and elevations to be drawn. He proceeded as if he was an architect or surveyor, and it has been argued persuasively that quattrocento perspective "not only was inspired by the geometry of surveying but arose within surveying practice, as a topographic technique."[41] Having established both the cultural and technical context within which this painting was produced, does it follow that Piero used a plan overlaid onto a circular measuring disc, like Alberti's horizon, so as to choreograph this particular composition? If so, might he have built a physical model of the scene to be depicted? Vasari referred to the practice whereby painters first draw a composition in plan, and he also relates that Piero was "very fond of making clay models which he would drape with wet cloths arranged in innumerable folds, and then use for drawing and similar purposes."[42] This method described by Vasari is a reasonable extension of the "other method" identified by Evans, as it permits the artist to sculpt the plotted profile of the head (and body) prior to drawing and painting it. Modeling the entire scene would seem to be a practical second stage in this process and is one that could have made good use of Alberti's "veil," a frame and screen through which to view distant objects. Alberti described this in *De pictura* to help artists translate three-dimensional figures onto the surface of a painting.[43]

Of course, while such an approach would have helped Piero to construct a mathematically precise and symbolically valuable composition, he would not have expected the viewer of this painting to retrace his techniques in order to make sense of what is in front of their eyes. Rather, the viewer looks for clues with which to interpret the *historia*, or theme, being depicted in the painting.[44] On the assumption that Christ represents the "ideal" man and is 6 feet tall, it follows that the mathematical beauty that passively pervades the composition would have prompted an informed fifteenth-century observer to meditate on the visual clues Piero provides in the painting. The question remains, however, who or which particular community would have wished to decipher its hidden meaning in order to appreciate the message it conveyed? Unfortunately too little is known about the painting's origins to be certain, and even its dating is a matter of guesswork. Without firm evidence, scholars have argued that the *Flagellation* was painted between the middle and third quarter of the fifteenth century.[45] In Florence during those years, Lorenzo de' Medici provided a focus for a group who would have been receptive to the ideas embodied in the painting. More pertinent to its provenance, so too would Federico da Montefeltro, who ruled over Urbino, the city where the painting was discovered.[46]

Federico knew the power of "humanitas," having been taught by the eminent humanist Vittorino da Feltre. Moreover, he, like Lorenzo, regarded Alberti highly. Federico built himself a great palace and library, surrounding himself with leading intellectuals, architects, and artists. Alberti was a frequent visitor, and they shared a common passion for the arts and architecture. Although the first printed edition of *De re aedificatoria* was finally dedicated to Lorenzo de' Medici, it is recorded that Alberti had at first intended dedicating it to Federico.[47] Piero della Francesca was perhaps Federico's favorite artist. He was chosen to paint the now famous diptych in memory of Federico's much-loved wife, Battista Sforza, who had died in 1472, only months after giving birth to his son and heir, Guidobaldo.[48] The *Triumphs* depicted on the diptych's outer panels contain many explicit emblems of authority, theology, and virtue. It shows two triumphal carts being drawn to one another, one carrying Federico, the other Battista. His is being pulled by white horses, hers by unicorns; he is being crowned by a winged Victory, who is accompanied by three cardinal Virtues. Charity is depicted with a pelican on her lap. As the pelican mythically fed her young with her own blood, it probably refers here to the sacrifice of Battista, who gave her body for her son.[49] Consistent with the cultured aristocracy of the fifteenth century, Federico was clearly the sort of patron who would have enjoyed meditating on the symbolism of the *Flagellation* as well as appreciating its conjunction of figures and architecture *all'antica*.[50]

Meditating on the Body of Christ

The figure of Christ in the painting stands in a circle inscribed in the floor grid, much as Vitruvius had described an "ideal" man bounded by a square and circle.[51] The traditional interrelationship of perfect body and the geometry of circle and square determines simple number sequences. It is well known after Vitruvius that a 6-foot square is circumscribed by a circle whose diameter is close to 8½ feet, since 6 times the square root of 2 (or 1.414) closely approximates 8½ (exactly 8.484). This "ad quadratum" method of proportionally relating squares (and their areas) to one another so that the diagonal of the first square becomes a side of the second, and so on, was well known in the quattrocento and employed by masons. Vitruvius refers to this method as wisdom received from Plato.[52]

The tradition that Christ embodied the perfect measures of the Vitruvian ideal and that these ancient and Christian values are combined at this point in the painting is indicated by the golden statue on top of the column. The statue has been interpreted as a representation of the sun—the source and provider of light, real and spiritual.[53] It could also represent a classical god or hero because of its nudity and pose. Marilyn Lavin has identified it as either Apollo or Hercules; both were considered classical forerunners of Christ. Lavin suggests, "Moreover, the silvery sphere in the statue's extended left hand is an imperial sign of universal sovereignty, frequently applied to Christ. In other words, Piero has given the statue attributes describing the pagan qualities that Christ himself embodied and superseded."[54]

The column on which the statue stands is Ionic, which, as Vitruvius presents it, is usually associated with female deities and their temples, "in keeping with the middle position they hold."[55] The Ionic may therefore be considered to be an inappropriate form to tie Christ against, though it may have been used here because it is "middling" and is intended to provide a clue to the principal numbers at this point in the painting. According to Alberti's discussion of the origin of the column types in *De re aedificatoria*, the Ionic has the proportions 1:8, because it is the mean between the extremes of the Doric 1:6 and the Corinthian and Composite at 1:10.[56] Meditating along these lines, an observer of the painting may conclude that as Christ is 6 feet tall, the Ionic column behind him is 8 feet, the statue height 2 feet, and therefore that the height of column and statue combined is 10 feet. He would be substantially correct. The Ionic column is visibly between these two columnar extremes and is only slightly shorter than the perfect mean, at 7¾ feet. By the same reasoning, the Composite columns of the Praetorium may be assumed to be 10 feet high, which indeed they are.[57] In this way the beauty of the architecture—its perfect proportions—can be interpreted through the dimensional significance of the body of Christ, though to understand the placement of the other figures relative to him would presumably require the observer to reconstruct the painting in plan.

Convenerunt in unum

As Christ is the means by which the perfect composition of the painting can be understood, I believe that the erased or discarded motto once seen on the painting has even greater significance than has been realized. This quotation originally was either attached to the gilt frame of the painting or was part of the painted composition itself, presumably like the text still visible on the platform edge of Pilate's throne.[58] It read "CONVENERUNT IN UNUM," meaning, literally, "They came together as one,"[59] and is probably an extract from Psalm II, verse 2, where it is presented (and in the King James translation) as: "*Adstiterunt reges terrae et principes convenerunt in unum adversus Dominum et adversus Christum eius* / The kings of the earth set themselves, and the rulers take counsel together, against the Lord [God], and against his anointed [Christ]." The psalm is concerned with the Jews and their persecution by the ungodly, and God's promise to support those who rise to their defense. This particular verse is associated with the Passion as the Church adopted it as the antiphon for the First Nocturne of Good Friday.[60]

The flagellation of Christ is the theme that is most obviously recognizable in the painting, and the lost motto relates to this. But how the three figures outside and to the right of the Praetorium relate to theme and motto has been hotly debated.[61] We may never know for sure whom they represent, though we must presume that Piero would have intended the *historia* being enacted was integral with the presentation of perfect body and ideal proportion that structures the painting.

Numerous explanations for the motto's significance have been put forward and in the context of specific identifications of the foreground trio.[62] My literal translation of this phrase—"they came together as one"—permits a more neutral reading that is not determined by dates or the need to prove the identities of the foreground figures in the painting; neither does it deny in any way its connection to Christ's Passion. His scourging and crucifixion was interpreted universally, as Bertelli has suggested: "Because the flagellation takes place at the centre of the earth [Jerusalem], it is a sacrifice that is relevant to all men; Greek, Latin and Arab."[63] Christ's figure is the divine source from which emanates all power, order, geometry, number, and measure; he embodies the heavenly perfection and truth that mankind should emulate on earth.[64] As the center and the measure of everything, Christ signifies universal truth. This truth pervades this painting and exists independent of the interaction by the three figures in the foreground. Piero presumably intended the painting to be legible at several levels and to have a general relevance for Christians and humanists, as well as the particular concerns of his patron.[65]

Alberti and Ficino retained a firmly held belief in the body-microcosm. It is reasonable to suggest therefore that the *Flagellation* was meant to be read as an erudite tract on mathematics and geometry and, more profoundly, as a declaration on sacred beauty in body and architecture—one that includes the principles for constructing spatial and architectural relations in perspective according to the universal laws of natural beauty. Alberti expressed similar concerns in his theories for the visual arts, and perfect number and geometry are among the qualities detectable in the fundamental organization of his buildings. We have lost the ability to perceive his buildings as he designed them; in any case, they have not been handed down to us intact and do not represent his original intentions.[66] Piero's paintings are by comparison far more pristine, and his *Flagellation of Christ* provides an opportunity for us now to appreciate the unity of body and building sought five centuries ago. As this theme of unity visibly come together as one in this painting, I believe we should abandon the title it has acquired by default and revert to the motto probably given to it by its artist or patron: CONVENERUNT IN UNUM. Recoupling these words with the painting may then encourage us to reflect on the unity that was once sought and what the modern era, with its dislocated systems, has been unable to accomplish.

6

Alina Payne

Reclining Bodies:
Figural Ornament in
Renaissance Architecture

Criticism and Historiography

It is commonly acknowledged that the appropriation of classical ornament constituted a defining feature of Renaissance architecture. Indeed, its deployment and design elicited a rich body of theory that is preserved in the numerous treatises of the period.[1] Yet despite this considerable act of attention, neither definitions nor a general theory of ornament was ever explicitly formulated. The orders claimed exclusive prominence in the literature, while the human figure that so often accompanied them—the masks, herms and terms, caryatids, figural bas-reliefs, reclining bodies on window and door pediments, and upright ones on roof parapets and stair balustrades—received no commentary (figure 6.1). Why they were there, whose province this sculpted matter belonged to, and how they were thought to interact with the columns and pilasters, cornices and entablatures, remain open questions.

Occasional insights can be gleaned from the literature of the period. For example, in the fourth book of the *Quattro libri* (1570), Palladio presents his reconstructions of the various Roman and foreign antiquities best known to his contemporaries. As we know, much of this was an exercise in imagination, for although some of the ruins now lost to us were still standing, many of the temples he illustrates were in bad repair and, worse, obscured by *tumuli* and medieval construction. A far greater figment of his imagination, however, was the figural sculpture with which he completes, and evidently believes he has embellished, parapets, pediments, colonnades, and niches. In fact, he admits as much when he describes the temples of Mars Ultor in the Forum Augusteum and the Temple of Minerva in the Forum Transitorium (or Forum of Nerva): "I have shown tabernacles with statues since the ruins *seem* to suggest this."[2] And as if to ensure that his readers do not think him entirely fanciful, he adds, "No one should marvel that I have shown such a wealth of statues in this building, because we read that in Rome there were so many that they seemed to constitute

6.1
Andrea Palladio, Detail,
Loggia del Capitaniato, Vicenza.
(Photo: Author)

another people" (figure 6.2).[3] The image, which belonged to Cassiodorus, was apparently as well known as Augustus's quip that he had found Rome brick and left it marble.[4]

But this is as far as Palladio will go with his comments on the sculptural matter attached to or placed on Roman buildings. Curiously enough he is even less forthcoming when he describes his own buildings. Although they too are inhabited by petrified bodies—parapet figures, reclining nudes on window pediments, caryatids or modified caryatids, figures on balustrades standing sentinel at entrances, not to mention varied figural bas-reliefs embedded in walls—none is mentioned even in passing (figure 6.3). It could be argued that as they were conceived and carved by others—such as Vittoria, Rubini, Zelotti, and India and their teams of sculptors, *scalpellini*, and *stuccatori*—they did not belong to the architect's province. Sketched into the facade by him, they awaited the input of others. Still, it seems difficult to believe that such an important component of a facade—one, moreover, that would affect its reception just as much as the columns and pilasters, and one that in some of Palladio's buildings takes on significant proportions—should be brushed off as if of no architectural consequence at all.

Although Palladio may be a good example to illustrate how often such sculptural devices were used, he may not be as instructive with respect to theory. His texts are very concise and factual, and his silence on the sculpture of his facades may not in itself be that singular. However, *not one* Renaissance author comments on the sculptural programs of his buildings and projects: not Francesco di Giorgio, sculptor though he was; not Alberti, who may well be expected to have done so since he wrote authoritatively on all the visual arts; not Serlio, despite his evident interest in the representation of personality types and character through architectural detailing; not Scamozzi; and certainly not Vignola.[5] And this silence extends beyond the architectural treatise. Even Vasari, who had explicitly set out to explicate art with categories that crossed mediums left architectural sculpture outside his purview.[6] The architects' and critics' collective gaze was firmly trained on the orders, and the sculpture they routinely included on the facades they designed was passed over in silence. Thus, we do not know how these figures were proportioned, if their dimensions were part of the larger network that embraced the whole facade, how their gestures were selected and how they were positioned, why some were languidly hugging pediments while others lined the roofs in *contrapposto*.[7]

Occasionally an author offers faint hints. In Book VII of *De re aedificatoria*, for example, Alberti assures his readers that in antiquity, "the use of statues was splendid (*egregius fuit usus statuarum*)," and he defines them as the ornament of public and private buildings alike.[8] Yet as promising as this may sound, it is only moderately relevant. In this section he describes everything as ornament (not only columns and cornices but also roofs and vaults,

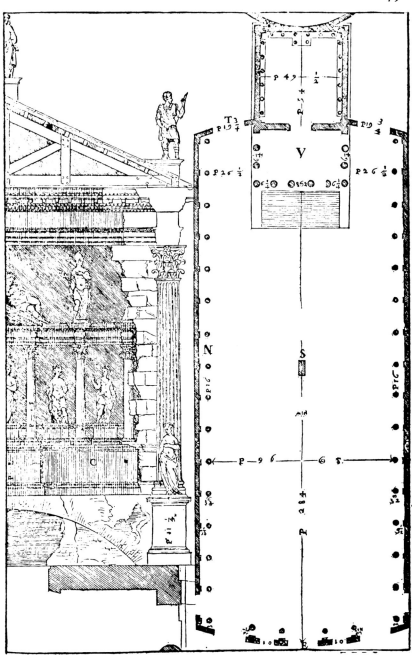

6.2
Andrea Palladio, *I quattro libri*
(1570), Forum of Nerva.

6.3
Andrea Palladio,
Palazzo Iseppo Porto, Vicenza.
(Photo: Author)

gates, streets, arches, and so forth). Moreover, this statement occurs in a passage focused on commemorative monuments and effigies, and thus does not directly concern architecture.

Gherardo Spini, a Florentine letterato who wrote a treatise on ornament in the 1560s, makes a more pertinent statement.[9] Unlike his predecessors he includes a short commentary on the acroteria in his systematic survey of all architectural ornament. For him, this device is the final touch in the sequence that starts with the column base and reaches all the way to the roof. And with great acuity, he declares it to be most successfully used when representing winged deities such as Fame and Victory.[10] It is clear from the context of his overall argument that Spini sees such figures, frozen in the act of taking flight and suggesting unfettered movement, levity, and weightlessness, as a necessary counterpoint to the load-versus-support dialectic that the columns and beams set up. Yet despite the perceptiveness of these observations, Spini remains unique among his contemporaries in discussing acroteria as a formal device of the facade and as sculptural ornament.

Given that such a blind spot affects commentaries of their own work, perhaps it is not surprising to see how few Renaissance architects analyze triumphal arches critically. This is not to say that they pass unnoticed, for the *taccuini* from the period are bursting with sketches that demonstrate how attentively their details were studied.[11] Palladio, for example, planned a separate book on triumphal arches and many of his preparatory drawings have been preserved.[12] What he would have said about them is hard to speculate on, though from scattered remarks we know that he admired their form and details. He specifically praises the *intagli* of the Arch of Titus as an example of "*edifici che furono fatti ai buoni tempi*" and describes the Arch of Constantine as "very beautiful."[13] Such an attentive examination of triumphal arches can be traced back to Alberti, who was the first to include them in his treatise on architecture and comment on their figural ornament. Thus, he recommended that "statues may be best set up on the ends of the beams where they project from the work to embrace the columns" (VIII, 6), yet he offered no comment on the visual function that such a gesture performs. Moreover, the passage is so brief, and had so little resonance even within Alberti's own treatise, that it did not generate a tradition of critical attention.[14]

An exception among his contemporaries, Serlio discusses triumphal arches in his Book III (1540) on antiquities at great length. Yet, like Alberti, he omits figural ornament from the discussion. Instead, he focuses on the agglomeration of profiles and the rich carvings that characterize these later products of Roman art. Although evidently drawn to them, he finds them licentious and confused, and he dismisses all triumphal arches one by one, with the exception of the least interesting of all, the Arch at Ancona.[15] His illustrations are no less biased, for he edits out all traces of extraneous ornament, figural sculpture in particular (figures 6.4 and 6.5). It may be that early criticism of the sculptures on the Arch of Constantine had set a precedent for such treatment; after all Raphael had dismissed them as the products of a "late" and exhausted style producing *figure sciochissime* (foolish figures), and Serlio may very well have been familiar with such a view from his days in the ambience of the Raphael and Peruzzi circles in Rome.[16] But even if true, such shortcomings in the execution of specific sculptural forms do not adequately explain why he should entirely neglect a whole class of ornament.

The absence of a discussion of figural ornament in architectural discourse has been accentuated by our own disciplinary biases and a scholarly tradition that came of age at the end of the nineteenth century. Such neglect is hardly surprising in an intellectual climate in which both representation and ornament were under attack.[17] Indeed, whether focused on tectonics or abstraction, on materials and building technique or empathy theories,

6.4
Sebastiano Serlio, *Il terzo libro* (1540), Arch of Septimius Severus,

6.5
Arch of Septimius Severus, Rome. (Photo: Author)

definitions of ornament that went back to Schinkel and Riegl, Wagner and Worringer did not include the human body.[18]

It is certainly true that Jakob Burckhardt devoted a fair amount of space to architectural decoration in his *Die Geschichte der Renaissance* (1867, 1878) as he drew attention to now frequently neglected items such as door surrounds, candelabra mullions, interior decoration, fireplaces, infilling of pilasters, friezes and window surrounds, altars and pulpits.[19] Yet he was also quick to distinguish between figural sculpture focused on the human body and decorative carving that drew on vegetal motifs. The former was excluded from this survey; even the latter received only an ambiguous accolade. Thus, he stated that "the great architects almost all loved ornamental work, and, if nonetheless they designed their buildings to be simple and grand, for them this factor has to be taken all the more deeply into consideration."[20] The emphasis on "simple and grand" as the business of architecture resurfaces later when he declares that "architecture, more than once threatened by the dominance of a decorative style, held to the course of its high destiny thanks to the activities of the great Florentines."[21] Even Wölfflin, who liked sculpture and was himself a great supporter of Adolf von Hildebrand, concentrated on the orders and the proportional relationships they set up on facades when he dealt with Renaissance architecture.[22] In his *Prologomena zu einer Psychologie der Architektur* (1886), Wölfflin argued that "ornament is an expression of an excess of force to form. The heavy mass produces no flowers. . . . Weight is overcome, the excess of striving force manifests itself in the rise of the gable and celebrates its greatest triumph in the plastic figures that, freed from pressure, unfold freely."[23] Yet when he talked about liveliness of surface or movement and excitement, he referred only to niches and pilasters, and sculpture receded into the background.[24]

That half a century later Wittkower should similarly ignore ornament, particularly figural ornament, need not surprise us.[25] For his generation, truth and honesty of structure were the ultimate goals of architecture, and so Alberti's adage that "the work ought to be constructed naked, and clothed later; let the ornament come last" (IX,8) rang a familiar note.[26] That Alberti meant no value judgment, but simply advised on a sequence of building operations so as not to damage finished parts if set up too soon, naturally escaped notice. Finally, in what became the principal reference work for modern scholarship, Heydenreich and Lotz attended little to ornament, figural or otherwise. On the few occasions when they did, as in the case of Alessi, they labeled his facades "pictorial" (*malerisch*). In a world focused on structure and its expression, on "space-time" and essential form, this was not altogether a compliment.[27]

Sculpture scholars have been equally disinterested in architecture with the exception of those working on Donatello and Michelangelo.[28] Around the turn of the century, some scholars brought architecture and sculpture together in the same work, as did Pietro Paoletti and Julius Baum.[29] Yet the echoes of these works remained weak. The treatment of the oeuvre of sculptor-architects like Ammannati and Sansovino is particularly revealing in this instance. Though we have exemplary studies on both, they tend to act out the prejudices of the field: some study their sculpture, others their architecture. Consequently, the two parts of one artistic personality remain essentially isolated.[30] Although there have been occasional efforts to redress the imbalance, such as Wolfgang Lotz's short but powerful formal analysis of Sansovino's sculpted frieze for the Marciana or the work on the sculptors associated with Palladio, this has not materially affected the interests, questions, and research among historians.[31]

For a world focused on abstraction and technology, neglecting figural ornament was perhaps inevitable. However, it is more difficult to explain why Renaissance authors should have done so too. And it is precisely because this omission is so baffling that it deserves attention. Located at the point where architecture and sculpture meet (or part), figural ornament, as dealt with at both the level of theory and practice, allows us unique opportunities to investigate how Renaissance architects defined ornament and construed the relationship between the visual arts.

Ornatus

What caused this gap between the practice of architecture and its commentators? One evident reason for the absence of a discourse on figural ornament has to be sought at the fountainhead of all architectural theory: Vitruvius's *De architectura*. His treatise, the blueprint for all those that followed from the Renaissance onward, entirely neglected this aspect. For Vitruvius, architecture precedes the other arts and supplies them with their context; paintings, mosaics, and sculpture are added later by other craftsmen, attached, embedded, and mortared into walls, roofs, and porticoes. As such, architecture is isolated away from this *Gesamtkunstwerk;* it precedes it and sets its parameters.[32] Implicitly, how the arts communicate with architecture is the sculptors' and painters' problem. Vitruvius's well-known vituperation against the irrational painted architecture of the second Pompeian style is only one example that confirms this bias: the painter fails to attend to the architectural narrative, and the whole is an unmitigated disaster.[33]

These structural characteristics of *De architectura* had a direct impact on the treatise writers of the Renaissance: Vitruvius excluded sculpture, and so did his readers. However, three other moves Vitruvius made affected decisively, if more subtly, the way in which a theory of architectural ornament was formulated. First, he suggests that the *ornamenta* might be isolated as a concern unto itself.[34] This is evident in Book IV, 2 where he discusses the elements above the column and supplies origins and prescriptions for their correct use. When he defines the *ornamenta* as *imago* (triglyphs and dentils as representations of beam-ends and purlins) in a subsequent passage, he reinforces the separation between building and ornament. Nevertheless, Vitruvius was ambiguous on this point. In Book III, for example, the orders are embedded in and indistinguishable from the building type itself. Yet his Renaissance readers privileged the notion of an applied ornamental screen that starts with pedestals, runs through columns and entablatures, and ends with acroteria.[35] Such a reading began to gain currency with Alberti, who declared the column to be "the principal ornament without any doubt" and became so established that the fact that Vitruvius had never stated as much was completely lost from view.[36]

If Vitruvius's first prophetic move was to suggest that ornament could be isolated as a concern, his second was to compare his endeavor in setting down the theory of architecture with that of Cicero, Lucretius, and Varro.[37] However, Cicero wrote on rhetoric, Varro wrote on the Latin language, and Lucretius wrote on the origin of things. These terms of comparison, though perhaps innocent enough for Vitruvius to use, were nevertheless not innocent of innuendo, particularly for Renaissance readers whose entire culture was so language driven and dependent on texts. For them, the subtle association of architecture, language, and rhetoric would have been implicit, whether Vitruvius had intended it or not.

Finally, Vitruvius made one other interesting opening in his treatment of ornament: his aesthetic category *decor* seemed to be of one family with the *decorum* of poetics and rhetoric.[38] And since *decor* particularly affected the appropriate deployment of ornament—which orders and decorative motifs were appropriate for which deity—and its definition came so close to that of *decorum,* the two virtually merged in the Renaissance reception of *De architectura.*[39]

These three aspects of Vitruvius's treatise may not seem significant in the context of the whole work, yet small gestures though they were, isolating ornament as a category, implying a *paragone* between architecture and the literary arts, and opening up ornament to the theory of *decorum* did not pass unnoticed by the reception. To be sure, ornament was already on the way to acquiring independent status in the Renaissance, as the contemporary *taccuini* with their endless records of carved details and measurements amply testify. Perhaps with the sole exception of the temple pediment, ornament produced the most powerful visual impact and gained an almost iconic currency as the most obvious way of declaring the appropriation of antiquity. No other aspect of ancient architecture had the same associative power when used as quotations; without its grid of classicizing pilasters, the Rucellai palace would have been just another Florentine block.

Once isolated, ornament could enjoy a semiautonomous existence. Separated from the main trunk of architecture, it could feed off other disciplines, especially those where ornament was a distinct category and claimed its own body of theory and critical vocabulary. Thus, when it came to a theory of ornament, it was difficult to resist the *paragone* that Vitruvius had so subtly proposed and not rely on the models provided by the literary arts. As his readers learned all to soon, the theoretical apparatus provided by *De architectura* was thin, at least when compared to that of rhetoric and poetics, where *ornatus* was part of a highly complex and developed analytical vocabulary and theoretical framework. Inevitably they turned to Cicero, Quintilian, and Horace for guidance to fill in the gaps.[40]

This process of appropriation of a theoretical apparatus from another discipline did not happen overnight. At first, architects were more concerned with identifying the forms that Vitruvius named, connecting and reconnecting signified and signifiers. From Alberti through Francesco di Giorgio to Bramante, Raphael, and Peruzzi, architects were preoccupied with little else. But as archaeological expertise sharpened and ever more authoritative translations and commentaries of Vitruvius's text became available, the interest in a theory of ornament formation and use increased, as did the isolation of ornament into a self-contained category. Already Alberti had intended the second half of his treatise to focus on ornament, even if he ended up broadening this topic; Francesco di Giorgio also focused on *colonne* separately and gave the orders their own chapter. Nevertheless, it is Serlio who consecrated the primacy and internal cohesiveness of ornament as an independent category by using it as the lens through which he looked on architecture. In Book IV, *Regole generale d'architettura sopra le cinque maniere degli edifici* (1537), columns, entablatures, and cornices combine and recombine into ever more complex systems, from door frames, through gates and fireplaces, until they become entire facade arrangements for town houses, villas, and palaces. Though he never made the connection himself, Serlio's Book IV may be seen as the complement to the *ornatus* section of any treatise on rhetoric or poetics. The gradual buildup from simple to complex forms, complete with their definitions, parameters for use, examples, warnings against abuses, and possible effects, constitutes the architectural equivalent of the structured presentation of literary *figure*.

Perhaps the consequences of isolating ornament into a self-contained category is nowhere more evident than in Gherardo Spini's *Trattato intorno all'ornamento* (c.1569). An author of poetry and scientific treatises, a member of the Accademia Fiorentina, involved with various literary and scientific circles, Spini was also in close contact with artists, among them Vincenzo and Ignazio Danti, Ammannati, Cellini, Dossio, and Bernardo Gamucci.[41] Perhaps, given his literary formation, treating ornament as an independent concern was a self-understood strategy for Spini, and it may be that his work illustrates the prejudices of his own discipline. Yet the very fact that he enters the architectural arena, focuses on ornament, and structures his text with the rigor of a treatise on rhetoric indicates that such trespasses were possible, latent in the discourse, and that he simply enacts links that were already there. Most important, he demonstrates that these links were associated with ornament.

For Spini, the cardinal points of his theory of ornament are *imitatione, corrispondenza, invenzione,* and *decoro,* categories customarily associated with the composition of a poem or tragedy.[42] Indeed, he says so outright when he concludes that "from here derives the similitude between the architect and the poet[,] for both delight with the same means in general."[43] Once he establishes this simile, Spini sets out to develop a rigorous theory of architectural *imitatio.* And he bases it on the treatises on poetics by Aristotle and Horace. To be sure, his efforts to derive every piece of the ornamental ensemble from construction is not new, though he is more consistent than most others. What is new is the reason he offers for this procedure: "Imitation is the representation and similitude of something that has been first produced by Nature or by Art," and he continues,

> Indeed imitation has great force to move man to pleasure and delight, given that his nature is intellectual; because while he recognizes through the means of the work which is being represented the intention of the artist, he feels delight above anything else, as there is no pleasure that equals that of the intellect and of learning . . . it will suffice that in imitating something the architect gives another the opportunity to recognize it, and who recognizes learns and concludes what everything is, as human beings naturally find pleasure in recognizing the things that they see.[44]

Clearly the shadow of Aristotle looms in the background and shows how, by way of ornament, architecture can enter the discourse on *imitatio* that united the figural and literary arts.[45]

That architectural ornament could be conceived of in this manner by the 1570s was not only a direct result of the gradual isolation of ornament as category but owed much to three other phenomena. First, the reception of *De architectura* was largely left in the hands of *letterati* and historians, who routinely imported literary theory to fill in its gaps. Second, the developing language of architectural criticism had borrowed heavily from literary criticism and so invited transference from one to the other. Third, the debate on the *questione della lingua* that shaped Italian culture in the sixteenth century offered striking parallels to what may be termed the *questione dell'ornamento,* that is, the debates on the correct use of architectural ornament.[46]

As far as the reception of *De architectura* was concerned, it had been in the hands of humanists since the time of Sulpitius and Pomponio Leto's Accademia Romana. Its language, already a hindrance to Vitruvius himself, who complained that he had to resort to Greek all too often due to a lack of appropriate Latin terms, was difficult to translate into an even less shaped Italian. As result it was in a "receiving mode": notions, concepts, and categories had to be named and, more often than not, were imported from the literary arts in which the translators were expert. When Barbaro, for example, translated *decor* with *decoro,* when he compared the *maniere del dire* with the *maniere del edificare,* when he talked of the *stile misto,* he both enriched the vocabulary of architectural theory and provided opportunities for a whole theoretical apparatus from the literary arts to seep through the porous wall of language.[47]

In some cases, more was at stake than the translation of terms. Criticism demanded its own vocabulary. To be sure, literary critics drew their most powerful similes and delivered the most incisive observations when using a vocabulary rich in images. Yet the attentive reading of detail, such as Serlio initiates and Scamozzi later fully articulates, depended in large measure on the practices of literary critics. The *questione della lingua* had prompted ever closer analyses of language, and works such as Carlo Lenzoni's *In difesa della lingua fiorentina e di Dante* (1556), where he sought to pinpoint the effects of consonants, vowels, and their combinations on the sound of words, were the natural outcomes of such attention. For him few consonants produced "weakness, lowness and sweetness," many produced "gravity and grandeur," and excessive use caused "inflation and difficulty."[48] Scamozzi's description of the effects of individual profiles, such as cymas, egg and dart, *cavetti,* and crown molds, on the work as a whole owed not a little to this tradition of analysis:

> It is a certain thing that the soft (*morbide*) profiles make buildings turn out well, in such a way that they have firmness and beauty: and as the manners that are too solid, and too swollen make them seem deformed, squat, and without grace; thus, to the contrary, styles that are not fleshy enough (*scarnate*), or too sharp as some use, make the work appear weak and dry: in such a way that the marble and any other noble stone becomes like wood, completely dry and without pulp (*spolpato*).[49]

Indeed, the parallelism between sixteenth-century projects to consolidate the Italian language and develop a systematic ornamental vocabulary for architecture is striking. Both architects and humanists were engaged in sifting through a thesaurus of forms and words and striving to identify criteria for their selection. The concern with setting up grammars on the one hand, and books of *regole* on the other, was only one of a series of similar responses to what were in effect similar conditions. When Vignola wrote his virtually textless *Regola deli cinque ordini* (1562) and Guillaume Philandrier his virtually imageless *Vitruvii Pollionis De Architectura Annotationes* (1544), both were reacting to the impact of the exegetical methods current in the literary circles of the Accademia della Virtù in whose great archaeological project they had both participated.[50]

In all these instances, theoreticians and critics acted in their own ways on that which Vitruvius had offered. And in so doing, they demonstrated that he had been too strong for his reception. What they talk about was what he talked about and in a world in which language and its formation took on such prominence they leaned toward the most rapidly expanding and most heavily used critical and theoretical apparatus available, that is, the apparatus provided by the language arts. Vitruvius had hinted that such a rapprochement was possible, and so it was.

Figura

The theory of the literary arts was not alone responsible for the architects' failure to include figural sculpture in their definitions of ornament and its functions. Yet this phenomenon of borrowing affected decisively the direction in which their attention was channeled, the issues they favored, and the problems they privileged. The remarkable *fortuna* of the *decorum* concept in architecture is one such consequence; so is the *vocabolario* mentality that invaded its treatise industry and caused a growing interest in *regole* and encyclopedias of parts; so is ultimately also the focus on the orders. Once conceived in terms of *maniere del parlare*, they necessarily took over the center stage of ornament theory, as the *genera dicendi* had taken over center stage in any treatise on rhetoric and poetics. In conjunction with Vitruvius, this set up the *forma mentis* with which ornament was approached.

It would therefore seem that we witness a parting of the ways between practice and theory, visual and verbal. The sculptural ornament so central to Renaissance architecture escapes theory and disappears into some form of collective blind spot. Yet is this cleavage one that separates the two on the surface, or are these truly noncommunicating vessels? Does the theory associated with the orders suggest nothing when considering figural devices?

The presence of the human body on a facade is no novelty in the Renaissance. If the Roman remains did not afford any other examples but the triumphal arches and written documents, that was certainly enough. But there was more, for free-standing sculpture was also a feature of Gothic architecture, and despite the shift in taste toward a classical vocabulary, it survived in the context of religious art, especially in the design of chapels, funerary monuments, and, most important, church facades. In all these cases, the religious

6.6
Andrea Palladio, detail, Palazzo
Chiericati, Vicenza. (Photo: Author)

origin of the device and its connotations remained strong: the figures are placed in niches as if in the consecrated space of the church. From the cathedral at Cremona to Donatello's *St. George* at Orsanmichele and *Annunciation* at St. Croce, the examples illustrating this type are legion. The same survival path is also true of acroteria figures. If they were missing from ancient temples, and architects knew of them only from Vitruvius, the Gothic figures on pinnacles certainly carried forward the notion of a petrified *gens,* negotiating the delicate transition between building and sky as a diaphanous intermediary.

A dialogue between figure and frame—that is, an exchange between sculpture and architecture—was certainly developing in this religious context. Tomb sculpture offered another powerful point of intersection for the two media. Still, rich though this tradition was, there were no examples of reclining, freestanding nudes on a pediment such as are most conspicuously evident in Palladio's palace facades (figure 6.6). In fact these architectural "*gisants*" seem to be a device newly invented in the Renaissance, which makes it all the more interesting to ask, Why was it deemed necessary? What function did it perform? Why were the figures in niches and parapets, the *statue* that Palladio mentions, insufficient? One precedent was certainly the winged victories framing the central opening of Roman triumphal arches (figure 6.7). Yet they were fully clothed, relatively flat reliefs, and contained within spandrels, not detached from the wall, literally reaching out into the viewer's space, without an evident iconographical function to elucidate their suspended position or their nudity.

Something approaching Palladio's device may be seen in the Loggia Cornaro by Falconetto; in Ammannati's Arco Benavides, in Sanmicheli's Veronese palaces, and in Sansovino's Marciana and Loggetta. As has been observed, all are indebted to some degree to

6.7
Detail, Arch of Constantine, Rome.
(Photo: Author)

6.8
Michelangelo, Medici Chapel,
Florence.

Raphael's late work, to his facade of the Palazzo Branconio, where statues in niches traditionally associated with a religious type were brought into the domain of the profane, literally leaping from religious three-dimensional icons to a purely decorative device that
allowed texture, light, shade, and movement to enhance the tactility of the architectural elements of the facade.[51] In Falconetto's case the theater-related context for the Loggia, the
tight three-way relationship among himself, Ruzzante, and their patron Alvise Cornaro,
may suggest why detached "live" figures should suddenly inhabit the blank window spaces

of a reconstructed *scaena frons*.[52] And in Sansovino's case as in Ammannati's, the origin of the winged victories in triumphal arches is still apparent, especially as they gracefully enhance similar arched openings. Yet although their figures are more outspokenly three-dimensional and nude than the Roman exemplars, there is still another leap from here to Palladio's pedimental figures.

It is possible to argue that the leap occurs in the wake of Michelangelo's Medici chapel at San Lorenzo and that his treatment of the sarcophagi with their reclining nudes, generically named Dawn, Night, and so on, is the missing link that connects Palladio's Palazzo Chiericati with medieval tomb sculpture and Roman victories (figure 6.8). An inhabitable sculpture or a sculpted piece of architecture, Michelangelo's chapel begged the kind of translation across media that I would like to suggest occurred here. The uniform use of marble for figures, furniture, and spatial container enhances the equivalence between them. Every dentil, volute, garland, and bead-and-reel appears to be of one family with the stone furniture, the sarcophagi, and the bodies placed on them. They are all seemingly carved by the same tools, the same hand; the architectural details belong to sculpture in the same way that the geometry of the bodies placed along pyramids and diagonals suggests that they belong to architecture. On the eve of the seventeenth century, Scamozzi suggested as much when he attempted to define architectural forms and was forced to resort to the Michelangelesque reclining bodies to reinforce the traditional image of the Vitruvian man (figure 6.9).

But not only bodies enter the architectural structure of the whole. A close look at the sarcophagus shows clearly that its lid has much of the so-called *tetto spezzato* (broken pediment) that was to become such a disputed architectural feature in the later sixteenth and seventeenth centuries. Moreover, this practice was put at Michelangelo's door by many later critics like Pirro Ligorio and Teofilo Gallaccini, who were exasperated with the excesses of the *epigoni*.[53] The same convex curve, very slight yet taut, the same scrolls and interruption in the middle that we find in the Porta Pia, we also find in the Medici sarcophagi. Nor does this effect of telescoping one member into another across media end here. The curve and counter-curve of the sarcophagus lid echo the curve of the niche pediments and garlands; its supports respond to the pilasters framing them; the reclining nudes refer to the figure of Lorenzo contained in his architectural setting. And, the same profiles make up the sarcophagus lid as the niche and door frames, thus suggesting continuity between them. As a final gesture, the scroll placed directly below the knee joints of the seated figure, and replete with connotations of mobility, simultaneously carries architectural connotations by recalling the Ionic volute (figure 6.10). Indeed, it is only by comparison with more traditional funerary monuments and with ancient sarcophagi that it becomes clear just how deliberately architectural the Medici ensemble is.

6.9
Vincenzo Scamozzi,
L'idea dell architettura universale
(1615), Architectural Forms.

6.10
Michelangelo, detail of
sarcophagus, Medici Chapel,
Florence. (Photo: Author)

Michelangelo had already proposed the human figure as ornament with the *ignudi* of the Sistine ceiling and in the facade of San Lorenzo in Florence. And certainly Palladio would have known this work and its offspring in the painted work of others.[54] But the impact of the Sistine ceiling should not obscure the kind of transposition possible between two three-dimensional arts like architecture and sculpture—and one that could have reached the Veneto through the confluence of relationships between Sanmicheli, Sansovino, Ammannati, Falconetto, and Palladio, in which patrons like Trissino and Cornaro played their part.[55] Indeed, Vasari tells us that "everyone was astounded" at the sight of the Medici chapel and goes on to describe its extraordinary impact, particularly on architects.[56]

Seen in this context, Michelangelo's anonymous naked figures set into a classical interior and reclining on a classicizing sarcophagus enhance and modify the tradition of the detached figures set up on triumphal arches or winged victories in the spandrels of the arch itself. Like them, from being sculpture they become architectural ornament. Palladio may talk of *statue* when he describes ancient building complexes, but in fact they have ceased to be unique objects authored by one artistic personality. In his pedimental figures, we witness a recession of authorship, a recession of the object as artifact to be admired and apprehended in its uniqueness. His figures stop being one exceptional object offered to close-up view, to be walked around and almost touched; they become one of many. According to the illustrations in the *Quattro libri,* there were fourteen such figures intended for the Palazzi Barbaranno and Iseppo da Porto (figure 6.11) and ten for the Palazzo Chiericati (and, if we add the parapet figures, another eight in the case of the former). Just as a column is one of many, just as the Corinthian capital is one piece of sculpture in the round among many, these figures too are exactly repeatable objects. Lifted high off the ground (not even on the first story as in the case of the Marciana, but all on the *piano nobile*), an intermediary layer of deep carving between the column capitals and the ground floor rustication, they are not presented as a unique artifact to be appreciated as the "original." Alberti said as much: "But I would have the ornament that you apply be for the most part the work of many hands of moderate skill."[57] Walter Benjamin's mechanical reproduction is far in the future, but the aura is nevertheless the issue here. Between architectural ornament and sculpture lies multiple reproduction; the aura is missing.[58] Neither unique accomplishments deserving of commentary in their own right, nor precisely quantifiable (like the orders that can be described piece by piece for a reader), these figural sculptures inevitably disappear through a fissure between image and text.

We are witnessing here the translation of a sculptural motif into an architectural one, and this is happening purely at the formal level, for there are no iconographic implications associated with it as there are with the figure placed within a niche. Nor is this a preferred

6.11
Andrea Palladio, *I quattro libri*
(1570), Palazzo Iseppo da Porto.

device for sculptor-architects like Sansovino or Sanmicheli. Palladio who crosses media less than others, is perhaps the most frequent user of the pedimental reclining nude in the sixteenth century, and his interest in this form is a testimony to its absorption into the professional architect's vocabulary.

Why do architects reach out for this device? Why add more sculptural incident to the facade? Certainly, when Renaissance architects wanted to signify a Gothic manner (as in the proposals for the completion of the facade of San Petronio in Bologna, for example), they covered the surfaces with figural sculpture. Why then skirt potential failure?[59] To say that they were necessary props for an *all'antica* appearance (as Palladio argued) is to stop short of the real issues. With this example I would like to argue that in a visual culture focused on *moti* and *istoria*, architecture seeks a point of contact. Palladio resists the humanization of the frame in the manner of Alessi, Serlio, and other north Italian architects, or indeed, that of the northern European tradition. Yet he uses it to explicate architecture more subtly and more effectively. From the late 1540s, Palladio begins to add figural sculpture to the *piano nobile.* The trend starts with the Palazzo Porto Festa; continues with the Palazzo Chericati, the early drawings for the Rialto Bridge, and the Palazzo Valmarana; and reaches a climax with Palazzo Barbaranno and Loggia del Capitaniato. These devices accompany a growing sculpturalization of his architectural members that seems to require an intensification of visual incident at the middle story.[60] His choice is for organic forms that literally lie beside and accentuate the swelling of a column, and so enhance the carrying message of a pilaster or the heavy, inert weight of a pediment.

We know that Palladio conceived of the classical frame of column/entablature/pediment in gestural rather than strictly tectonic terms.[61] This is especially evident when he discusses junction points of the frame, such as bases and friezes, that is, the points where the columns meet the platform or where the roof beams meet columns: "Likewise, since it is most appropriate that those things upon which a great weight is placed are squeezed, they [the ancients] placed bases under the columns, which, with their torus and scotiae seem (*paiano*) to be crushed by the weight above. Thus, they also introduced triglyphs in the cornices, modillions and dentils, to represent the ends of those beams in the attic which are placed to support the roof."[62] Clearly, for Palladio, bases and triglyphs exist no less in a world of representation and fiction than in one of loads and structure. For him, "abuses" in the use of ornament are those instances that violate this fiction. These are the *cartocci,* a manner of brackets or scrolls that occasionally supported columns but most often appeared in entablatures as *mensole triglifate* (brackets as triglyphs). Palladio's target is clear:

> For this reason instead of columns or pilasters which have to carry some weight one should never place *cartelle,* also called *cartocci,* which is a sort of involuted form which strikes the intelligent as extremely ugly, and to those who are not knowledgeable brings confusion rather than pleasure, and produce no other effect except to raise the expense. Similarly these *cartocci* will not be made to project out of entablatures; since it is necessary that all the parts of the cornice be made towards some effect, and display that which would be visible if the work were made of wood, and in addition, since it is appropriate that in order to support a weight something hard and able to resist is required, there is no doubt that these *cartocci* are entirely superfluous, since it is impossible that a beam or any other member produce the effect they represent, and feigning to be soft and tender, I don't know with what reason they can be placed under something hard and heavy.[63]

This concern for expressive tectonics is not without precedent, though it builds up gradually over the course of two centuries. Alberti likened columns, beams, and arches with bones and ligaments, the wall with flesh (III, 14);[64] Francesco di Giorgio described the *fregio pulvinato* (curved frieze) as "little squashed pillows (*piumacetti*)";[65] Gherardo Spini described the entasis as *tumefazione* (bruising), found etymological grounds to suggest that the torus represented a muscle under stress, like the chest of a straining horse, and described the egg-and-dart motif as gravel squeezing through mortar under the pressure of the floor beams.[66] But none of these authors associated this organismic reading of ornament with the structural frame as consistently as did Palladio. Nor was their reference to *imitatio* as unequivocal. Of course, not being a *letterato* like Spini, Palladio does not resort to Aristotle to ground his argument. But his terms of expression—*fingere* (to seem), *dimostrare* (to demonstrate), *pare* (to appear), and *piacere* (pleasure aroused in the viewer)— testify to the assimilation of the theory of literary *imitatio* and its almost unself-conscious application to architecture.

What do the two strands of this argument—about figural sculpture and the exchanges with literary theory—reveal about the definition of ornament in Renaissance architecture? As the discourse on *imitatio* developed in the literary and figural arts slides imperceptibly into the reading of Vitruvius, ornament increasingly blends structural and corporeal references. By Palladio's time, the ornamental screen is understood to swell and contract as if it were a muscle. In this scenario, the human figure completes the story—the architectural *istoria*— of load carried by support. As figural ornament takes up the space halfway between the inert wall of the building and the street of moving bodies, it gestures the structure. In so doing, it beckons the viewer "in" as seductively and effectively as the strategically placed *figura* that Alberti recommended painters include in a well-structured painted *istoria*.[67] Located at the intersection of literary theory, figural *imitatio,* and architecture, ornament could and did slide between the artificial barriers with which scholarship so often separates disciplines. Yet it is precisely from its location on this edge that ornament facilitated dialogue and exchange between the arts and tied Renaissance architecture into the fabric of its culture.

7

Simon Pepper

Body, Diagram, and Geometry in the Renaissance Fortress

The late quattrocento treatise of Francesco di Giorgio Martini was the first to provide comprehensive coverage of both the practical and theoretical issues that preoccupied Renaissance military architects.[1] Francesco illustrates a wide range of fortress designs, many showing the way to the future of the Italian pointed bastioned system. Not a few of them were built by the author himself in the Marche and in southern Italy.[2] This is Francesco's practical side, which commands respect from historians of military technology. There is another dimension to Francesco's work, however, which addresses the origin and meaning of the architectural language of antiquity. It is impossible to ignore Francesco's preoccupation with the human body, either as an analogy for the city and its component parts or—in a sometimes almost literal sense—as a generator for the forms and proportions of buildings and their parts—cornices, columns, and capitals at one level, the plan of a church at another.[3] One of the most frequently reproduced of Francesco's drawings shows a city model in the hands of a man (figure 7.1). It is explained in the text by reference to the story about the plan of Alexander the Great, proposed by his architect Denocrates, to found a new city on Mount Athos in the shape of a human body.[4] The artistic formula was the by then conventional medieval depiction of a city in the hands of its protective saint. Another well-known Francesco drawing shows a walled city in the shape of a human body, with a towering fortress supported like a crown on the head. Walls enclose the body, with towers ringing the feet and elbows. Here the fortress is likened to the "head" of the city and described as "the most noble member," overlooking and overseeing with its "eyes" the body of the city and like a "doctor" acting quickly to deal with problems "because even small injuries untreated become fatal."[5] The ruler-doctor is of course closely related to the idea of the doctor- architect formulated by Alberti (Book X), and Filarete (Book XV) and, in "real life," entered directly into the common currency of diplomacy

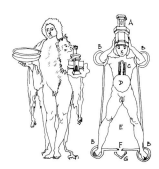

7.1

Two views of the anthropomorphic
city, after Francesco di Giorgio
Martini. *Left:* Denocrates holding
the vase and city model, draped
in the lion skin of his "Hercules
outfit" worn to attract Alexander's
attention, an early example of
the architectural penchant for
outlandish dress (from codex
Magliabechiano, II, I, 141, f.27v).
Right: The human body as the city
(from codex Saluzziano 148, f.3r).
The original is annotated:
A. Roccha, B. Torrione, C. Tempio,
D. Piazza, E. Chorpo della citta,
F. Porta, G. Rivellino.

when subject addressed ruler.[6] Francesco's analogy speaks more clearly than many others of the central importance of the ruler's fortress as the seat of secular power in Francesco's ideal scheme. It reveals much about Renaissance concepts of power and the representation of power.

Not surprisingly Francesco's treatise is the starting point for many of the recent publications exploring the cultural and political role of fortresses and the importance of fortress imagery in the political art of the Renaissance.[7] It is easy to dismiss such cultural concerns as peripheral to the technical evolution of Renaissance fortifications and the wider military revolution that drove it, but almost certainly unwise for any historian to reject such potential keys to understanding. Yet it is as difficult for me, as for Hale,[8] to accept that the late sixteenth-century Portuguese Fort Jesus, in Mombasa, could actually have been laid out in the form of a human body,[9] or that the trace of Poggio Imperiale, the important Florentine fortress built at the turn of the fifteenth and sixteenth centuries overlooking the border of Sienese Tuscany, could be explained in the same way.[10] Francesco's anthropomorphic analogy was not a design guide. In the transitional phase of the new fortifications, however, elements of the medieval tradition were certainly retained and new forms introduced, and it is often difficult to reconcile these features with the direct line of development leading to the triangular bastion and the generally much simplified lines of fortresses that had been designed to resist gunpowder artillery.[11] Here the quattrocento improvements to the Castelnuovo in Naples provide a range of examples well illustrating the conflicting objectives that provided creative tension in the design of a major Italian fortress, one of the first to be adapted to the gunpowder age.

The core of the Castelnuovo was medieval (figure 7.2). The central keep with its irregular quadrangle and cylindrical corner towers originated in the late thirteenth century and had already been substantially rebuilt on the same plan in the early fifteenth century. The corner towers and much of the curtains were then reconstructed once again in the middle years of the century following the castle's capture in 1442 by Alfonso V of Aragon and I of Naples at the end of his war of succession against René of Anjou. The Aragonese rebuilding program was largely complete by 1451, although the outer skin of *piperno* and the elaborate projecting *merlatura* around the tops of the towers remained to be finished during the 1450s; the decorated portal with its sculptural decorations illlustrating Alfonso's triumphal procession was not completed until the late 1460s.[12] During the 1450s a double gallery was added at the top of the upper curtains, possibly to provide additional protected firing positions for crossbowmen. In the 1460s the lower walls were thickened by the construction of a broad platform running around the base of the keep on the three landward-

7.2

Castelnuovo, Naples and its
merlatura after a drawing by
Francisco de Holanda, 1539–1540
(Escorial, 28.1.20, f.53v). The
central keep and the tallest towers
are medieval; the Aragonese gun
gallery around the base of the keep
dates from the mid-quattrocento;
and the outermost Spanish circular
tower-bastions and ramparts date
from 1503–1519. The elaborate
curved *merlatura* crowning the wall-
heads of both inner and outer
works dates from the early
sixteenth-century Spanish
enlargement. It is quite different
from the conventional rectangular
tooth-and-gap crenellations shown
in the well-known Tavola Strozzi
view of the fortress (Museo
Nazionale di San Martino, Naples)
and the depictions in Ferraiolo's
Cronaca Napoletana figurata
(Pierpont Morgan Library N.Y., ms
801, f.115v–16). Both of these
earlier pictorial sources postdate
the main Aragonese
reconstruction. The scale of the
wall-head *merlatura* shown in the
early and later drawings is also very
different. The later *merli* are very
big and probably enclose sheltered
casemates for small guns firing
through the horizontal "letter box"
embrasures, which are clearly
shown in Francisco de Holanda's
drawing. A very functional
arrangement (if this is what it is)
has been dressed in a traditional
fortress image.

facing sides. This artillery platform was the principal modern feature of the Castelnuovo and provided firing positions for a large number of guns, delivering more or less horizontal fire onto the approaches to the castle. A medieval barbican was further developed during the quattrocento and served effectively as an advanced gun platform during the second siege of 1495, when the French, who had seized the castle earlier in the same year, held out for almost five months.[13] Shortly before the French invasion of 1494-1495, Francesco di Giorgio himself added a number of low-level gun positions on the floor of the ditch, and Francesco, who assisted the Aragonese in their recapture of the castle in the second siege of 1495, may even have played some part in the design of the major refortification program to add a new outer circuit of large, round bastions.[14] It was actually built in the early years of the sixteenth century after Francesco's death. The early sixteenth-century round bastions and the curtain ramparts connecting them were equipped with a particularly elaborate system of protected gun positions, apparently designed to appear as a large *merlatura*, the distinctive tooth-and-gap projections forming the battlements on the top of medieval walls.[15]

By the early sixteenth century, therefore, the seat of royal power in Naples presented an interestingly confused image. The newest outer works were capped by a *merlatura* that served a practical enough purpose, but was apparently designed to look like the upper works on old-fashioned fortifications. The mid-quattrocento *merli* on the keep were also unusually prominent. The 1460s gun platform was decorated with striking fluted and spiral (and on one the landward-facing towers not shown in this illustration, diamond) patterns in the masonry, which, as a diverse selection of decorative devices on a fortification has, to my knowledge, no precise parallel.[16] In order to enter the castle, one crossed two ditches and the new line of outer works before passing through a gateway designed as a triumphal arch and bearing a marvelously detailed Renaissance sculptural depiction of a Roman triumph, a theme that would be pursued in different media by other emperors and their artists.[17] This particular triumph recorded an actual Neapolitan event in 1443 in which Alfonso celebrated his victory over the Anjevins with a procession through the city, starting from a breach in the wall. It featured members of his court, as well as distinguished foreign visitors, and with the king borne in a four-wheeled cart fashioned into the likeness of a castle.[18]

The local inspiration for the so-called Aragonese arch was almost certainly the gate built from 1234 by Frederick II at Capua. This earlier gate used classical architectural and sculptural forms featuring the figures of *Justitia* and the emperor in a composition that any visitor approaching Naples from the north would understand as an "unambiguous advertisement for the Roman imperial monarchy whose restoration had been the aim of the Hohenstaufen dynasty since the middle of the twelfth century."[19] The Capua gate, like that at the Castelnuovo, was flanked by two battlemented towers, "built in an unusual style of chamfered stonework, elaborately worked."[20] Indeed, it may not be fanciful to connect the unusually elaborate masonry of the low-level gun platform in Naples with another echo of Frederick's gate. Built just over two centuries after Frederick's Capuan gate, the Aragonese arch of the Castelnuovo was among the first of a new wave of Renaissance and baroque gates that constituted the main decorative architectural element in early modern fortifications and that often also "told a story," albeit less explicitly than at Naples.

The *merlatura* was clearly significant as well as functional. The battlemented upper works and the brackets that supported them and allowed missiles to be dropped down the face of a medieval wall were important elements in medieval fortification. In England and France, a royal license had to be obtained before a castle or town could be crenellated, making it a mark of favor and prestige as well as of increased strength.[21] Moreover, it is not uncommon to find vestigial crenellations in the form of a zigzag brickwork course or a row of brackets in much later buildings. Alfonso's triumphal "chariot" employed a similar architectural device. If something was important symbolically, it was worth wrecking. Marino Sanuto reports that the *merli* of Brescia were stripped off by the French when they captured the city in 1509. Sanuto records the incident in connection with a number of French outrages, and it may be that this kind of *merli* stripping was regarded by both the French and the Brescians as a form of civic degradation, for by this date a medieval *merlatura* would not have fundamentally influenced the defensibility of the walls.

Francesco di Giorgio sought to achieve a meaningful overall framework for the city-fortress using anthropomorphic analogies and images. If "literal" anthropomorphism was always likely to prove unhelpful to the practical fortress designer, geometry was a different proposition. Accurate surveying and well-planned lines of defensive fire were essential to the new art of siege warfare.[22] On flat sites, the designer had opportunities to propose elaborate geometrical schemes of crystalline regularity. In practice, of course, there were many objections to the arbitrary use of geometrical forms because military architecture had to respond to different topography. This was the message hammered home remorselessly in the later sixteenth-century treatises by authors such as Bellucci who saw themselves primarily as professional military men and urged their readers to discount the advice of architects or *dottori*, "for books don't fight."[23] Even so, this fascination with geometrical form remained an inescapable aspect of military architecture, and it was a topic that evidently proved compelling to many of those working in the field. It was shared by architects as different as Antonio da Sangallo the Younger and his arch-rival Michelangelo, whose thrusting "zoomorphic" fortification forms—part biological, part geometrical in inspiration—have long intrigued art historians.[24]

The Renaissance architect who first attempted to reconcile ideal geometry with a proto-modern fortification layout was Filarete who in his mid-quattrocento treatise had anticipated Francesco di Giorgio's borrowings of anthropomorphic—even biological—analogies concerning the gestation of a building in the mind of an architect "for seven to nine months" and later "sickening and dying unless it receives medical attention in the form of regular maintenance."[25] Filarete's geometry was based on the circle and two interlinked squares—a close relative of the classic Renaissance circle and square combination, which, as illustrated in the various *homo ad circulum* drawings, was to be idealized by Luca Pacioli in his *De divina proportione*:

Nature, that divine agent, has endowed the human fabric with a head conceived in proportions that correspond to all other parts of the body. Thus the ancients, having taken into consideration the rigorous structure of the human body, constructed all their works, and above all their sacred temples, according to these proportions; for here they

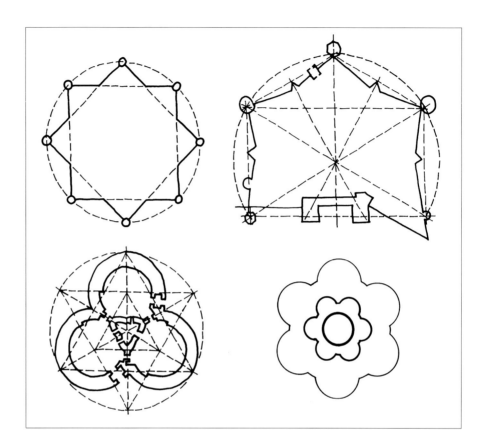

7.3
Geometry in fifteenth- and
sixteenth-century fortress plans.
Upper left: Filarete's diagram
of Sforzinda. *Upper right:* Yedikule,
Constantinople (Gabriel's
geometrical analysis). *Lower left:*
Kilid Bar, Dardanelles, central
structures. *Lower right:* Deal
Castle, Kent, England, 1539–1540.

discovered the two principal figures without which no realization is possible: the perfection of the circle, first among all regular forms, and the equilateral square.[26]

The simple circle of walls was probably the oldest ideogram of the city, helped, as Chiara Frugoni points out, "by the fact that this symbol had already been adopted by classical art on coinage, a medium that circulated everywhere and was an important vehicle for the familiarization of this imagery." This remained the convention in the Byzantine world, while in the West, "the walls describe a quadrangle, or more often a hexagon, and in any case a polygon and, from the ninth century onward, an octagon."[27] Frugoni illustrates a number of medieval ideograms employing octagonal walls formed from two interlinked squares. It may be that familiarity with these images stimulated Filarete's decision to combine all of these elements: circle, octagon and two interlinked squares. Filarete's scheme is evidently partly an ideogram and partly the plan of an ideal city. Possibly it is also an attempt to come to terms with ideas about new fortification forms that were current in some circles as early as the mid-fifteenth century and anticipated by many years postmedieval fortresses actually built in the West.[28]

For the ideal city of Sforzinda (figure 7.3), the circle becomes a circumferential waterway, part moat and part distributor for the canals that penetrate the city itself, an idea that reappeared in Leonardo's urban plans for Milan, prepared for another Sforza.[29] The walls are generated by the two overlaid squares. Gates are located in the reentrant angles, serving radial roads that do not mesh properly with the orthogonal planning grid of the buildings and open spaces in the center of the town. The salient angles of the walls are fortified with round towers, which, like other buildings in the city, continue the play of circle and square by having, according to his text, square rooms inside the cylindrical drums of the towers (posing some more formal problems where they touched and gave a wall of zero thickness, although these are wisely avoided by having no drawings to support this particular description).[30] Filarete's anthropomorphic references recur too, sometimes combined with the geometry with considerable subtlety and depth of meaning. The square plan of the garden of the prince was "made into a circle" and, in Susanne Lang's words, "divided like a map of the earth, [containing] high mounds from which the water in the canals flowed and to which it all returned—a strange image which takes on a new significance when we assume that the canals stand for the veins and arteries of a man, so that here we may have that identification of man with the universe . . . which played so large a part in Medieval and Renaissance thought."[31]

The cranked sawtooth plan of Sforzinda's walls is not quite the same as the classic polygonal bastioned solution (figure 7.4), but it was a powerful symbol of novelty in urban fortification, as well as a profoundly satisfactory demonstration of Renaissance geometry as a unifying element in urban design. This surely must have been its primary function. Filarete's sawtooth plan, however, did have a certain logic of its own in fortification terms. Francesco di Giorgio illustrates a number of schemes with similar features, and it was widely used in smaller fortresses and fieldworks in the sixteenth century and appears on the pages of a number of the later treatises. However, the earliest example of this kind of purist geometrical thinking to be carried into practice in military architecture is to be found not in Italy, but in the works carried out in Ottoman Europe in the aftermath of the fall of Constantinople.

In the winter of 1457–1458 the Golden Gate of Constantinople—the official entry point for Byzantine emperors arriving by land at the Sea of Marmara end of the Theodosian Walls—was transformed into the centerpiece of a new fortress complex by Mehmed the Conqueror.[32] With only slight deviations caused by irregularities in the original Byzantine

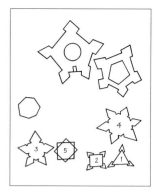

7.4

Evolution of a fortress plan. Diagram illustrating studies for the Florentine Fortezza da Basso by Antonio da Sangallo the Younger, March–April 1534, redrawn from Uffizi U758A recto. The drawing dates from the early involvement of Antonio, who arrived in Florence to work on the project shortly after receiving an invitation from Alessandro Vitelli on March 10, 1534. All the major decisions had been taken on the design when the foundation stone was laid on July 15, but other marks on this sheet place the fortress on what was to be its eventual site by the Porta San Gallo. The architect numbered his preliminary studies 1 through 5 (as indicated) before developing two versions of a five-bastioned fortress with different courtyard treatments. The final solution employs five bastions.

walls, Yedikule (the Castle of the Seven Towers) forms a regular pentagon, with each of the four new curtains facing into the city cranked inward to form a reentrant fortified by a small triangular tower (figures 7.3 and 7.5). The three new towers were roofed on the two upper levels, where guns could be accommodated on a platform 3.5 meters wide. The triangular and semicircular subsidiary towers in the reentrant angles of the curtain also provided wide and open platforms suitable for guns and were built out from the main curtain gallery so that the passage around the walls was not interrupted. The towers of the Golden Gate and the adjacent section of the Theodosian Walls took their form from a much earlier time and, in the cases of the two flanking octagonal towers, were rebuilt in 1754–1755.[33] The massive towers of the Golden Gate were modified to form a keep with residential accommodation, but the *aga* commanding the fortress occupied a house in an area of formal walled garden just "inside" the Golden Gate. On the central axis of the fortress was placed a mosque. The overall pentagonal geometry, which has been analyzed by Gabriel, finds echoes only in the most formal of Western European medieval schemes (notably, the Castel del Monte in Apulia) and in a much later generation of bastioned works. Some of Yedikule's detail is highly formalized too, in particular, the faceted masonry on the central great tower, with its elaborate fluted base moldings, reminiscent of the decorations on the base of the Castelnuovo in Naples but probably antedating them.

Yedikule was started nearly ten years before the Ottoman sultans began the construction of the Topkapi Palace on Seraglio Point and made it their favored state residence, and it may be that the fortress incorporated such features of "polite" architecture because of its special status as a royal fortress, which initially housed the treasury and many distinguished state prisoners and probably accommodated the sultan in an emergency.[34] However, Yedikule was not the only early Ottoman fortress to be designed on geometric lines. Between 1459 and 1462, two new coastal fortresses were built at the narrows of the Dardanelles where Europe and Asia are only 1,200 meters apart. The fortress of Kilid Bar (Key to the Sea) stood on the European shore, and Cianak Kale (sometimes Sultaniye Kale) on the Asian side in the modern town of Cianakkale.[35] The two fortresses are strikingly different.

Cianak Kale is rectangular, with round corner towers and multifaceted semicircular intermediate towers on its outer enceinte (figure 7.5). In the center a substantial rectangular keep with a broad platform on its roof is equipped with a thick, curved parapet, indicating that this platform, like the mural towers, was designed to mount artillery. Western observers noted guns mounted on the platform in the sixteenth and seventeenth centuries.[36] The side facing the sea was modified in the nineteenth and twentieth centuries to house modern coastal artillery, some of which saw service in the Dardanelles campaign of 1915. Although lacking the picturesque charm of the Ottoman fortresses built earlier in the same

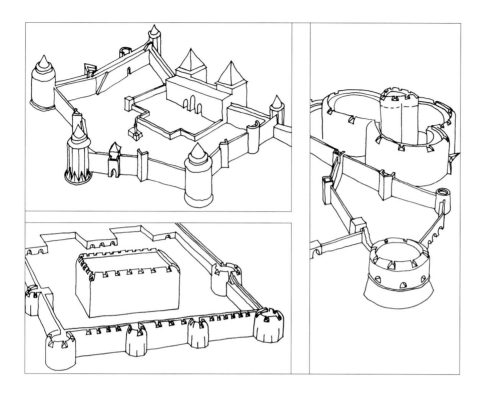

7.5
Ottoman fortresses of the mid-fifteenth century. *Upper left:* Yedikule, the castle of the Seven Towers, Constantinople (after reconstruction by Gabriel). The rectangular mass is the modified Byzantine Golden Gate. *Lower left:* Cianak Kale, on the Asian shore of the Dardanelles. *Right:* Kilid Bar, "Key to the Sea," on the European shore of the Dardanelles (after air photographs). Both of the Dardanelles forts have been modified to accommodate modern coastal artillery, but the original Ottoman cores remain.

decade at Constantinople and on the Bosphorus, Cianak Kale is very clearly a product of the new gunpowder age and demonstrates a high level of technical competence in the Ottoman architects.

Kilid Bar is of even greater interest for its geometry. A central trefoil plan keep (six floors high from the evidence of embrasures) is surrounded by a larger trefoil curtain, which itself towers over lower outer works (figures 7.3 lower left and 7.5 right). The keep and its trefoil curtain are rotated so that a series of separate courtyards are formed at ground level, and the gun positions on the parapets have a large number of overlapping fields of fire. Formally the geometry of the plan is very sophisticated, encouraging further speculation about Western influence.[37] Here too the works are now incomplete. The big guns that closed the seaway were located outside the geometrical castle at the water's edge, where a lengthy section of the battery wall is now missing. The views published by Western travelers, as well as a fifteenth-century drawing illustrating both castles, show that the fifteenth-century gun battery wall extended right across the front of the castle.[38] However, it is the central keep and its curtain that are of importance here for their formal geometry, which is unlike anything that survives in the West until we encounter the rounded clover-leaf coastal forts (figure 7.3 lower right) built on the south coast of England in the 1540s by King Henry VIII's architects.[39]

No one knows who designed the post-1453 Ottoman fortresses. Necipoglu has recently observed of Yedikule that "this star-shaped fortress [was] designed according to new Italian theoretical concepts of ideal planning."[40] She cites Restle and Raby, who in turn mention the advice reportedly received by the sultan on the post-1453 fortresses from the Florentine community in Pera. Mehmed II's interest in Western history and his appointment to the Ottoman court of Western scholars, artists, and artisans are well known. It has even been suggested that Filarete himself planned a visit to Constantinople in 1465, by which time Mehmed's fortresses would have been completed, but Babinger is dismissive of Filarete's participation, while assuming the participation of unspecified Italians in the conqueror's fortification and bridge-building programs.[41] The chronology is confusing too, raising the interesting possibility that Filarete was not the only mid-quattrocento architect experimenting with the star-shaped planning diagram. On the ground we are left with fascinating, if incompletely understood, early geometrical demonstrations at Yedikule of the kind of mid-quattrocento geometry pioneered in Italy by Filarete, and at Kilid Bar of sophisticated cinquecento forms.[42] Both generally failed to reappear in Ottoman military architecture and, in a wider perspective, represent what is really a footnote in the development of the Italian bastion.

The footnote, however, died hard. Filarete's original diagram of the overlapping squares appears more than a century later, in undiluted form, as the basis for the defenses of an ideal fortified town in the mid-sixteenth-century treatise of Maggi and Castriotto.[43] More significant to those of us who seek evidence that this pattern of thinking informed the designers of actual projects is its appearance (together with numerous copies of Francesco di Giorgio's quattrocento designs) among the drawings of Antonio da Sangallo the Younger, who with Sanmichele was probably the most prolific of the large-scale fortification designers in the first half of the sixteenth century. Sangallo had been engaged in March 1534 by Alessandro de' Medici, the recently installed imperial duke of Florence, to design and build the Fortezza da Basso to strengthen the city's defenses on the flat northern approaches—and, of course, to secure the new dynasty in the former republic. It was the latter function that has gone into the history books with Segni's celebrated denunciation of the plan "to place on the necks of the Florentines a yoke of a kind never experienced before: a citadel, whereby the citizens lost all hope of ever living in freedom again."[44] Alessandro was assassinated shortly afterward, and the project was completed for Cosimo I in the surprisingly short period of two years, albeit at the sacrifice of the more ambitious features of Sangallo's early scheme, which had all the makings of an "ideal" fortress.

Formal ranges of arcaded barrack blocks and stables surrounded a vast piazza laid out inside a five-bastioned enceinte that Sangallo had placed astride the northern city walls of Florence. The gateway into the city was the most sophisticated piece of urban architecture to form part of the eventual scheme, with a secure "airlock" entry system, smoothed-off upper surfaces to deflect shot, and a diamond-and-ball motif on the low-level masonry that made play in the balls with the Medici *palle* emblem and won praise for its *bellezza* from Vasari (who had evidently not seen the low-level masonry on the Castelnuovo at Naples). At the center was a fortress-within-a-fortress that was never to be realized but features in various stages of development in the early drawings. One of the most interesting sheets (U758A recto) illustrates the five-sided fortress on the Prato road leading through the Porta San Gallo (figure 7.4). It contains a series of numbered geometrical variations on the idea of the polygonal fortress: triangle, square, two interlocked squares, five-pointed star, six-pointed star (formed from two interlocked triangles), and a six-sided polygon. Above are two polygonal fortress designs—one with a circular core, the other with a hexagonal core. These cores could represent courtyards (as at Caprarola) or variations on central *mastio* arrangements (as at the Castel Sant' Angelo, Rome, where the imperial mausoleum drum stands in a courtyard surrounded by two concentric rings of Renaissance fortifications). Other Sangallo drawings (U759A recto and verso) suggest the latter.[45]

In all of these cases, Sangallo's sketches reveal the level of graphic play inherent in the development of polygonal bastioned fortress architecture. Like the preliminary sketches in so many other architectural schemes from the Renaissance to our own time, these exploratory diagrams actually convey more about the ideas informing the project than any of the more finished design drawings. In the absence of written sources to shed light on the thinking of Sangallo and his collaborators, they are our best window into the designer's mind. Sangallo's sketches also strongly recall both Francesco di Giorgio and Filarete in the idealizing, geometric approach that is seen to have been adopted here in the initial stages of an important state project. The kind of geometry that two generations earlier had fascinated Filarete and his contemporary designers of the new Ottoman fortresses still preoccupied a very pragmatic working military architect—one of the most experienced fortress builders of his time—who was writing no treatise but working on the urgently prosecuted construction program for the Florentine citadel that would not only symbolize but enforce the pattern of power in the late Renaissance city.

8

Harry Francis Mallgrave

Dancing with Vitruvius: Corporeal
Fantasies in Northern Classicism

When historians of architecture speak of the fulsome building forms of a Johann Lucas von Hildebrandt or Christoph Dientzenhofer that appear north of the Alps around 1700, the assumption often seems to be that this late baroque exuberance (like its Franco-Italian counterpart) was born of a sustained process of Renaissance development. Such was not actually the case. Northern architects, it is true, had for more than a century eyed both the classical forms and humanist ideals of the South, but they and their patrons—for reasons of religion, politics, and a viable late Gothic tradition in building—were at the same time slow in introducing the new forms into practice. Classically inspired buildings scarcely appear in northern Europe before 1550, and this is also the case with regard to treatises.[1] By this date, Sebastiano Serlio, Michelangelo, and Guilio Romano had already steered the Italian Renaissance along its mannerist path. Moreover, it is not until the very end of this century that a significant, if somewhat singular, interpretation of the classical ideal (one drawing its inspiration as much from a fascination with Vitruvius as from Italian models) finds artistic resonation in the North. Yet even this belated interest is rarely seen in the work of leading architects; it is found, rather, in the architectural fantasies of a few imaginative painters and engravers.

One of the first of these influential artists was the Netherlander Jan Vredeman de Vries (1527–c. 1606), a designer, painter, and occasional architect. Born in the Friesland town of Leeuwarden, he studied painting before migrating to Antwerp, where he assisted Coecke van Aelst on the decorative design of the provisional triumphal arches built in 1549 for the entry of the future Habsburg emperor, Philip II, into Antwerp. This brought Vredeman into contact with this learned publisher of various editions of Vitruvius and Serlio, as well as with a small circle of other classically minded artists who included the architect Cornelis Floris, the designer of the northern mannerist Antwerp Town Hall (1561–1566).

8.1a–b
Jan Vredeman de Vries,
"Perspective Designs" from
Perspective (Amsterdam, 1604–
1605). (Photos: Lee Ewing,
courtesy of the National Gallery,
1998)

Vredeman subsequently immersed himself in the writings of Vitruvius and Serlio, although he continued to earn his living primarily as a decorative painter and engraver. His career was victimized by the religious persecution of the time, and he, in effect, lived a migrant's life: seeking refuge and work in Aachen, Liège, and Antwerp once again, before moving to Wolfenbüttel in 1585. He next settled in Hamburg, worked as a painter in Gdánske (Danzig) for the Polish court, and later worked in Prague in the service of Emperor Rudolf II. Only in the last decade of his life, near the end of the sixteenth century, did he return to the northern provinces of the Netherlands, now in revolt against Spanish rule. Throughout his wanderings, however, he continued to publish his increasingly famous engravings. Between 1555 and 1587 he produced twenty-seven publications consisting of 483 prints. His work in this field eclipsed his fame as a painter, as well as the notice of his few architectural commissions.

The themes of Vredeman's architectural musings are wide ranging, though they are always elaborate and complex in their visual delineation (figure 8.1). With respect to the theme of the body and building, they are more generally characterized by an absence of human form (at least by living human form), resulting in a quasi-Chiricoesque vision of unpopulated buildings, courtyards, and streetscapes presented with the stark qualities of stage sets. It is an architectural world of fantasy different from the real one, largely classical in inspiration but also personally eccentric in its willful predilections. Vredeman's buildings and perspectival exercises (often intended as drawing manuals for rendering compound forms) assume shapes and proportions determined less by need or existing convention and more by an artistic striving for novel forms and combinations. In this last regard, he was particularly successful.

Nevertheless, his full corpus of work was by no means completely devoid of human forms. In his *Architectura oder Bauung der Antiquen aus dem Vitruvius* (started in 1577), Vredeman used the columnar system of Serlio to explore the emotive possibilities of the five orders. He does not simply present the mathematical rules for the orders, as so many before him had done, but rather seeks to adapt them to the different cultural and climatic conditions of the North and to invest them with ornaments of his own creation. In another short book produced in 1577, *Theatrum vitae humanae*, he couples the orders with human figures and other allegorical attributes.

Although often characterized as a mannerist, Vredeman and his designs rather suggest aspects of the baroque in the playfulness and overt violation of classical norms. And it must be stressed that his personal fascination with classical motifs and symbolic attributes appeared against an architectural backdrop that was still largely Gothic in character. This was the period in the Netherlands noted for its use of high curvilinear or scrolled gables, of which Henry-Russell Hitchcock has written so eloquently.[2]

Vredeman's sometimes laconic fantasies, however, provide but a muted initiation into the more effusive rites of the German painter and engraver Wendel Dietterlin (c.1550–1599), who was certainly one of the most talented (if least studied) figures of this time. In the lone illustrative treatise, or column book, of this visually inebriated artist, the line between body and building becomes altogether blurred. If Vredeman's depopulated designs exude a near-modernist angst of an imagined and strange classical metropolis, Dietterlin's fantasies were rather a forerunner to the late baroque fever of Piranesi, especially to the darker or more manic of his creations.

Born in Pullendorf near Lake Constance, Dietterlin moved as a youth to Strasbourg and trained as a decorator and fresco painter. It was a field in which he enjoyed considerable success, with his commissions eventually taking him to Hagenau (1583), Overkirch (1589), and Stuttgart (1590). In the last town, while painting the ceiling of the Lusthaus for the duke of Württemberg, Dietterlin befriended the classical architects Heinrich Schickhardt and Daniel Schlossberger, from whom he learned, as he tells us proudly, "the correct distribution of the five columns."[3] In the early 1590s Dietterlin returned to Strasbourg and devoted himself entirely to the production of his textbook on the classical orders. The first and second volumes of *Architectura von Ausstheilung, Symmetria und Proportion der fünff Seulen*

8.2 (right, and facing page)
Wendel Dieterlin, Plates from
*Architectura von Ausstheilung,
Symmetria und Proportion der fünff
Seulen* (Nuremberg, 1598).
(Photo: Lee Ewing, courtesy of the
National Gallery, 1998)

appeared in 1593 and 1594; separate German and Latin/French collected editions appeared in 1598.

The restiveness displayed in Dieterlin's 203 engravings almost defies verbal description (figure 8.2). The volume is divided into five books, thematically presenting the basic geometry and proportions of the five orders. The presentation includes an iconographic interpretation of each order's decorative and more esoteric attributes. The Vitruvian and Serlian traditions are here filtered through Dieterlin's artistic imagination in a way that produces a completely surreal result, one that an early twentieth-century biographer termed "almost impressionistic" in its imagery.[4] The column book's full title—*Architecture of Distribution, Symmetry, and Proportion of the Five Columns and All Their Related Art Work of Windows, Fireplaces, Doorways, Portals, Fountains, and Epitaphs*—suggests the range of elements to be subsumed under this new style of design, as the columns as well as their appurtenances,

for the painter, are grounded in "one foundation and principle." It is an anthropomorphic principle that Dietterlin wants to convey, but in a way that also transposes the "obscure and difficult" aspects of classical theory into something that offers "delight and grace to the beholders."[5]

Such an admission, however, does not fully prepare the reader for the rich panoply of decorative attributes that follow. Classical architecture for Dietterlin comes alive, albeit in an almost tormented manner. The allegorical distinction between organic and inorganic is effaced in his engravings. Human figures, threatening demons, exotic creatures, and mythological beasts become extensions of the architecture, peering out from its darkest lithic niches, indeed sometimes tearing at its very fabric. The sense of fantasy and humor exhibited here is almost unparalleled in Renaissance treatises, and the book is clearly the work of someone living on the fringes of its canon. The catharsis of emotions can be so wildly spent because classicism is known only through textbooks and a few isolated examples. With this artist, the mysterious organism of Renaissance architecture teems with life and assumes near-nightmarish proportions.

If we turn to the work of the third northern artist of this period to deal with the classical theme, Peter Paul Rubens (1577–1640), we find a somewhat more correct but no less vivid understanding of what classical architecture is all about. The vocabulary of classicism for Rubens remains the architecture of the South, that is, the architecture of the "other"— a sensuous array of forms that in their overt materiality and dress are still quite removed from the colder and more prosaic architecture of the North.

Rubens's contribution to the spread of classicism in the North has been consistently unappreciated, notwithstanding the many books that have been devoted to his love of antiquity and the various artistic influences that he absorbed during his extended stay in the South. He made his way to Italy in 1600 in the employ of Vincenzo Gonzaga, the duke of Mantua, and it was in this last town that he was introduced to a full range of Renaissance development: from the mathematical rule of Leon Battista Alberti to the mannerist playfulness of Guilio Romano. During two stays in Rome, he studied the writings of Serlio, the most recent buildings of Vignola and Carlo Maderno, and in particular the late work (painterly and architectural) of Michelangelo.[6] Certainly it was the buxom and corpulent forms of the latter that lay nearest to Rubens's plump sense for artistic expression.

Also vital to his architectural schooling was his seven-week stay in Genoa in the summer of 1607. Here the already famed artist, inhabiting the Palazzo Grimaldi and charged with painting portraits of the local nobility, fell in love with that city's palaces. He used his spare time to draw the facades of these richly polychrome works and had his traveling companion and disciple, Deodat del Monte, take interior measurements.

Within a few years after returning to Antwerp, this student of classicism purchased a house on the Wapper Canal and set about converting it into a "Renaissance Palace," as it was known locally. This was not his lone foray into architectural practice. Around 1615 Rubens became active in the design of a Jesuit church in Antwerp, a work whose overall design is generally attributed to Pieter Huyssens. Yet Rubens, who was responsible for the painted and plastic decoration, may also have had his hand in larger aspects of the design. Anthony Blunt credits the painter for the superimposed arcades of the interior, the design of the main altar, various other interior details, and the Italianate features of the exterior, including the ponderous proportions of the church's three-story facade.[7] What are perhaps the most interesting features of the design, however, are the baroque-like qualities of the detailing. Their author was a skillful and imaginative artist well schooled in evolving Latin tendencies. It seems that Rubens, long regarded as the first baroque painter of the North, may also have been the North's first baroque architect.

Rubens speaks of the significance of the church's design in his preface to his *Palazzi di Genova,* his little-noted architectural folio published in 1622. In it the painter's architectural sensibilities become fully transparent, and the two-volume work is a remarkable production, especially in view of its appearance during difficult political times. Dedicated to Don Carlo Grimaldi of Genoa, it is altogether polemical in intention:

> We see in our country the architecture that is called barbaric or Gothic slowly perishing and disappearing. We see some enlightened men introducing into our country, for its embellishment and decorative glory, a true symmetry that follows the rules of the ancient Greeks and Romans. We find examples of this in the magnificent churches built by the Holy Society of Jesus in the towns of Antwerp and Brussels. Because of the dignity of the divine office, we begin to change the temples to a better style.[8]

Later in his preface Rubens speaks of the functionality of these palatial examples (figure 8.3). He especially admires their cubic forms (itself a critique of Gothicism) and smaller scale (smaller than Roman or Florentine models), which he argues are better suited to the more urban and more modest needs of the North. Altogether, he illustrates nineteen Genovese palaces and four churches. The work fills out two volumes and contains 139 plates, mostly plans, elevations, and sections. Rubens had one of his favorite engravers, Nicolas Ryckemans, prepare the plates.[9]

Still one has to ask what features in these palaces appealed to Rubens's sense of form. If we accept him as the painter that he was—a superb colorist known for his fleshy and portly figures—the answer has to be just these corpulent attributes: the restrained and sometimes rustic plasticism of the architecture, its massiveness, proportion, and pleasing native polychromy. The Ligurian setting to these works no doubt conveyed to him a sunny and lively richness, qualities quite foreign to northerners reared on brick and half-timber buildings and living within a somber atmosphere so rarely displaying strong effects of shadow.

Rubens's most significant folio production was exceedingly ill timed, however, to have an immediate impact. Its appearance in 1622 followed by a few years the start of the Thirty Years War, which would radically reconstitute the overall political landscape of Europe and create the political entity of Holland (thereby ensuring the ascendancy of Amsterdam over the formerly preeminent trading center of Antwerp). It would also bring to a grinding halt, as wars are prone to do, nearly all architectural activity, including the writing of treatises.[10]

We thus have to look to the period after 1648 to search for an afterglow to these sublime architectural leads, but by this date the lines of continuity are already effaced, or nearly so. The psychology of the time—as art historians were once fond of saying—was simply wrong. The *Compendium architecturae civilis* (1648) of Georg Andreas Böckler, for in-

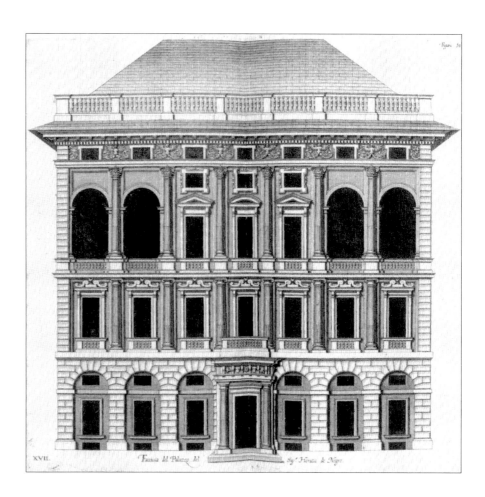

stance, is largely undistinguished in its intent and content. *Architectura civilis* (1649) of Johann Wilhelm is concerned almost solely with the transmission of structural expertise in the wake of declining technical skills brought on by the lengthy military conflict. Only in the classical work of Pieter Post (1608–1669) do we find an echo of the imaginative spirit of Vredeman de Vries and Rubens resurfacing.

Not coincidentally, Post was also trained as a painter. A friend and collaborator of the classical architect Jacob van Campen, he turned to architecture in the 1640s as the war was winding down. After several decorative ventures, his first large building commission, the Huis ten Bosch for Amalia von Solms in The Hague (started in 1646), established his reputation. It consisted of a nine-square plan with the colossal reception hall in the center, the *Oranjezaal,* enclosed above by a dome resting on a tall drum. His monograph of the building, *De Sael van Orange* (c. 1653), preserves the novelty and grandeur that this Palladian building must have signaled to his contemporaries. A richer monograph of Post's designs published in 1715, *Les ouvrages d'architecture,* contains various other Renaissance-inspired works. Both Post and van Campen (the court architect to the House of Orange and the designer of the Amsterdam town hall) surely owe a debt to Vredeman and Rubens, although their obligation to the Renaissance style of Palladio appears equally as strong.

Post's and van Campen's fascination with Palladio was not entirely unique in the North. Two later monographs by the Swede Eric Jönsson Dahlberg (1625–1703) and the Dane Lauritz Lauridsen de Thurah (1706–59) demonstrate that Palladianism was quite strong in these two countries as well.[11] This northern extension of the movement forms an interesting parallel to what was also taking place in Britain.

In Germany, meanwhile, Dietterlin's fire was scarcely to be rekindled. The most important writer on the arts in the second half of the century was the Wallonian Joachim von Sandrart (1606–1688), who published his *L'Academia todesca della architecture, scultura & pittura* in 1675–1679. Again a painter by trade—in fact, Germany's most highly regarded portrait painter of the seventeenth century—Sandrart had trained in Nuremberg and in Utrecht in the 1620s with Gerrit van Honthorst. He toured the northern Netherlands in 1627 with Rubens, visited England in the following year, and in 1629 began a six-year tour of Italy, where he befriended many of the leading painters of the day, including Domenichino, Claude Lorrain, Nicolas Poussin, Pietro da Cortona, and Pietro Testa.

When Sandrart returned to Germany in 1635, he did so already as a painter of high repute, but the war soon forced him to seek safety in Amsterdam. He later claimed his hereditary estate near Ingolstadt, where he lived in comfort while carrying out commissions for German and Austrian nobles. In 1670, however, Sandrart sold his estate and moved to Augsburg; three years later he returned to Nuremberg. In both cities, and no doubt inspired by pedagogical events taking place in France and Italy, he founded academies of classical art, from which derives its title.

What is most apparent about *L'Academia todesca,* a learned, two-volume treatise, is the labor and patience that Sandrart brings to the discourse. Its tripartite structure deals with architecture, sculpture, and painting to varying degrees within the established humanist tradition, and Sandrart supplements it (in the spirit of Vasari) with numerous biographical sketches of famous artists, past and present. The work is dedicated to the youth of "the world-renowned German nation, to the most praiseworthy and most excellent champions and lovers of art." In the preface, the author, after sketching the major moments of recent art from Michelangelo and Dürer to Bernini, speaks of the honor that he feels in transmitting to the German people the principles and techniques underlying this new art of classi-

PLAFOND des Parade Zimmers.

8.4

Paul Decker, *Furstlicher Baumeister oder Architectura civilis* (Augsburg, 1711). (Photo: Lee Ewing, courtesy of the National Gallery, 1998)

cism. It is as if time has stood still or been pushed back a full century, and classicism is discussed as something entirely new to northern sensibilities.

Sandrart's treatment of the architectural orders is historically and theoretically exhaustive. Vitruvius remains the acknowledged "teacher and guide," but the humanist tradition of Alberti also figures prominently in his instruction. Sandrart's discourse on architecture, in fact, is entirely focused on the style of the high Renaissance, although he was by birth a child of the baroque.

L'Academia todesca nevertheless remains an essential text within the northern classical movement, which in the late seventeenth century was making significant inroads in theory and design. Still, we have to point to a military event to find the lever that gave the Germanic lands their most important push in this direction: the defeat of the sultan's armies at the gates of Vienna in 1683. This ended the threat of Ottoman intrusions from the South and invigorated the cultural aspirations of the Habsburgs.

The last event allowed the grandiloquent and orotund creations of Fischer von Erlach, Johann Lucas von Hildebrandt, Jacob Prandtauer, Georg Bähr, Daniel Pöpplemann, Johann Michael Fischer, and Johann Balthasar Neumann, again to mention but a few. For their inspiration we can look not only to Italian sources but also to the new cultural force of France and the rich perspectival and scenographic breakthroughs of painters like Andrea

Pozzo and the Galli-Bibienas.[12] As a mediating force of these tendencies, we can also point to the richly inventive work of Paul Decker (1677–1713). Trained as a painter in his native Nuremberg, before studying architecture under Andreas Schlüter in Berlin, Decker gained a post as a court architect in Bayreuth shortly before his early death, which precluded the translation of his artistic energies into built form. What we know of his talent was published in his *Fürstlicher Baumeister oder architectura civilis* (1711–1716), containing his ideal design for a palace (figure 8.4). The highly corpulent forms of the architecture combine the drama of Borromini with the grandiloquence of Fischer von Erlach's first designs for the Schönbrunn (c. 1688). Decker's ceiling frescoes also display a mastery of quadrature, or the use of illusionistic effects, which was just making its way northward from Italy and Vienna. One might also discern in these imaginative creations a faint remembrance of the corporeal fantasies of Dietterlin, for here the body once again insinuates itself as a prominent feature of the classical medium. What makes this characteristic of Decker's designs doubly interesting is that these allusions, now consciously clothed in the allegorical gown of the late baroque, are a full century removed from their inspirational source.

9

Vaughan Hart

On Inigo Jones and the Stuart Legal Body: "Justice and Equity . . . and Proportions Appertaining"

The first half of the seventeenth century saw a fundamental change in the popular style of English architecture. As is well known, the work of the court architect Inigo Jones introduced the fashion for building *all'antica,* that is, for the coherent display of the antique orders on facades following Renaissance building practices common throughout Europe. In this chapter, I propose that the "body" of these columns on Jones's court buildings was seen as expressing the body of Jones's royal patron, since the body of the king was universally celebrated as the very pattern of symmetry and perfect proportion in Stuart art. The related idea that these newly introduced architectural canons of symmetry and proportion, in embodying the king's perfection, were seen to represent royal authority in the form of the monarch's traditional legislative prerogative will also be examined.

The King's Body as the Perfect Microcosm

The general link between the body and building was made explicit in the only book on architecture published in Stuart England. Henry Wotton, in *Elements of Architecture,* advised his readers "to pass a running examination over the whole edifice, according to the properties of a well shaped man."[1] In antiquity, the Roman author Vitruvius had recorded that the various columns imitated male or female features and shapes (IV.i.6–8), from "masculine" Doric to "maidenly" Corinthian, and the human basis of the columns' proportions was probably well understood by Stuart builders following the characterization of the five orders by John Shute in his architectural treatise of 1563.[2] Indeed with reference to Vitruvius, Wotton noted that the height of the Tuscan order "shall be six diameters, of the grossest [thickness] of the pillar below. Of all proportions, in truth, the most natural; For our author tells us, *lib.3.cap.I.,* that the foot of a man is the sixth part of his body in ordinary measure, and man himself is as it were the prototype of all exact symmetry."[3]

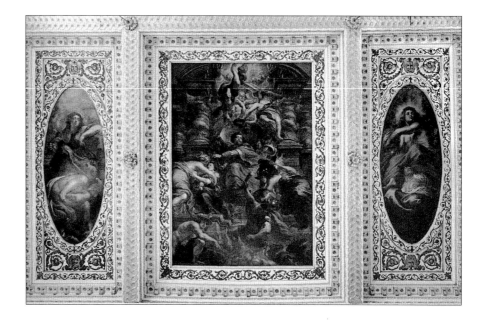

9.1
The column and the king's
body, on Rubens's ceiling to the
Banqueting House. James is
here portrayed as Solomon, the
archetypal wise judge.
(Photo: Author)

Inigo Jones studied these ideas in his *Vitruvius,* where he noted that "the body of man well-proportioned is the pattern for proportion in buildings, . . . the round figure forms the body of man."[4] Jones's close study of proportion is evident in his numerous drawings of figures for masque costumes and in his study of human heads within his *Roman Sketchbook.*[5] But what ideal body in particular might the Stuart populace and Jones himself have seen reflected in well-proportioned court architecture?

Perhaps not surprisingly, the king's body was commonly celebrated in Stuart art as the exemplar of earthly harmony, and as such the ideal microcosm and "pattern" of perfect proportion (figure 9.1). The court poet Ben Jonson urged that, when viewing James's body,

Read him as you would do the book,
Of all perfection, and but look,
What his proportions be;
No measure that is thence contrived,
Or any motion thence deriv'd,
But is pure harmony.[6]

For the Stuart apologist George Marcelline, the body of James's son, Charles I, was in succession "composed of the purest mould that lodged in the bosom of Nature, . . . so that indeed he seems the masterpiece of Nature."[7] Marcelline here extended this praise of Charles through the body-building metaphor, in proclaiming the "stateliness of the building" and "rareness of the edifice."[8]

This idealization of the royal body echoed the medieval concept that the king possessed not only a human or physical body, but also a divine or mystical one, a legal and religious concept termed the king's "two bodies."[9] One body was subject to decay, while the other was an embodiment of the monarch's authority and prerogatives, and as such was immortal. Ernst Kantorowicz notes that "the anointed King appeared as a 'twinned person' because *per gratiam* this King reflected the two natures of the God-man, 'man by nature and, through his consecration, God by grace.'"[10] An important sign of the immortality of the monarch's body in the popular imagination was his supposed power to cure the "King's Evil" through touch. James often wrote that the king was two persons: as a man he was mortal, and as sovereign he ruled with divine power, as the successor to the Old Testament kings and to Christ. When James spoke before the Lords and Commoners in 1610 he observed, "The state of monarchy is the supremest thing upon earth. For Kings are not only God's lieutenants upon earth, and sit upon God's throne, but even by God Himself they are called Gods . . . a King is truly *Parens patriae,* the politic father of his people. And lastly Kings are compared to the head of this microcosm of the body of man."[11]

James thus placed himself at the "head" of the body politic conceived as a microcosm. As John Shute had earlier made clear when dedicating his treatise on the orders to Elizabeth, a body-politic is a commonwealth; its parts form an integrated whole, with a head to rule and everything in its place and in proportion.[12]

The Body of the Column and the "Two Bodies" of the King

The idealization of the king's body in court policy and art equally emphasized the Stuart monarch's role as a Christian prince directly empowered by God. Traditionally Christ's body was cultivated as the ultimate human embodiment of divine proportion—hence Vitruvius's famous description of the perfect, Euclidean body of man encompassed by a circle and a square (III.i.3), to which Jones's observation on the geometry of the human form most directly referred, became represented by Cesare Cesariano in his edition of *Vitruvius* of 1521 as a crucified figure. Alternatively, in the English translation of *Lomazzo,* the perfect human figures were represented as Adam and Eve.[13] But following Stuart court rhetoric it was surely the king's "ideal" body that Jones especially identified with the Vitruvian form, and, moreover, it was surely the idealized body of his royal patron that Jones sought to emphasize through the symmetry and proportions of his court architecture.

9.2

The verse entitled "Her Maiestie resembled to the crowned pillar" in George Puttenham's discussion of proportion in *The Arte of English Poesie* (London, 1589). (Photo: Cambridge University Library.)

More particularly, the "body" of the column would naturally enough have expressed the preeminent political theory in Stuart England, that is, the theory of the king's "two bodies." Like the king, the antique column following Vitruvius's description was composed of two bodies: one visible, based on human features, and the other invisible, based on ideal human proportions. And the body of the king and that of the column were both considered as material *and* transcendent. The column's constituent ornament was, like the physical body of the king, subject to decay, while the essentially invisible canonical proportions of the column were by their nature immortal, like the king's "divine" body. Proportions were certainly conceived of as invisible, the Elizabethan philosopher John Dee describing "the necessary, wonderful and secret doctrine of proportion," and Wotton observing the talismanic capacity of architecture to "ravish the beholder . . . by a secret harmony in the proportions."[14] Whatever the physical state of a facade *all'antica*, it was the proportions of the individual elements—and of the column in particular as the principal ornament—that lent harmony to the whole design. The monuments of Rome may have been ruined, but their proportions were perceived by many Renaissance artists and architects as still intact, and the stones of Stonehenge, although much decayed, evidently preserved in Jones's view the "harmonic proportions, of which only the best times could vaunt."[15]

Elizabethan poets had clearly associated the column's form with the royal body. In George Puttenham's discussion of proportion in *The Arte of English Poesie* (1589), a verse is column shaped and entitled "Her Majesty resembled to the crowned pillar" (figure 9.2).[16] The body of the queen and that of the antique column were frequently linked in royal heraldry, such as in the famous engraving by Crispin de Passe Senior of Elizabeth standing between two Corinthian columns (1596). Here the Virgin Queen is, appropriately enough, associated with the order of the Corinth virgin. John Shute even elevated the humble Tuscan order to regal status in representing the column as "Atlas, King of Mauritania." In the Stuart era, proportionate ratios were seen to express British social order in Jonson's satire of Jones within *A Tale of the Tub* (1633), for in this play a character named "Inigo Jones" exclaims, "A knight is six diameters; and a squire / Is five, and somewhat more: I know't by compass, / And scale of man."[17] Jonson here parodied Jones's association of social and architectural order, as conventionally expressed through the body-column analogy. Court propaganda made clear the link between the king's body and Jones's columns. A sermon preached in 1620 at St. Paul's by the bishop of London and written by the king to proclaim the restoration of the cathedral through Jones's new facades *all'antica* made reference to "the body of the King, a building not made with hands, but shaped of flesh and blood"; for the king "himself shall come, and stretch his body upon the body, afford his own bodily presence, . . . mark the pillars and pinnacles, and make it his princely care."[18]

However, if Jones's columns were indeed seen to express the authority of the king's "two bodies," royal authority was defined by the right (or otherwise) to make law. It is the specific idea that through its unprecedented display of the orders, court architecture proclaimed to the Stuart populace this legislative power of the monarch, which I now examine.[19] In associating court architecture and statute law, it is first necessary to understand the uncertain legal status and powers of the Stuart king that this architecture sought to consolidate. The very legitimacy of Stuart rule, which all early court art and public pronouncements sought to affirm, much concerned James following the Act of Union and his succession in 1603 to the newly created "British" throne (he had been king of Scotland since 1567). The monarch's role defined in relation to natural law was the central theme of Shakespeare's tragedies (*King Lear,* for example, was performed at court in 1606), and the tradition of natural law informed James's insistence to Parliament that his position at the "head" of the body politic was as God intended.

Moreover, the Stuart period was largely characterized by the battle between the institutions of court and Parliament concerning their respective statutory powers. This conflict led to Charles's eleven-year period of "Personal" or prerogative rule, when he made law without the consent of Parliament following its dissolution in 1629,[20] and after 1642 defined more dramatically the battle lines of the English Civil War. English medieval monarchs had cultivated the right to make law by statute in Parliament because it was seen as an essential aspect of their sovereignty, and it was argued that their "immortal" body was an expression of this right. Hence, royalists maintained that the king alone made the law in Parliament, acting with its advice and consent but without actually sharing the right to legislate, a concept known as the "order theory of kingship" and equated with the king's "immortal" or "legislative body."[21] On the other hand, the common law was frequently advanced by members of the legal profession to emphasize the individual rights of the subject and the duty of the monarch to protect those rights. The concept of the king's "legislative body" was also countered by Parliament's three estates—the Bishops, Lords, and Commoners—some of whom argued the so-called community-centered view that the king shared law-making powers with them.[22]

The mutual harmony of natural justice and Stuart statute law was frequently celebrated in court masques and poetry. Thus, Ben Jonson eulogized the first visit of the newly crowned monarch to Parliament in 1603 by presenting Stuart England as the home of harmonic justice, symbolized by the descent from heaven of the Greek goddess of law and personification of justice, Themis, together with her daughter, Eunomia, who were "but faintly known / On earth, till now, they came to grace his throne."[23] Successive court masques made clear the king's relationship with the law as the source of earthly harmony, a harmony physically expressed through Jones's ordered stage settings with their architecture *all'antica*. In James's masques, personifications of Peace (Irene) and her heavenly sisters Harmonic Justice (Dice) and Law (Eunomia) were presented as royal virtues set within Jones's piazzas and column-lined, porticoed temples. In George Chapman's *The Memorable Masque of the Two Honourable Houses, or Inns of Court* (1613), Eunomia serves as a priestess in a temple to Honor formed from "an octagonal figure, whose pillars were of a composed order, and bore up an architrave, frieze, and cornice."[24] Under Charles, the justification of prerogative rule came to influence all court art, especially the masques.[25] The figures of Minos and Numa, royal lawgivers of Greece and Rome, stand in Jones's ornamental proscenium for the *Triumph of Peace* (1634) (figure 9.3). This masque emphasized that there can be no peace without law, and only from their mutual harmony can justice prevail. All three virtues were clearly represented to the court through Jones's Roman architecture, as the embodiment of the civil order and decorum that the law upheld.

Jones's interest in civil decorum and the philosophy of ethics in particular is evidenced by his close study of Xenophon, Aristotle, Plutarch, and the Renaissance moral philosophy

Figures of Minos and Numa, royal lawgivers of Greece and Rome, in Jones's proscenium for the masque *Triumph of Peace* (1634). (Photo: Chatsworth House)

of Alessandro Piccolomini (Jones's copies of these authors' works are preserved at Worcester College in Oxford), while his faith in the power of architecture to lend decorum to society is attested by his Stonehenge thesis in which he argued that it was on being taught the "Roman manner of architecture" that the ancient Britons acquired Roman civil order.[26]

Jones's court architecture can thus be seen as a public statement of the Stuart monarch's legal legitimacy and law-making powers, equivalent to similar court-bound justifications made in the masques for which Jones designed settings *all'antica.* For the "perfect" numbers and canonical proportions that Jones employed to order the elements on his facade designs (such as that of the Banqueting House in Whitehall),[27] in reflecting the absolute, divine qualities of the royal body, must inevitably have been seen to reflect the absolute, divine right of Jones's royal patron to rule by statute law as traditionally represented by the king's "immortal" body. According to this view concerning the purpose of Jones's work, royal decorum was expressed by architectural decorum, the "order theory of Kingship" was represented by the use of the orders, and the balanced, natural justice of statute law and "equity" was matched by the Vitruvian canons of symmetry and proportion. The individual column thus stands in Jones's designs as a "pillar" of royal justice.

The representation of the king's traditional "legislative body" through the newly introduced architectural orders might well have seemed natural enough to Stuart courtiers.[28] The English translations of architectural terms central to the Vitruvian canon have a natural counterpart in well-established legal terminology widely employed in Stuart statutes: proportion and harmony, order and decorum, symmetry and balance, licentiousness and the rule, scale and measure all obviously feature in the theory of both disciplines, while "ordinance" is defined as both the rules governing the design of the orders of architecture (particularly their proportions) and, especially in France, as a law of the king.[29] The Italian theorist Daniele Barbaro in his commentary to *Vitruvius,* first published in 1556, had explained the concept of architectural proportion through citing those of equity and justice in his introduction to Vitruvius's book 4. Medieval legal disputes frequently centered on issues of scale and measure, while judgments were passed with reference to proportion. Echoing Barbaro, this tradition was to provide a precedent for the first English explanations of the principle of harmony implicit in the orders.[30] John Dee in his "Mathematical Preface" to the English *Euclid* (1570), in outlining the mathematical arts to his readership of artisans and builders, noted "what proportion, 100 has to 75 . . . which is *sesquitertia:* that is, as 4 to 3. . . . Wonderful many places in the civil law require an expert arithmetician, to understand the deep judgment, & just determination of the ancient Roman lawmakers." Dee continues by echoing Barbaro that "in the laws of the Realm . . . justice and equity might be greatly preferred, and skillfully executed, through due skill of arithmetic, and proportions appertaining."[31] Only following this legal discussion did Dee go on to explain the role of proportion in architecture with more traditional references to Vitruvius and Alberti. Dee's emphasis on number as the key to architectural and legal practices represented an attempt to bring both "arts" into line with the values, or rather what would increasingly become the value-free claims, of natural science. Both arts thereby conformed to nature's laws through their particular dependence on Euclidean geometry.[32]

Inigo Jones would have seen these ideas when studying Barbaro's *Vitruvius* and Dee's "Preface,"[33] and in fact he even translates Barbaro's comment that "Euruthmia is the tempering of the proportion applied to the matter as equity is to justice." As if to echo this association, Jonson's poetry equated the language of Vitruvian architectural theory with qualities of moral solidity and justice.[34] Indeed Wotton would also use a legal metaphor when explaining the rules of proportion through translating the Roman rhetorician Quintilian on painting: "Parasius did exactly limit all the proportions so, as they call him the Law-giver, because in the images of the Gods and of Heroic personages, others have followed his patterns like a decree."[35]

Hence the early texts on architecture by English theorists used both a practical and a metaphorical legal analogy to explain the principles of proportion, and as such would surely have further justified the Stuart use of the orders to express the traditional legal concept of the king's "two bodies."

Stuart London and the "Ideal" Commonwealth

The ideals of natural law and justice lie at the very heart of the well-governed state, whether princely or republican, as Shakespeare's *Merchant of Venice* (c. 1600) made clear to the Stuart citizen. James stressed the antique-biblical role of the king as the wise judge, lawgiver, and indeed builder through his identification with Solomon and Augustus. James's cultivation of the role of peacemaker also emphasized these judicial qualities, as a type of supreme justice of the peace.

Through new, well-ordered building facades, London was to be physically transformed under the Stuarts into the seat of royal justice, a city conceived in succession to Rome as the (Protestant) imperial center from which law and order emanated. The law was itself used as an instrument to realize this symbolic objective. In building statutes that James issued in 1615 and 1619, London was projected as a second Rome restored by its new Augustus. Indeed the expression of the king's legislative authority through the control of new building work was a central tenet of these statutes.[36] The statute of 1615 implied that an ordered uniformity was expected of all new facades, and the statute of 1619 stipulated no "jutting, or cant-windows," "the windows of every whole story, to be of more height than breadth," "a sufficient peer of brick, between the windows for strength," and "the windows of every half story [basement] to be made square every way, or near thereabouts." James concluded by commanding officials such as justices of the peace to enforce these statutes. From 1630 onward Jones himself served as a justice of the peace, a role perfectly compatible with his celebration of Stuart justice and peace in the masques, and he is likely to have been directly involved in the implementation of these statutes.[37] Certainly Jones had been a member of the 1618 commission charged with the enforcement of the first statute of 1615.[38] Indeed Jones's Banqueting House facade, with its vertical walls, tall windows, column "piers" between each window, and square windows in the basement half-story, clearly exemplified James's statutes, albeit transformed by Vitruvian principles. The masquing hall was commenced in 1619, the same year as the second statute quoted above (figure 9.4).

But to conclude, the expression of the justice of the king's "legislative body" was less through the practical regulation of architecture than it was through the first use in Britain of proportion to "organize" architectural design through the device of the column. Again taking the Banqueting House as an example, the column-lined interior of this masquing hall has the proportions of a double cube; in 1610 Marcelline had described the cube's "triple dimension of length, breadth, and depth" as a "figure" or "number of justice."[39] Harmonic proportion thus clearly represented civil order and justice to the Stuarts. The bishop of Bristol, John Thornborough, in warning against the disunity of Britain apparent in 1641 on the eve of the Civil War, noted that "a commonwealth may fittingly be resembled to musical instruments; . . . the harmony is in the unity of proportion with agreeable consent of distinct sounds."[40] For Thornborough, the Stuart monarchy justly distributed its virtues "equally, and graciously among all, by geometrical proportion."[41]

The iconography of Jones's projects in London for the court also celebrated the theme of Stuart justice and legal authority. At St. Paul's, for example, the work on which was car-

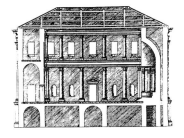

9.4

The Banqueting House, London
1619–1622. Photo: Author.

9.5

Jones's design of 1617 for a new
Star Chamber (revised section,
John Webb, c. 1660). (Photo:
Worcester College, Oxford)

ried out during the years of Charles's "Personal rule," the statues of James and Charles that surmounted the royally funded portico made clear that the king's prerogatives were invested in his body, here upheld both literally and symbolically by Jones's majestic Corinthian columns.[42] Indeed, his design of 1617 for a new Star Chamber, a column-lined basilica with an apse "celebrating" the bodily presence of the royal judge, made the link between the royal prerogative and Stuart architecture *all'antica* explicit (figure 9.5). It was in the high court of the Star Chamber that the king met with the Privy Council to issue royal proclamations (among other duties), and it became a powerful symbol of royal authority independent of Parliament and the judiciary.[43]

Jones's Star Chamber was designed to form part of a new Whitehall Palace, of which the Banqueting House was the only element to be constructed. On the Banqueting House ceiling painted by Rubens, James was portrayed as the archetypal wise judge, Solomon, set within antique columns (explicitly cast as "pillars" of royal justice), and the palace was itself conceived as a modern rival to Solomon's temple (figure 9.1). The palace became the focus of the Platonic harmony of heaven and earth in the masque *Albion's Triumph* (1632), which closed with, "a prospect of the King's palace of Whitehall and part of the city of London seen afar off, and presently the whole heaven opened, and in a bright cloud were seen sitting five persons representing Innocency, Justice, Religion, Affection to the Country, and Concord, being all companions of Peace."[44] The god of justice thus presented the proposed palace within the court as a Stuart temple of harmonic law, just as a series of new, well-

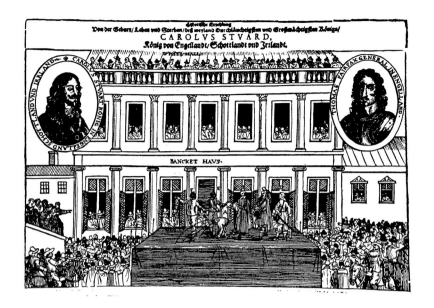

9.6
The execution of the king's
"legislative body" in 1649 before
the Banqueting House facade, as
engraved by Marx Anton Hannas.
(Photo: Nuremberg Germanisches
Nationalmuseum, HB.24726)

ordered buildings were being planned in order to proclaim the king's "legislative body" throughout the capital. Hence, the opposing strands of Stuart society, from Puritan to Catholic, would be united by the universal harmony of law and architecture in Charles's ideal commonwealth.

Whitehall Palace was destined to form the backdrop not to this Stuart apotheosis but, true to antique dramatic precedent, to royal tragedy. One of the most decisive of Parliament's acts during the Stuart period, its decapitation of the king's "legislative body" in 1649, was enacted appropriately enough in front of the Banqueting House facade (figure 9.6). The defacing of the cathedral's Corinthian portico and its statues during the Civil War is testimony to the popular identification of Jones's architecture with royal authority.[45] The modern era of constitutional government was to have a new style of architecture from its surveyor, Christopher Wren, for which neither the king's body, nor indeed the human body in general, would, much as in Parliament, be viable as the absolute "rule." For Wren, the new measure of architecture was geometry divorced from human proportion; columns now imitated the natural growth of trees.[46]

It might be observed by way of an epilogue that the most influential latter-day ideal figure, the Corbusian "Modulor man," no longer grasps at perfect Euclidean geometry nor is he made to span the cross. Inigo Jones would no doubt have found him grotesque. But echoing the seventeenth-century ideal body, this human figure, a form both more universal and more democratic, is once again shaped in the image of its time.

Karsten Harries

Sphere and Cross: Vitruvian Reflections on the Pantheon Type

The following reflections were occasioned by an aspect of the Vitruvian account of the origin of architecture that deserves more attention: when Vitruvius likens his first builders to wild beasts, he also insists on what makes them different. This, to be sure, can hardly surprise us, but I do find it surprising that what he mentions in the first place is not their extraordinary ability to use their hands and fingers, or their capacity to imitate, learn from, and improve on what they observe, but their "not being obliged to walk with faces to the ground, but upright and gazing upon the splendour of the starry firmament."[1] How are we to understand this remark, which links human verticality to the firmament? It brings to mind the often told tale of Thales who, looking up at the stars, fell into a well, to be ridiculed by that pretty Thracian servant girl for whom he did not have any eyes. What did the stars matter to Thales? What do they matter to us earthlings? What does the sight of a splendor that the ancients thought essentially inaccessible, a permanent order open only to eye and spirit, beyond human reach, what does this vision of cosmic permanence have to do with the origin of building?

I want to underscore the verticality of humans in Vitruvius's account. To be sure, in sleep and death, we return to earth-bound horizontality. Such horizontality, however, does not circumscribe our being. Unlike the other animals, we are not obliged by our bodies "to walk with faces to the ground." But if the human animal is thus free to look up to the firmament, such freedom is more than a gift of the upright body: "Nature had not only endowed the human race with senses like the rest of the animals, but had also equipped their minds with the powers of thought and understanding, thus putting all other animals under their sway."[2] The human body's verticality signifies spirit.

Such verticality also possesses a temporal significance. When Vitruvius links humans with the upward gaze, he understands them as beings able to rise and look up out of the horizontal temporal condition that circumscribes the lives of the other animals to the seemingly ageless order of the firmament. He thus understands human beings as subjected to time and death by their earth-bound bodies, yet led by their ability to look up to the firmament to dream of immortality, understands the human body in the image of the cross, as the intersection of time and eternity.

Did the sublime spectacle of the starry sky, which the ancients thought to be a perfect sphere, awaken the spirit sleeping in Vitruvius's proto-humans, somewhat as the snake's promise, "You will be like God," opened the eyes of Adam and Eve? Did it awaken them at the same time to their own subjection to time, to their mortality, even as it allowed them to glimpse in the heaven's unchanging order possibilities of a more perfect, more spiritual dwelling? Is human building to carry something of this promise into this death-shadowed world? Or did Vitruvius also associate "the splendour of the starry firmament" with the light- and life-granting sun, the hearth of the cosmos, being represented by the warmth-giving hearth of his primitive home? This much at any rate seems clear: by linking the origin of the first house to the awe-inspiring sight of the inaccessible unchanging order of the sky, Vitruvius places human building between animal shelter and the divinely ordered cosmos, even as he invites us to understand human dwelling as an intersection of animal horizontality and divine verticality.

In the introduction to Book II, Vitruvius disclaims originality for his account of the origin of building, acknowledging, without naming, his debt to "those writers who have devoted treatises to the origins of civilization and the investigation of inventions."[3] The most important of these would appear to have been Cicero's teacher, the Stoic Posidonius.[4] Vitruvius's description of the human being as the being who looks up to the firmament is quite in keeping with the Greek understanding of the human being as *zoon logon echon,* which becomes the Latin *animal rationale.* Possessing reason, the *erecti homines* are not bound to their particular places, as are the *prona animalia.* Standing up and gazing at the firmament, admiring its order, they rise above their natural subjection to the power of place. In the *Phaedrus* Plato thus attributes wings to the soul, which are to carry it to its true home where the gods dwell. Related is the biblical understanding of humans as beings who, created in the image of God, look up to God. Calvin thus suggests that reason, intelligence, prudence, and judgment are given to us not just so that we might govern our lives on earth, but that we might transcend these lives even unto God and eternal blessedness, while Zwingli links our humanity to our ability to look up to God and his divine, timeless word.[5] The human animal transcends and measures himself by a timeless logos. Every attempt to speak the truth is witness to such self-transcendence, for when I claim truth for what I have to say, I claim more than that this is how I now happen to see some matter: the truth I claim is in principle open to all. And even if the truth should ever elude us human knowers, even if Simonides should prove right and truth belong to God alone, the mere attempt to speak the truth is sufficient to show that we are not bound by the body and the accident of its spatial and temporal location, that we do indeed look up to and measure ourselves by a timeless logos, figured by the firmament. Building too should be informed by such a logos, and so we find Vitruvius insisting on symmetry and harmony, prefigured by both the divinely ordered cosmos and the similarly ordered body of the well-shaped human being.

And yet the reference to the biblical understanding of human being as created in the image of God is accompanied by a warning: the snake's promise suggests that human verticality carries with it the danger that, by claiming a higher place, a permanence and plenitude denied to them, human beings, like the proud, spherical proto-humans of Aristophanes in Plato's *Symposium,* lose their proper perfection and place and instead of rising beyond their mortal condition become less than they were. Gazing at the stars, Thales thus fell into a well, while Icarus, lured by the splendor of the sun, flew high above the earth, only to fall and perish by that very splendor he pursued: *cadet impostor dum super astra vehit.*[6]

With such warnings in mind, let me return to Vitruvius. Were the souls of his first builders comforted by the firmament, as their bodies were comforted by the warmth of the fire that first frightened them? But what promise does such cosmic order, such deathless beauty, hold for us embodied and therefore ephemeral mortals? Will we not inevitably run out of time, even though sun, moon, and stars will continue to rise and set long after we are gone? Can we take comfort from such repetition, from the sun's daily and annual course, from the ever-repeating cycles of nature, from the return of the seasons, from sunrise and sunset, ebb and tide? Does such unending repetition not only serve to make conspicuous what separates our existence, stretched out between birth and death, from the endless circling of a world that seems indifferent to our desires? This difficult-to-bear gap that separates our lifetime from world time seems to condemn our dwelling on earth to insignificance?[7] Does gazing "upon the splendour of the starry firmament" help us to accept ourselves as we are: embodied, vulnerable, and mortal? Will it not rather make it more difficult for us to take pleasure in whatever reminds us of the passing of time? Pleasure in the gifts of the earth? In ourselves? Or does it call us, like Plato's *Phaedrus,* to a transfigured, winged dwelling and to a similarly transfigured spiritual architecture that, unburdened by gravity, answers to the vertical dimension of our being? A spherical architecture perhaps?

The Roman Pantheon, whose one great eye opens its body to the starry firmament, invites interpretation as an attempt to raise this Vitruvian insight into the verticality of human being to the level of great architecture. Not that the builders of the Pantheon neglected the horizontal whose significance Vitruvius so clearly recognized. Present in the spine that joins the rotunda's entrance to its apse, such horizontality must have been far more assertive when the journey to and into the interior still led through a propylon, followed by a long colonnaded court, up five steps to the portico and into the domed cylinder, where its forward thrust was quieted by the calm verticality of the round interior: "The seamless circles around and above the great interior described both the cosmos and Roman rule. The role of giving the Pantheon life was assigned to the sun, the master planet. . . . Because of its form the Pantheon is an activated, light-drenched place, expanding and revolving, visibly connected with the heavens through its cyclopic eye."[8]

There is something reassuring about this sunlike eye, about the vertical axis thus established, a would-be *axis mundi* that seems to proclaim that our journey has ended, that we have arrived at the world's center. We want to rest in this space, in this ageless, domed ring, which promises security and peace.

It is part of the sublimity of this space that its center should be inaccessible to us. Hardly a space in which embodied mortals feel easily at home, this is a sacred space that does not seem to want to open itself to the human world beyond. Here verticality and geometric order triumph over horizontality and the often chaotic everyday in a way that fails to do justice to the requirements of human dwelling—not a criticism, to be sure, of a building meant first of all to celebrate the imperial power of Rome and its gods. The world in which we get born, work, love, and die is left behind, shut out by this space, animated by the light entering from above and transfigured by the time-defying power of the sphere inscribed into this space.

More than the building itself, it is precisely the Pantheon's spherical soul, so indifferent to our frail flesh, that offers itself as a sublime symbol to those wanting to celebrate the boundless freedom and immortality of the human spirit, capable of a self-elevation that leaves the body and thus the whole human being far behind. It is therefore only to be expected that spherical buildings in the image of the Pantheon should have become an object of special concern for the architects of the Enlightenment, in this age when faith in the incarnation and bodily resurrection was increasingly being called into question and an abstract immortality had to offer ersatz for the concrete immortality promised to the Christian. As Sergio Villari observes, Enlightenment "architects seemed almost obsessed by the sphere's solemn and cathartic form. Every one of them planned at least one building in such a form: during little more than a decade, from 1785 to the last years of the century, more than ten such spherical buildings may be counted. Neoclassical architects believed they saw in the sphere, an ancient symbol of eternity and perfection, the ineffable presence of the sublime."[9] In such utopian designs, the Pantheon's spherical soul leaves behind its earth-bound body.

Best known of these is Claude Nicolas Ledoux's experimental design of a spherical house for the agricultural guards of Maupertuis. It belongs with the enthusiasm that then greeted the first balloons, which promised a godlike freedom from the tyranny of place, being capable of flying across boundaries and whatever false walls divided human beings from one another.[10] Heralds of a freer, more genuinely humane world, "these balls of air are the first invention linked to the concept of world revolution. The balloon rises into the sky—as a sign that reason on earth is extending its sway. Such a revolution has this subjective aspect that human beings want to find themselves, want to give themselves a human countenance. This subjectivity is the divinity of religions. The attack on the latter is the greatest presumption and thus liberation. The airship is a practical presumption of that sort."[11]

Ledoux's spherical house is another such practical, or rather impractical, presumption, it too the sign of a spiritual revolution of which we moderns are the uneasy heirs, a revolution that would liberate the human subject from its subjection to the body—would liberate human beings from themselves?—just as it would liberate architecture from the body of building. Anthony Vidler calls attention to the way Ledoux's sphere,

> which rests lightly on the ground, supported by buttresses that serve as bridges to the main entrances, is triangulated between, on the left, a rude shed of branches and leaves—the traditional shelter of shepherds—and, on the far horizon, the rising sun, whose rays bathe the scene in bucolic splendor. The original "type" of the rural hut is here mediated through the "type" or origin of nature into a symbolic form of universal guardianship.[12]

But *mediation* is hardly the right word. This figure of solar plenitude refuses to engage the landscape. Quite the contrary, it is protected from it by its moat, which also prevents it from rolling. The house here becomes a ball that wants to roll, perhaps even a balloon that wants to rise into the air—a figure of an altogether new freedom.[13]

The reference to the Pantheon is more evident in Vaudoyer's appropriately named House of a Cosmopolite (1785), another spherical design marking the threshold of the modern age. This is a house for someone at home everywhere and therefore nowhere, a sphere that refuses even to touch the earth—a sublime house perhaps, home for some disembodied, eternal spirit, but hardly a home for mortals. Once again the Enlightenment's enthusiastic reception of what it experienced as the sublime invention of the balloon comes to mind; Vaudoyer's design dates from 1785 and thus follows by just two years Montgolfier's first balloon flight, a widely celebrated symbol of the spirit's victory over humanity's gravity-burdened, earth-bound existence.

The sphere, this "image of perfection,"[14] presents itself as a natural symbol of such a victory. When Ledoux conceives his cemetery at Chaux in the image of the Pantheon but accentuates the power of the sphere, he provides an enlightened age with a striking image of immortality. Related is Boullée's project for a cenotaph for Newton. Boullée is right to invoke the sublime, which has long been linked to a movement of self-transcendence that leaves behind the body and its bonds: "Sublime mind! Prodigious and profound genius! Divine being! Newton! Deign to accept the homage of my feeble talents! Ah! If I dare to make it public, it is because I am persuaded that I have surpassed myself in the project which I shall discuss. . . . By using your divine system, Newton, to create the sepulchral lamp that lights thy tomb, it seems that I have made myself sublime."[15] It seems only fitting that this sublime creation should be a tomb.

Boullée begins by opposing his feeble talents to Newton's divine genius, where once again divinity means subjectivity that has left behind its imprisonment in base matter. Such a leave taking or self-elevation is presupposed by the new science and its ideal of objectivity: the scientific spirit and the turn to the sublime belong together. In a flight of spirit, Newton thus raises himself beyond the earth in order to "define," godlike, its shape. In the image of this scientifically defined earth, Boullée designs his cenotaph, enveloping, as he puts it, Newton within his discovery and thus within his own self, enveloping spirit within spirit, for "how can I find outside you anything worthy of you?"[16] It is thus Newton's own spirit, which is also the spirit of the new science—indeed of the Enlightenment, of the dawning modern world—that uses the architect to build Newton his proper home, or rather sepulchre.

After this sublime rhetorical flight, we, like Icarus, are brought down to earth, and not to that earth transfigured by reason into a sphere Boullée wanted to represent, but to soil and dirt. We are forced to descend by the architect's decision to surround his "sepulchre in the shape of the earth . . . with flowers and cypress trees." Flowers and trees have to sink their roots into the dark, moist earth, and this is now no longer that earth spirit is able to define and comprehend, but a *mysterium tremendum et fascinans* that resists understanding.

Small wonder that Boullée himself "experienced a certain dissatisfaction that made me want to include inside the tomb ideas that I thought it would be impossible to include, because I could scarcely glimpse how it could be possible."[17] Did Newton's vast genius not embrace the entire universe? If the only fitting monument to Newton would have to envelop him within his own discovery, would such a monument not have to represent that universe whose laws Newton discovered rather than just the earth: "I wanted to give Newton that immortal resting place, the Heavens."[18] Boullée thus chose to transform the interior of his sphere into a "perfect reproduction" of the starry sky, leaving the spectator alone with its immensity and the tomb as the only material object. But did Newton and, inspired by his achievement, Boullée not prove that the human spirit can take the measure of such immensity? Here lies the key to the Enlightenment's understanding of the healing power of the sublime: the embodied self will end in some grave; but what it experiences as a threatening abyss, the terror of endless time and infinite space that threatens to reduce to insignificance the limited life span given to each human being, becomes a source of delight once human beings learn to recognize the spirit's power of flight, learn to recognize themselves as beings of reason. Like the Tower of Babel, Boullée's monument too would found a community, one presided over by a new divinity, personified by Newton. This then is the worldwide community of all human beings who recognize that they are joined by reason, a reason that knows that the universal is higher than the particular and raises us above the body-centered selfishness that normally divides us.

But once more Boullée's design brings us down to earth. Immense as Boullée meant his creation to be, the magic of the starry sky within the sphere is unmasked as no more than a remarkable piece of theater by the ingenious architecture meant to make it possible, by the earth on which this cenotaph stands, by the sky above—and by the silent paper that supports all this. Representation of a representation of an appearance of the cosmos and thus three times removed from reality, Boullée's starry sky is in fact much more a representation of the firmament of ancient cosmology, of the closed world of the ancients, than of the infinite universe of the moderns. His sphere encloses only an inevitably finite artistic representation of the boundless cosmos and thus invites thoughts that Newton too might have replaced nature with an artifact, might have taken the measure only of a human representation of nature—thoughts that return us to the *mysterium tremendum et fascinans* of the infinite other, the earth, the mystery of death, the terror of time, which is the other side of the absorbing mystery of our individuality. Boullée's sublime design leaves us alone with ourselves, even as we recognize ourselves to be members of the human community. But this community remains altogether abstract, offering no shelter to mortals.

The simple geometry of the spherical buildings designed by the architects of the Enlightenment seems to deny gravity. The flight of spirit here leaves the body behind. In a design like Ledoux's House for the Agricultural Guards, the architect's vision is thus allowed to outstrip the capabilities of the builder, which did not prevent the establishment of an influential paradigm: born of modernist self-assertion, the ideal of a spiritual, earth- and body-defying architecture was to inspire much subsequent architecture. How many modern buildings look as if they could be stood on their heads, ready to roll, to move, even to fly?

The Enlightenment's enthusiastic reception of the first balloons, Le Corbusier's love affair with the airplane, and Tatlin's preoccupation with his flying machine, the Letatlin, belong together. They all dreamed of an Icarian, birdlike dwelling, of an architecture for an ideally disembodied, ghostly humanity. Modernism is ushered in by a return of the old Gnostic dream of escaping the all-too-material prison that is our body, of flying into that boundless openness demanded by our godlike freedom.

It was a version of that dream that let van Doesburg demand of architecture "a floating aspect (insofar as this is possible from a constructional standpoint—this is the problem for the engineer!) which operates, as it were, in opposition to natural gravity."[19] The "as it were" is telling: such opposition can be no more than an appearance. "No matter how it is combined, matter is always subject to gravity. It makes no essential difference whether architecture employs load and support, tension and compression construction, or no construction at all."[20] The painter here has an advantage. In his counter-constructions, van Doesburg thus floats planar surfaces in an indefinite space, recalling Malevich's slightly earlier suprematist compositions, which similarly float geometric shapes on a white background that figures the infinite void. Van Doesburg, to be sure, was unwilling to pursue such dreams only as a painter; he wanted to see them realized in the world as architecture. And did not the new technology lead the way toward such realization? "Through modern technique material is transformed, *denaturalized.* The forms which thereby arise lack the rustic character of antique forms. Upon this denaturalization or, better, *transnaturalization,* the style of our age is largely based."[21] In structures like Rietveld's Schroeder House (1924), such hopes for a truly modern, denaturalized architecture that would answer to human beings that had finally learned to master the earth and in the process become themselves denaturalized begin to find their realization.

At first glance such designs may seem to have little to do with the spheres of such Enlightenment architects as Ledoux, Boullée, Vaudoyer, Lequeu, or Sobre. The sphere is a simple geometric solid, while van Doesburg will have nothing to do with such solidity: "The new architecture is *anti-cubic;* that is to say, it does not attempt to fit all the functional space cells together in a closed cube, but projects functional space cells (as well as overhanging surfaces, balconies, etc.) centrifugally from the center of the cube outwards. Thus height, breadth, and depth plus time gain an entirely new plastic expression."[22] More important is the way this architecture too emphasizes simple geometric forms, invites an inversion of up and down, and appears to deny gravity.

Of a piece with such attempts to elide the appearance of gravity are attempts to elide every appearance of the hand:

the best handwork is that which betrays nothing of handwork. this perfection is dependent upon our environment: and absolute purity, a constant light, a clear atmosphere, etc. are the qualities of our environment which become qualities of the work. your studio must be like a glass bell-jar or hollow crystal. you yourself must be white. the palette must be of glass. your brush sharp, square and hard, always free from dust and pure as a surgical instrument. there certainly is more to learn from medical laboratories than from artists' studios: the latter are cages smelling of sick monkeys.

your studio must have the cold atmosphere of the mountains at an altitude of ten thousand feet, the eternal snows must lie there. cold kills the microbes.[23]

In van Doesburg's sterile cold studio, we breathe the air of that sublime Platonism that found such provocative expression in these words spoken by Socrates in the *Philebus*:

I do not mean by beauty of form such beauty as that of animals or pictures, which the many would suppose to be my meaning; but says the argument, understand me to mean straight lines and circles, and the plane or solid figures, which are formed by turning lathes and rulers and measures of angles—for these I affirm to be not only relatively beautiful, like other things, but they are eternally or absolutely beautiful, and they have peculiar pleasures, quite unlike the pleasures of scratching. And there are colors, which are of the same character, and have similar pleasures; now do you understand my meaning?[24]

Plato's Socrates already disliked the hand-made look: too present here were body, decay, death. The spirit demands a spiritual home. And what testifies better to the death-defying victory of spirit over matter than the sphere? Should architecture then not look to the sphere and carry something of its ageless promise into our imperfect, contaminated world? It is therefore not surprising that in the very beginning of his essay, Boullée should chide Vitruvius, who is accused of having been familiar only with "the technical side of architecture."[25] Indeed, had Vitruvius made more of that remark that has his primitive builders look up to the sphere of the firmament, he might have recognized the poetry that according to Boullée alone lifts building to the level of art and makes it architecture. Refusing to define architecture as the art of building, Boullée insists instead that it is first of all a product of the mind, and mind seeks order and perfection. In the sphere, he too finds the natural image of perfection: "It combines strict symmetry with the most perfect regularity and the greatest possible variety; its form is developed to the fullest extent and is the simplest that exists; its shape is outlined by the most agreeable contour and, finally, the light effects that it produces are so beautifully graduated that they could not possibly be softer, more agreeable, or more varied. These unique advantages, which the sphere derives from nature, have an immeasurable hold over our senses."[26] "Nature" here has nothing to do with mud and excrement. This is a "denaturalized nature," the kind of nature figured by the firmament. It is this nature Boullée would have the architect study. In its image he would have him build.

The paradigm of such architecture, the Pantheon, often has been called sublime; the sublime again has long been linked to a sense of not feeling at home in the world. Sublimity in architecture and the requirements of dwelling do not easily go together. Inevitably sublime architecture turns a cold shoulder to the body and its requirements. A spherical home like Ledoux's House for the Agricultural Guards seems almost a contradiction in terms.

The Roman Pantheon, to be sure, while it may have a spherical soul, has a body that very much belongs to the earth. It does not want to roll or fly, but to hold its place, while opening itself to the sky. Its hemispherical dome rests firmly on a cylinder of the same radius, recalling a long tradition of round earth-bound grave monuments that includes the chambered Neolithic tomb in Newgrange, Ireland, and the so-called Tomb of Agamemnon in Mycenae. All of these are much less accomplished works of architecture. The Pantheon spiritualizes this tradition, transfigures it by virtue of the power of geometry even as it asserts more strongly the power of the vertical against that of the horizontal. But precisely this transfiguration threatens to make us strangers in this divine space: we would have to be able to fly to place ourselves at its center. The clarity of the geometrical idea, appropriate to a representation of cosmic order, here threatens to triumph over a fuller humanity. This is no criticism: this is, after all, not a house in which embodied mortals are to find shelter, but a temple for all the gods, and thus no god in particular, in keeping with the cosmopolitan and at bottom secular, proto-modern religiosity of Hadrian's Rome.

Still, the living body seems to have little place inside the Pantheon, and it is hardly surprising that its most immediate successors should have been houses for the dead, such as the mausoleums of Diocletian and Maxentius. The Pantheon's earth-bound geometry speaks not only of eternity but also of death. If its oculus represents the sun, it interprets it as a source of light rather than of life. It seems only fitting that the Pantheon should face north.

Vitruvius himself, however, despite my suggestion that the Pantheon raises his insight into the verticality of human being to the level of great architecture, had a rather different idea about how temples should be oriented:

> The quarter toward which temples of the immortal gods ought to face is to be determined on the principle that, if there is no reason to hinder and the choice is free, the temple and the statue placed in the cella should face the western quarter of the sky. This will enable those who approach the altar with offerings or sacrifices to face the direction of the sunrise in facing the statue in the temple, and thus those undertaking vows look toward the quarter from which the sun comes forth, and likewise the statues appear to be coming forth out of the east to look upon them as they pray and sacrifice.[27]

More important to us humans than the sun above is the rising sun, which presents itself as a symbol of the ever repeating victory of the life-giving power of light over the forces of darkness: *ex oriente lux*. Compare the function of sunlight in the Pantheon with its function in the chambered tomb at Newgrange, where "the entrance is so arranged that at the winter solstice the rising sun shines through a specially formed aperture, down to the entrance passage and into the burial chamber at the heart of the mound." Here "it is clear that we are looking at more than just a burial place."[28] This tomb is not just a place of death, but expresses a conviction that darkness will not have the last word, that life on earth will triumph over death. Important here is the way the light of the midwinter sun promises renewed warmth and life. Light is tied to the gift of life. It is the severance of this tie that makes the Pantheon a less than happy space. Its sublime, spiritualized light does have the power of transporting us, as our everyday cares and concerns are bracketed. In time we are given a fleeting deliverance from the burden of time, a semblance of redemption. And so understood, it figures the redemptive power of much great art, which provides relief from the burden of life. The price exacted for such relief is our engagement in the world: we cease to really live. Such sublime art is born of an inability to forgive ourselves and accept our essential temporality. And so understood, the Pantheon's cold beauty, this symbol of eternal plenitude and spiritual self-transcendence, also figures death.

As Vitruvius knew so well, architecture should be linked not to eternity and death but to life, should allow mortals to find shelter. In conclusion, I return to the upright posture of Vitruvius's first builders that raises them above the ground they share with the other animals. Contemplating the firmament, they must not only have been challenged by its unaging perfection, but also been put in their place. Unlike the immortal gods, these images of a transfigured, transnaturalized humanity, mortals can maintain their verticality only with effort; their bodies belong to the earth, to which they return in sleep and in death. Full self-affirmation demands an affirmation of this twofold belonging that is never without tension. But the tension is difficult to bear and again and again tempts us with dreams of a more perfect dwelling, of buildings in the image of the sphere. Yet to affirm ourselves as the mortals we are, we have to affirm not only that vertical dimension of our being that links us to a timeless logos, but also that horizontal dimension that binds us to the earth and into time. To build houses fit for mortals, we must resist the temptations of the sublime, look up to the spherical firmament and what it figures, but also ahead and down; we must learn to make room for vertical and horizontal, for the cross.

11

Alberto Pérez-Gómez

Charles-Etienne Briseux: The Musical Body and the Limits of Instrumentality in Architecture

Instrumentality and Tradition

Entering a new millennium, we are bombarded by stories of technological accomplishment and informed that this is only the beginning of a great technological era ushered in by the computer revolution. In architecture, computers are no longer merely utilitarian instruments to make architectural production more efficient; they are now being promoted by their incredible capacity to generate "new forms" that are totally "other" from our traditional orthogonal building practices. The generative patterns of these forms resemble both cultural artifacts and natural phenomena, and appear to transcend many of our old dualistic assumptions, particularly the opposition between "rational" and "irrational" design.

This exciting new instrumentality, however, is based on mathematical models and often becomes a self-referential exercise in structural determinism. This encourages fashionable architectural projects that are oblivious to their cultural context, their intended programs, their historical roots, their ethical imperatives, and the experiencing body. Indeed, cyberspace would make no sense if we were not first and foremost mortal, self-conscious bodies already engaged with the world through direction and gravity. We do not merely *have* a body, we *are* our bodies, inextricably woven with *our* world. Trying to think in a totally dark room for more than a few minutes is enough to convince us of the reality of this unarticulated, preconceptual ground of being that includes the legacy of architecture as its external, visible order.

All this notwithstanding, the obsession with instrumentality rages unabated in architectural practice and almost always underscores the most celebrated "leading-edge" positions in architectural theory. What are its limits? Does it have limits? Or is it truly humanity's unavoidable "destiny": our vehicle for transcending stylistic conundrums and making a better place for all of us in a world with limited resources? Is this our only option for self-transcendence after the failures of the modern ego?

After two hundred frustrating years of testing instrumental discourses in architecture, following the mode of theorizing introduced by Durand, it is clear that other alternatives must be contemplated. We have inherited scientist theories and rational methodologies that tend to disregard values other than efficiency and economy. Values involving speculative language or historical experience cannot be understood as mathematical variables and therefore have been derided as subjective opinion.

The origin of our instrumental obsession needs more explication, for it is complex and profoundly imbued with the myths that make us human. The rich ambivalence of instrumentality is particularly explicit in mid-eighteenth-century technical theories, especially in engineering, music, and architecture. When theory becomes exclusively a prescriptive instrument, it effectively subverts the traditional relationship between thinking and making. Yet these instrumental theories allow us to probe their myths of rationality and their theological assumptions, and to understand how our own concepts of nature and culture have become more polarized and problematic.

To pursue the topic of instrumentality, we must clarify the role of discourse in premodern architecture, a discipline that traditionally involved long apprenticeship. The beginning of our tradition, as reflected in Vitruvius's *Ten Books,* has rendered certain essential aspects of architectural knowledge as *techné,* a stable discourse founded on *mathemata* that could be transmitted through a "scientific" treatise. It also acknowledged that important questions of meaning and appropriateness could not be articulated in this way. Appropriateness (*decorum*) was always considered in relation to "history." The architect, for instance, had to know the stories recounting the origin of the different orders of columns and their relationship to the natural world, including the way they represented the gendered human condition and embodied particular characters. The appropriateness of a chosen order depended on this knowledge and the architect's understanding of other relevant precedents. In crucial issues of proportion, which was considered both the epitome of regularity and a transmissible *mathesis* that served as an ontological bridge between the works of humans and the observable cosmos, the practicing architect always had to adjust dimensions during execution according to the conditions of the site, the scale of the work, and the limitations of human perception rather than strictly following the dictates of theory.

Historically, instrumental and prescriptive intentions appear mostly as partial aspects of architectural discourse, unable on their own to account for the potential meaningfulness of the operation they addressed or helped to realize. Practical apprenticeship, with its acts of *mimesis,* remained the principal education of the architect until the late eighteenth century. Theoretical intentions, however, were subject to transformation. Here I examine the polemic between two instrumental theories in late seventeenth- and eighteenth-century France: the work of Charles-Etienne Briseux and his criticism of the earlier writings of Claude Perrault. My characterization of Briseux's intentions will also draw from the eighteenth-century musical theories of Jean-Philippe Rameau, himself motivated by a technical and instrumental interest. Rameau was a prolific writer and composer at the center of a fascinating debate with Rousseau, Diderot, and D'Alembert on the nature of musical principles, and both Briseux and Rameau quoted each other to support their respective theories. Rameau is still respected as the music theoretician responsible for a systematic theory of tonal composition that accounts for the most popular forms of Western musical expression. Briseux, on the other hand, is practically ignored by architectural historians.

Briseux in Context: *L'Art de Bâtir*

Praised by Jacques-François Blondel as being a "cultivated architect,"[1] Briseux worked for the *fermier général* Daugny to design and build his private residence. He was a fashionable domestic architect in Paris, as well as the designer and builder of the Abbey of Saint-Just-en-Chausse in Picardy, conceived as a palace with a portal decorated with classical orders. Given this reputation, his outspoken criticism of Perrault in his second book, accompanied by his support for the much earlier architectural theories of François Blondel and his praise of Ouvrard and Alberti, may seem surprising and anachronistic. However, his argument was based not on mythology or cosmology, but on a radical belief in inductive methods from science as a model for architecture. Of course, this is not unlike Perrault, whose radical position derived from identifying Cartesian science with architecture.

Briseux is usually qualified as a reactionary theoretician yearning for absolute, universal principles and ignoring the cultural basis of architecture at a moment "when character theory was not sufficiently developed."[2] In fact, Briseux was well aware of the theories of character that had been articulated by his contemporaries, often reiterating their expectations and the problems of architectural expression. Briseux was a rigorous theoretician, perhaps more coherent than the famous Jacques-François Blondel, the most important yet eclectic teacher of architects in France during the middle decades of the eighteenth century.

In his first book, *L'Art de Bâtir des Maisons de Campagne où l'on traite de leur distribution, de leur construction et de leur Décoration,* published in Paris in 1743, Briseux appears to be keenly aware of the importance of cultural differences in architecture as he discusses the distribution of country houses and how the architect must know the different regions' local customs in order to locate certain elements in the *distribution* of a house.[3] Much of his advice on the design of country homes is practical. He provides projects for seventeen different house widths and four different morphologies, revealing an obsession for "combinations" that is reminiscent of seventeenth-century epistemology. His argument is that previous authors treated the issue of distribution only lightly, concentrating instead on the theory of the orders. Distribution, he claims, in relation to the size of the lot and "the status (*qualité*) of the people that will inhabit the house" is a very important issue that deserves special consideration.[4]

In *L'Art de Bâtir,* Briseux argues that the classical orders are appropriate only for palaces and public buildings. As they are exclusively suited for the representation of public functions, he mentions them only at the end of his book. This treatment of the orders is significant, since it suggests that they are no longer central to architectural theory. In his later work, this position results in a crucial difference between his theory of proportion and those of his predecessors, including both Perrault and his opponents. Briseux's interest was always fueled by concrete problems encountered in the practice of domestic architecture during the early eighteenth century, particularly issues of appropriate social representation. He wrote to provide architects with "generative" theories, and his discourse was never simply critical or speculative. In this, he could not be more distant from that other important writer of the mid-eighteenth century, the Abbé Marc-Antoine Laugier, whose *Essai sur L'Architecture* (1753) emphasized that theory should flesh out the "metaphysics" of the discipline.[5] Although Briseux quoted the same sources for authority—in particular the scientific endeavor of Newton—his interest was different. Despite his heated polemic, he shared with Perrault an interest in applied science and a desire to provide a truly useful theory.

The first volume is filled with alternative planning solutions for buildings of different sizes and often includes several options for the same form, that is, the same basic outline in plan and the same proportions. The second volume discusses materials and construction problems, such as how to make good foundations and design gables. In part 6 of the second volume, Briseux examines aesthetic issues.[6] The topics here are a prelude to the much-expanded discussion in his later treatise. He believes that in addition to *convenance,* architecture should express "natural beauty, noble as it is simple, which pleases the eye by symmetry and by the just relationship among the parts and the whole."[7] Two kinds of decoration are possible, he adds: with or without the classical orders. When using classical orders, the greatest beauty depends on the harmony of their parts. When not using classical orders, beauty depends on the harmonious assemblage of the simple masses that constitute the building. To avoid producing "tasteless sculpture," an architect should aim for "noble simplicity," a most difficult accomplishment in all the arts. It is important to note that beauty for Briseux, as for Perrault, must be visible, and *convenance* seems to obtain priority among architectural values. In fact, some of the attributes of Briseux's "natural beauty" were similar to Perrault's "positive beauty." However, Briseux insisted on proportion as a true *cause* of this beauty, while Perrault had discounted this notion. For Briseux, this was an issue, most emphatically when the question concerned an architecture without the orders, one whose "representational" role was more ambiguous than the traditional public institutions. This was a "case" that Perrault's classical theory, rooted as it was in the Golden Age of Louis XIV, never actually considered.

Although Briseux states that harmony is "essential," this topic takes up barely four pages in *L'Art de Bâtir*. Much more emphasis is placed on the surface aspects of decoration. This implies that harmony (and indeed, the meaning or *sens* of architecture) is an "event" of experience. Anticipating the much later work of Nicolas Le Camus de Mézières, he insisted that an architect must carefully consider the interior decoration of each room while composing the distribution of a plan. This emphasis on the qualities of interior space was an important innovation in theoretical discourse. It indicates that architects now felt the need to introduce such qualities deliberately into lived space, which had become homogenized and geometrized following the scientific revolution. Lived space was losing its intersubjective status as a cosmic place, and now needed to express human situations. Briseux says that the first apartments one enters should satisfy more for the "nobility of their forms" than for the richness of their ornament.[8] Harnessing the rhythms of human desire, the experience should gradually become more intense, so that "the spectators' admiration may increase in the measure that they progress through the rooms."[9] Each room should be characterized by attributes related to its use, but without expressive exaggeration. Both Gothic and figurative ornaments may be used, as long as they are not monstrous and remain appropriate to the use of the room.

L'Art de Bâtir was only the beginning of an ambitious project to address the character of all decorative elements in architecture, including profiles of moldings, ironwork, cabinetmaking, the framing of alcoves for beds, the design of balconies, and the use of paint and varnish. This emphasis on the experience of domestic spaces marked a significant shift from seventeenth-century and Renaissance theories. Those earlier architectural treatises had developed a theory of proportion that was linked to a cosmic order and the public space of larger political or religious buildings-a "space of appearance" distinct from the private or social realms. The assumption was that framing public rituals provided the only real possibility for a meaningful practice.

Briseux, in contrast, presumed that the practice of architecture was primarily domestic, the house contributing its character to frame a space of social interaction. Various social functions, such as the role of a functionary in office, or the *function* at which a theatrical performance takes place, constituted a new social world, no longer the same as the public

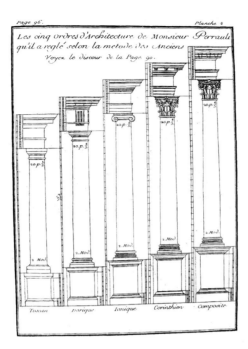

space where political and religious rituals used to occur.[10] It was through these "representational characters" that the space of social interaction was maintained in the eighteenth century. Briseux's most important theoretical work, *Traité du Beau Essentiel dans les Arts* (1752), described an essential beauty in architecture that was universal yet conventional, privileging domestic and social programs over traditional public institutions.

Briseux's *Traité du Beau Essentiel: Avant-propos*

It has been assumed that Briseux's *Traité* was a nostalgic reiteration of traditional theories, an indictment of Perrault's theory, and a reactionary statement that architectural beauty is based on nature rather than cultural traditions. I have suggested elsewhere that Briseux sometimes misrepresented Perrault's position, simplifying the complex argument for "arbitrary beauty" that the earlier architect had developed in his *Ordonnance for the Five Kinds of Columns after the Method of the Ancients* (Paris, 1683).[11] Nevertheless, a close reading of Briseux's text reveals a subtle and sophisticated theory.

Briseux's polemic was written seventy years after the publication of Perrault's treatise, at a time when Newton's natural science had become a model of truth, not only in the exact sciences but also in the arts and humanities. The differences between Perrault's modified Cartesianism and the scientific framework of Newtonianism accounts for many aspects of this debate.[12] However, a reconciliation between the renewed faith in proportions and the prevalent expressive theories of architecture could not have occurred without the "evidence" of a practical music theory. This was provided to Briseux by his friend, the composer Jean-Philippe Rameau, whose theory of harmony clearly described compositional practices.

Briseux recognized that Perrault was not opposed to proportions per se, that his main argument concerned the perfectibility of past proportions and their improvement.[13] At times, however, Briseux misrepresented Perrault's theory by claiming that it disregarded the role of proportions in architectural beauty and that its use of proportions for the orders contradicted its denial of their importance.[14] Deemphasizing Perrault's interest in the ability of human conventions to limit the licentious imagination, Briseux accused Perrault of nothing less than endangering the epistemological integrity of architecture, making it a "blind practice" at the mercy of craftsmen for whom "precision has no importance."[15]

Indeed, while Briseux enthusiastically stated that difference of opinion advances the arts and sciences, embracing the modern future orientation of knowledge, he argued that this "spirit of inquiry" can be abused and can become a source of terrible problems. In the case of Perrault, he claimed that an obstinate adherence to a certain position, probably "motivated by the false honour of defending a singular system," led him to lose sight of the truth. Thus, Perrault had defended a system of proportions that evidently "had no relation to the beauty of buildings." Briseux speculated that Perrault had defended his theory so obstinately because he was offended by François Blondel's criticism and had become insensitive to his own knowledge, the opinions of other authors, and the "unquestionable evidence of experience."[16]

According to Briseux, Perrault had asserted that the choice of proportions depends more or less on the taste, experience, and intelligence of "those who compose the modulation." Music appears to be integral to this argument, although this "had escaped M. Blondel" in his own polemic against Perrault.[17] This realization did not lead Briseux to a simple denial of subjectivity, putting forward a traditional theory of analogy between the macrocosmos and the microcosmos. On the contrary, Briseux also believed that it was ultimately the architect, an enlightened subject, who must make the final decisions about appropriate proportions. This became an argument for a "good" instrumental theory that coincides with our experience of harmony in great architecture, in the same way that correct proportions are important in music, nature, bodily health, and other phenomena.

Briseux understood Perrault's position as a questioning of "real" theory. Principles, in Briseux's opinion, could not be generated by convention alone because the arts seemed to demonstrate (despite the unquestionable reality of historical and cultural differences) a universal dimension that supported the impossibility of conceiving of nature and culture as truly autonomous, independent realms. Principles for Briseux are either "natural" or simply not real, as it is self-evident that human expression speaks about something other, that necessarily grounds it. And while proportions invariably must be adjusted in view of their appropriateness to a task, they are absolutely indispensable for the architect to bring about meaningful work. This underscores the work's capacity to appear as universally significant, that is, beautiful and good. Starting with Perrault's theory, Briseux emphasized, truth has been concealed "behind the veil of the false and the arbitrary."[18] Architects had abandoned their principles, ushering in an epoch of architectural decadence.

Briseux obviously considered Perrault's theory influential enough to offer a lengthy, point-by-point refutation.[19] Given the minor influence of Perrault's system of proportions on the early eighteenth century, the reason behind Briseux's concern must have been this threat of a "crisis of principles."[20] In addition, Briseux must have been keenly aware of the potential of Perrault's theory to become a powerful instrumental device, capable of dictating how to proceed in architectural practice, a capacity that he both admired and feared. Briseux considered Perrault's *Ordonnance* extremely obscure and full of contradictions, a criticism that Perrault himself had directed toward earlier theories to justify his own. Briseux carefully justified his belief in the analogy between architecture and music. This crucial part of the argument, including a reflection on music's expressive power, was based on Rameau's contemporary music theory and practice.

Briseux stated that harmonic relations are the main source of musical pleasure, although the public is not entirely aware of this. We perceive them (*on sent ces rapports*), and this harmony is "recognized," even if conceptually we may not know which specific ratios are involved. Similarly, in architecture, the "spectator has but a natural taste, and does not measure geometrically through vision all parts of a building that may be ruled by proportions before recognizing an agreeable impression and the sensation of beauty."[21] A "natural trigonometry," adds Briseux, seems to be involved in the judgment of proportions and enables beauty (and value) to be recognized. The architect, he emphasizes, must be responsible for applying these proportions. Briseux concluded his critique of Perrault and his *Avant-propos* by stating that despite all of this, "it is not enough to follow proportions; it is important that taste, perfected by experience, help the architect to make a final choice." This crucial "contradiction" will be unraveled later when we return to the text.

The Music Lesson
Briseux cited the theories of Jean-Philippe Rameau to support his contention that a profound affinity exists between harmonic relationships and nature.[22] Briseux used Rameau's

theory of the "fundamental bass" to develop his own theory of harmonic proportion in architecture, praising the musician and quoting from his *Traité de la génération harmonique* and from his report to the Académie des Sciences in 1720.[23] Conversely, Rameau extensively mentions the remarks of "M. Briseux Architecte" to support and defend his own theories.[24] He paraphrased Briseux's method, claiming that the best architects had considered the length of their plan as the base for all other parts of the building—a length that was then subdivided into the same proportions that generated musical harmony from a vibrating string—literally, a c(h)ord-to derive (*tirer*) all the beautiful parts of an elevation.[25] He claimed that Briseux had demonstrated how the buildings of the Greeks and the Romans, "admired universally," were based on proportions with their origin in music. Therefore, concluded Rameau, music is the most evident source of principles for the composition of all arts that depend on taste.[26]

Rameau was fascinated by the coincidence between mathematical rationality and musical harmony. This, of course, was an old observation, perhaps first noted in the Western tradition by Pythagoras and then developed by Plato, and it was central to the mathematical liberal arts of the *quadrivium,* in both the Middle Ages and the Renaissance. The relation between musical harmony and proportion had been the cornerstone of Renaissance theories of architecture, but its transcendental justification had been questioned by Perrault, who claimed that these proportions had no cosmic correspondence. However, Rameau's theory was significantly different from that of his predecessors, and for this reason we must pay attention to its implications.

His *Nouvelles Réflexions* provides a short summary of his ideas. This "demonstration" shows that "the unity, the simple action, the simple resonance of a sounding [vibrating] body provides the law [a single law] to all music, *both* in theory and in practice."[27] This "unity" or "simple resonance" is the fundamental principle of music, he claims, and it should therefore "not be indifferent to all arts and sciences." When the string resonates, it contains not just the basic sound, but also the sounds that one hears when the string is divided by rational numbers. In other words, the bass contains its harmonics: its third and fifth. (If the primary sound is a natural C, the additional sounds that the ear can distinguish are natural E and G.) The principle that determines the structure of chords also determines the succession of notes. The intervals of the third and the fifth in the perfect chord are also perfect intervals for the progression of the fundamental bass. As it turns out, these few basic principles can be developed into a comprehensive system that shows the logic of tonal music and its syntax of chords. The major influence of Rameau's system throughout the eighteenth and nineteenth centuries, and even up to the present day, has more to do with tonal syntax than harmonic generation. Although its principle of division is fully graspable by reason, its "first principle" (like Newton's "Cause" of universal gravitation) may be beyond our faculties. In Rameau's later writings (which most offended *philosophes* such as D'Alembert and Diderot), he extended his theory beyond the realm of music, making it the basis of a metaphysical system for all arts and sciences, and eventually religion and the universe as a whole.[28] Curiously, these assertions were accompanied by "experimental proofs" in a truly Newtonian spirit. He even "reversed" the traditional roles of mathematics and music: it was now music that provided the basis for mathematics, and musical experience of harmony became the basis for perceiving truth in the arts and sciences.[29] Perhaps not surprising, Rameau eventually associated this principle of the resonating body with God's presence in nature.[30]

Rameau's accomplishment was to provide the first truly instrumental theory of composition, which could apply a harmony that traditionally had been the subject of intellectual contemplation and was believed to originate in the supralunar realm. This was no small accomplishment. During the seventeenth century, Johannes Kepler started by transforming the musical theory at the basis of celestial harmony. Since Pythagoras, it had been based on ratios among the first four natural numbers. Such a theory, offered Kepler, "does violence to the natural instinct of hearing."[31] In the sixteenth century Zarlino had added the numbers 5 and 6 to the previous tetradic theory, while Vincenzo Galilei (Galileo's father) refused to accept that harmony could be reduced to abstract concepts. Kepler wanted to uncover "causes" that might both satisfy the ear's judgment and also establish "a clear and evident distinction between the Numbers that form musical intervals and those that do not."[32]

Kepler's harmonic theory presumed an equivalence between geometric awareness and musical consonance. "The circular line [representing the string of a musical instrument] can be divided geometrically in 2, 3, 4, 5, 6, 8, but not 7, 9, 11, 13, not because of a defect in our intellect or an imperfection in the science of geometry, but by nature."[33] Checking his theory against empirical data, he concludes that music "is not a human invention, subject as such to change, but a construction that is so rational and natural that God the Creator has impressed it upon the relations of the celestial movements."[34] Kepler's celestial music can be experienced only from the central vantage point of the sun. It can never be perceived by earthlings; man's reconstitution of it is purely intellectual. "We know the score, but can never attend the performance," he wrote. Keeping this in mind, we may grasp more easily how previous theories of proportion, particularly during the Renaissance, could not have been considered human creations. Theories of music and architectural proportion remained within traditional *theoria:* they could be understood only through observing the Creation in the mind's eye. Coincidences could be discovered in human *techné*, but could not be objectified and transformed into instruments for artistic or architectural practice.

Modern philosophy and science were compelled to actualize geometric constructions, initially to demonstrate the presence of God himself. The emphasis on systems and geometric methods in architectural theories in the second half of the seventeenth century indicated a desire to construct mimetic artifacts using the very operations they believed God had used in the Creation. Rameau's theory of music, in this light, was a final transformation of musical discourse from *theoria* to *techné*. The test of his theory, however, was its total and proven coincidence with experience, a point Rameau made many times. While celebrating the mathematical precision of music theory, he emphasized that one need not be a musician to recognize harmony; for example, we can hum a note and easily change it into a fifth. This copresence of a sounding body with its third and fifth, posited Rameau, is an unchanging "law" of acoustics. This transformation from heavenly harmony into both embodied experience and rational concept was a powerful incentive that fueled both "rational" scientific speculation and "intuitive" creative practices, avoiding the seemingly inevitable split that would happen in the nineteenth century between science and art, between rationalism and romanticism, and between culture and nature. Furthermore, this theory-practice also supported the belief in a universe created "for us" (*propter nos,* as Copernicus had written). It suggested a purposefulness in both nature and cultural artifacts. This, we shall see, was precisely Briseux's attitude in his *Traité*. In this regard, both Briseux and Rameau appear to be traditional. According to Voltaire, the great thinkers of the Enlightenment, all disciples of Newton by 1735, presumed the existence of God. For Voltaire, the discoveries of natural science had made atheism impossible, and there were indeed very few atheists (or agnostics) among eighteenth-century intellectuals. The theories of Briseux and Rameau must be counted among the many extrapolations of Newtonian monism into other disciplines that appeared in the eighteenth century. During the eighteenth century, the existence of God would have been dubious if the human order of things had been completely dissociated from the natural order of Creation. Harmony was deemed a manifestation of both natural and revealed truth.

Nevertheless, when Rameau complained about the uselessness of previous theories of music, he was expressing a similar criticism as Perrault was. He was seeking a truly instrumental theory of composition that would stand the test of embodied experience. Harmony was the fundamental principle of music because it is both given in nature and constructed by a cultivated musician.

A further difference between Rameau's theory and earlier musical discourse is its emphasis on expression. While Rameau became increasingly convinced that he had discovered a principle that could ground all human knowledge, his compositional practice was based on cultural expression[35] and had nothing to do with manifesting a "transcendental"

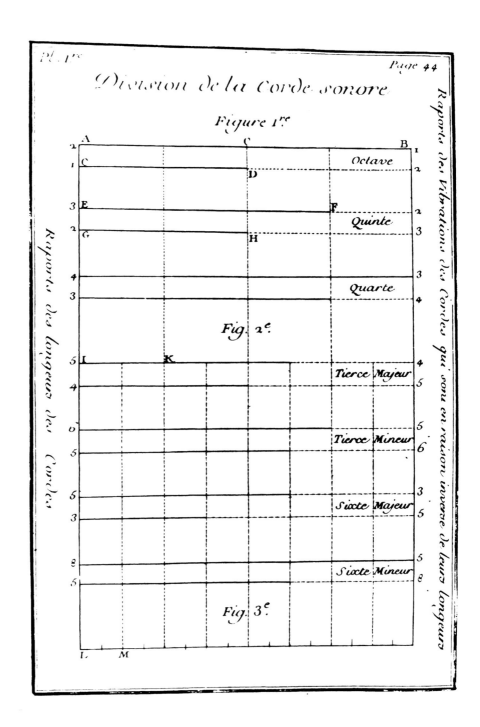

11.2
The divisions of a vibrating
string into harmonic tones.
(From Briseux's *Traité du Beau
Essentiel*)

order, as ancient and medieval music theory had proposed. The mutual reinforcement of instinct and reason was not confined to the listener's response but was essential for the compositional process.[36] This is significant, for the issue of expression had also become crucial for architectural meaning after Perrault's critique of architecture's transcendental foundations. Rameau understood musical expression as a close setting of a text. Although music was based on harmony, it also had to be perfectly responsive to the meaning of the words. The singing voice reconciled music (nature) and language (culture) into a coherent expression. A harmonious voice—the perfectly shaped human breath or spirit—could thus attain communion with the universal mind.

For Rameau, music as science was almost all encompassing. There was no separate domain in music left untouched by rational objective principles: this Briseux would retain for his architectural theory. Yet in Rameau's view, instinct and sensibility could also reveal principles that are known through reason. Numbers revealed laws, laws revealed harmony, but all this could be perceived directly by instinct, regardless of one's education. This argument was also invoked by neoclassical architects, such as the celebrated J.-G. Soufflot, who defended his obsession with proportions in the design of St. Geneviève in Paris. There is an identity, he declared, between taste and proportional rules when both derive from nature.[37] For Rousseau, on the other hand, music as expressive art was almost all-encompassing.[38] Reiterating Perrault's argument for architecture, Rousseau claimed that musical harmony is man-made, a product of culture. This criticism led to the possibility that theories of human disciplines such as art and architecture could be based on custom and convention, on history rather than nature. Yet Rousseau seems to qualify this polemical position in his article on "Harmonie" for the *Dictionnaire de musique.* After paying tribute to the principle of the *corps sonore,* he concurs that theory, having had no principles, finally came to be based on reason. First he reiterates his critique of Rameau: "This system, no matter how ingenious, is not at all based on nature. . . . It was established only on some analogies or convergences that can be overturned tomorrow by an inventive man who finds more natural ones."[39] Rousseau seems to prefer Tartini's system because its "laws of harmony seem to arise the least arbitrarily."[40] Harmony exists, however, and if we must have it, harmonic theory is necessary. Even if it is never more than conjecture or hypothesis, such a theory should be able to show how everything is linked and how "the true system of nature leads to the most hidden detours of art."[41] Not surprisingly, eighteenth-century architectural theories concerned with character and expression, ranging from Boffrand and Briseux to Ledoux, never failed to mention the ultimate need to reconcile art with nature.

Rameau's nature, similar to Newton's, was permeated by rationality and believed to be totally intelligible to the mind. This concept would have a triumphant future in the nine-

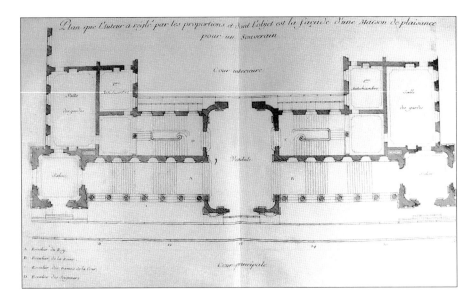

11.3

Briseux's design for a country house (*maison de plaisance*) for a king. The title of the drawing implies that the plan, regulated by proportions, is intended to generate a facade of appropriate character. (From Briseux's *Traité du Beau Essentiel*)

teenth and twentieth centuries as the unstated premise of applied science. It pervaded scientific speculations seeking a unified theory of "everything" in which self-similarity might be the universal rule. Although expression for Rameau was unconcerned with cosmic transcendence, it was still based on a traditional *mimesis.*[42]

Briseux's *Traité du Beau Essentiel*: The Text

Briseux's *Traité* opens with a characterization of nature as the origin of the "true idea of beauty," the source of all rules.[43] Nature, our "fecund mother," leaves nothing to chance and always acts in a predictable and wise manner, evident in the perfect mathematical ratios that govern all her works. While avoiding any evocation of cosmic harmony, Briseux retains the traditional theme of the human body as a visible (empirical) model for proportional ratios. The body's external parts, he writes, provide a "true idea of symmetry and harmony; of symmetry through the identity of parts, and of harmony through the precise proportions which relate the parts among themselves and with the whole."[44] Part 1 demonstrates how historical texts advocate harmonic proportion as the basis for a meaningful architecture. He claims the evidence is clear in Vitruvius's theories, in the Holy Scriptures and the Temple of Solomon, in the works of more recent European theoreticians, and in the great architecture of the past.

In part 2 Briseux describes the origin of harmonic proportion in nature (figure 11.2)[45] "It was observed . . . that the vibrations of resonating strings were in inverse proportion to their length." The subdivision of a string (cord) into its natural fractions (2, 3, 4, 5, or 6 parts) produces harmonic consonances (a chord). The ancients "inferred" from this "experiment" a common principle of beauty based on nature that could "strike the soul" uniformly, producing an agreeable effect. Experience has shown that "the Creator" established a more natural sympathy between certain sounds and the emotions of our soul than between the soul and inanimate objects. Nevertheless, having discovered that harmonic proportions also ruled the human body, the ancients concluded that similar proportions must be present in other sensible phenomena that were perceived as pleasing and significant. This effect would not change even if different senses were involved. "So the ancient architects came to choose harmonic ratios as a principle for their art."[46]

Briseux was convinced that acoustic harmony and visual proportion are analogous, based on the common effect of their mathematical ratios. His quest was to prove that harmonic proportion is visible on the surface of objects, a source of sensuous pleasure and expressive potential, rather than a hidden correspondence with the supralunar world. Like musical consonance, he claims, architectural harmony is derived from nature and therefore is "sympathetic" with the human soul, which perceives it with pleasure. In this way, multiplicity is resolved into "noble simplicity," the unquestionable cause of essential beauty. The "fibers and all other parts that compose the mechanism of the body" are ruled by proportions related to their function (*usage*).[47] Similarly, the humors of our body need to maintain a certain "quantitative" proportion for us to be healthy. This internal disposition must also be manifested externally. All objects of art must be regulated by similar principles in order to be "sympathetic" to humans.[48] Indeed, nature itself is rational, creating an analogy between the "fibers that compose the mechanism of hearing" and the harmony of the resonant body.[49]

To justify this extrapolation further, Briseux invoked Newtonian science, particularly Newton's optical theories. His theory of the rainbow, claims Briseux, proved how its seven colors reveal the same proportions as the intervals among the seven tones of a diatonic musical scale and present "a natural painting that the Creator reveals to our eyes to initiate us into the mysteries of the System of the Arts.[50] In the same empirical (and monistic) vein, Briseux argued that nature always operates in a simple and uniform manner, so both auditive and visual pleasure are based on "the perception of harmonic relationships analogous to our human constitution." This principle must be true not only for music but for all the arts, since "one same *cause* cannot have two different *effects*."[51] Although Briseux's theory of perception is passive and proto-psychological, the relationship he imagines between the soul and the organs of sense perception is not unambiguously dualistic (like Descartes' and Perrault's). He argues that our senses are touched in a similar way by commensurate objects. The mind judges both sights and sounds in the same way, "which becomes an indispensable necessity, a sort of law that has been imposed by Nature and that, though appearing under different forms, can never be denied." Like Perrault, Briseux believed that perception happens *through* specific, autonomous senses. Yet he criticized Perrault's statement that the distinction between vision and hearing makes the musical analogy untenable for architecture. Objects of perception "rattle" our nerves (note the analogy to sound), which are the instruments of our various sense organs.[52] The nerves are vivified by "spirits that run through them, proceeding all from the same blood and thus penetrating the brain." The fluids for the eyes are the same as for the ears, and all nerves are made of the same substance. If our passions have greater sympathy for music than for inanimate objects, it is because music is "alive." Similarly, we are touched more by the sound of the human voice than by instrumental music. This still suggests a faith in the primacy of meaning as "presence": "When there is a relationship and convenience (*convenance*) between the objects and our disposition, the objects touch us agreeably, as if by a physical necessity."

To Briseux it is evident that the poetic power of harmony can change our lives. Thus, his architecture is meant to operate in the erotic realm, like previous architecture in the Western tradition.[53] Although this transformative power of harmony is evident to our senses, it remains distinct from our intellectual judgment yet necessarily coincides with it. The "bitter-sweetness" of eros, the human condition of identity-difference, of completion-incompleteness, is translated as quantitative harmony and dissonance. The experience of meaning is so unique and extraordinary that Briseux identifies it with rational (mathematical) truth, the only formulation of truth that could claim universal legitimacy at that time. This was ultimately at the heart of his debate with Perrault, who seemed to imply that architecture had lost its capacity to reveal such truth for humanity.

Harmony operates across the senses because our soul participates in the mathematical order of Creation. Our soul, elaborates Briseux, can be affected by either perception or sensation. Sensation is a judgment that derives from a received impression, without examining its causes.[54] "Sensation is not the cause of the perception of proportions, it is merely the occasion. But the perception [of proportions] that is born from a sensation can also take place without said sensation, through the imagination or the force of memory." This highlights the difference between Briseux's position and traditional theories and is one more point of contact with Perrault: the absolute hegemony of mathematical reason. "Pleasure emerges from the perception of proportions."[55] By the mid-eighteenth century, these proportions were believed to be truly present in the human (sublunar) world, although they were made to appear through the application of theories in human works, such as architecture and music, revealing the correspondence of beauty and truth. According to Briseux, human pleasure was based on a recognition of humanity's potential wholeness and purposefulness and its participation in the order of Creation. This recognition relied on both experience and reason.

While Briseux believed in a mathematical structure that links the external world to the human intellect, he was confident that this was demonstrated through intuitive, embodied, synesthetic perception. Rameau had also given priority to tactility, arguing that "all our senses are modifications of touch," to support his view that harmony is the source of universal meaning.[56] Briseux and Rameau used the same argument to legitimize the need for "corrections" in practice, while claiming the absolute validity of harmonic theories.

Briseux was interested in a truly instrumental theory of proportions capable of solving the problems of architectural "expression" that had been emerging in the first half of the century (figure 11.3). In this he is closer to Perrault than he may have wished to appear. Perrault's criticism of the age-old veneration of proportions stemmed from a keen observation of the "confusion" among previous writers and from an obsession to reconcile the differences between theory and practice that, in his opinion, originated not in rational discourse but in faulty craftsmanship. Briseux, like Perrault, wished to establish a truly workable system founded on very simple ratios that are "the most agreeable."[57] Following the simple divisions of the monochord, architects decided to choose "as a fundamental base the length or the height of each object" (figure 11.4).[58] The similarity with Rameau's terminology in this passage is not accidental: *basse* or bass is a homophone of *base* or base, also in French. A few pages later, Briseux praises Rameau as a dexterous musician, author of the theory of harmonic generation that demonstrated that a sounding object produces not only its main sound but also the fifth and the third of that sound, as well as its octave.[59] Rameau, claims Briseux, showed the "friendship" between harmonic relationships and nature, and the relationship between the number of vibrations that generate sounds and the eye's capacity to discern "arithmetic progressions in the vibration of strings."[60]

Thus, in order to "regulate" the main parts of a building into a harmonious composition, one must start by establishing the total length of the facade as if it were the c(h)ord that produces the bass.[61] This should be divided into as many equal parts as are needed to proportion the main elements harmonically. Each part should then be subjected to a similar operation. The height, which should be in harmonic proportion to the length, should be subdivided to establish the dimensions of plinths, stone courses, and other elements. When the orders are used, the intercolumnar distance (between the centers of Doric triglyphs or Corinthian modillions) serves as the base dimension for the main parts.[62] The module of the order can then be used for smaller elements. Briseux "demonstrated" the presence of such harmonic ratios in all great architecture, from Palladio and Scamozzi to

11.4
Detail of an elevation by Briseux, showing the way to proportion the elements of a facade in height, starting from a baseline one-fourth the length. (From Briseux's *Traité du Beau Essentiel*)

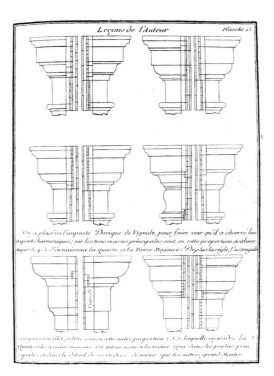

On a placé ici l'imposte Dorique de Vignole, pour faire voir qu'il a observé les
rapports harmoniques; car les trois masses principales sont en cette proportion arithmé-
tique 3. 4. 5. D'où naissent la Quarte et la Tierce Majeure : De plus la règle, l'astragale

compris son filet, est dans cette autre proportion 4. 5. 6. laquelle engendre la
Quinte et la Tierce mineure. Cet auteur a suivi la même règle dans les parties principales et dans le détail de ses Ordres, de même que les autres grands Maîtres.

11.5

Briseux's analysis of Vignola's
proportional rules, offered as
a historical demonstration of
the author's principles. (From
Briseux's *Traité du Beau Essentiel*)

Bernini and Borromini, an argument that he would repeat in the history of architecture included in the second part of his treatise. These "demonstrations" consist of drawings that
show the *son grave* or bass tone as a subdivided line, placed under the elevations of the
works in question and "generating" the harmony of their main parts. In chapter 4, Briseux
returns to his debate with Perrault and claims that despite Perrault's "opposition to proportions, he followed them, with such affectation that he applied them where it wasn't necessary, and ignored them when they were essential," hardly following the ancients as he
(Perrault) had wished to do.[63] He subjects Perrault's proportional system to his "harmonic
test" and concludes that Perrault's proposition does violence to the principle of harmony,
unlike the systems of Palladio, Scamozzi and Vignola, which he determines are correct. Perrault's proportions were derived not from the observation of nature but from the numerical average of the largest and smallest precedents for each part of the five classical orders,
and in Briseux's opinion, had "visibly altered the beauty" of the classical orders and were
therefore despised by most architects (figure 11.5).

Briseux obviously could accept diversity of tastes, but he was adamant that taste could
not be the sole basis of architecture. We must remember that Perrault had indeed subverted

the Vitruvian hierarchy by stating that *accoutumance* was "the main authority in architecture" even when it was contrary to reason,[64] and that beauty (traditionally associated with meaning and thus truth) was established by arbitrary authority, while a "positive foundation is [rather] the usage and the useful and necessary objective which is the aim of a building, such as solidity, health, and commodiousness."[65] For Briseux the "experience" of meaning was primary, yet it had to be based on the unambiguous truth of mathematical ratios. Vitruvius, we may recall, had indeed spoken about "appropriateness" (*decorum* in Latin, translated into French as *bienséance*) and related it to cultural conventions (the "state of things," or *thematismos*), but had separated this issue from the other aspects of meaning ruled by proportion (such as symmetry and eurythmy). He had inferred that "history"— the stories concerning traditional usage and particularly the origin of the classical orders— was the mode of discourse that might enable the architect to comply with this aspect of his work. Perrault, in contrast, made "appropriateness" (*bienséance*) the primary value, based on human history rather than on myth or cosmological analogy, but then related it to a simplified system of proportions that could change with taste. Briseux took up the challenge of integrating appropriateness into a holistic sense of value (beauty), but could not accept that true principles, symbolized by proportional ratios, were subject to historical change. "The followers of Perrault think highly of taste," claims Briseux, and this is pure vanity because they are only copying; they deny that proportions make their work beautiful. The relationship between proportions and beauty is a real cause-and-effect relationship, in architecture as in music and science, and this is validated by our experience. The problem becomes worse, argued Briseux, when these architects build without the orders.[66] Then they truly lack a model, and their work becomes totally arbitrary.

This is indeed the crux of the argument. Briseux's instrumental system retains its metaphysical claim: if architecture seeks the "experience" of beauty, it is also about truth. It cannot depend exclusively on the cultural world for its significance. Its meaning must refer not to some speculative supernatural world but to a more-than-human world. This is a fascinating insight that even today must be pondered seriously. His theory also enables a new mode of domestic or social architectural practice that is no longer based primarily on the classical orders. Yet Briseux's argument depended on the Enlightenment belief in mathematical reason as the only sure guide for metaphysical certainties.

In Laugier's discussion of ornament and structure in his theory of the primitive hut, the classical orders of columns (traditionally deemed to be "ornament) yielded the only essential parts of the actual building and were regarded as the "first principles" of architecture. Conversely, rococo architects had collapsed structure and ornament, transforming the trabeated elements of churches into convoluted, naturalistic elements. Briseux and Perrault similarly believed that it was possible to synthesize theories of expression with the use of architectural proportions. In a section devoted to "the rights of Taste" Briseux wrote: "Everyone agrees that the general ordonnance [notice the word from the title of Perrault's treatise, with its legal overtones], and the disposition of all parts of a building are the province of Genius and Taste, while they must be subject to the Laws of symmetry and convenience, and consequently to certain proportions perfectly analogous to the type of building (*genre de l'Edifice*), to its character, to its position, and to each one of its parts."[67]

Briseux was acutely aware of the ancient association between "character" and musical "modes." He criticized a gateway in the Hôtel de Matignon because each part was regulated by different "modes," like mixing major and minor tones in music.[68] Both ancient and modern architects, he argued, assigned a particular character to each mode. We must therefore not only follow proportional rules, but choose specific ratios related to the masculine or delicate character that one may wish to convey. Briseux emphasized that previous writers on the orders were certainly aware of this. Vignola, for example, used only 2, 4, and 6 in his Doric order: 3, 4, and 5 in his Ionic: and 5, 6, and 7 in his Corinthian.[69]

Proportional differences among the classical orders had traditionally conveyed their specific meaning and character, over and above their particular ornamental syntax. Even Perrault understood this argument and supported it in his *Ordonnance*. The Greeks, we may recall, had associated *ethos* with musical expression, relating musical modes (the sequences of notes in the diatonic scale, using different sets of intervals) to particular "functions": the "dorian," for example, was manly, magnificent, and appropriate for combat, while the "phrygian," of divine inspiration, was orgiastic and pathetic, appropriate for dithyrambic music such as Dionysian rituals. Tonal music, which was institutionalized for European composition by Rameau, inherited these associations and applied them to the major and minor scales. During the eighteenth century, these associations were taken for granted. Although Perrault emphatically differentiated music from architecture, he could not question the "natural" principles of musical harmony, though he could claim that modern music was superior to ancient music. It seemed that character in music was potentially "positive," associated with the truth of mathematics as an inherently human capacity or *Ursprache,* and not subject to custom or change.

In apparent contradiction of his emphatic arguments, Briseux often repeated that it was never sufficient to follow proportions slavishly. "Taste, guided by a judicious reflection and enlightened by experience, should make choices that are convenient to the task at hand."[70] Like his contemporaries, Briseux acknowledged that "genius is without doubt the first creator of beauty in art," but it needs solid principles.[71] Proportions are never a limitation; they are "infinitely diverse," and "experience" is crucial for genius. If taste became diversified to the point of dissonance, thought Briseux, it was due to a lack of education and a weakness of the senses. While taste is always potentially in tune with harmony, these two deficiencies can cause it to become arbitrary.[72] Briseux used *arbitrary* not as the positive result of human authority, like Perrault, but as a negative adjective. Humanity was susceptible to different impressions. Nevertheless, those that are generally accepted and stem from geometric principles are founded on invariable truth. These truths, argued Briseux, could not be changed but through a choice of proportion. This choice is therefore essential, being the source of the mediocre, the beautiful, and the exceedingly beautiful.[73]

Echoing Rameau's argument for a theory of music based on reason but also instinct, Briseux emphasized that it is not enough for an architect to have been born with (good) taste: "Besides feeling the beautiful, one must also know its character and its cause." Natural talent should be perfected by "experience," accompanied by "solid reflections and invariable rules" such as proportions based on nature, calculation, and experience.[74] Briseux elaborates on the "different means that lead to essential beauty" in part 5. Noble simplicity is the very character of beauty.[75] Nevertheless, this is not as simple as unison in music (the harmony of octaves). Instead, it must be like a chord, with enough variety to resolve into unity. Thus, the modes and the orders should be coherent, and ornament should be appropriate to the intended character and "must appear to be useful and in its proper location." We should also pay close attention to the "status of the potential inhabitants of the building."[76] A majestic character is convenient only to palaces, while a courteous (*galant*) character is appropriate for a simple country house. Furthermore, the duty of the architect is to convince the client not to request an architecture that may represent a superior status.

In the second volume of the *Traité,* Briseux devotes significant space to the history of architecture.[77] We should remember that the introduction of history as a component of theoretical discourse in architecture was a recent development, dating back only to the genealogical enterprises of the seventeenth century. Before then, theory had sought to align the present with a mythical past that was believed to be fully recoverable and associated with a cosmic order. In Briseux, as for Perrault, change is real, and progress is possible in architecture. The lesson learned in this *mythistoire,* however, is that architecture degenerates when proportions are abandoned. His story of beginnings is remarkably free of myth: agriculture came first, and then necessity led humanity to build a "safe retreat" for each family. The primitive hut was not an ideal vision but merely a construction of mud and bricks, as the first buildings were merely useful. Only in the following centuries, he claimed, did people add decorative elements. Then, through reflection and experience, architects discovered proportion, which was naturally pleasing to humans because God had devised it and used it in all his works. Briseux thought that "health, commodiousness, and solid-

ity" (*salubrité, commodité, solidité*) came first. It is important to emphasize that here Briseux used language identical to Perrault's description of the "positive foundations" of architecture. Although Briseux mentions Cain as the first builder of cities and acknowledges Villalpando's argument that all classical orders derive from the Temple of Solomon, he was noncommittal with regard to more traditional religious stories about the beginnings of architecture.[78] Briseux associated the discovery of reason and architectural proportions with the Western tradition. He obviously believed that nature and humanity were rational, yet in his story, reason and mathematical ratios are also discoveries of the Western mind, incorporated in its Judeo-Christian heritage. They are a product of civilization rather than a found natural "state." Without engaging in a polemic that might have revealed the true fallacies of his theory, he simply stated that the Greeks brought architecture to its perfection and the Romans continued this tradition through the works attributed to great emperors. In the Middle Ages there were two sorts of architecture: one "offensive, massive and without taste," and the other, gothic, "which is admirable, of astonishing boldness and accomplishment," and ruled by general proportions. After a brief discussion of medieval architecture, he proceeds to praise the "re-establishment of ancient architecture in Rome" and the more recent architecture in France after Francis I.

In this context, Briseux compiles the rules of the orders from diverse authorities. He compares not their specific proportions, as Fréart de Chambray had done in the previous century,[79] but diagrams of their intercolumniations. For details, he always compares his source to his own interpretation, drawing the "base" line with its subdivisions and showing whether the ancient proposition is compatible with his own. Curiously, his own versions are never identical. The concept of harmonic proportion is infinitely flexible, and thus it never becomes a strict prescription (figure 11.6). This is the paradoxical result of his fully modern desire for an instrumental theory, tempered by its inevitable limitations. Briseux's theoretical assumptions thus allow him to "discover" harmonic relationships in all the great authors he studies, aligning history with nature in a transparent and rational way.

In the third part of the *Traité,* Briseux deals with the important subject of "corrections," trying to account for the statements of previous authors concerning "the changes which the situation, or the height of buildings" may cause in their final appearance.[80] We have noted that Briseux's concept of taste, never entirely arbitrary or subjective, was responsible for the ultimate choice of proportions. Taste could actually improve rules, even tight rational systems such as Perrault's. With humans and rational nature sharing the same substance, Briseux's taste had an intersubjective character that could only improve the true natural systems of proportion. Briseux's notion of taste, however, remained distinct from later eighteenth-century concepts suggesting that genius could override rules.[81] In fact, as we have seen, he thought that most contemporary architects who "praised taste" as the legitimizing force behind their work (such as Perrault) were merely copying precedents. This is a revealing concept, showing Briseux's traditional understanding of imagination as "reproductive" rather than "productive," as would later be the case for the romantic genius, who might believe that art works could be created *ex nihilo.*

In view of this, it is interesting to note how Briseux regarded optical corrections to harmonic proportions (figure 11.7). After asserting that "the route of proportions is the most certain" and that the abandonment of this route leads to architectural decadence,[82] he agreed with Perrault's refutation of optical correction in architectural practice. It should be remembered that optical correction had appeared (explicitly or implicitly) in all classical theories of architecture in the lineage of Vitruvius.[83] Traditional theories had argued that the position of the human eye does not allow one to grasp the intended perfection of proportional ratios and that adjustments therefore are necessary. The aim was never to fool the eye but to make the intention of mathematical perfection, mimetic of the heavenly star dance, evident to humanity. The proportions of the building were experienced in an "approximate" way in the human realm, never in a mathematical space. Following the

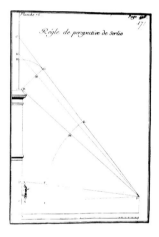

11.7
An illustration, after Serlio's Renaissance treatise, of the principle of optical correction. (From Briseux's *Traité du Beau Essentiel.* While Briseux, like Perrault, disagreed with Serlio's recommendation to adjust proportions in order to compensate for optical distortions, he believed adjustments of proportions were necessary for buildings to express their appropriate character and respond to specific sites and situations.

scientific revolution in the seventeenth century, the eye became a privileged medium to apprehend the perfect mathematical order in nature. This led to a belief that humans could directly perceive (in the mind's eye, the pineal gland or point of perspectival conversion) the undistorted truth of the world—its quantitative properties. By the time of Perrault, this Cartesian understanding led to a distrust of optical correction as a strategy to bridge theory and practice. The modern mind in its geometric space seemed capable of perceiving proportional relationships through unmediated vision, without error.

Optical correction is one aspect of traditional theory that Briseux criticized explicitly, but not without qualification. Engaging Vitruvius's and Serlio's versions of this issue, he writes: "These reasonings are not without foundation, but their principle is too general."[84] Corrections are necessary, states Briseux, according to "the situation and its extension," but are not to be regulated by optics. There is a tension here between the epistemology of perspectival vision and the experienced reality of architectural meaning. "If optics are used the proportions will appear defective from any other point." Once human vision had been identified with perspectival vision, optical correction would produce only distortions. Yet Briseux believed that specific situations do demand adjustments, which he associated with architecture's role to express appropriate character. "The eye perceives correctly (the rule of common sense[!]), but proportions can and should be adjusted."[85] In other words, Briseux already assumes that the eye sees in perspective and that our perception of the world's truth is based on vision.

Resituating the Body

Both the musician Rameau and the architect Briseux were concerned with modern epistemology and tested the limits of instrumental theories in their respective practices. It could be argued that the limit of instrumentality (in the sense of transparent know-how) is reached in their work. Their limitations in implementing their theories, as well as their success in their respective arts, were conditioned by the priority of experience described today by phenomenology, particularly in the work of Maurice Merleau-Ponty. In their eighteenth-century understanding, this was rendered as a bodily knowing that integrated consciousness with the senses through the intimacy of touch.

In the long run, however, this synesthetic premise worked better for music than for architecture. The absolute hegemony of vision in the nineteenth and twentieth centuries, leading to our world of simulations, consecrated sight as an autonomous sense. Vision, with its associated perspectivism and relativism, is adamant about cultural differences and diversity of expression; harmony is simply a delusion. Yet in later modernist theory, Le Corbusier's *Modulor,* for example, was intended to operate in a very similar way to Briseux's theory of harmonic proportion, bringing instrumentality to practice through a mathematics of the ineffable. Le Corbusier realized that while Archimedes and Copernicus could only invent geometry in their heads, we can now "feel the intense joys of geometry" with our senses.[86] Indeed, like Briseux (but unlike Kepler, who thought we could know harmony but not experience it), we now attend the performance, but unlike the eighteenth century, we can never claim to fully know the score. This might be the most persuasive argument against instrumentality as a reductive methodology for "theory" to dominate "practice." This critique was "incorporated" in the paradoxical *Modulor:* the instrument is subjected to the test of bodily experience and is always a personal process or story that engages bodily making and perceptual faith; it never becomes a neutral methodology.

Despite this evidence, in architecture and the visual arts we continue to doubt our capacity to be touched and, more recently, even discount it as a possible delusion to be "corrected" by deconstructive criticism. For vision in particular, the body remains a Cartesian obstacle rather than our very means to attain a sense of value: a sense of truth, beauty, and goodness. Thus, architecture seems less capable than music to profit from this eighteenth-century lesson. Despite later conflicting theories and atonal systems, Rameau's theory still accounts for the most universal modes of musical expression on our compressed planet. The tonal traditions of classical and romantic music and pop music are pervasive and continue to touch human emotions beyond language. For Rameau, the experience of harmony was analogous to an objective knowledge of truth, a confirmation of a rational nature and a rational mind, fully transparent and synonymous with the light of divine providence. While we retain the experience of completion in harmony, as in erotic encounters ranging from art to sexuality, the knowledge it offers is not the objective knowledge of mathematics, positive science, or dogmatic theology. It is effectively an unveiling that always partially conceals. What we know most certainly is what we know less clearly, and which also conveys a sense of purpose to our lives. We can experience harmony that is both given (natural) and made by us (cultural). However, the experience of recognition in a work of art, here and now, is not objectifiable as a concept independent of the experience itself.

Heidegger has written succinctly that the problem with modern instrumentality is that it merely "brings about" objects while traditional *techné-poiesis* always "brought forth" things-in-the-world. As we engage our instruments, the challenge is to find how they may first transform the maker. This may lead to a nondualistic fine-tuning of our internal disposition and our capacity to engage the shared flesh of the world. Only then may the products of contemporary technology be truly transformative for others, revealing our humanity through (rather than in opposition to) our very mortality, and thus existing in solidarity with a more-than-human world.

12

Richard Sennett

The Foreigner

The foreigner is perhaps the most threatening figure in the theater of society. An outsider calls into question society's rules, the sociologist Georg Simmel believed; the foreigner exposes the sheer arbitrariness of society's script, which insiders follow, thinking its lines have been written by Right, Reason, or God.[1] Yet this cannot be the whole story, for the foreigner may also gain another knowledge through his or her own exile, denied to those who remain rooted to home; knowledge about living a displaced life. And this knowledge Western civilization, from its very origins, has honored, if painfully.

The Second Scar of Oedipus

The exile's knowledge about living a displaced life shapes the first two of Sophocles' Theban plays, which the playwright makes dramatically apparent in two scars on King Oedipus's body. *Oedipus Rex* turns on a fact that seems of little artistic interest in itself—just a cog in the machinery of the plot. The king's ankles bear a scar as a result of a wound he received as a child; the very name *Oedipus* in Greek means "one with pierced ankles." The king has wandered, lost touch with his origins. When the characters in the legend come to the point where they must know the king's true identity, they are able to recover this truth by looking at his body. The process of identification begins when a messenger declares, "Your ankles should be witnesses."[2]

Were the evidence King Oedipus seeking not about incest, we might pay more attention to his scar. Despite the great migrations in his life, his body contains permanent evidence about who he "really" is. The king's travels have left no comparable signatures on his body. His migratory experience counts for little, that is, in relation to his origin; in his origins lie his truth. Indeed, it is a commonplace that among the polis-proud Greeks, exile, dispossession, and migration have been of far lesser account than the marks of origins and of belonging. One thinks of Socrates' refusal of exile as evidence of the belief that even death as a citizen was more honorable than exile. Or of Thucydides' remark that foreigners have no speech—by which he meant that their speech counts for nothing in the polis; it is the chattering of those who cannot vote.

Yet the marks on Oedipus's ankles will not be the only marks on his body. He will answer the wounds others made on him at the beginning by gouging his own eyes out. The second wound balances the first; the first wound marks his origins, the second his personal reckoning of his life. Twice wounded, he has become a man whose life can literally be read in his face. When Freud wrote about oedipal guilt, this second scar seemed the end of the story. Yet in Sophocles' drama, this tragic, willed act sets in motion a new phase in the life of the king.

Oedipus sets out again into the world as an exile, thinking that perhaps he could return to his origins, to the mountain, "*my* mountain, which my mother and my father while they were living would have made my tomb,"[3] yet this return is not to be. As *Oedipus at Colonus* opens, he has come instead to the *deme* (village) of Colonus, a mile northwest of Athens, where the Delphic oracle has told him he will die; the prophecy will be fulfilled differently than he had imagined at the opening of the play. The two wounds on Oedipus's body are thus a scar of origins that cannot be concealed and the wanderer's self-inflicted scars that do not seem to heal. Unlike Freud's image of guilty consummation, Sophocles tells the story of a life that cannot stand still.

The Greeks would have understood Oedipus's unending journey as resonant with the Homeric legends, particularly the legend of Odysseus. In Greek practice, later to be codified in Roman law, there were certain circumstances in which foreign exile was in fact honorable, more honorable than Socrates' way. *Exsilium* entitled the person convicted of a capital charge to choose exile instead of death, a choice that spared friends and family the shame and grief of witnessing the execution. Sophocles introduces to *Oedipus at Colonus* a moral dimension to the very act of migration, in depicting Oedipus as a figure who has been ennobled by his uprooting. But how, precisely, has that happened?

At a haunting moment in *Oedipus at Colonus,* Oedipus tries to tell the young Theseus what he has learned in his exile:

> Dear son of Aegeus, to the gods alone it happens never to die or to grow old; all else is confounded by almighty Time. The strength of the land wastes away, and the strength of the body; faith dies and faithlessness comes to be, and the same wind blows not with constancy either in the friendships of men or between city and city. To some now, and to others later, the sweet becomes bitter and then again pleasant. And if in Thebes it is

now fair weather for you, Time in his course will break to pieces the present pledges of harmony for a small word's sake.[4]

The speech seems to foreshadow Simmel's image of the outsider as a man possessed of a threatening knowledge: *nomos* is not truth; ordinary things in themselves are illusory. And yet Oedipus does not speak to Theseus in despair. Since the king blinded himself, he has not lost faith in the world: rather he sees it in a new way, as a place of provisional loves, temporary attachments, insecurity. In his blindness, Oedipus has accepted the world on these terms: they are all he or Theseus can hope for. Oedipus dies at Colonus at peace. The second scar has led him to dwell in the world, uncertainly, painfully, yet aware.

Something of that same knowledge informs the Judeo-Christian tradition.[5] The people of the Old Testament thought of themselves as uprooted wanderers. The Yahweh of the Old Testament was himself a wandering god, his ark of the covenant portable; in the theologian Harvey Cox's words, "When the Ark was finally captured by the Philistines, the Hebrews began to realize that Yahweh was not localized even in it. . . . He traveled with his people and elsewhere."[6] Yahweh was a god of time rather than of place, a god who promised to his followers a divine meaning for their unhappy travels.

Wandering and exposure were as strongly felt to be the consequences of faith among early Christians as among Old Testament Jews. The author of the "Epistle to Diognatus" at the height of the Roman Empire's glory declared that "Christians are not distinguished from the rest of humanity either in locality or in speech or in customs. For they do not dwell off in cities of their own . . . nor do they practice an extraordinary style of life. . . . They dwell in their own countries, but only as sojourners. . . . Every foreign country is a fatherland to them, and every fatherland is a foreign country."[7]

This image of the wanderer came to be one of the ways in which St. Augustine defined the two cities in *The City of God:* "Now it is recorded of Cain that he built a city, while Abel, as though he were merely a pilgrim on earth, built none. For the true City of the saints is in heaven, though here on earth it produces citizens in which it wanders as though on a pilgrimage through time looking for the Kingdom of eternity."[8]

Rather than settling in place, this "pilgrimage through time" draws its authority from Jesus's refusal to allow his disciples to build monuments to him and his promise to destroy the Temple of Jerusalem. Judeo-Christian culture is thus, at its very sources, about experiences of displacement.

Yet no more than Oedipus do these Judeo-Christian homilies preach sheer renunciation of the world. If ordinary social relations do not reveal divine purposes, they nonetheless are morally important. In the world we must learn to accept ourselves and each other as insufficient creatures, unfinished works. We can attain closure, if at all, only in another life. By uprooting ourselves, in spirit or in fact, from our daily circumstances we might come to such realizations of our finitude. This wound of displacement is the Judeo-Christian version of the second scar: we deprive ourselves of rootedness, that we can become consequent human beings.

The two scars on the body of King Oedipus represent a fundamental conflict in our civilization between the truth claims of belonging and origins versus the truths discovered by displacement and wandering. The second scar is not so much a dismissal of society as a hard lesson about how to live with its rules, customs, and beliefs. Only by a painful act of self-denial or self-injury can one come to experience the *nomos* as the problematic, uncertain reality it is.

The Foreigner's Scar in the Modern World

This ancient conflict has taken on a new form in the modern world. On the one hand, the "disenchantment of the world" of which Max Weber wrote has meant that people experience the arrangements of society as mere conventions that can be changed at will. On the other hand, and perhaps because living in a truly disenchanted condition is more than most people can bear, modern society has generated a deep need to deny the ethical dimensions of disenchantment conveyed by the second scar. Community, identity, roots: these human relations represent borders to be sealed rather than boundaries to be crossed. The passion for closure appears only in nationalistic and ethnic strife, but also within gentler states, in the experience of sexual, religious, and racial differences—as though truth lay in finding out who we "really" are, as though our lives lay in the secrets of Oedipus's first scar. The notion that we might traverse the complexities of society only by willing painful ruptures in ourselves seems truly foreign and strange.

I want to explore these general assertions and reckon the modern presence of the second scar, in focusing on events in a time and place that seems utterly removed from the beginnings of our civilization. Although historians today are rather perversely suspicious of dates, the Revolution of 1848 marks a moment in which the modern passion for identity, roots, and origins bursts forth in Western culture, a passion declared for community especially in its nationalist form, at the expense of the estranging journeys of self-transformation. In these nationalist explosions of 1848, the native—using that word in its largest sense—rebukes the foreign.

The Revolution of 1848 lasted four months, from February to June. It began in Paris, and by March its repercussions echoed throughout central Europe, where movements sprang up proclaiming the superiority of national republics over the geographic parceling of territory made by dynasties and diplomats at the Congress of Vienna in 1815. Events had something of the same combustive character as did the disengagement from Russian hegemony that spread across these same nations in the last four months of 1989.

The generation of 1848 also marks a contrary implosion in modern culture as well. After the revolutionary fervor subsided, something like a knowledge of the second scar appeared in the arts—a research into the possibilities and consequences of displacement, an inquiry into how the everyday could be made strange. The ensuing conflict between modern art and society is one way in which our own time still echoes the passions of the Homeric legend, the tragic playwrights, the prophets of the Old Testament, and the early Christian believers.

The Native Self

It may be a truism that all societies fear outsiders, an ethnocentrism that the psychoanalyst Erik Erikson calls incisively "pseudo-speciation," meaning the propensity to treat those unlike oneself as not really human. In the nineteenth century, nativity—that core identity with which one seemed born—became a highly self-conscious cultural construction, as self-conscious an effort as must be the desire to render the everyday world strange and foreign. It certainly is true that the voices heard in 1848 throughout Europe celebrating place, blood, and inherited ritual were not those of men and women who had learned suddenly to speak. The tangled history of nationalist sentiment was as old as the nation state. Yet in 1848 those who spoke about nations had to account for new ways of speaking about society, principally in the emerging domain of anthropology, and even more sought to relate the sentiments of blood and soil to that most modern of all discourses: discourses about the self.

As Isaiah Berlin has shown in his study *Vico and Herder,* the eighteenth century thought in anthropological ways that would be rejected in the nineteenth century. In the eighteenth century, the word *native* had two meanings that we continue to employ today but lacked one meaning used in the nineteenth century. In the *Encyclopedia,* Diderot used *native* as an adjective to describe any person's origins; he used the noun *native* to describe a non-European. (Montesquieu would make a play on this second usage in *The Persian Letters* by having his Persians treat the Parisians like aboriginal natives.) Lacking in these usages was the sense that natives were the ancestors of Europeans; the native was an "other" rather than a kinsman. Prior to Darwin, early nineteenth century English and French accounts of Inuits, Laplanders, and Africans described native peoples as the first humans out of which civilized Europeans evolved to their present glory—for reasons these early ethnographers could not really explain. These accounts, moreover, connected the world of the European peasantry to "savage" life abroad; to be civilized meant to live in a court or a town.

The savants of the Enlightenment earlier employed their own anthropological understanding for the most liberal of reasons; they sought to affirm the dignity of human differences. To Herder, in Berlin's words, "it is [people's] differences that matter most, for it is the differences that make them what they are, make them themselves."[9] This assertion that human beings are culture specific was in the eighteenth century more than a plea for taking sheer anthropological variation seriously. It was an attack on what we today call Eurocentrism. Voltaire believed that "it is terrible arrogance to affirm that, to be happy, everyone should become European."[10] In different places, different people find different ways to attempt happiness, that most difficult of feats.

To Voltaire, the knowledge that others do not die of foods we are afraid to eat, that others in fact find happiness in tasting them, ought to give us pause about our own convictions—indeed ought to arouse our desire to taste the unknown. The perception of differing values ought to make the perceiver more cosmopolitan. That perception about aboriginal natives then crossed to the usage of *native* as an adjective describing any person's birthplace. The best hopes of 1789, for instance, drew on this cosmopolitanism; one did not have to live in Paris or to be French to believe in the liberty, equality, and fraternity proclaimed in the French Revolution. In *Reflections of a Universal Citizen of the World* (1784), Kant argued that the capacity for reasoned political judgment develops when a person learns to feel at home and derives stimulation among a diversity of people. This "universal citizen" learns correspondingly what is common to them all, aboriginal Indian, Persian, Pole, and Frenchman alike.

European powers had for generations practiced imperialism in the name of destroying aboriginal peoples as heathens, devils, and animals, justifying the carnage by religious doctrines of "pseudo-speciation." The contrary eighteenth-century celebration of natives, as in Rousseau's writings about the noble savage, constituted in fact a bitter play on words. Rousseau seems to have been much struck by the stuffed figure of an American Indian in full ceremonial dress who was put on display in Paris in 1741 by a taxidermist; the taxidermist had posed the Indian in a pensive mood. This "savage" Rousseau imagined to be a man whose reflectiveness was more acute and profound than the bewigged, gossipy, thoughtless Parisians who came to the taxidermist's shop. The noble savage stood, like Kant's citizen of the world, for a more universal, deeper humanity, a personage freed of the petty habits and the moral blindness that passed for civilization.

Herder understood something ahead of his time: the perception of difference might make people more ethnocentric, since there is no common humanity to which they can jointly appeal. Nativism in turn would create blindness and indifference toward others—a blindness justified by conceiving of the native as a man or woman innocent of the world. The natives who appear in Manzoni's writings on the Italian peasantry after 1848 have crossed into that innocent territory, for instance. Sometimes Manzoni does indeed depict them to be like Rousseau's noble savage—self-conscious and knowing. Removed from the cities that were the seats of Austro-Hungarian power, they have guarded the democratic values of an earlier, free Italy. More often Manzoni claims, as Tolstoy will later, that the peasantry is morally superior because peasants have no awareness of themselves in time and history, are free of the gnawing poison of too much thought, of thinking beyond the confines of life as it is given. Manzoni's "man of the soil" does not look in the mirror of history; he simply lives.

The politics of this cultural movement used a newer language of legitimacy than did those who had earlier argued for constitutional regimes, democracy, or other political ideals in their homelands, echoing the eighteenth-century ideals of the American and French revolutions. The language of the Slavophiles or the Sons of Attica represented the triumph of an anthropology of innocence over the worldly politics of difference. In 1848, the revolutionary nationalists rejected the very idea of a nation as a political creation because they believed that a nation was enacted instead by custom, by the manners and mores of a *Volk;* the food people eat, how they move when they dance, the dialects they speak, the precise forms of their prayers: these are the constituent elements of national life. Law is incapable of legislating these pleasures in certain foods: constitutions cannot ordain fervent belief in certain saints: that is, power cannot make culture.

The loathing of intellection and self-consciousness, characteristic of so much modern intellectual culture, coagulated in this rhetoric of nationalism. As I have tried to show elsewhere, by 1848 the self as a psychological phenomenon had become a political issue, for a labyrinthine self-consciousness, a burdened selfhood, seemed the mark of a rotten social order, and it seemed possible that political action could lighten that burden.[11] The man or woman of the city appeared to carry the heaviest psychological burden. A century before 1848, Rousseau had imagined, in his *Letter to D'Alembert,* that those who fled towns would become more introspective and self-knowledgeable human beings, like the noble savage. In 1848, the burdens of selfhood are to be lifted, in towns and countryside alike, through recourse to images of an unknowing innocence. The romantic movement had inflated the realm of individual sensation and reflection to a moral condition; the revolutionaries proposed to deflate it by a return to the native, collective self.

The new anthropology crossed with this psychology in 1848 in visually sophisticated ways. In the posters calling for national unity composed in the spring of 1848 by Chodluz and others, for instance, the people are shown responding to the call for an uprising dressed in work clothes or peasant costume. In the revolutionary posters of 1790 and 1791, poster artists frequently dressed the poor in military uniforms or in the colors of their political clubs. Two generations later, in responding to a great historical event, the people do not dress for the occasion. Nor in the posters of 1848 are the masses given especially dramatic expressions of rage or patriotic zeal: everything is done to signify that the people are not self-conscious: they are just being themselves. Gone are even the allegorical, classical figures that emblazoned the posters of the revolutions of 1830, such as Delacroix's *Liberty Leading the People*. For the revolutionary nationalists of 1848, the unawareness of the *Volk* of itself, its lack of a mirror, was a source of virtue—as against the vices of self-consciousness and self-estrangement of the cosmopolitan bourgeois whose mental outlook is on a diorama of mirrors that reflect back endless hesitations and second thoughts. The native self would be liberated from all this.

This crossing of anthropology and psychology in the concept of a native self supported a renewed sociological emphasis on the truth of origins, the truth of the first scar. The seeming spontaneity and lack of cosmopolitan self-consciousness of natives renewed that emphasis first through denying history's hold over a people's inherent character. Petöfi's appeals for a Magyar revolt exclude from whatever it is to be a "real" Magyar-the centuries-long interaction of Magyars with the Turks, Slavs, and Germans, though these historic encounters in fact colored the practice of religion, created a complex cuisine, and altered the structure of the Hungarian language itself. In place of this history, Petöfi preached a version of Magyar-ness, as if from generation to generation it had been both unchanging and self-sustaining.

The ingredients of the native self that crystallized in radical thought in 1848 gave a corresponding, fixed geographic imperative to the concept of culture: habit, faith, pleasure, ritual, all of which depend on enactment in a particular territory. This is because the place that nourishes native culture rituals is composed of people with whom one can share without explaining, that is, people like oneself. Both the time and soil of the true native are freed of the cursed turns and inner questioning of the cosmopolitan.

The eighteenth-century code of national honor would have found this celebration of everyday life degrading. In that older code, you placed a foot soldier—whether mercenary or not, French or not—in a blue-and-red flannel uniform fitted with gold braid, epaulets, and stamped ceremonial buttons. No matter that it was a useless costume or worse than useless during military engagement, no matter that he might be starving in barracks. This ceremonial robe gave him a place in something greater and grander than himself; it glorified his condition as a Frenchman. Similarly, in peacetime, monarchs like Louis XIV sought to legitimate their policies through elaborate ceremonies; the "progresses," "turnings," and "audiences" threw into dramatic relief the glory of the state, its magnificent constructions elevated far above, if "unnatural" in relation to, the sphere of everyday life.

The ideology of the native self preached by Kossuth, Manzoni, Garibaldi, Mickiewicz, and Louis Blanc—that a people should glory in themselves as they ordinarily were marketing, feasting, praying, harvesting—meant that honor was to be found in an anthropology of authenticity rather than of arbitrary signification. Native rituals, beliefs, and mores represent forms of being rather than doing, to make Heidegger's distinction, embodied in time-tested and permanently cohering form, inseparable from native territory.

We may recognize beliefs in this rough sketch that overflowed in 1848 about nativity and true identity the origins of many twentieth-century totalitarian practices. Modern totalitarian states capitalize on the virtues of the native self, legitimated repressive institutions as reflections of that selfhood impulse rather than as constructions that might be problematic and in need of constant discussion; civil police or neighborhood revolutionary committees, for instance, can be declared permanent organs of spontaneity, seeming only emanations of what "everybody" wants welling up from the folk-life. Yet to think about the legacy of 1848 in terms of totalitarianism alone clouds our understanding of how the quest for a native self continues to permeate more democratic forms of life.

Nineteenth-century aspirations established the modern ground rule for having an identity. You have the strongest identity when you are not aware you "have" it; you just are it. That is, you are most yourself when you are least aware of yourself. This doctrine of spontaneity as truth has served as much as a touchstone in the arts as in everyday life; it diminishes our pleasure in sheer artifice for its own sake and makes the practice of courtesy seem fake.

Perhaps more consequently, the belief in a native self has infected what Americans have come to call multiculturalism. The terms on which cultural differences appear in our society are not those that Voltaire imagined, the appearance of differences that stimulate people to cross borders of identity. Rather, these borders are increasingly sealed, as though the sexual, racial, religious, and ethnic differences between people constitute native distinctions. It has become common to criticize gays, blacks, and radical feminists for having become separatist in their thinking and behavior. It is highly unusual, however, for the people making these criticisms to speak of gay impulses in themselves, or—seemingly even more bizarre—moments when they become black. The dominant culture speaks instead of inclusion and absorption, offers in place of the disturbances of difference the balm of assimilation, as though that dominant center is more fundamental and solid, as though those who differ must seek to return to native ground.

Yet 1848 also set in motion the forces that would lead modern culture to draw again on the passions of the second scar, through entirely modern means. The failed revolution set in motion profound doubts about the stability and certainty of everyday life, that *nomos* that the nationalist revolutionaries celebrated. This subsequent *critique de la vie quotidienne,* to use Henri Lefebvre's phrase, appeared most strongly in the arts. But that artistic impulse to dislodge the everyday, the rooted, and the fixed also appeared among those revolutionaries who had to make something of their own lives as permanent exiles. We can see these counter-currents at work, for instance, in the paintings of Edouard Manet, and the writings of the revolutionary socialist Alexander Herzen. I next show in some detail how they regained that oedipal knowledge of the second scar in ways that speak to our own struggles today with the scar of nativity.

Manet's Mirror

Edouard Manet was a painter of place but no realist, as we commonly understand that term. He did not seek to achieve in painting the effect of surprising life in the raw, as did photographers of his time. Nor did his record of Paris share much in spirit with Zola's declarative, indignant literary portraits of the city's whores, abandoned children, or families dining on roasted rats. Manet's art is capable of stunning direct political statement, as witness the painting he made in 1868, *The Execution of the Emperor Maximilian,* but the artist's vision of the city relies on other means for its effects.

In recording everyday life, Manet made use of visual gestures that trouble the eye, wrench it from object to object within the frame of the painting, and often suggest that the real story of the painting is happening elsewhere, off the canvas. A painter completely at ease in Paris, interested in the smells and shadows of its daily round, Manet yet imagines what is positive about the very experience of transforming these familiar stimuli into strange and foreign sensations. By the work of his brush, rather than in the record of his life, Manet made the second scar appear as a work of art.

This work comes to consummation in Manet's last major painting, *The Bar at the Folies-Bergères,* done over the winter of 1881–1882. The painting has an interesting history. In 1879 Manet proposed himself to the Municipal Council of Paris as the painter of murals for the new Hôtel de Ville; these would show the effect on the life of the city of new constructions: the steel bridges, the poured cement sewers, the wrought-iron buildings . These would be murals of modern Paris. Manet's proposal was rebuffed, and it is significant that this, the great work he turned to after his denial, does not present one of the scenes envisioned for his murals of Paris, but rather turns to an institution more familiar, more sentimental, more kitsch even: he paints a picture of the Folies-Bergères.

The Folies-Bergères of Manet's time was a place of sensual license. Both female and male prostitutes drifted among its crowds. The Folies-Bergères was not itself, however, a whorehouse, if conveniently located to several, a fact that meant that it was possible for women to frequent it for amusement , which surprisingly respectable women in surprisingly respectable numbers did. This, then, was a risqué place but a public one, filled with noisy crowds drinking and flirting, the air perfumed by cigars, coffee, and cheap Beaujolais. Parisians went to the Folies when they wanted to relax. Though it is difficult to imagine Mazzini or Kossuth treating it as native ground, the Folies-Bergères represented a more realistic, actual version of a place in which ordinary people could feel *chez eux*. A comfortable spot, in the nineteenth-century it was frequented far more by locals than tourists.

Such is the scene Manet will reinvent. We are shown a woman standing behind a bar pensive, sad, unsmiling, an isolated figure in the midst of noise (the painted figure is based on Suzon, a barmaid at the Folies-Bergères whom Manet knew). The viewer is drawn into this scene through the use Manet makes of mirrors, which create a special experience of displacement. The barmaid is painted so that she stares directly out at the viewer. The mirror in front of which she stands is also directly opposite the viewer; Manet reinforces this full frontal alignment by how he places the barmaid's arms and hands on the bar. Her arms are extended and her hands are turned out, as a ballet dancer would turn out the legs in the full-frontal address of the body. Directly to the right of this figure we see her back reflected in the mirror, the flat mass of her black dress exactly the size of the body, so that the reflected figure lacks perspectival diminishment; the reflection seems in the same dimensional plane as the body. I say we see her reflection in a mirror, although optically this is impossible; we could not be facing her directly and seeing her reflection to the right of her at the same time. Today the viewer accepts this impossibility; it seems visually logical, if optically impossible. However, Charles de Feir, in his *Guide du Salon de Paris* (1882), spoke for many of Manet's contemporaries in finding this strange mirror a sign of the painter's faulty technique.[12]

In many of Manet's late paintings, the modern viewer's sense of optical displacement is reinforced by some seemingly minor, arbitrary gesture that further detaches the scene from representational fact. In *The Bar at the Folies-Bergères,* this occurs in the way Manet paints two gaslights reflected in the mirror; they are disks of pure white that lie flat on the picture plane. These lanterns cast no shadow and show no penumbral refractions as mirrored lights usually do, nor indeed are they even painted in the round. Again, Manet's contemporaries found in these strange lights a sign of the painter's weakness. In *I'Illustration,* Jules Compte remarked of them that "Monsieur Manet has probably chosen a moment when the lamps were not working properly, for never have we seen light less dazzling".[13]

Today we can see these white disks to serve the same purpose as the displaced reflection of the barmaid's black dress. They set up the painting so that we focus on the only significant experience of depth and recession in it. In the upper right corner of the painting, reflected in the mirror, we see the man the barmaid is looking at, staring intently into her eyes. However, just as the barmaid's back cannot possibly be reflected to her immediate right, this intent gentleman in his top hat asking her a question with his eyes, who inspires in her a look of such sadness, cannot exist optically, for he would entirely block out our direct, unobstructed view of Suzon, who is in turn looking straight in front of her. The painting is set up so that the viewer, you or me, is standing in front of her. But of course you or I do not resemble the particular person reflected in the mirror. Due to the full frontal positioning of the subject in relation to the viewer, there is no way to look at *her* without this reflexive disturbance occurring. The drama Manet creates in this painting is this: I look in a mirror and see someone who is not myself.

This aspect of the painting did speak to Manet's contemporaries. Some sought to pass off the disturbance with a joke (the *Journal Amusant* of May 27, 1882, made a woodcut of the painting with the gentleman reflected in the mirror drawn in, standing before the barmaid and blocking our view), but most critics reacted with anger to the disturbing questions about the viewer created by Manet's painting: "Is this picture true? No. Is it beautiful? No. Is it attractive? No. But what is it, then?"[14] Their distress could have mostly to do with the story being told by the painting: a man propositions a young barmaid, who responds to him with a look of infinite sadness.

Such a story is as apt a Victorian homily as one could imagine. The lonely young woman in a vice-tainted public realm was a homily Edgar Degas painted more directly, for instance, in *L'Absinthe* (1876). In Manet's painting, the optic disturbance relieves the woman of serving such a neatly moralizing purpose. A question is raised about the story of the painting by making the viewing of the painting inseparable from the story being told. In the same painterly way, the objects placed on the bar are given a heightened life. The bottles on the bar are painted fully in the round; they contrast with the abstract disks in that mirror, which shows us another self from the one we might prefer to call our own. Although the mirror runs full length across the painting, Manet allows only two of this crowded collection of objects to show in reflection, although optically *all* should show. These optical ghosts of bottles, flowers, and fruit seem the most solid objects in the painting.

This is how scarring works in the *Bar at the Folies-Bergères*. Displacement creates value: both reflexive value, that is, a value given to the viewer as part of the thing seen, and again to the very physical world itself, whose character and form we are forced to observe by looking at its transmutation in a distorting mirror. By contrast, there is but an illusory solidity to those objects that have not been subjected to this displacement. Were Manet a philosopher (which he emphatically would protest he was not), he might point to this as the real intention of his painting: the solidity of undisplaced things, as of selves that have not experienced displacement, may indeed be the greatest of illusions. And yet Manet's is no art of negation (or of deconstruction, as we might say today). Like Oedipus's speech to the young Theseus, this painting aims to arouse more than visual suspicion. Displaced vision takes us on a journey in which we see a new value in bottles, in light, in faces as optical constructions. The mirror is Manet's instrument to make us take that journey with our eyes.

Of course, it could be said that all great art contains the power to arrest and seize the eye through the unexpected. But we do not look at the objects Chardin painted in the way we stare in Manet's mirror. Self-consciousness about the act of looking is not what Chardin aims at. Similarly in music, there are endlessly surprising events in a quartet by Haydn that keep the music fresh, but the surprises do not aim to make the listener think about the very act of hearing, whereas Manet's near-contemporary Satie had that aim, as does the music of John Cage today or the art of Duchamp. Displacement in its modern artistic form aims at making an audience question the conditions and terms of perception; it promises that something of unexpected value will appear through this self-questioning—something unforeseen, other, foreign.

The story of Alexander Herzen's life forms a fitting complement to the painting of the Folies-Bergères, for it reveals how one man forced into exile gradually began to look into something akin to Manet's mirror in order to make sense of his life. More, it translates that artistic practice into a sociological form—one that suggests how the journey into foreign territory might be taken off today.

The Foreigner

In the early spring of 1848, it seemed to Parisians like "Daniel Stern" (the nom de plume of Marie d'Agoult, Franz Liszt's one-time companion whose chronicles of 1848 are a vivid record of the upheaval) that the "foreign colony will empty in a few days, as our friends return to the places which call them."[15] Given the nationalisms being trumped in the press, her expectation seems logical. Paris in the 1830s had filled with foreigners, principally from Poland, Greece, Russia, and Bohemia. The political question the surge of revolutionary nationalism in 1848 posed to all those who had become foreigners—whether as political exiles or economic émigrés—was, Why aren't you home among your own kind? How indeed could you be Russian somewhere else?

Yet by late April 1848, Daniel Stern had noted that, oddly, few of the émigrés had left for home. "They are still to be found arguing in the Palais Royal, receiving emissaries from abroad, hectoring; they are full of hope, but no one has packed his bags."[16] The comforts of Paris alone did not hold the Parisian émigrés who failed to respond to the call of their own nations; in part, the answer to their immobility resulted from a familiar cruelty. Their web of mutual contacts abroad was outdated; time and events had passed them by.

But more than this, as Daniel Stern noted, the exiles had changed. "It is as though they have looked in the mirror and seen another face than the one they thought they would see," she wrote.[17] Her image employs the figure of Manet's mirror, in which what is reflected back to us is so unlike what we expect to see. It seemed to Alexander Herzen, as he watched in the Café Lamblin his companions plot, telegraph, argue, and yet remain, that they had need of this mirror; otherwise they, whom history had left behind, would become their own jailers in the prison of regrets.

Herzen was the illegitimate son of an aging Russian nobleman and a young German woman (hence his name, which is roughly equivalent to "of my heart" [*Herzens*]). Inspired by the uprising of 1825, he was as a young man active in radical Russian politics as these politics were then understood, that is, he was a proponent of constitutional monarchy and liberal reforms. For this he suffered internal exile and eventually expulsion from the Russian empire. In April 1848 Herzen joined the exile colony in Paris; he did so to move away from Rome, which was in its own first moments of nationalist awakening. Like others of his generation, he thought of himself at first as in temporary exile, expecting to return to his native land when political circumstances made it possible. But when this possibility arose, he too held back.

On June 27, 1848 the revolution came to an end in Paris. Troops swept through the city, indiscriminately shooting into crowds, deploying cannon in random barrages into working-class neighborhoods. The forces of order had arrived. Herzen, like the other foreigners who had remained in Paris of their own free will, were now finally forced to leave. He went to Geneva, then back to Italy, then back to France, arriving finally in London in August 1852, an ailing middle-aged man who had lost his wife to another man, had set himself publicly against the Slavophiles dominating radical discourse in his homeland, and spoke English haltingly in the manner of novels he had read by Sir Walter Scott. "Little by little I began to perceive that I had absolutely nowhere to go and no reason to go anywhere."[18]

When he arrived in England, Herzen seemed to many a broken figure, yet he did not break. Here, the working out of the second scar began. Herzen recognized that his wanderings could not be understood simply as the play of historical circumstances over his hapless person. Rather than history's victim, he was a man who had chosen to cut himself off. Had he been more diplomatic, less fervent, in advancing his own opinions, he could have survived and perhaps flourished as others had done. He could have perhaps even retained the interest and affections of his wife. Exile was his self-chosen fate, his self-chosen wound.

The imagery of exile and uprooting invites a kind of romantic self-indulgence. Such self-indulgence appeared among those who made an *émigration intérieure* in the 1830s in the wake of the new bourgeois regime of Louis Philippe in France; the rejects of this vulgar regime wore their alienation from society like a badge of honor. The same self-inflation—how sensitive I am! how little I fit in!—marks a strain of modern self-consciousness up to the present day. Herzen's exile was too painful for this game. But precisely in acknowledging that it was a personal responsibility, "by degrees, a revolution took place within me," he wrote. "I was conscious of power in myself . . . I grew more independent of everyone."[19] He began to reconstruct how he saw the world around him: "Now the masquerade was over, the dominoes had been removed, the garlands had fallen from the heads, the masks from the faces," and "I saw features different from those that I had surmised."[20]

The working out of the second scar took a decisive step when, in England, he decided not to return to Russia. In this great drama of exile, Herzen confronted two dangers. One was the danger now of forgetting too much, the other of remembering too much. A foreigner, he saw, could be demeaned by the desire to assimilate, or be destroyed by nostalgia.

Herzen saw these dangers exemplified by two men. Ivan Golovin was, like Herzen, a political refugee from the 1840s, but Golovin had wandered for no noble reason; a small-time crook barred after a few years from the Paris stock exchange, Golovin now exploited his fellow exiles, flitting from scene to scene. "What had he left Russia for? What was he doing in Europe?" Herzen demanded. "Uprooted from his native soil, he could not find a center of gravity."[21] The importance of Golovin's defects became magnified by Herzen's reflections on himself in London. Golovin's character, Herzen wrote, "bears the stamp of a whole class of people," those whose very desire to assimilate had led to a loss of self, "who live nomadic lives, with cards or without cards at spaces and in great cities, invariably dining well, know everybody, and about whom everything is known, except two things: what they live on and what they live for. Golovin was a Russian officer, a French *braider* and *hobbler,* an English swindler, a German *Junker,* as well as our native Nozdrev Khlestakov [characters from Gogol]."[22]

Herzen came to understand, by contrast, that one of the gifts that exile made him was the experience of resistance. Sheer adaptiveness and flexibility were the marks of men who lacked "a center of gravity." And Herzen came to believe this exile gift had a wider social implication: to accept resistance is to solidify the self. A society of Golovins, of "protean selves," of endless adaptive people, as in the managerial world, is an empty shell.

What does the experience of resistance mean? It cannot be a matter of asserting the closures of the native self, closures that exiles experience in nostalgia or longing for a homeland. Herzen explored that danger in his encounters with Father Vladimir Pecherin. In the mid 1830s the young Pecherin had taken up the chair of Greek at Moscow University but in the next few years felt himself suffocating in his homeland. In Herzen's words, "Round about was silence and solitude: everything was dumb submission with no hope, no human dignity, and at the same time extraordinarily, dull, stupid and petty."[23] Pecherin, the young classics professor, decided to emigrate; he surprised none of his contemporaries, who were also suffocating in Mother Russia. Pecherin boarded a boat for England, landed, and suddenly entered a Jesuit monastery. In this he surprised other young people around him, who could not understand how he could revolt against one system of authority only to submit to another.

When Herzen landed in England, he sought out Pecherin, to make his acquaintance and to ask if some of Pecherin's youthful poems might be reprinted in Herzen's publication, "The Bell." They met in the Jesuit monastery of Saint Mary's Clapham. Pecherin is avid for news; he disowns the value of his Russian poems yet is avid for the younger man's opinion. As their relations unfold over the years, Pecherin seems to him a man who has surrendered the will to live, transforming his remembrance of the mother country into ever more seductive hues. Memory, longing, and passivity become inseparable conditions of his life. Pecherin's erosion in exile recalls to Herzen lines he had written in Geneva in 1850 just after he had quitted Paris with the other central European refugees. For the first time it dawned on many of them that they were in permanent exile, which triggered in them the dangers of closure in time: "All émigrés, cut off from the living environment to which they have belonged, shut their eyes to avoid seeing bitter truths, and grow more and more acclimatized to a closed, fantastic circle consisting of inert memories and hopes that can never be realized" and again, "Leaving their native land with concealed anger, with the continual thought of going back to it once more on the morrow, men do not move forwards but are continually thrown back upon the past." Pecherin concluded that the exile could be enslaved as well by his or her own powers of memory, those "questions, thoughts and memories which make up an oppressive, binding tradition."[24]

How does Herzen propose to avoid these dangers? The foreigner must confront memories of home, yet memory must be displaced, refracted, so that he or she is not suddenly seized by the past, acting out the injuries received long ago and now instead playing another role in that old drama. Yet in the ever-enlarging compass in which Herzen sees his own life, displacement now takes on a larger, more positive, more general social value. It teaches men and women how to live in society without expecting society to make them whole men and women. That expectation is what Herzen discovers he has been resisting. Simply to adapt and fit in would give him a place in society, but he would occupy it as an empty man. To give himself over to longing for the past would also make him whole of sorts, as Pecherin remained whole, but that native wholeness would be bought at the price of passivity.

To live in society without expecting society to make one whole: this precept crystallizes in Herzen's thinking and writing around the very idea of home, the place of one's native self. In London, he says, suddenly he has become Italian:

> And now I sit in London where chance has flung me—and I stay here because I do not know what to make of myself. An alien race swarms confusedly about me, wrapped in the heavy breath of ocean, a world dissolving into chaos . . . and that other land— washed by the dark-blue sea under the canopy of a dark-blue sky . . . it is the one shining region left until the far side of the grave. . . . O Rome, how I love to return to your deceptions, how eagerly I run over day by day the time when I was intoxicated with you![25]

"Home" is not a physical place but a mobile need; wherever one is, home is always to be found somewhere else. As Herzen's life unfolds in England, a sunless land of overly practical, if kindly, people, the home he needs will change countries, from a place of snow to sun, from the intimate village outside Moscow to the languid cafés of Rome. Herzen will always have a home so long as he can change how it looks. This ironic, bitter knowledge about his need for "home" came to Herzen as an older man; he acknowledged that he would never feel complete. Finally he came to terms with insufficiency. It is permanent: the scar does not heal. And this same power of displacing "home" was what he hoped for others who did not pack their bags when the borders opened in March 1848, who did not return to the loved world of their childhood, their language, their soil.

The genius of Herzen's writing is to make us understand that this journey of exile is a journey for those inside a culture as well as those who come from outside. How can human beings manage their emotional attachments? How can connection to others, in either the present or the past, be shaped? True enough, the foreigner, as Simmel imagined him or her, knew these attachments to be arbitrary, but that does not make them unreal. Rather, the voyage of displacement in a life offers at least the possibility of recommitting to these attachments under the aegis of the will.

Like Manet, Herzen sought to understand displacement not as something gone wrong, but as a process with its own form and possibility. In particular Herzen saw that his displacement from Russia had created a new kind of freedom in his life—a freedom he felt to be so new, so modern, that he could not claim to define it. When he exercised his will, he acquired not the power of closure but openness and became capable of living in indeterminacy.

That is why the story told in these pages is a story about the present as well as the past. Rather than the closure of identity, as preached by the revolutionaries of 1848, these emblematic figures of the later nineteenth century sought to open up the boundaries of the everyday world, and the human passage through it, to the powers of indeterminacy. They show us, in the practice of an art and the conduct of an exile, the possibility truly contained in a diverse, multicultural society: boundaries of identity to be crossed rather than borders to be sealed. Perhaps most strange to our everyday way of thinking, that passage requires acts of will, of self-control, rather than simple surrender to the other. Herzen, the greatest émigré of the nineteenth century, willed himself to make this passage in his memories. We have to will it in our dealings with one another. Indeterminacy as an expressive achievement rather than blind chaos, an achievement in experience requiring resolve, judgment, and art: this is our second scar.

Vitruvius Crucifixus: Architecture, Mimesis, and the Death Instinct

This chapter takes its point of departure from a discussion of links between representations of Vitruvian man and the 'dying,' crucified Christ. The theme of death is then taken further as I argue that the principle of harmony that underlies proportional systems may be understood in terms of Freud's death instinct—the instinct that seeks to bring everything to a peaceful resolution. I explore how psychoanalysis might offer an insight into how proportions help us relate to architecture by providing a mechanism that facilitates the way in which we read ourselves into the built environment. Representations of the human figure inscribed into plans and other drawings of the Renaissance might therefore be understood as emblematic of an attempt to relate to a building by a process of mimetic identification.

Vitruvius's comments on the subject of proportions have proved to be highly influential within the history of architectural theory. They have provided the grounding for much subsequent theoretical work on the relationship between buildings and the human body. The tradition of relating the layout of temples and churches to the form of the body is captured explicitly in the drawings of Francesco di Giorgio, where the ghostlike figure of a human body is quite literally mapped onto the plans and elevations of buildings. It is these drawings, along with those of Fra Giocondo, Cesariano, Leonardo da Vinci, and others, that Rudolf Wittkower addresses in his discussion of proportions in his seminal work on the centralized church of the early Italian Renaissance.[1] Joseph Rykwert and John Onians, among others, have continued the tradition of scholarship stemming from Wittkower's earlier insights on the links between the human body and buildings. It could be argued, however, that the full significance of Vitruvius's comments has yet to be understood. The concern of these scholars has been largely for the symbolic meaning of these proportions and the mathematical ratios that underpin them. So far there has been little investigation

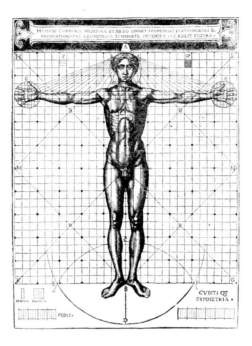

13.1
Vitruvian man within a square,
after Cesare Cesariano,
De architectura (Como, 1521).

into the question of how the use of these proportions might help human beings relate to buildings at a psychical level.

Traditionally, proportions have often been viewed as something "out there." It is perhaps only for God to recognize them. If we are to pursue an existing model of how we might identify with those proportions, at best we might perhaps follow the logic of the *Phaedrus,* where Plato argues that when we sense something "harmonic" our souls recognize the fundamental order of the universe.[2] According to Plato, souls are mixed in the *chora* of the universe of the same substance as the universe itself. The tension that exists between the imperfect mortal body and the perfect immortal soul, composed as it is of the stuff of the universe, is set right by recognition of the essential harmony of the universe, revealed in a harmonious sound or image. It is this Platonic tradition that informs more recent ontological enquiries, notably the work of Hans-Georg Gadamer in *The Relevance of the Beautiful.*[3]

Questions about the body, however, and about the way in which human beings identify with the world have been central to much recent theoretical debate, not least in the domain of psychoanalysis. It is to psychoanalytic theory that we might turn for fresh insights into these issues and to further our understanding as to how the use of proportions might offer a mechanism to enhance the way in which human beings relate to their built environment at a psychical level.

Vitruvius Crucifixus

We start with one of the most famous illustrations on the theme of proportions, that of Vitruvian man found in Cesariano's 1521 edition of Vitruvius's, *De architectura* (figure 13.1). This is one of two images with which Cesariano illustrates Vitruvius's comments on the human body, which is so perfectly proportioned that it may be inscribed within either a circle or a square:

> For if a man be placed flat on his back, with his hands and feet extended, and a pair of compasses centred at his navel, the fingers and toes of his two hands and feet will touch the circumference of a circle described therefrom. And just as the human body yields a circular outline, so too a square figure may be found from it. For if we measure the distance from the soles of the feet to the top of the head, and then apply that measure to the outstretched arms, the breadth will be found to be the same as the height.[4]

One of the intriguing aspects of this illustration is the similarity that the figure bears to images of the crucified Christ. There are a number of incidental parallels between the two persons and a clear stylistic indebtedness to the crucified Christ in representations of Vitruvian man. In some, for example, the head slumps to one side. But in this one by Cesariano, not only is there a scroll above the head of the figure reminiscent of the INRI of the crucifix, but the hands and feet are displayed precisely as though they have been affixed to the cross. The parallels extend to Cesariano's other famous image of Vitruvian man. Alongside the image of Vitruvian man inscribed within the square, Cesariano includes a second image of Vitruvian man, a man spread-eagled within a circle, his hands and feet touching the circumference of that circle (figure 13.2). As Vitruvius describes in the original text, here the man is "stabbed" in his midriff by one arm of a pair of compasses, while the other arm is used to circumscribe the figure, "striking" the hands and the feet. Vitruvian man is thus "wounded" in the same parts as Christ. But it is the first image—Vitruvian man inscribed within a square—that is more immediately reminiscent of images of the crucifix.

The links between Christ and Vitruvius have been observed by a number of scholars. The two, it has been noted, were near contemporaries.[5] Furthermore, Vitruvius's comments on the ideal proportions of the human figure, which should also be present in the layout of temples, exerted a major influence on the design of Christian churches throughout the Renaissance. Not only do we find proportions of idealized human figures inscribed in various plans of Christian buildings, but representations of Christ himself take on the proportions of Vitruvian man. As has been observed, Brunelleschi's wooden crucifix in the

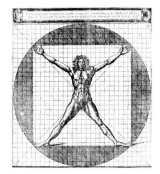

13.2
Vitruvian man spread-eagled, after Cesare Cesariano, *De architectura* (Como, 1521).

church of Santa Maria Novella in Florence shows Christ with the proportions of the *homo ad quadratum,* the distance between his outstretched hands matching his height from head to toe.[6] Nor is it out of place that Brunelleschi should have chosen to portray Christ, the very manifestation of God on earth, with the perfect proportions of Vitruvian man, proportions that echo the cosmic harmony of the universe. With Brunelleschi's crucifix, Christ has become "Vitruvianized." Yet the Renaissance was as much about the Christianization of a Vitruvian tradition as it was about the Vitruvianization of a Christian one. Hence we find in Cesariano's illustrations a clear allusion to the crucified Christ, which develops the links between architectural form and the crucifixion of Christ, already evident in the cruciform layout of the medieval basilica.

This connection—this Christianization of Vitruvian man—is corroborated by Vitruvius's manuscripts. Two variants in the text describe the way in which the hands are held out in the figure of Vitruvian man. The manuscripts here vary between the use of the (more common) form *manus pansas* and the variant *manus spansas.*[7] The verb *pandere* simply means "to open out," or "to extend." The hands are "outstretched." In the variant, the verb *spandere* is used. This has a secondary meaning of the way that a priest holds out his hands "in prayer."[8] The variant *manus spansas* therefore marks a religious moment in the representation of Vitruvian man. From Vitruvian man with his hands "outstretched," we move to Vitruvian man with his hands "outstretched in prayer." In this shift from *manus pansas* to *manus spansas,* from the hands "outstretched" to the hands "outstretched in prayer," Vitruvian man becomes in effect Christianized. In this shift we recognize not only the Vitruvianization of the Christian world but also its corollary, the Christianization of the Vitruvian world. In effect, Vitruvian man adopts the posture of Christ on the cross. Vitruvian man becomes crucified: *Vitruvius crucifixus.*

Freud and the Death Instinct

How might psychoanalytic theory help us to understand the role of proportions? It is through the emblem of Vitruvian man on the cross—the dying, crucified Vitruvian man—that we might approach the theme of death and through this engage with one of the central themes in psychoanalysis. And it is through a creative and deliberately indulgent reworking of Freud's work on death that we might begin to understand the role of proportions in helping the individual to identify with the built environment.

The theme of death is fundamental to Freud, especially to the later Freud, the metapsychological Freud. Freud's later theory is centered around the conflict between eros and thanatos, between love and death, between life instincts and death instincts. Eros, as the life instinct, serves to counter the tendency toward thanatos, the death instinct, and acts as a force to complicate life. It continuously counteracts and delays the death instinct. Eros is therefore set in opposition to thanatos, that which seeks resolution and quiet. Thus, the death drive becomes for Freud one of the fundamental impulses within human behavior.

The death drive can be seen to emanate from the moment of birth itself, a violent trauma that upsets the pleasure of the time in the womb. For Freud the time in the womb relates to the development of the *id,* the faculty that absorbs and enjoys pleasurable sensations. The id is the domain of the unconscious. Herbert Marcuse defines the id as follows: "The 'id' is free from the forms and principles which constitute the conscious, social individual. It is neither affected by time nor troubled by contradictions: it knows 'no values, no good and evil, no morality.' It does not aim at self-preservation: all it strives for is satisfaction of its instinctual needs, in accordance with the pleasure principle."[9]

The womb provides the id with a refuge, a state of placid protection and constant gratification. With birth this freedom from disturbance is lost forever. Yet the memory of this period in the womb remains, and subsequent life is governed by a desire to regain this lost quietude, this lost paradise. Life is dominated by a regressive compulsion, a desire to return to the womb. This striving for integral gratification dominates all subsequent life. Thus, for Freud, the drive toward equilibrium that results is none other than a "continuous descent toward death," where death finally provides that longed-for resolution and quiet. According to Marcuse, "The death instinct is destructiveness not for its own sake, but for the relief of tension. The descent toward death is an unconscious flight from pain and want. It is an eternal struggle against suffering and repression."[10]

From this drive toward equilibrium, Freud develops the "nirvana principle"—the urge to return to the nirvana of the womb—which becomes for Freud "the dominating tendency of mental life, and perhaps nervous life in general."

Related to the nirvana principle is the pleasure principle, which is, in effect, one expression of the nirvana principle: "The effort to reduce, to keep constant or to remove internal tension due to stimuli [the 'Nirvana principle' . . .] finds expression in the pleasure principle; and our recognition of this fact is one of the strongest reasons for believing in the existence of death instincts."[11]

At a straightforward level, then, we might recognize an apparent parallel between the drive for harmony within the principle of architectural proportions that Vitruvius recognized and the drive for resolution that underpins the death instinct in Freud. There is an obvious point of comparison between the state of equilibrium sought in proportions, and the equilibrium of the nirvana principle. The harmony sought in the proportions of Vitruvian man—the "dying, crucified" Vitruvian man—matches the harmony sought in Freud's death instinct. Proportions offer a mechanism that strives for a resolution, a rec-

onciliation of tensions. The aesthetic gratification of harmonic proportions in architecture might therefore be seen to represent a return to the nirvana of the womb, to the sensory realm of the protected. Yet this realm need not be a closed, interior space a womblike space. Indeed, according to the logic of the argument, open architecture would have a similar effect, providing that it is harmonious.

By itself, however, this model appears to be somewhat inadequate. It cannot account for the stimulation that may be induced by this release of tensions. Harmonious architecture may equally prove to be innervating. It is as though the gratification of aesthetic contemplation might serve not so much to resolve the death instinct as to transcend it.

Here we might refer to the work of Herbert Marcuse, a somewhat unlikely figure in this context in that his work has been concerned largely with the theme of eros rather than thanatos. Yet he offers a further interpretation of the interplay of eros and thanatos in the moment of aesthetic contemplation and thus sheds some light on this question. According to Marcuse, the distinction between eros and thanatos is not fully resolved in Freud. Marcuse goes on to suggest that these two seemingly opposite drives have a common origin and may therefore be reconciled. For Marcuse, the crucial images that bring together eros and thanatos are Orpheus, the poet who plays so beautifully on his lyre that he is able to hold even wild animals spellbound, and Narcissus, the beautiful youth whom Aphrodite punishes for spurning the advances of Echo by making him obsessed with his own image (figure 13.3). His frustrated attempts to grasp his own image reflected in a pool lead to his despair and death. On his death Narcissus's body turns into a flower of the same name.

Marcuse picks up on the models of Narcissus and Orpheus. For Marcuse, the images of Orpheus and Narcissus reconcile eros and thanatos:

> They recall the experience of a world that is not to be mastered and controlled but to be liberated—a freedom that will release the powers of Eros now bound to the petrified forms of man and nature. These powers are conceived not as destruction but as peace, not as terror but as beauty. It is sufficient to enumerate the assembled images in order to circumscribe the dimension to which they are committed: the redemption of pleasure, the halt of time, the absorption of death; silence, sleep, night, paradise—the Nirvana principle not as death but as life.[12]

In this fusion of the Orphic and the Narcissistic world, Marcuse sees a reconciliation of eros and thanatos. In this sense, he goes beyond Freud to offer a vision in which art plays a creative role. It is a world that embodies the principles of both eros and thanatos, a static world, a world at rest, but a fundamentally poetic world. It is a world where "static triumphs over dynamic; but it is a static that moves in its own fullness—a productivity that is sensuousness, play and song."[13]

The nirvana principle—the return to the womb—gives us a sense of the real meaning of "death" in the death instinct. Death is not death as finality, as absence of life. The death instinct calls for a death that is not death, a death that transcends death, a death that is put in the service of life. This death is akin to the death of Christ on the cross (to return to our starting point)—a death that gives others life. And it is akin to the death of Narcissus—the ecstasy of the narcissistic absorption into the self—which results in the birth of a flower. It is in the resurrection from the cross, the blossoming of the flower, that the death instinct is realized and death itself is transcended.

The myth of Narcissus also gives us an insight into the way in which we interact with our environment. Unlike Orpheus, who worked with song, Narcissus was obsessed with contemplation and aesthetic beauty and as such relates more to the realm of architecture. Marcuse's model of Narcissus comes from the world of myth and painting. We should also consider, however, the motif of Narcissus as Freud pursued it.

In Freud, Narcissus becomes one of the two models of object love: anaclitic and narcissistic. According to Freud there is a primary narcissism in everyone. This narcissistic love can take four forms. To quote Freud, a person may love:

1. What he himself is.
2. What he himself was.
3. What he himself would like to be.
4. Someone who was once part of himself.[14]

Freud sees narcissism as a negative mechanism—a regressive, childish delusion that in effect prevents us from recognizing the "other" in the "other." Narcissism, for Freud, would mean that we constantly see ourselves in the other, and cannot fully grasp the alterity of the other. Anaclitic love, by comparison, is preferable, because it respects otherness. Here, however, I want to read Freud against Freud and suggest an alternative approach to narcissism, in line with a number of more recent theorists: that there is something positive in narcissism that needs to be rescued.

Narcissism in Freud refers to a mechanism for potential engagement with the other, even though the other may in fact be the self. Subjects read themselves into the other, see themselves reflected in the other. In effect the figure of Narcissus is emblematic of a mode of engaging with—identifying with—the other. It becomes, in other words, a means by which the subject can identify with the object. Narcissus stands for the "refusal to accept separation from the libidinous object."[15] As Marcuse explains:

Primary narcissism is more than autoeroticism; it engulfs the "environment" integrating the narcissistic ego with the objective world. . . . The striking paradox that narcissism, usually understood as egotistic withdrawal from reality, here is connected with oneness with the universe, reveals the new depth of the conception: beyond all immature autoeroticism, narcissism denotes a fundamental relatedness to reality which may generate a comprehensive existential order.[16]

Narcissus, for Marcuse, offers a model of a "non-repressive order, in which the subjective and objective world, man and nature are harmonized."[17] In this respect narcissism retains a sense of the childishness that Freud associates with it, in that the dissolution of the self into the other parallels that stage in childhood when the subject-object split has yet to be developed. The model of Narcissus gazing at his own reflection without recognizing it as such would therefore parallel the period preceding the mirror stage, as defined by Lacan, in which the child has yet to recognize its own reflection. In this context, however, narcissism should not be seen as an immature regression into a childish state, but as a positive development that broadens the subject and overcomes the divide between the self and the other.

The myth of Narcissus offers us an insight into the way in which human beings relate to the world. This relatedness involves identification with the object at the level of the symbolic, by which the image of the object is, in effect, a reflection of the subject. This identification between subject and object operates within the realm of the unconscious. In effect, an unconscious—narcissistic—identification takes place.

Adorno and Mimesis

This is a mechanism that Adorno has already observed in the context of architecture. In "Functionalism Today," the only article of his specifically devoted to the question of architecture, Adorno addresses the way in which humans constantly attach symbolic meaning to the built environment: "According to Freud, symbolic intention quickly allies itself to technical forms, like the aeroplane, and according to contemporary American research in mass psychology, even to the car. Thus, purposeful forms are the language of their own purposes. By means of the mimetic impulse, the living being equates himself with objects in his surroundings."[18]

This last sentence, "By means of the mimetic impulse, the living being equates himself with objects in his surroundings," surely holds the key to exploring the whole question of how human beings situate themselves within the built environment, and it points to an area in which the domain of psychoanalysis may offer crucial insights into the mechanism by which humans relate to their habitat. It begins to suggest, for example, that the way in which humans progressively feel at home within a particular building is precisely through a process of symbolic identification with that building. This symbolic attachment does not come into operation automatically. Rather, it is engendered gradually through (in Adorno's terms) the mimetic impulse. Mimesis here should not be understood in the sense used, say, by Plato, as simple imitation. Rather, mimesis in Adorno, as indeed in Walter Benjamin's writings, is a psychoanalytic term, taken from Freud, that refers to a creative engagement with an object. It is, as Adorno defines it, "the non-conceptual affinity of a subjective creation with its objective and unposited other."[19] Mimesis, as Freud himself predicted, is a term of great potential significance for aesthetics.[20]

To understand the meaning of mimesis in Adorno, we must recognize its origin in the process of modeling, of "making a copy of." In essence it refers to an interpretative process that relates not just to the creation of a model but also to the engagement with that model. Mimesis may operate both transitively and reflexively. It comes into operation in both the making of an object and making oneself like an object. Mimesis is therefore a form of imitation that may be evoked by both the artist who makes a work of art and also the person who views it. Yet mimesis is richer than straight imitation. In mimesis, imagination is at work and serves to reconcile the subject with the object. This imagination operates at the level of fantasy, which mediates between the unconscious and the conscious, dream and reality. Here *fantasy* is used as a positive term. Fantasy creates its own fictions not as a way of escaping reality but as a way of accessing reality, a reality that is ontologically charged, and not constrained by an instrumentalized view of the world. In effect mimesis is an unconscious identification with the object. It necessarily involves a creative moment on the part of the subject. The subject creatively identifies with the object, so that the object, even if it is a technical object—a piece of machinery, a car, a plane, a bridge—becomes invested with some symbolic significance and is appropriated as part of the symbolic background through which individuals constitute their identity.

It is important to recognize here the question of temporality. Symbolic significance may shift, and often dramatically, over time. What was once shockingly alien may eventually appear reassuringly familiar. The way in which we engage with architecture is therefore not a static condition but a dynamic process. The logic of mimesis dictates that we are constantly assimilating to the built environment and that, consequently, our attitudes toward it are forever changing. The very process of assimilation within mimesis, as it is used here, implies an appropriation, a "claiming" of the object, and it is here perhaps that parallels with hermeneutics are most obvious.[21] The understanding of mimesis as a form of creative appropriation echoes the theme of Narcissus's trying to reach out and appropriate his own image. Benjamin evokes this theme in his description of the mimetic impulse: "Every day the urge grows stronger to get hold of an object at very close range by way of its likeness, its reproduction."[22]

The assimilation that mimesis demands with the inanimate world reveals the link with the death instinct. The action of mimesis constitutes an almost chameleon-like process of adaptation. This process, as Miriam Hansen observes, "involves the slippage between life and death, the assimilation of lifeless material . . . or feigning death for the sake of survival."[23] The origin of this process lies in the instinctual mechanisms of self-preservation. Animals, when trapped in potentially life-threatening situations, often freeze into seemingly lifeless forms rather than run away. Through this action, they attempt to blend with their environment and thereby escape the gaze of the predator. A similar trait is found in humans. "The reflexes of stiffening and numbness," as Adorno and Horkheimer note, "are archaic schemata of the urge to survive, by adaptation to death life pays the toll of its continued existence."[24] Thus, somewhat paradoxically, the feigning of death preserves life. "Death" is used in the service of life. This is a tactic that represents not simply the subordination of the self to nature, but also an overcoming of nature, a defense against the dissolution of the self. Benjamin himself distinguishes between a mimesis of pure sublimation of the self, which seeks to blend in with the environment purely defensively, and a mimesis of "innervation" which sees the environment as a source of empowerment. A mimesis of innervation stresses the creative act of self-expression against a given background. And it is precisely this active—rather than defensive— form of mimesis that offers a basis for creative expression in art.

Mimesis therefore constitutes a form of mimicry, but it is an adaptive mimicry, just as when a child learns to speak and adapt to the world or when owners take on the characteristics of their pets. In fact it is precisely the example of the child's "growing into" language that best illustrates the operation of mimesis. The child absorbs an external language by a process of imitation and then uses it creatively for its own purposes. Similarly, within the realm of architecture, we might see mimesis at work as architects develop their design abilities; this process also allows external forms to be absorbed and sedimented as part of a language of design. Clearly, mimesis goes beyond straightforward mimicry, if by mimicry we understand a response that is merely instinctual. Mimesis necessarily involves a sense of volition and intentionality on the part of the subject. It does not simply look back and mimic what is already given, but it relies on a process of creative engagement, of conjuring up something for the future. It is in this moment that the magical base of mimesis manifests itself. Like the magician who plans the trick, mimesis contains within it the sense of control of some organized project. Yet what distinguishes mimesis from magic is that it does not attempt to deceive in the same way. Thus, for Adorno, art as a form of mimesis is "magic delivered from the lie of being truth."[25] In distancing itself from the illusionistic claims of magic, mimesis surpasses magic while nonetheless remaining within its conceptual orbit.

Although mimesis involves a degree of organized control and therefore operates in conjunction with rationality, this does not mean that mimesis is part of rationality. Indeed, in terms of the dialectic of the Enlightenment, we might perceive mimesis as constitutive not of rationality but of myth, its magical "other." Mimesis and rationality, as Adorno observes, are "irreconcilable."[26] If mimesis is to be perceived as a form of correspondence with the outside world that is articulated within the aura of the work of art, then Enlightenment rationality, with its effective split between subject and object and increasing emphasis on knowledge-as-quantification over knowledge-as-sensuous-correspondence, represents the opposite pole. In the instrumentalized view of the Enlightenment, knowledge is ordered and categorized, valorized according to scientific principles, and the rich potential of mimesis is overlooked. All this entails a loss, a reduction of the world to a reified structure of subject-object divides, as mimesis retreats even further into the mythic realm of literature and the arts. At the same time, mimesis might provide a dialectical foil to the subject-object split of Enlightenment rationality. This is most obvious in the case of language.

Language becomes the "highest level of mimetic behavior, the most complete archive of non-sensuous similarity."[27]

Mimesis for Benjamin offers a way of finding meaning in the world through the discovery of similarities. These similarities become absorbed and then rearticulated in language, no less than in dance or other art forms. As such, language becomes a repository of meaning, and writing becomes an activity that extends beyond itself, so that in the process of writing, writers engage in unconscious processes of which they may not be aware. Indeed writing often reveals more than the writer is conscious of revealing. Similarly, the reader must decode the words resorting to the realm of the imagination, which exceeds the purely rational. Thus, the activity of reading also embodies the principles of mimesis, serving as the vehicle for some revelatory moment. For Benjamin the meaning becomes apparent in a constellatory flash, a dialectics of seeing, in which subject and object become one for a brief moment, a process that relates to the experience of architecture no less than the reading of texts.

Vitruvius Crucifixus

Architecture, along with the other visual arts can be viewed as a potential reservoir for the operation of mimesis. In the design of buildings, the architect may articulate the relational correspondence with the world that is embodied in the concept of mimesis. These forms may be interpreted in a similar fashion by those who experience the building, in that the mechanism by which human beings begin to feel at home in the built environment can also be seen as a mimetic one.

Mimesis, then, may help to explain how we identify progressively with our surroundings. In effect, we read ourselves into our surroundings, without being fully conscious of it. "By means of the mimetic impulse," as Adorno comments, "the living being equates himself with objects in his surroundings." Understood in the terms of our discussion of Narcissus, this mimetic impulse might be seen as a mechanism for reading ourselves into the other. We relate ourselves to our environment by a process of narcissistic identification and mimetically absorb the language of that environment. Just as Narcissus saw his own image in the water without recognizing it as his own image, so we identify ourselves with the other symbolically, without realizing that recognition of the "other" must be understood in terms of a mimetic identification with the other as a reflection of the self. And this refers not to a literal reflection of our image, so much as the metaphorical reflection of our symbolic outlook and values.

The aim throughout is to forge a creative relationship with our environment. Seeing our values reflected in our surroundings feeds our narcissistic urge and breaks down the subject-object divide. It is as though—to use Walter Benjamin's use of the term *mimesis*—in the flash of the mimetic moment, the fragmentary is recognized as part of the whole, and the individual is inserted within a harmonic totality.

Within this framework we can begin to address the role of proportions, which can be understood as emblematic of an attempt to relate to the built environment, not through empathy but through identification. The use of the human figure—and the use of human proportions, albeit of an idealized human figure—represents an enabling mechanism by which this process might be enhanced. The human figure is "reflected" back out of the object. The human figure is echoed—to use a term from the myth of Narcissus—in the building. Yet, here equally, the limitations of proportions are exposed. If proportions are to achieve their objective, they must offer a framework for a creative engagement with the world. The subject must be able to abandon itself in assimilation with the nonidentical. Once proportions become codified into an instrumentalized system, however, they enter into a terroristic standard of totalitarian rule, a logic of domination. Human values are imposed on the environment, rather than humankind's subjecting itself to the environment, assimilating to it in a process of mimetic identification. It is a case of *natura naturata* versus *natura naturans.*

In this respect, the tradition in the Renaissance of inscribing human figures into the plans of buildings, the elevations of columns, and so on can be seen as a form of mimetic device that vicariously evokes the desire for identification. The figure inscribed within the plan becomes a mimetic emblem for a physical body within the actual building. The emblem must be understood here as a device that is "magically" invested with the properties of an originary object, much as in the sacrifice when the victim is offered up as a substitute for others. Thus, the figure incised in the ground plan transcends mere representation. The figure takes on a symbolic significance, that can be understood only beyond the framework of Enlightenment rationality. It is precisely this investment that locates such devices within the realm of the mythic. These emblems become vehicles of identification, the objects of wish fulfillment, that evoke the principle of the sacrifice, as Lévi-Strauss has described it: "For, the object of the sacrifice precisely is to establish a relation, not of resemblance, but of contiguity, by means of a series of successive identifications."[28]

Hence we might read these inscriptions of the human body as being informed by a mimetic impulse, an attempt to relate to an inanimate object. They act as mimetic devices, vicarious objects of identification, charged with symbolic significance like the victims in a sacrifice.

It is here that the significance of the image of *Vitruvius Crucifixus*, Vitruvian man as the dying, crucified Christ becomes apparent. The theme of sacrifice also operates at a broader level. In our mimetic engagement with the built environment, it is precisely the self that is sacrificed. The subject effectively surrenders the self to the other in order that it might live on through a creative engagement with the other. Narcissus can therefore be seen as the quintessential emblem for aesthetic contemplation. Gazing at his own reflection, he identifies with the image, surrendering himself to it. In trying to grasp the beauty of that image, he drowns, only to give life to a flower. He thereby enacts the sacrifice of mimesis.

This sacrifice—this surrendering to the other—remains a precondition of aesthetic experience. As in the myth of Narcissus, the sacrifice transcends death. In the shock of aesthetic recognition, the subject is forced open and exposed to a meaningful relationship with the object. The subject is decentered and broadened. The subject identifies with the object, and it is in the forging of new identities during the dynamic process of mimetic assimilation that death itself is resisted and overcome. Hence, we might recognize the 'sacrifice' that lies at the basis of all architecture. As such, myths of sacrifice, which have filtered into architectural folklore, might be understood within the framework of mimesis.[29] It is as though the sacrifice of a human life is required in order to animate the inanimate stone. And we might read this sacrifice replicated in the sacrifice of the self within the mimetic identification of aesthetic experience.

In this process, we can recognize an almost mystical moment that shares something of religious ecstasy and the experience of love. If love, in Lacanian terms, is what fills the gap between the self and the other, mimesis can be seen to be the aesthetic equivalent of love. Hence we find terms with clear references to the world of love, like *jouissance,* being used to describe aesthetic experiences, while thinkers such as Julia Kristeva have made explicit comparisons between aesthetic experience and love.[30] And if the "death" of Vitruvian man can be seen as a sacrifice that transcends death and thereby serves the life instinct, a sacrifice where thanatos is put at the service of eros, the erotic character of this moment is evoked by Cesariano's other image of Vitruvian man spread-eagled within a circle (figure 13.2).

For Benjamin, art, through mimesis, takes on a quasi-religious turn, in offering the possibility of a return to some lost paradise following the fall of humankind through the instrumentalization of the world. If we are to understand mimesis as offering access to some form of paradise, then this promise is evoked in the mimetic emblem of Vitruvian man. Just as the death of Christ on the cross opens up the possibility of a life after death, just as the death of Narcissus gives rise to a flower, so the emblematic death of Vitruvian man leads to the possibility of a deeper, more meaningful engagement with the built environment.

The aesthetic gratification that results from this mimetic moment—the recognition of the self in the other, the self as part of, at one with, the whole—induces the nirvana principle. The narcissistic gratification of the self-reflected back in this stimulating engagement with the environment recreates the sensuous oneness of the womb, the integral gratification of the womb. The memory of the nirvana of the womb is recognized, and a state of pleasurable bliss is reached.[31] All conflicts are resolved as the death instinct is both realized and transcended. The vital experience that flares up in this sensuous engagement evokes the blossoming of the flower on the death of Narcissus. And in the *jouissance* of this intensely poetic moment, paradise is regained.

14

Marcia F. Feuerstein

Body and Building inside the Bauhaus's Darker Side: On Oskar Schlemmer

The apologists and the historians of the Bauhaus have always presented it as the
shrine of reason in an unreasonable, confused world. . . . This picture is a distortion
of what was thought or done. . . . The Bauhaus remains interesting and relevant
because it had an irrational, strong dark side.[1]

In the writings of Sigfried Giedion, Hans Wingler, and James Marston Fitch, the products of the Bauhaus were canonized as its image was sanitized and rationalized. These seminal polemicists of first-generation Bauhaus-inspired modern architecture promoted a hygienic aesthetic, ostensibly based on function, clarity, precision, and *Sachlichkeit* (objectivity). Walter Gropius, the first Bauhaus director, codified this sanitation in the exhibit he co-curated for the Museum of Modern Art (MoMA) in 1938.[2] Joseph Rykwert's study, "The Dark Side of the Bauhaus," in which he framed the "other" Bauhaus as an irrational, imprecise, and illogical proposition illuminated an inherent instability within the Bauhaus edifice.[3] The largely unexplored work of Oskar Schlemmer, artist-architect and Bauhaus master, reveals inconsistencies in the institution's official history that are greater still than those first explored by Rykwert.

Oskar Schlemmer based his oeuvre on the notion of merging the human body with the space it occupied and defined. The ambiguity inherent in this procedure is apparent in Schlemmer's relatively unknown proposal for the design of the first international Bauhaus exhibit house (1923) in Weimar. His project, *Hausbau Bauhaus,* demonstrated a playful, ambiguous, and irreverent dwelling built on unstable ground. It combined individual and collective bodies unbound from a dark world filled with static inhabitants.

Lather, Rinse, Repeat

Although Walter Gropius portrayed a Bauhaus that was singularly rational, it was not immune to the cultural and political conflicts of the Weimar Republic. Gropius and Herbert Bayer, co-curators of the MoMA exhibit documenting Gropius's nine years as Bauhaus director, subjected the "fringe" elements (read chaotic) of the institution to a thorough sanitization.[4] The manner in which Gropius and Bayer represented Johannes Itten in the exhibition catalogue exemplifies this program. Rather than using the now-familiar photograph of Itten with his cleanly shaven head, monklike glasses, and flowing crimson robe, they published a photograph of him wearing a business suit and sporting a conservative haircut.[5] The result of Gropius's and Bayer's sanitation was an internally coherent image of the Bauhaus educational pedagogy. The myth that Gropius and Bayer constructed was renewed in the early 1970s when their catalogue was reprinted, four years after Rykwert published his essay on the Bauhaus's "Dark Side."

Peter Gay described this generation of postwar Germans as "disinherited" and "incomplete" (*Halbheit*), a reaction to the unprecedented horror of and loss from war.[6] Unable to find clarity and peace within their lives, they searched for leaders and ideologies whose rejuvenating and healing messages promised a return to simple and clear values: positive and negative, right and wrong. Gropius and a number of his faculty who witnessed the war firsthand also committed themselves to training a new kind of individual. While they believed in the Bauhaus utopian view before war broke out, after the war this training was a social necessity.[7] It produced "educated men": designers who would create and build prototypes within up-to-date laboratories, thereby directing German industry, promulgating new German design principles, and building a new German identity.

Wassily Kandinsky explained that this method of training "implanted" narrowly focused information into the student body, thereby transforming the students through the dictates of prescribed "lessons."[8] This process inadvertently opened the door to Mazdaznan, a popular Christian mystical cult that for a time had a pervasive and insidious influence on the intellectual and pedagogical culture of Gropius's Bauhaus. Many of the Bauhaus faculty and students sought this return to clarity through Mazdaznan "methods" of purification, rather than seeking lucidity through a rational approach that eventually was envisioned by Gropius and later mythologized by the MoMA exhibit and subsequent Bauhaus polemicists. Its adherents were cleansed and reeducated after following a rigid order of bodily training. This process developed "new" men and women empowered as positive forces to make sense of the postwar chaos.[9]

Itten and George Muche, both Bauhaus masters, followed precepts developed by the Mazdaznan leader Otoman Zar-Adusht Ha'nish. Itten, a follower of Zar-Adusht Ha'nish since 1907, imported a number of Mazdaznan precepts into the *Vorkurs*, the foundation and entry into the Bauhaus education. He also introduced the healthful living patterns of the Mazdaznan belief system into the Bauhaus canteen, including a macrobiotic diet.[10] The primary goal of Mazdaznan was a complete purification of humankind—in essence, a return to paradise. This process of purification, of which the macrobiotic diet was part, would eradicate "all prenatal influences and errors of ancestral relations"[11] and recreate the original Aryan people—the white race of Zarathustra.[12]

Oskar Schlemmer, knowledgeable of Mazdaznan precepts,[13] chose an alternative method of building his vision of the "new man." Unlike Itten, Schlemmer's new man was the key to spatial design. Schlemmer, who was skeptical of Itten's educational program, observed that the exclusive and cultic forces that Itten promoted undercut the student's education, resulting in a split between believers and nonbelievers.[14] When the Bauhaus canteen began serving only the Mazdaznan diet, Schlemmer sardonically noted that "paying so much attention to the stomach and to what passed one's lips might rob one of one's spontaneity" and wondered if "purity was guaranteed by a pure stomach."[15] Schlemmer's work is central to the story of the Bauhaus's darker side. His ideas, like his personality, were complex and at times seemingly impenetrable. Here I focus on a narrow range of Schlemmer's work that reveals his speculation about the human body in relation to space-making during his tenure at Gropius's Bauhaus.

Costume

Architectural space for Schlemmer was less a container for the body than an aspect of the body transformed. The entirety of Schlemmer's oeuvre speaks of space filled with, through, and as body. Schlemmer's body-based knowledge is apparent throughout his strange and nightmarish paintings, as well as through the uncanny sculptures he set in motion. Schlemmer's students studied the body as art, science, and spirit. This credo was key to his course, *Der Mensch,* which Schlemmer saw as an extension of Gropius's principle of "creating a new unity . . . a unity having its basis in Man himself and significant only as a living organism."[16]

Schlemmer's course promoted an anthropomorphic theory of costume design. The *Vordruck* (form) that Schlemmer developed—a male form (figure 14.1)—was central to his teaching.[17] Schlemmer and his students used copies of his *Vordruck,* reproduced by the Bauhaus print shop, as the basis for their studies of human proportion and costume design. Using a standardized body form like the *Vordruck* was consistent with the Bauhaus's general program of type and standardization. Schlemmer argued for the production of costume as the philosophical and compositional expression of key body types. These types were related to specific actions and spaces deformed by, and in conflict with, a "pure," clear, and clean (read "standardized") image of a human body. Schlemmer's costume designs constituted a conundrum: they attempted to formalize a theory that was at once playful and disruptive, yet they were typological and restrictive for the human body that inhabited his costumes.

Costume, architecture, body, and space were dynamic and inextricably linked for Schlemmer. Moreover, his theory of the relation of the human body and costume is no less a theory of the relation of body and architecture. The dynamism within the theory reveals

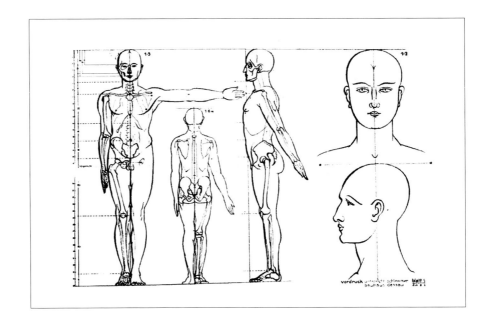

14.1
Vordruck (Form) with human skeleton (*Vorkurs "Der Mensch," Der Knochenbau des Menschen,* 1928–1929). (© 2000 Oskar Schlemmer Theatre Estate, Collection UJS, I-28824 Oggebbio, Italy)

an original theory of type. For Schlemmer, human types were artificial constructions based on the various natures of man and his life experiences. Schlemmer formalized his idea of human beings as a composite of a number of interactive circumstances. This variety of human circumstances contributed to continually changing human *compositions*,[18] paralleling a political theory of human archetype advanced by Eric Voegelin.[19] For Voegelin, archetypes were the outcome of changing human experiences. Voegelin's theory provided a method based on archetypal images (*Urbild*), the essence of which was a mixture of two specific yet ill-defined phenomena: life and human nature. These phenomena—and the human images to which they relate—continuously change owing to time and situation. This "primal way of seeing" (*Urweise des Sehens*), according to Voegelin, fabricated archetypes into dynamic compositions that grew from a variety of circumstances and occurrences.[20]

Schlemmer's theory of costume, like Voegelin's archetypes, is based on human images that negotiate within distinct constructions derived from human nature. Schlemmer's theory of type both promoted and questioned the reconciliation among various categories of human existence. His costume designs represented difficult and ambiguous human relationships that measured and represented the human condition. For Schlemmer, his "being" was and always would be an artificial construct—an "art figure" (*Kunstfigur*)—that emerged from the "transfiguration of the human form."[21] In his essay "Man and Art Figure" (1924) and using his standing human form, *Vordruck,* Schlemmer realized his theory of costume. Each version of *Vordruck* was "clothed" by a particular 'law' or rule (*Gesetze*), creating unique two- and three-dimensional postures as exaggerated expressions of Schlemmer's principles of costume. Schlemmer thought of these costumes as a figural language with peculiar shapes and profiles signifying four distinct ideas about the body, based on the interaction of two "acts"—body and costume—that shaped distinct actions.[22] The exterior layer of the costume molded the concealed human body into fragmented or restricted forms of movement. This interaction between body and costume created a third condition. The triadic relation among quotidian living, space, and movement created four distinct characters that Schlemmer named: "Ambulant Architecture," the "Marionette," a "Technical Organism," and "Dematerialization" (figure 14.2).

"Ambulant Architecture" was a "spatial-cubical construction" of "laws of the surrounding cubical space . . . transferred to the human shape" (figure 14.2a).[23] It is a solid and heavy cubic body whose large masses tower over a small base, creating a compressed, bound, architectural-like body. The "Marionette" consisted of curves and circles (figure 14.2c), representing "functional laws of the human body in their relationship to space," through the "egg shape of the head, . . . club shape of the arms and legs, [and the] ball shape of the joints."[24] Schlemmer derived the Marionette from his studies of human joints. The third costume, "Technical Organism" (figure 14.2b), revealed "laws of motion of the human body in space," such as "rotation, direction, and intersection of space: the spinning top, snail, spiral, disks."[25] It was a composite of moving parts creating a curvilinear and orbiting space. The "Dematerialization" costume (figure 14.2d) represented "metaphysical forms of expression."[26] This costume was a dialogue between the outer costume-as-body and the underlying human body. It consisted of a dynamic figure moving vertically and horizontally while rotating about its vertical axis, alternating between leaping and standing positions—balance and a loss of balance. These costumes are "theatrical" yet "dramatic," transforming the actor into a character. "Theatrical costume amplifies an actor as well as his character without eliminating him."[27] Schlemmer's principles of the human body amplified the very notion of the human being, recharacterizing the body as a space-making being. Each of Schlemmer's costumes signifies a "theoretical" body that implies distinct shape and motion patterns.

The costume types implied a certain kind of life and pattern of movement—a dance that followed strange and unexpected rhythms.[28] Schlemmer designed these costume types

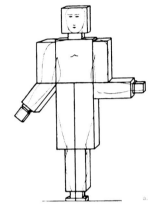

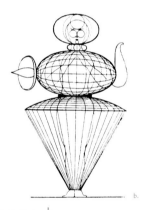

14.2a–b
Theory of costume.

a. Ambulant Architecture (*Wandelnde Architektur,* 1924).

b. Technical Organism (*Ein technischer Organismus,* 1924).

through a process of "hollowing out" and "piecing together" various elements, which were then inhabited by human bodies that enacted the "orders" or "statutes" that the costume type implied.[29] Schlemmer believed that there was no singular human "essence." Rather, humans were a composite of ideas that ordered and reordered the human-made world. Each of Schlemmer's theoretical body-costumes resulted in a perceivable space that was constructed by virtue of the moving costume. The four bodies replicated (rather than imitated) these body-based forces as space-making types.

Hausbau Bauhaus

Schlemmer's proposal, Hausbau Bauhaus, for the 1923 International Bauhaus Exhibition in Weimar contrasted sharply with the realized Bauhaus exhibit, *Haus am Horn,* designed by Georg Muche (figure 14.3). Muche created an object-like building with a central void. This void, surrounded by insulating compartments (rooms) of singular functions, drew the inhabitants into its center, isolating them from the land and community.[30]

Schlemmer's conception of interior space in *Hausbau Bauhaus* was never fully developed, although the drawing became the basis for a later project for the Folkwang Museum in Essen.[31] Schlemmer represented a deeper and perhaps darker familial isolation in his painting *Fünf Figuren im Raum (Römisches)* (1925) (figure 14.4). In the painting, Schlemmer represented detached human figures who have been compressed within various spaces, grouped together by discrete architectural elements.[32]

Schlemmer's *Hausbau Bauhaus* formed an interactive program of engagement between the building and the bodies who inhabited it, wherein the building merged inside and outside—body and building. This merging generates a spirit of playfulness and camaraderie throughout the extended familial community.[33]

The two words *Haus* and *Bau,* in Schlemmer's title, have a poetic rhythm that seems more appropriate for a libretto or chant than a prototypical house design. Its syntactical formation is based on the simple symmetry of two "bau" bracketed by two "haus." Yet Schlemmer does not create a mirror or bilateral symmetry "Hausbau Uabsuah." Rather, *Haus* contains *Bau* in his title, evoking both the present Bauhaus and a future house to be built. *Haus* signifies house, home, and domesticity. The verb *hausen*—variously signifying "to live," "to house," and "to dwell"—refers to family (*Hausarzt:* family doctor or *Hausmutter,* mother of the family) and implies an inside rather than an outside (*Haustarif:* internal pay scale, *Haustelephon:* intercom). *Bau* means building, construction, growth, and cultivation. *Bau* frames structures and creates boundaries within a Heideggerian framework of human living. Schlemmer's play with these words connotes the action or making

14.2c–d
Theory of costume.

c. The Marionette
(*Die Gilderpupp,* 1924).

d. Dematerialization (*Die Zeichen im Menschen Entmaterialisierung,* 1924). (© 2000, Oskar Schlemmer Theatre and Family Estate, I-28824 Oggebbio and Photo Archive C Raman Schlemmer, I-28824 Oggebbio, Italy)

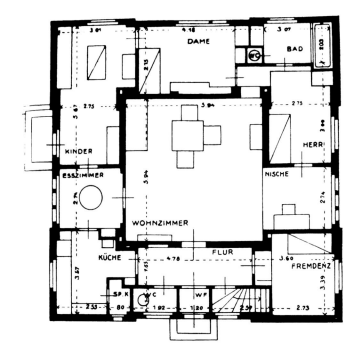

14.3
Haus am Horn, Weimar, 1923
George Muche with Adolf Meyer.
(Bauhaus Archiv, Berlin)

of the house as house building. The title is intentionally ambiguous—typical of Schlemmer's open-ended, unresolved, and skeptical position.

A year before his *Hausbau Bauhaus* project, Schlemmer wrote a short essay with the same title.[34] The essay, both sardonic and spirited, is a description of the early modernism of Gropius and his colleagues, with jokes about popular modernist themes (hygiene, glass, and mobility) and such theorists as Paul Scheerbart and Bruno Taut. Schlemmer also satirizes the new Bauhaus (*sans* Itten) proposed by Gropius. The resulting school and its house were intended to be a "real utopia."[35]

The earliest sketch for *Hausbau Bauhaus* is relatively small (8.1 by 12.2 centimeters) and at first glance seems banal (figure 14.5). It is hastily drawn on the back of a scrap of paper. The second image, *alte Skizze (Weimar)* from 1928, is larger and precisely drafted and rendered in pencil. The third image, *Vorentwurf für das Museum Folkwang* (1928), is also precisely drafted and rendered with color.[36]

On the earliest sketch, a portion of printed text appears through the substrate of the paper and the sketch itself. The text, barely perceptible, nonetheless forms a series of equally spaced vertical rows, forming an underlying visual structure for the drawing of the house.

A door interrupts the frame of the drawing, enticing the viewer to "enter" the scene and the space beyond—perhaps into another room. Unlike Muche's insular project, Schlemmer's design consists of two different spaces: the outside corner of the house and part of its adjoining natural setting, which includes a terrace, trees, and a field. The house has a flat roof and an ionic-like column and is occupied by a group of people. A human figure peers through a window; another figure lounges on an upper deck, and something is wrapped around a pole. People engaged in friendly, sociable activity fill the site next to the building. It is daytime; something is flying in the air. And looking farther, there are hints of a human profile whose eyes are formed by the sun and the flying object.

Schlemmer's sketch followed the graphic and proportional structure that he uncovered from the traces on the scrap of paper and then refined from his own marks. Within the conceptual framework that Schlemmer constructed, the found object is understood as a fragment, the whole of which is unknown. All that is known is how the fragment and the traces recorded on its surface provoked Schlemmer's conception of the larger work. Beginning from this graphic fragment, he designed the fragment of a house for the fragment of a site. The design of both the house and its site continues beyond the edges (read site) of the paper. The embedded profile further divides the open space of the exterior. Schlemmer reveals a synthetic and composite approach to design: the plan opens toward and contains

14.5
Oskar Schlemmer, Hausbau,
Bauhaus, 1923. (© 2000
Oskar Schlemmer Theatre and
Family Estate, I-28824 Oggebbio
and Photo Archive C Raman
Schlemmer, I-28824 Oggebbio,
Italy)

the exterior. The general structure of the ensemble contains two kinds of space: a space of social action that fills and establishes the architectural space, and a liminal space between inside and outside. The barely discernible human profile merges both types of spaces. Schlemmer's sketch also indicates three modes of structure and use. In the first mode, the space (solidly filled with humans and human action) provides a social structure implying a familial unity with the inside and outside, as well as an asymmetric sense of continuity. The second mode is the architectural space of the house itself. The third is a space of contextual ambiguities that assembles the project either onto a wall (as a wall painting) or into a scene of the future building.

People integrated with the building actively populate Schlemmer's design sketches. Like his costumed dancers, they are compressed and expanded, gesturing at and to the building. They are codependent. Yet it is curious that both the house and the bodies that populate the scene share unknown and unforeseen foundations that have nothing to do with either bodies or buildings. Rather, they grow from Schlemmer's own playful dialogue between his particular conception of architectural space and the form that represents that space. Unlike Muche and Itten, Schlemmer's proposal for a house was no less a representation of human interaction. Yet Schlemmer's proposal, *Hausbau Bauhaus,* began with a piece of paper—a form—that he used for the original sketch and the idyllic, and mysterious and untraceable, building it produced. In the process of building up the project from found fragment to ambiguous dwelling spaces, he established a dialogue between the "site" of the original paper fragment and the "forms" he designed within the building and its site.

Schlemmer's sketch pictured new houses and ways of living whose relaxed camaraderie within the Bauhaus community was both myth and reality.[37] The community of this drawing was not a regimented life of Itten's Mazdaznan cult. Rather, this was a mixed community, somewhat disorganized, almost leaderless, and with an equality among groups and individuals. Throughout these projects, an indistinct form, human or otherwise, remained ambiguous, lightly drawn, and essentially within the background. This background propelled his *Hausbau Bauhaus* into an architectural structure of bodies and building, playfully composed from built-up fragments of "forms," yet incomplete. The second and third drafts of the *Hausbau Bauhaus*, which became proposals for the 1929 opening of Essen's Folkwang Museum, were abandoned. Schlemmer's never-to-be-completed project for the Bauhaus revealed a light and nuanced hand. Yet this hand was coupled with dark and ominous visions revealing deeply rooted concerns—both the future of building houses and for the isolated bodies that would occupy them during increasingly ambiguous and lawless times.

15

George Dodds

Desiring Landscapes/Landscapes of Desire: Scopic and Somatic in the Brion Sanctuary

*I saw . . . the pleasant location; . . . the ornate green plants; the delectable and
moderate hills decorated by small and shady groves; . . . And here . . . I directed with
great pleasure my eyes upon this heavenly picture, and I feasted my eyes and looked
upon this beautiful and rare image and divine picture with all [my] senses, so that in
myself the aroused and impetuous vibrations, which had liquefied the soul by their
sweetness, revealed even more pleasure. . . . Not less I marveled at the skill with
which teacher Nature spread out all the Arabian perfume especially and in
abundance* in this lovely body.[1]

The Brion family sanctuary in San Vito di Altivole is arguably the best known of Carlo Scarpa's more than seventy projects for gardens and landscapes. This aspect of his work, largely overlooked in the literature, ranges from small, temporary installations to large-scale parks.[2] Scarpa is better known for the many museums and exhibitions he designed, in which he carefully honed his ability to direct the visitor's vision through subtly manipulating his or her body. In the design of the Brion sanctuary (1968–1978) Scarpa combines the scopic and somatic dimensions of his architectural production, engaging visitors in his personal desire for landscapes and gardens.[3]

The circumstances of the Brion project are distinct among Scarpa's previous landscape and garden commissions. Unlike his garden for the Venice Biennale (1952), the temporary landscape for the Italia '61 Exhibit in Turin (1961), and the gardens for the Fondazione Querini-Stampalia (1950–1963) and the Museo di Castelvecchio (1957–1964), the Brion project was privately funded. Moreover, Scarpa was unrestrained by the archaeological, museological, and institutional programs that limited these earlier works. The Brion commission is further distinguished by its nominal programmatic requirements for a site that posed few, if any, spatial limitations beyond its L-shaped configuration. This is not to say that there was no *preesistenze ambientali* into which Scarpa intervened.[4] Beyond the obvious physical and historic context of the existing public cemetery of San Vito di Altivole, there was the town itself and the contiguous landscape on which Scarpa's conception of the garden complex was largely contingent.

Onorina Brion commissioned Scarpa to design the tomb, honoring her husband Giuseppe's wish to be buried in the town of his family's origin.[5] To secure a plot of land for the project contiguous with the public cemetery, the Brion family was required to purchase far more property than was originally envisioned.[6] Consequently, Scarpa assumed the task of inventing an expanded program for the project to exploit fully the possibilities of the 2,000-square-meter site.[7] Scarpa's program included a shelter for the graves of additional Brion family members, a funeral chapel, a water garden with a pavilion for private meditation, "cloistered" walkways, a cypress grove for the burial of local clergy, and the symbolic use of specific plants.[8] The centerpiece of the site and program is an elevated *prato* (or lawn) surrounded by a continuous concrete wall, at the center of which is an arched canopy. Beneath the arch—which Scarpa called the "arcosolium," one of many Latin terms he used to describe the garden complex—are the sarcophagi of Onorina and Giuseppe Brion. Scarpa's program for the sanctuary is not limited to an assemblage of architectural objects, however; it includes the historic and mythic dimensions of a culturally constructed site wherein the viewing body negotiates between landscape-as-representation and landscape-as-experience. The Brion garden's visual program includes specific views borrowed from both its walled interior and the surrounding landscape, while its somatic program engages one's syncopated movement into and through the garden complex.[9]

Bodies, Landscape, and Painting

This story of the scopic and somatic dimensions of the Brion sanctuary begins with three views: from the loggia of the Palazzo Chiericati in Vicenza, from inside the *Albergo* of the former Scuola di Santa Maria della Carità that houses the Accademia Galleries in Venice, and from Carlo Scarpa's apartment in Asolo. These three views are key to understanding a critical aspect of the Brion sanctuary and Scarpa's larger interest in the corporeal dimension of landscapes and gardens, both real and fictive.

Giuseppe Mazzariol, Scarpa's lifelong friend who, as the director of the Fondazione Querini-Stampalia collaborated on the design of its garden, recalls that Scarpa's fascination with landscape began when he was a young boy, while visiting relatives at the Villa Tacchi in the Veneto countryside.[10] When Scarpa was growing up in Vicenza, he enjoyed a relatively close relation to the agrarian landscape, which was much nearer the city center than it is today. It was still possible, for example, to glimpse a view of the countryside from Palladio's loggia of the Palazzo Chiericati, which, when it was built, was located at the boundary between city and rural landscape.[11] During an interview with RAI television in 1972, Scarpa sat on the balcony of his apartment in Asolo (another important locus in this story) recounting his first architectural memories: playing marbles in the loggia of the palazzo.[12] Writers on Scarpa have presumed that the point of this recollection was Scarpa's first consciousness of Palladio's architecture. Yet just a few years after the RAI interview, Scarpa referred to Palladio's attempt to copy antique Attic bases, such as those in the columns of the Palazzo Chiericati, as "rubbish."[13] Perhaps there was more to Scarpa's memory than a game of marbles and Palladio's loggia. During the early twentieth century, the piazza on which the palazzo fronts (today the car-covered Piazza Matteotti) seemed more field than piazza. It is no less likely that in a city with a limited amount of public green space but rich in views of distant mountains, the view from the loggia across the piazza to a framed view of countryside may have had an equal impact on the young Scarpa as did Palladio's loggia. The combination of the two—Palladio's hybrid building, half palazzo and half villa, and the view of the nearby landscape—seems to have had an enduring influence on the entirety of Scarpa's work, particularly in relation to his design of the Brion sanctuary.[14]

When Scarpa was thirteen years old his mother died, and his family moved back to Venice; as a result, this direct connection to the Veneto landscape, if not closed to him, was at this stage of his life significantly altered. As a student of painting at the Accademia in Venice, Scarpa encountered a Veneto landscape that differed substantially from the landscape views associated with the Palazzo Chiericati or the Villa Tacchi. This was an idealized Veneto, the Veneto of the Venetian school of painting to which the Accademia was singularly devoted.

The Accademia Galleries contain the core of the Venetian school, displayed in twenty-four rooms that Scarpa reorganized and redesigned between 1944 and 1959. The first space one enters on the *piano nobile* of the Accademia is the former chapter room of the Scuola di Santa Maria della Carità. Here many great Trecento paintings and artifacts from the Veneto are exhibited. Among these is the *Vision of St. John the Evangelist* by Jacobello Alberegno, the center of which is dominated by the body of God the father enclosed in a mandorla (figure 15.1). The almond-shaped mandorla is a common iconographic device found in early Christian, Byzantine, and Gothic art works; it typically frames the body of Christ or the Virgin Mary.[15] First appearing in Greek and Roman mosaics and vase decorations, often in vague egg-shaped forms, the mandorla has always signified a separation between quotidian human experience and an "other" realm.[16]

The former *Albergo* of the *scuola*—adjacent to the chapter room—is the last gallery on the museum's circuit. In the *Albergo,* Titian's *Presentation of the Virgin* still hangs in the room in which it was originally installed in 1539 (figure 15.2). Mandorla-shaped mountains are the focus of the painting's background. In the foreground, the child Mary ascends the steps of the temple, enclosed in a luminescent mandorla amid an idealized architectural setting influenced by the architecture of Jacopo Sansovino and Sebastiano Serlio.[17] The background landscape that Titian constructed had both liturgical and personal significance for the artist. It evoked the iconographic relation of the mandorla-shaped mountain to the body of the Virgin Mary as the Christianized *magna mater* (underscored by the glow-

15.1
Detail, *Vision of St. John the Evangelist,* Jacobello Alberegno (© Accademia Galleries, Venice; from Francesco Valcanover, *The Galleries of the Accademia*)

ing mandorla) and the artist's relation to his home of Pieve di Cadore in the Dolomites, where such mountain types are common.[18]

Scarpa positioned Alberegno's painting in the chapter room so one can view both it and Titian's *Presentation* simultaneously through the broad doorway of the *Albergo.* These two works, one representing the beginning and the other the zenith of the painting patrimony of the Veneto, appear simultaneously in the visitor's cone of vision once having seen the entire collection. Describing his arrangement of sculptures in the Museo di Castelvecchio in Verona, Scarpa explained that by positioning works of art in certain ways, visitors can be encouraged to move their bodies in relation to the works being viewed so as to heighten their critical appreciation.[19] The juxtaposition of Alberegno's mandorla to Titian's mountains and the child Mary surrounded by a mandorla of light seems to demonstrates Scarpa's complex understanding of the body's relation to both works of art and landscape. This relation was not simply scenographic, but involved both the physical movement of one's own body through the museum and the iconographic tradition of Venetian painting in which the distinction between bodies and landscapes is often obscured.[20]

Presentation of the Virgin, Titian, Albergo Room of the Scuola della Carità. (© Accademia Galleries, Venice; from Francesco Valcanover, *The Galleries of the Accademia*)

During a lecture in Madrid in the summer of 1978, Scarpa commented that his work was located inside a longstanding and deeply felt tradition.[21] Scarpa's relation to the Venetian school of painting must be considered a key part of this tradition, an aspect of which is the representation of bodies as landscapes[22] and landscapes as bodies.[23] In the Venetian school, the body that was represented in this manner was invariably female and often nude.[24] Johannes Wilde compares Giorgione's portrait *Laura*—in which "the flesh has been rendered in a variety of tints, among them a very intense red"—with the "colour sensations [one experiences] in the south in the deceptively transparent air which precedes a sudden storm in the summer." Wilde concludes that in this manner, Giorgione has purposefully demonstrated "that figure and surrounding are inseparable, and that plastic form only exists in a space full of light and atmosphere."[25] The key here is not so much the ancient and more generic association of nature as feminine, but rather the particularly Venetian tradition of the fleshy female anthropomorphizing of landscape.[26] Naomi Schor has argued that the paintings produced in Venice during this period had long been gendered female, largely because of their emphasis on the presentation of the (beautiful) detail over the representation of the (sublime) whole. Sir Joshua Reynolds, Schor argues, codified this gendering of the Venetian school in his *Discourses on Art* (1769–1790).[27] For Reynolds, the role of the invariably male artist, was both to correct the many defects found in nature and edit out *her* multitudinous and distracting details.[28] In this way, "the scattered beauties of nature," as Boullée characterized a similar process in his architectural treatise of the same period,

15.3
Framed view of Asolo's *rocca,*
Gipsoteca canoviana, Possagno.
(From © *Casabella continuità*
222, 1958)

could be reassembled and made sublime.[29] Naomi Schor argues, "To focus on the detail . . . is to become aware . . . of its participation in a larger semantic network, bound on the one side by . . . ornament, with its traditional connotations of effeminacy and decadence, and on the other to become aware that the normative aesthetics elaborated and disseminated by the Academy . . . is not sexually neutral. . . . The detail . . . [therefore] . . . is gendered and doubly gendered as feminine."[30]

The relation between the gendered and eroticized ground of Venetian painting and the physical ground of the Veneto—the Veneto as signifier and signified—is a key to Scarpa's understanding of landscape and garden and the role that the body, particularly the female body, played in the gardens he designed. Whether Scarpa was consciously aware of the historicity of gender in relation to detail is unclear. The role of detail in the construction of a feminized and eroticized landscape, particularly in relation to Venetian painting, was, however, well known to Scarpa from numerous sources.[31] To understand better how omnipresent this notion was for Scarpa on a personal level, his apartment in Asolo may hold a key. From one side of his apartment, the view was of the green slopes of the hilltop town and the verdant plains below. Scarpa had a magnificent view from the other side of the town, dominated by its *rocca*. Both views, at least in the 1960s, had changed relatively little during the centuries since Pietro Bembo resided there, resulting in his *Gli asolani* (1495–1505), dedicated to Queen Cornaro, in which "the author explores a Platonic and anti-sensual conception of love in a beautiful garden."[32] Arrigo Rudi, Scarpa's longtime associate on such projects as the Museo di Castelvecchio and the Banca Popolare di Verona, recalls standing on Scarpa's balcony in Asolo as Scarpa pointed out specific sections of the landscape, comparing them to details from various paintings of the Venetian school.[33] Scarpa considered these bits of vista as details, not fragments, which he associated with details of paintings, related to both the region's tradition of landscape painting and its general history.

Scarpa's personal desire to locate views of an idealized Veneto landscape often extended into his architectural designs so that the occupant encounters carefully framed views of a related landscape. The Gipsoteca canoviana in Possagno is perhaps the earliest example of Scarpa's constructing views of this type. His addition, built alongside the exiting nineteenth-century Canova sculpture gallery, frames a view of Asolo's *rocca* (figure 15.3). This view was originally foregrounded by Canova's sculpture grouping *The Three Graces*.[34] Although Canova's sculpture group remains, the view has long since been obscured behind the unchecked growth of vegetation contiguous with the museum. The *rocca* of Asolo, located midway between Possagno and San Vito di Altivole, is also the focus of a seminal view Scarpa constructed from the Brion sanctuary. It was this image of the Veneto landscape—feminine, full-bodied, and full of details—that Scarpa wanted to see for himself, and perhaps wanted others to see, from both the Canova gallery and the garden he constructed for the Brion family.

At the time of his death, Scarpa was at work framing a similar landscape view in Monselice at the home of his patron and friend, Aldo Businaro. As part of his renovation and reorganization of the villa compound called "il Palazzetto," Scarpa designed an apartment for himself above the garage at the edge of the property. His design of this apartment was prompted by his being forced to vacate his flat in Asolo a few years earlier due to the owner's desire to reoccupy the space.[35] Scarpa lived in the Asolo apartment for ten years (1962–1972). He loved the small medieval city, relating to its history, fabric, and relative isolation.[36] After leaving Asolo, Scarpa and his wife ultimately relocated to an apartment above the stables of the Villa ai Nani in Vicenza. This was Scarpa's last permanent home. While living there, he often visited the Palazzetto for extended periods, in part to hide from students and clients but also to regain a more direct connection to the Veneto landscape.[37] The design of the apartment at the Villa Palazzetto was intended to recreate, at least in part, another lost aspect of Scarpa's former living arrangement: the view from his apartment of Asolo's

15.4
View of Monte Ricco from Scarpa's unfinished apartment, "Il Palazzetto," Businaro Estate, Monselice. (Photo: Author)

mountaintop *rocca*. From the Palazzetto apartment, left unfinished at the time of his death, Scarpa had constructed a framed view of the mandorla-shaped Monte Ricco (figure 15.4). This view fulfilled two of Scarpa's seminal desires: to frame views of Veneto landscape corresponding to details of both Venetian paintings and the lost view he associated with Asolo.

The Palazzetto apartment relates to another important experience of loss that Scarpa associated with this particular landscape. Here in Monselice, while painting this same *rocca* many years earlier, Scarpa finally realized that his competency as a painter was not equal to his desire to paint.[38] Although he gave up his aspiration to paint, focusing instead on the design of exhibitions, buildings, and gardens, the concepts and techniques of painting continued to influence his productive activities.

The painterly undercurrent of Scarpa's thinking is implied in his description of the design process for the Brion project, recounted in his lecture in Madrid:

> I suddenly decided that at this point there ought to be a water element that would interrupt the perspective. I like water very much, perhaps because I am Venetian. . . . At this point I thought of devoting part of the site to the making of a small, "tempietto." . . . Having thought about this, I decided I needed an element in the background. Here there is a pure sky like there was today [in Madrid], very beautiful. . . . At this location I felt the need of a dark value. From the first it seemed that the scheme called for a dark de-

pression at this point, otherwise the perspectival value would not have had any sense. These are the reasons that I have made it this way.[39]

Scarpa's use of a painterly vocabulary in describing landscape and architectural decisions is fundamental to understanding the Brion enclave. In his Madrid lecture, Scarpa described the perspectival view he was constructing—not in terms of converging lines and vanishing points typical of the Florentine-based method *disegno*—but in terms of figures and atmospherics. He focused not on line but on the values of colors, dark and light, near and far, and the direct use of materials, all essential characteristics of *colore,* the method and philosophy of Venetian Renaissance painting.[40] In the *colore* method, bodies and the spaces between them are built up simultaneously from the direct application of fields of color, without elaborate preparatory drawings. Space in such paintings tends to be a function not of linear perspective, but of a combination of chiaroscuro, intensity of color, degree of detail, and relative size of objects.

The design for the Brion project was also influenced by his study of literature. Commenting on the design process and the locale, he cited a number of key works on which he reflected while designing the project: the garden landscapes of Francesco Colonna's *Hypernotomachia Poliphili,* where the chaste body of Polia is pursued in the dream of Poliphilo; the garden of Professor Canteral in Raymond Roussel's *Locus Solus,* where preserved bodies float in a strange and magical watery substance called *acqua micans;*[41] and the funereal landscapes of Edmondo De Amicis, who picturesquely describes cemeteries inhabited by young women eating and drinking.[42] The female body situated in a landscape or garden figures prominently in all of these visual and textual narratives. This may help explain why the design drawings for the Brion sanctuary, more than any of Scarpa's other projects, abound with images of nude females. Although these images often appear somewhat ghostlike, they reflect the manner in which Scarpa imagined the living body physically engaging the Brion sanctuary, both directly and as a site from which to view a distant, idealized landscape.

Memoria Causa

Perhaps the most important interpretation of the Brion sanctuary is Scarpa's own. The little-known monograph that he edited, *Memoria Causa,* is his only book. Scarpa apparently never wrote about architecture, owing to what Francesco Dal Co calls his "hypersensitivity to the written word."[43] *Memoria Causa* consists of a hardboard folder holding eleven unbound and folded folio sheets.[44] The only text in the monograph, save for spare captions to the nineteen black-and-white photographs, is an inscription, in Latin, on the

15.5
View of propylaeum entrance to
Brion sanctuary (left), San Vito
di Altivole, from *Memoria Causa*.
(Photo: © Guido Pietropoli)

first folio: "The images contained on these sheets are of the monument constructed in memory of Giuseppe Brion, his wife Onorina, and their children."[45]

The first photograph in *Memoria Causa* is a now-familiar image of the entrance from the public cemetery.[46] It is a close-up of the stairs and interlocking circles that form a vertically oriented mandorla. The image, rendered in stark chiaroscuro by the ambient lighting, is the frontispiece of the monograph, much as the entrance itself is the frontispiece for the entire garden complex (figure 15.5). The entrance introduces many of the project's essential themes: the asymmetry of left and right, the construction of thematic views, the negotiation of interrupted passages, the model of Venetian private gardens, the iconography of Venetian Renaissance painting, oriental and Arabian gardens, and, perhaps most important, the movement and orientation of the visitor's body in relation to the garden's organization.

Scarpa called this entrance the "propylaeum"[47] and its interlocking circles the "eyes" of the garden, underscoring both its hierarchical importance and its somatic implication.[48] By Scarpa's own account, the propylaeum is the critical origin point or navel of this garden-as-body.

The view from the public cemetery into the propylaeum was originally obscured behind a low-hanging weeping cedar (*Cedrus atlantica*), lost during a severe winter in the mid-1980s.[49] Scarpa intended visitors to encounter the stairs and mandorla only after moving aside the branches of the cedar, which he described as "a kind of tent."[50] On the left-hand side of the entry portal are stairs with a conventional ratio of rise to tread; the ratio of the right-hand stair is doubled, discouraging normative use. In two earlier plan drawings of the enclave,[51] in which many provisional ideas for the project are depicted, the stairs fill the entire passage. In a composite elevation-section study of the propylaeum made somewhat later,[52] the stairs are shown in their current left-sided position. Beneath this elevation Scarpa drew a line to the stairs, noting, "*Spostare a destra . . . tutti vanno a destra,*" one translation of which is, "Move to the right-hand side . . . everybody to the right." Guido Pietropoli, unable to explain the logic of the notation, elsewhere observes that by providing two different stairs and by locating the conventional stairs off-axis, Scarpa required the visitor to make a conscious choice between left and right.[53] That Scarpa interrupts the passage and requires a change in the direction of the visitor's path is not in itself remarkable, as he often structures entrance scenarios to gardens in this manner, such as the Fondazione Querini-Stampalia and the Museo di Castelvecchio. What is significant is the manner in which Scarpa codes this particular choice, signifying an asymmetry of value.

The drawing sheet, the drafted base of which is by Petropoli, is filled with Scarpa's marginal sketches of the interlocking ring and mandorla motif,[34] one of which frames a miniature landscape of poplar-like trees standing on an empty *prato.*[55] This small and hastily drawn sketch is important, as it shifts the meaning of the double rings away from that of an isolated and self-referential icon,[36] an interpretation that permeates the literature on both Scarpa and the Brion sanctuary, to that of a frame. Moreover, the constructed view of the enclosed garden, overlaid with the mandorla—a sign of the Virgin Mary, the *magna mater* and, by extension, the vulva—is a doubly gendered female, signifying both the garden-as-mother and the equally old association of the tomb-as-womb.[57]

The relation of the body of the Virgin and the enclosed garden underscores another of the garden's important themes: the *hortus conclusus.* The conflation of the mandorla and the enclosed garden is a fundamental part of Marian iconography associated with the Song of Songs.[58] The *hortus conclusus* is an enduring garden type in Scarpa's oeuvre. It was the model that Giuseppe Mazzariol prescribed for Scarpa's design of the Fondazione Querini-Stampalia garden, and it is part of one of his last projects, the Villa Mateazzi-Chiesa, Ponte Alto, Vicenza (1974–1975).

Pietropoli intuits the mandorla at the entrance as the doorway to the precinct. It is more window than doorway, however; its limited size and raised position, in concert with the water channel beyond, underscore that this was a threshold that was not to be crossed. The implicit prohibition against transgressing the mandorla reflects its roots in both ancient and Christian cultures. Its iconographical traditions include female corporeality, sacrality, and the separation of the quotidian world from the realm of the "other." Moreover, the vertical mandorla is part of a pancultural tradition that recognizes the asymmetry of the left (associated with matter and gendered female) and the right (associated with spirit and gendered male).[59] Standing at the top of the stairs, the visitor is part of the unfolding iconography of the enclave as one's body is literally and figuratively oriented. Looking through the mandorla toward the "other" realm of the consecrated sanctuary (*camposanto*) to the east, the visitor again chooses between left and right. Robert Hertz explains that at sites of sacrality, of which Catholic burial grounds are a part, the body often becomes a kind of *gnomon,* a marker of solar orientation. By orienting the body to the east, "the parts of the body are assigned accordingly to the cardinal points. . . . The full sunlight of the south shines on our right side, while the sinister shade of the north is projected on our left."[60]

In a transverse section of the propylaeum, Scarpa represented himself facing the mandorla at the top of the stairs.[61] The view from Scarpa's position in the section is of a simple *prato.* While the elevated and walled *prato* suggests analogies with the tradition of Venetian private gardens, the superimposition of the mandorla onto this view prompts more personal meanings for Scarpa.[62] In numerology the mandorla is associated with the number 11. While Scarpa's personal association with this number has been much discussed in the literature,[63] the role of the mandorla in this regard has yet to be recognized. The mandorla's numerical equivalence to the number 11 derives from the intersection of the two circles—one representing spirituality (signified by the number 1) and the other representing perfect unity (signified by the number 10).[64] As if to underscore this numerical association, directly above Scarpa's body in the drawing, he notes the dimension: "11 cm."

Most of the human figures in Scarpa's many drawings of the mandorla window, including his own, are positioned facing east, tacitly signifying the role of the propylaeum in orienting the body of the visitor. In an elevation study of the entrance, Scarpa inscribes each of the circles with a female and male body, respectively, ostensibly representing the unbroken union of Onorina and Giuseppe Brion and emphasizing the entrance's gendered asymmetry. The left-hand stair in the Brion propylaeum—the one designed for "our bodies" and gendered female—leads to matter, to the bodies of the Brions beneath the arcosolium and the direct pleasures of the garden as a *locus amoenus,* a site of direct physical pleasure. Scarpa imagined this part of the garden filled with children playing and women eating and sipping wine,[65] as described by Edmondo de Amicis's in *Constantiniopoli.* Scarpa explained, "I read that the women of Constantinople gladly take walks in the cemeteries there—sometimes to picnic. The memory of these things left something in me."[66] The right-hand stair is the beginning of a very different and more difficult journey, physically and conceptually. It is a journey of the spirit to the island designated for private meditation. Here the visitor experiences the enclosed garden from afar, as a rationalized object of contemplation.

"Spostare a destra . . . tutti vanno a destra."

Of three aedicular structures within the Brion enclave—the island pavilion, the funeral chapel, and the arcosolium—the island pavilion is the only one that encourages human occupation. Scarpa returned to the island often, even before the pavilion was constructed. He explained, "This is the only private [place in the garden]—all of the rest is for the public, for the playing of children. . . . The pavilion I made for myself. I go there frequently and meditate. . . . It is the only one of my works that I gladly come back to see."[67]

Among the more than a thousand graphic documents in the Scarpa Archive in Trevignano di Montebelluna (CSA) for the Brion project is an inordinate number of drawings of the water garden and island pavilion. Scarpa continued drawing this part of the enclave long after its construction was ostensibly complete. In *Memoria Causa,* the absence of any photographs taken from or of the island demonstrates both Scarpa's desire for it to remain private and that, in his mind, its design was not yet complete.[68] Yet among his many drawings for the Brion project, the studies for this site are the most populated. Understanding the unique scopic and somatic programs that are in play in the island pavilion helps explain why these drawings are so filled up with bodies.

An elevation study of the pavilion helps explicate this point (figure 15.6). In the center of the drawing Scarpa sketched the figure of a nude female. The nude consists of two superimposed bodies (two sets of eyes, shoulders, and so on) representing a single body that is moving along the vertical axis of a slot in the pavilion's fascia. The pavilion consists of four attenuated composite columns, asymmetrically disposed about a platform supporting a boxlike roof and fascia. Subtending the fascia is an *involucrum,* which in Latin signifies an "envelope" or "wrapper" covering the front of an object.[69] This continuous panel is bifurcated by the slot and the moving nude. At the base of the slot is a pair of arcs creating a kind of viewfinder. In the drawing, Scarpa aligns the head of the nude with the slot and viewfinder. What is it about the island pavilion that prompted Scarpa to study it so assiduously? Why does he create a continuous and apparently superfluous wrapper around the pavilion, only to slice a slot along its centerline? Why does the nude figure occupy the center of the pavilion and the slot?

From the vantage point of the nude, the view is of a simple *prato* enclosed by the apparently continuous perimeter wall and a circular water element, consistent with the iconographic tradition of the *hortus conclusus.*[70] This vista from the island would have been possible, however, without the pavilion, its viewfinder, and the concrete seat-planter that

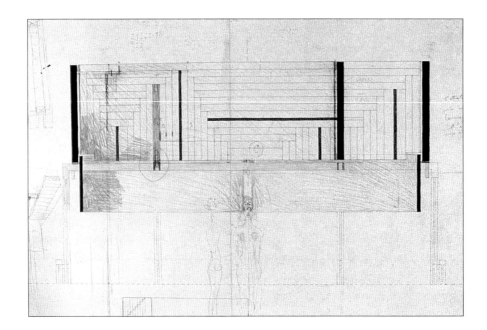

15.6
Elevation study, pavilion, private island, Brion sanctuary, San Vito di Altivole. (Carlo Scarpa Archive, Trevignano di Montebelluna, Tobia and Afra Scarpa)

Scarpa provides the visitor. Moreover, the *involucrum* interferes with this vista. Visitors must adjust their eye levels to gain an unobstructed view of the walled garden, either by using the viewfinder, as does the nude in the elevation drawing, or by sitting, as do the corpulent nudes in Scarpa's numerous other studies. Why then does Scarpa create a view of the garden from this locus by such elaborate means, only to obscure it?

The studied manner by which, in his design drawings, Scarpa directs potential vistas from the island indicates the importance of the views and the manner in which they were to be apprehended. There are two distinctly different and equally important views from the island. The first is of the interior walled garden of the sanctuary. The second view is of the distant landscape. The moving nude in the elevation indicates how Scarpa intends for the visitor to discover these views. The claustral wall that surrounds the garden is key to this process, which is equal parts discovery and concealment (figure 15.7).

The wall was the first construction completed at the site and was designed to work in tandem with the pavilion and its viewfinder. During his frequent visits to the Brion construction site, Scarpa often expressed concerns about the height of the claustral wall. He worried that it would not be high enough to efface the view of the adjacent agricultural fields and the incursion of postwar buildings contiguous with the cemetery.[71] In two section drawings, Scarpa highlights his concerns about the relation of the surrounding landscape to the enclosed garden. In one of the drawings he represents a human head using the top of the wall as a kind of surveyor's level. In yet another drawing (ACS 70 129 27) Scarpa represents himself, his eye aligned with the top of the wall and his gaze fixed on the distant landscape. Ennio Brion, the son of Giuseppe and Onorina Brion, confirms that had the family not objected to Scarpa's original plans, the wall would have been still higher.[72]

Although most of the discussions of the Brion project in the Scarpa literature focus on what is contained inside its walls, the drawings of wall and the pavilion indicate that the landscape outside is equally important. Scarpa incorporated various devices throughout the garden complex to prompt the viewer to look beyond the immediate enclosure—not in a general way but to specific objects or places in the landscape. The island pavilion is the most conspicuous example of this practice.

The Veneto landscape that Scarpa desired to see from this prospect was not the actual Veneto landscape that, by the late 1960s and early 1970s, had been visually marred by unchecked development. By constructing highly selective views of the landscape beyond the *hortus conclusus*, Scarpa prompted the visitor to make connections between foreground and background, culture and history, the Veneto as physical place and as idea. Without the editing effect of the garden walls, Scarpa could not have constructed the views he desired.

Unlike Scarpa's architectural restorations, the landscape instauration of the Brion garden did not require the physical alteration of the surrounding landscape. Through his

15.7
Claustral wall, Brion sanctuary, San Vito di Altivole. (Photo: Author)

15.8
View from sitting position, island pavilion, Brion sanctuary, San Vito di Altivole. (Photo: Author)

architectural interventions, Scarpa changed the manner in which the landscape is viewed—Scarpa constructing images of both a *hortus conclusus* and a *locus amoenus*. One of the requisites of the pastoral landscape of a *locus amoenus*—the site of sacred and profane love—is the absence of utilitarian and often quotidian buildings of any kind.[73] Viewed from the concrete seat, the garden appears to be a simple rectangular shape wrapped by a continuous wall—the *hortus conclusus*. Beyond that there is a distant moutanious landscape. (figure 15.8)

The other key view from the island, is seen from a standing position, with knees slightly bent, looking through the binocular viewfinder (like the nude in the drawing). From this position alone, can one align the bottom of the *involucrum* with the top of the claustral wall, deleting all of the surrounding landscape, save those objects isolated in the viewfinder (figure 15.9). One of these objects is, like the view framed by Scarpa's addition to the Gipsoteca canoviana, the *rocca* of Asolo.

A very similar view of Asolo appears in the background of *Sleeping Venus*, begun by Giorgione and completed by Titian (figure 15.10). In the painting, the hilltop *rocca* of Asolo and the castle of Queen Cornaro[74] are represented behind the nude and reclining Venus just as the mandorla-shaped mountains in Titian's *Presentation* dominate the view behind the body of the Virgin Mary, enclosed in a mandorla of light. In *Sleeping Venus*, the recumbent body of the nude oscillates between an idealized goddess and an eroticized courtesan, between body-as-object and body-as-landscape, between a distant and unattainable paradise and a singularly sensual and attainable experience.

15.9
View from standing position
(through "viewfinder"), island
pavilion, Brion sanctuary, San
Vito di Altivole. (Photo: Author)

The views of the Veneto landscape from the island pavilion provoke a process of recovery, the whole of which has been forever lost, but the details of which persist, piece by piece, as if in a dream. In the *Hypnerotomachia Poliphili*, one of the many texts with which Scarpa was preoccupied during the design of the Brion project, Poliphilo dreams that he and Polia arrive at the island together. Yet the glass door and narrow passageway to the private island in the Brion sanctuary are wide enough to permit only one body to pass at a time. Scarpa's prompts—"*spostare a destra*"—lead one on a somnabulatory path. On this path one dreams alone and awakens, like Poliphilo, alone, but with the memory of a complex landscape in which both carnal and divine love are the object and the viewing body is the subject.

Conclusion

The shift in bodily position encouraged by the prospects on the meditation island signifies far more than the pictorial reconstruction of oneiric or eroticized landscapes. The visitor's apprehension of the Brion garden involves both the construction of specific views and the absence of others; it engages both a conceptual body and the physical body of the visitor. The movement indicated by the female nude in the elevation drawing, for example, recalls the kind of bending motion prompted at all of the critical thresholds in the Brion enclave. At the entrance to the island pavilion, however, the visitor enters upright and alone, through an opening in the involucrum that corresponds to human proportions. Yet to obtain the prospect of the claustral garden and idealized pastoral landscape, visitors must reenact the bending motion one final time. Bowing to the level of the viewing device or resting on the concrete seat, visitors adjust their bodies to the position prompted by the architecture to find the views constructed by the architect.

Unlike the arcosolium, the funeral chapel, and the family pavilion—all of which are thematically associated with death—the island pavilion is for the living. As if to signify this, Scarpa sketched a couple in the midst of coitus in the margin of one of his drawings of the pavilion. Although sexual climax is also a metaphor for death (*petit mort*), in Scarpa's drawings for this project, one finds less a contemplation on death than a complex, layered study of the interaction of the living body with the lively art of building. Scarpa's drawings of bodies in the Brion project express the mimetic program of the garden architecture in the richly layered context of the Veneto's landscape and culture. His drawings for the island pavilion, the fortress-like perimeter wall, and the propylaeum indicate that the mechanics of vision and the construction of specific views are critical to the garden's perceptual program. More than simply representing the static image of vision at work, however, Scarpa's drawings are themselves viewing devices of a sort. In them one can see the architect at work, mimetically interpreting the form and movement of the human body in a culturally constructed landscape.

While Scarpa has fabricated these elaborate views prompting references to landscapes and bodies from sixteenth-century paintings, this should not be interpreted as a nostalgic attempt to construct a naive or scenographic landscape. Scarpa does not attempt to connect the viewer directly and physically with these ideal images. It is only through an elaborate artifice of separation that they are made visible.

The Brion sanctuary ought not to be reduced to either a simple parody of Poliphilo and his lost Polia, Martial Canteral's garden with its weird and wonderful floating bodies, or the distant and obtuse images of Titian's courtesans laid out like the Dolomites made flesh. The Brion sanctuary is not about the body-as-object or the body-as-other; it is about how our bodies, not simply as sensing organs or viewing devices, but as sentient beings fully engage in culturally specific constructs, vegetal and mineral, landscape and building. This is a lesson that, arguably, seems to have become peripheral in the practice of architecture during Scarpa's lifetime, and perhaps our own too. It is an issue to which Scarpa constantly returned in his drawings and built works. By placing the sign of the mandorla, Scarpa's personal sign, at the navel of this garden-as-body, he wrote himself into the telling of this collection of stories, constructing a labyrinth from which not even he could escape. Scarpa's mortal remains are part of this place, buried in its margins like the objects in his copious marginal design drawings. The Brion sanctuary is a teaching place; it reminds us how one can engage more fully in a world that is constantly finding more efficient and enticing ways to deflect and distance the sentient body with visually consumable icons.

Ennio Brion recounts that Scarpa claimed to be designing the Brion project even in his sleep,[75] fulfilling Gio Ponti's aphorism that gardens should be based not on designs but on dreams.[76] The Brion sanctuary demonstrates that it may be possible and even desirable to dissolve the distinction between the world we dream and the one in which we dwell or, in the case of Scarpa and the Brion sanctuary, between desiring landscapes and landscapes of desire. It may be mere happenstance that at the end of the circuit through the Accademia in Venice, one can view simultaneously Jacobello Alberegno's painting of a mandorla enclosing the body of God the father and Titian's *Presentation of the Virgin* with its mandorla-shaped mountains. Or it may be yet another example of how body, landscape, and physical movement often combine in Scarpa's work to produce moments such as the view from the former *Albergo* of Santa Maria della Carità or the view from the island pavilion in the Brion enclave. These moments that Scarpa frames are windows into a human dimension of architectural production that intentionally obscures the distinction between bodies and landscape, or as Johannes Wilde explained, where "figure and surrounding are inseparable."

Marco Frascari

A Tradition of Architectural Figures: A Search for *Vita Beata*

Beata est ergo vita conveniens naturae suae.[1]

The fashionable practices of many contemporary architects produce architectural bodies without qualities. These buildings are miserable figures without proper body images. These patched-together atrocities are lifeless forms bringing together fragmentary body parts in a kind of anatomical Lego game. The wanting results of these designs in effect create architectural corpses that, on the one hand, become pathetic expressions as Mary Shelley's ogre or, on the other hand, the vaudeville fiend as Mel Brooks's updated version of the Frankenstein's tale. The prevailing way of thinking that these deceptively nimble designers use are entwining wreckages of building-remains on their glinting workstations seems better suited for the pathologist's dissecting table than the drawing tables of discerning and discriminating architects. Happily and gruesomely clicking on the mouse at their workstations, these designers seek cockatrices, and produce behemoths and Leviathans such as the Bilbao Museum or the addition to the Cincinnati School of Architecture. The architectural bodies without qualities that these architects have created result from a process whereby prosthetic gadgets, mechanical carcasses, and perfunctorily Cartesian morbid remains supplant the time-honored theory of signature that sees the portrayal of edifices as embodied constructs.

The graphic and photographic representations pervading contemporary topical architectural journals eulogize the deforming devices and procedures that these architects use. The employment of these malicious practices takes the place of the traditional use of corporeal figures as inaugural mechanisms of sound analogical design. Yet these widely published designs simulate human nature, suspiciously avoiding the more critical and nettlesome issue of how to assimilate a corporeal dimension within the context of contemporary architectural practice.

The majority of fashionable architects seem to suffer from an agnosia by which, to paraphrase Oliver Sacks, in their nuptial relations with Lady Architecture, they constantly mistake their allegorical consort for their hats.[2] The imagery they produce and their architectural imagining reflect body-looks not body-images. By *body-image*, I am referring to the schema of the "imaginal body" as theorized by Paul Schilder, which I am appropriating into the sphere of architectural imagination.[3] The imaginal body for Schilder consists of a meaningful body-image that is formed in the mind. This image is not merely the product of sensation, representation, or perception; it results from a coalescing of the three, generating an understanding of one's body that is fairly different from one's literal anatomical condition. The body-image is a powerful and vivid animated presence similar to the phenomenon of phantom limbs following an amputation.[4] The merging of visible bodies and invisible *body images* become gestalts, interweaving human anatomy and posture with cultural and social conventions.

This manner of perception—consisting of body icons combined into a complex amalgam of personal and cultural imaginal representations—is a potentially powerful tactic of architectural design. Comprehending the subtle role played in design by body gestalt images points the way toward reuniting architectural production and the production of human well-being—a union that has been considerably belittled by the monstrosities of contemporary architectural practice.

Within the domain of architectural production, the idea of the body-image is a peculiarly Venetian tradition of ideas in which architectural design is recognized as an allegorical process of assimilating bodies—bodies with qualities—into the conception of buildings. Within this tradition, body icons are brought into play to arrange buildings for a *vita beata*.

The concept of *vita beata* began with Seneca and was introduced into architectural discourse by Leon Battista Alberti.[5] The concept was subsequently assimilated into Venetian architectural design by the compelling trinity of Falconetto, an antiquarian painter-architect, Alvise Cornaro, a dietitian-architect with Galenic biases, and Angelo Beolco, a tragicomic play writer whose pen name was Ruzante. This Venetian tradition searches for a *vita beata* by posing the possibility of a sympathetic dance between bodies and buildings, and interfacing design and construction brings into play edifications gathered from the interaction between corporeal images and building images as a means for allegorically apprehending space and form.

A simple categorization of a beatific life lies between the designations of the French *le bonheur* and the Italian *l'allegrezza*. *Vita beata* results from an architectural landscape designed for a "happy existence." Ruzante describes the *vita beata* poetically in his tragicomic plays. Beatific existence for him is a way of life free of any temporary impairment caused by psychic commotions. The attainment of a *vita beata*—the virtue of being in good spirits—is the primary scope of human existence.[6]

Antonio Averlino, the renaissance architect known as Filarete ("lover of virtue"), is the only architect to have directly addressed the Stoic topic of virtuous happiness. Filarete points out in his *Trattato* that implementing a *vita beata* through architecture is an ethical requirement for architects, since a beatific edifice increases the potential for investing in psychic talents of its inhabitants.[7] Filarete distills the essence of this powerful idea in his affirmation that a properly designed and erected building will *cresce l'animo* (nurture the soul) of its inhabitants.[8] His view of the architecture for a *vita beata* poses a real possibility of a dialogic dance between bodies and buildings. He argues that by playing an analogical game of body images, architects should mold and construct the bodies of both humans and buildings. This analogical design is a way of figuring out how to attain the correct balance of psychic and physic interaction in a design—the *allegro ma non troppo* in architecture.

Following Filarete's argument, one can envisage an architecture that results from the power of working out bodily experiences into a virtuous condition. Within the Paduan Galenic-Aristotelian intelligentsia, the allegory of Madonna Sofrosina denotes this virtuous condition.[9] Within this tradition, body images emerge from experiential stockrooms, becoming procreative graphic presences that bring forth the beatific sphere of design, albeit not necessarily belonging to the sphere of gifted vision.

Construing architecture through body-image ensures that the imaginal force of human bodies is impressed, received, and vividly transmitted into the built environment. This compelling approach predominantly takes part of the elaboration of the corporeal images evoked by mimes and dancers, especially when counterpoised to culturally specific images of everyday people.[10]

To help clarify and appreciate the tradition of a qualitative corporeal design for a *vita beata*, I will analyze the design practices of Valeriano Pastor. Pastor, a practicing architect in the Veneto and a professor at the Istituto Universitario di Architettura di Venezia (IUAV), had been a student of Carlo Scarpa. He also collaborated with Scarpa on a wide range of projects during a twenty-year period.[11] I will examine the work of the master (Scarpa) through the work of his pupil (Pastor) to help amplify the perception of this intellectual tradition that is peculiar to the Veneto, while at the same time underscoring its sequential nature. Pastor's use of body-images in architectural imaging evolved from his training and collaboration with Scarpa. It cosubstantiates space and construction by

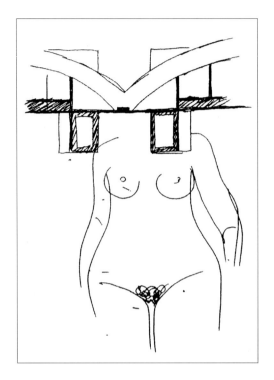

16.1

Valeriano Pastor, sketch for the
District School Center near
Dolo. Nude female torso in a
detail study sketch of the
ribbed vaulting in the school's
laboratories.
(From *Anfione Zeto, 1,* 1989)

means of metonymical and allegorical design transmutations that are fundamentally haptic in nature. In Pastor's design method, this imaginal tactic, based on Stoic foundations, upholds the medium of architectural drawings as a principal means of thinking through corporeal images. For Pastor, architectural drawings are not limited to envisioning the future construction of a building; they are also a figurative means of thinking about the body's interacting with other bodies. In this procedure of architectural imaging, the substance of a design follows from corporal experiences constructed and construed within a corpus of body images. These thoughtful embodiments bring forth the virtuous nature of architecture—an indispensable condition for implementing a *vita beata*—by dealing with the visceral character of building to foster high spirits.

Pastor's body-images establish potential architecture by delineating the relation of the visible and material icons of construction to the immaterial and invisible signs of edification. He accomplishes this by inhabiting the space of his architectural drawings with a physiognomic "otherness"—invisible and subtle lines of thought. The body figures in his drawings reveal the noetic geometry underpinning architectural detailing, establishing the material qualities necessary for a beatific inhabitation. Pastor evolved this Stoic imaginal tactic from the soft Epicurean ideas of Scarpa into a sharp Lucretian imaging.

The examination of a few of Pastor's sketches for the District School Center near Dolo, partially built between Stra and Mira, on the Brenta Canal may explicate Pastor's use of the symbiotic relation of body and building in a corporeally conscious design.

In the drawings for this never-to-be-completed building, one finds clues of both a particular attitude toward the body and a general anticipation of how the body of the projected building will interact with its future inhabitants. Pastor's drawings demonstrate how, by foreseeing corporeal reasons, architectural images can anticipate the interrelation of inhabitation, construction, and imagination. The mystery of the incarnate building in these drawings is never entirely conjured using the skin and the bones of only one specific body image. They are not Frankensteinian hodgepodges of heads, torsos, and limbs but rather Stoic assemblages of analogical empathies informed by the quotidian world, enhancing the *wunderkämmer* of architecture.

Pastor juxtaposes the darkness of the spring of the vaults with the image of a nude female torso in a detail study sketch of the ribbed vaulting in the school's laboratories revealing the "*natura*" of a construction (figure 16.1). In another design drawing for the school, Pastor represents a perspectival view of a passage with vaulted corbels. In the passageway, two naked mime-like figures are walking, underscoring the vaults above through the rhythmic expression of their cantilevering muscles (figure 16.2).

Although the manner in which Pastor expresses various characteristics of body postures and attitudes in his architectural drawings is clearly influenced by Scarpa's *ad rem* body figures, they are ultimately quite distinct in a number of key areas. Pastor's images constitute a system consisting of three particular classes: the nude mimes, the dancers in leotards, and the shadow people of the quotidian. These classes correspond to three design realms. Pastor explains the gestalt of his design procedure: "The architectural event can be seen as the result, or rather, process, of interaction among three 'realms'—the program, construction and use. Each has specific traits and operative modalities . . . but none can be independent without impairing the others. Each tries to take over, but non-systematic design can be imposed other than dialogue and conflict—as experience of participation has shown."[12] A sectional drawing of the central space of the school, rendered in shadow, demonstrates this tripartite interaction, architecturally and corporeally (figure 16.3). Naked mimes are the essential expressions of Pastor's architectural mimesis of Lady Architecture, creating the counterpoint for the designed elements around them as they portray a tale. Jean Dorcy, a voice for the silent theater, describes the power of the mime: "[It] is neither a natural

16.2
Valeriano Pastor, sketch for the District School Center near Dolo. Perspectival view of a passageway with vaulted corbels and two naked mime-like figures.
(From *Anfione Zeto, 1,* 1989)

impulse nor a physiological reflex; censored and elaborated by the intellect, as by an architect, it therefore offers us sharp images."[13] Dorcy continues, "The stage is a place where space changes nature, size and architecture according to the body occupying it; . . . scenic spaces becomes a sky, a meadow, or a garden, thanks to the magic of a dancing body."[14] The dancers in Pastor's drawings describe spaces by magically delineating the tension of the surrounding structures.

The shadows in Pastor's drawing set the stage for the dialogue between potential use and programmatic requirements. The presence of these ordinary individuals in Pastor's drawings enables one to comprehend the role of the two other classes of body-images he uses. The mimes are metonymic figures evoking the constructive nature of the spatial container. The dancers are dynamic and metaphoric figures outlining the spatial representation with crossing paths reflecting the disposition of the building. These two body types reveal the invisible side of architecture, transubstantiating the corporeality of time, tempo, and weather within the atemporality of design. The dancers' symbolic movements add perceptual details to future spaces, while the mimes' dynamic actions condense events while evoking constructional principles.

The ordinary people in Pastor's drawings suggest, in contradistinction, the protean potential of architecture with a distinct regional expression. The regional expression of bodily figures is not unique to Pastor's drawings. In "Les Techniques du corps," Marcel Mauss discusses the wide range of activities that shape the mutable human body. These activities include styles of caring, gender formation, styles of work, exercise, sexual postures, dance, and ritual. While these activities seem innate, they are actually acquired expressions of cultural values. Particular expressions such as work positions or other aspects of the body differ, sometimes radically, from culture to culture. Individuals raised in a climate of surgery, drugs, orthopedic devices, and constraining social fashion image their body differently from those who have been raised to use meditation, movement postures, herbs, sensitive manipulation, and acupuncture to maintain sound health.

Building-bodies are as regional as are body-images.[15] Pastor's fusion of bodies, for example, originate in part in the *Venetianitas* of Bellotto's *Capricci,* in Canaletto's camera views,[16] and through Scarpa's design *pansophia* to the Venetian *Orbus Pictus* of allegorical representations such as Zorzi di Castelfranco's *La Festa Campestre* and Gianbellino's *Allegoria Sacra.*

As transfigurations of the built world through similarity and contrast, Pastor's allegorical depictions of human images become primary causes for composing through differentiation. Pastor points out that "composing through differentiation" is a design tactic he

16.3
Valeriano Pastor, sketch for
the District School Center near
Dolo. A rendered sectional
drawing of the central space of
the school demonstrating a
tripartite interaction, architectural
and corporeal.
(From *Anfione Zeto, 1,* 1989)

acquired by monitoring Scarpa's design procedures: "The idea of composition through differentiation comes from reading Scarpa's works and from work experience I had with him, seeing him designing, when he was developing forms identifying autonomy for each element of composition."[17]

In the drawings of both the master and the pupil, the body-images are an extension of the lively process of architectural design. They do not sketch the body images after the delineation of the project is complete to solve anthropometrical problems or to simulate and dissimulate design intentions. The delineation of these figures takes place during the outlining of the design, if not before it. In the dynamic of design imaging, these body icons amplify the perceptions of time and space through striking empathies. The active and static moments of these graphic pantomimes metonymically distill the body into building tectonics. In Pastor's architectural drawings, images of mimes and dancers merge with the walls, beams, windows, doors, floors, and other building elements. Pastor evokes space and

Valeriano Pastor, sketch for the District School Center near Dolo. A sectional construction detail including a group of figures located near a section through the vaulted walls. (From *Anfione Zeto, 1,* 1989)

construction in his drawings through metonymies of touch and metaphors of synesthesia. Engaging the space of the drawing with lines of corporeal thought, the body types Pastor uses produce constructive and volumetric delineations. They transfigure the invisible characteristics of spaces and tectonic forms into visible geometries of construction.

Revealing future construction and construing of buildings, Pastor's tension between flesh and geometry advances Scarpa's phantasmagoric use of body images. Pastor transfigures the design strategy of the images of the Vitruvian man: conflating Cesariano's grotesque bodies, Leonardo's aerobically moving four-limbed figure, the analogical *charkas* of Francesco di Giorgio's Italian mimes, and the silently evocative solar plexus of Le Corbusier's corporeal mime, the Modulor.[18]

A sectional construction detail of the Dolo school demonstrates how Pastor uses a body image to generate a constructive geometry. In this sketch, a group of figures is located near the section of the vaulted walls. Their body postures evoke an everyday event (figure 16.4). A naked man seen from the rear is different from the others, however. Balancing on a single leg, this mime evokes, through the tension of his muscles, the co-temporal tension in a structure that is out of plumb. Moreover, the other leg and the torso of the mime have the same inclination as the centerline of the vaulted wall. The parallelism between the two lines underlines Pastor's design intention. The posture of this figure is the poetic substance of the design.

This naked man is a corporeal mime as theorized by Jean Louis Barrault. The originating concept of Barrault's art of mime is the "*counterpoid.*"[19] The *counterpoid* is the corpo-

Valeriano Pastor, sketch for the District School Center near Dolo. Sectional drawing with a running female. (From *Anfione Zeto, 1,* 1989)

real basis for assisting the imagination to disclose the intangible. Through his body, the corporeal mime evokes that which is not present. Through the tension and perturbation of their musculature, corporeal mimes express the imaginary existence of an object. The invisible object is made tangible by the mime's virtual use of the object and the effect this use has on the mime's body, revealing a presence, in absentia, through a projection.

In a sectional drawing of the Dolo school, Pastor represents a running woman, substantiating the evocative power of this analogy. In this simple drawing, Pastor establishes the reciprocal relationship of the mime's dynamic repetitive movement and the profile of the beam (figure 16.5).

In a section of the main building a cheerfully dancing female figure captures, in a graphic *counterpoid,* the countenance of the entire edifice (figure 16.6). By depicting the dancing female balancing on only one foot, Pastor graphically acknowledges the intangible dynamic of the structural asymmetry of the building section.

Pastor's drawings imply a fortunate union of human bodies with the constructed bodies of buildings. These buildings have been designed with body images that seem to have the capacity to combat our atavistic terror of time and space. Demonstrating that the matrix of the body is the same as that of building-bodies, Pastor's drawings reveal the bittersweet sense of the work of the architect, where the infinite possibilities of body-images are employed in order to locate the pattern of time and space to be embodied in any construction intended for fostering a *vita beata.*

Vive feliciter.

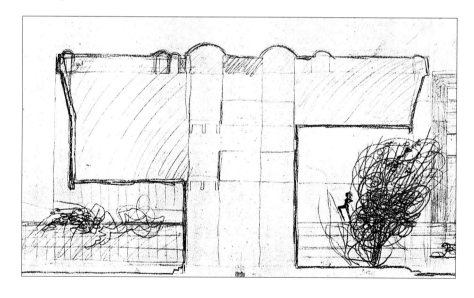

16.6
Valeriano Pastor, sketch for the District School Center near Dolo. Sectional drawing through the main building with dancing female. (From *Anfione Zeto, 1,* 1989)

17

David Leatherbarrow

Sitting in the City,
or The Body in the World

Despite the seemingly reasonable assumption that conditions as distinct as being in and outside an architectural enclosure require equally distinct ways of thinking about the body and the settings it inhabits, Joseph Rykwert suggested at the end of "Meaning and Building" that the two should be seen as one—that architects should think about the body within an interior in the same way they imagine it within the environment.[1] Perhaps this suggestion made some years ago now seems uncontroversial, for widely shared notions about the unity and centrality of individual experience, the continuity of space, and of the several scales of architectural design (from an interior to the building to the neighborhood) assume the indivisibility of the interior and exterior and of our experience of them, even if most design projects actually focus on one scale and site or another—the room or the street. What is more, the central motif of modern architectural space—whereby the inside and outside of a building are connected—suggests that these two topics can be seen as part and counterpart. Yet aside from the suggestive elaborations of the concept of the environment in ecological theory (Max Oelschlaeger's writings, for example) and the social science of everyday praxis (the texts of Pierre Bourdieu or Henri Lefebvre), architecture's role in establishing this connection remains rather unclear, or unclearly discussed, perhaps because the vocabulary of space we normally use to discuss the environment is conceptually vague and technically narrow. Further, and paradoxically, when architects concern themselves with the vicinity as well as the building, the more comprehensive territory is often treated as if it too were an "object of design." This involves substituting a singular vision for the range and diversity of interests, motifs, and patterns that typically characterize an urban setting.

This chapter takes up Rykwert's invitation to consider the designed interior as part of the environment and to do so from an architectural point of view, intending to complement but not restate arguments made by others concerned with "material culture," such as those named above. In the arguments that follow I introduce and partly redefine the term *topography,* to name a horizon of architectural work that is more inclusive than the outer walls of a building and is indicative of the existence it sustains, a wider horizon of physical and spatial conditions that traces typical human affairs. Because I oppose totalizing design practices, I also outline a kind of architectural work that recognizes its own limitations, not, however, territorial limitations—the edges of a parcel of land a client happens to own—but limitations on one's ability to envisage and project a "complete world." I consider what Rykwert called the "semantic" aspects of the built world, as well as the habits and histories of the human body within it; I mean that situated and ambulatory locus of the memories and anticipations through which each of us knows and lives in the world. Just as I want to observe the building being "occasioned" by its vicinity, I want to see the body emerging out of the lived world, but also disappearing into it, testifying to the world's ontological priority. Rykwert's concluding passage still provokes reflection on the status of the body: "Every moment of perception contains a whole personal and collective past, our body is the incarnation of that past; and with every moment of perception this past is reordered and revalued."[2]

In the first years of the twentieth century, no other architect proposed the interconnection between the interior setting and the environment more insistently than Frank Lloyd Wright. Because he wrote so much, it is risky to suggest that any single theme is primary in his texts, but the notion of organic unity, to which he returned repeatedly, must be seen as among his most important. The late, more or less midcareer, summary presented in *The Natural House* can be taken as an adequate account of his understanding of this concept. He explained that after the Winslow house of 1893 his conception of the wall changed; simply put, it was no longer the side of a box.[3] The wall was still a means of protection against environmental inclemencies, but it had become both less and more than that. After being reduced in length or interrupted in its perimeter continuity, it took on the role of bringing "the outside world into the house and let[ting] the inside of the house go outside." Obviously doors and windows had done that before the "box" was broken, but not as fully. The wall was becoming a screen, a means of spatial extension that would permit the "free use of the whole space without affecting the soundness of the structure." The milieu into which the interior was extended, or with which it was now connected, was not only the building's immediate vicinity but also the greater region surrounding the site.

The step was consequential, for the abbreviation of the wall led to changes in what was built on either side of it, in the building's furnishings and gardens. Not only were they reshaped in what was to become the Wrightian manner—extended and superimposed horizontal planes—but more basically, they became subject to design and construction technique and shaped as if they too were permanent parts of the house, of the same fabric or weave, parts of a single, "simple," "integrated," and "organic" whole. "Breaking the box" thus extended not only the house but also the authority and responsibility of the designer. Wright intimated this in an account of the ruined finances of his early clients:

> The clients themselves usually stood by interested and excited, often way beyond their means. So, when they moved into their new house, quite frequently they had no money left . . . and had to drag their old furniture into their new world. Seldom could I *complete* an interior because the ideal of 'organic simplicity' seen as the countenance of perfect integration naturally abolished all fixtures, rejecting the old furniture, all carpets and most hangings, declaring them to be irrelevant or superficial decoration. The new practice [of organic design] made all furnishings so far as possible integral parts of the architecture.[4]

The same was true for the building's outward extension: no "planting was to be done about the house without cooperating with the architect." Nor was a sculpture or painting to be "let in" unless approved by the architect. Whenever this restriction was ignored, there was "trouble." Clients, Wright wistfully noted, sometimes held onto furnishings and rearranged garden layouts, compromising unity for the sake of familiar forms. So did the sculptors, painters, and gardeners with whom he sometimes worked. At best, and "only in a grudging and dim way did most of them even understand" the idea of such a synthesis. But there was a way to avoid this sort of trouble: Wright would make designs for all of it—all of the furniture, the gardens, and applied art—on the assumption it was better to "design *all* as integrated features" (figures 17.1 and 17.2).[5] Thus, from lamp to table, table to room, room to room, and all of this to the site, he composed everything as if it were a single "world," each setting and scale on the verge of others. And the divergence went further: just as the house was "integral" to its site, the site was to its region, and the region was to the nation, for his was an American architecture that expressed the essential characteristics of a people and place at all of its scales. Wright's project for the Living City, embodied in the Broadacre City model, elaborated this territorial claim.

The result of organic unity or "plasticity" would be harmony, he said—essentially the same as the harmony of nature, which is always self-same throughout, purposeful and beautiful. This idea of harmony was clear to Wright even in his early years, for already in 1896 he observed that in nature, all things "harmonize with the whole." Never is one figure shown in relief at the expense of the rest; nature shows that "all arrangement is organic and

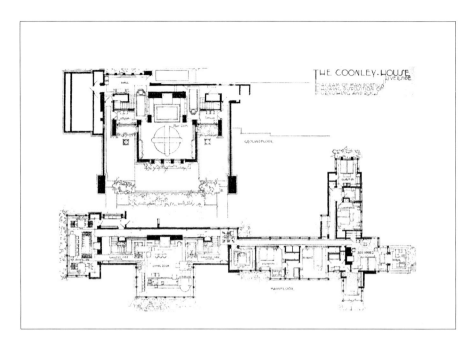

17.1
Frank Lloyd Wright, Coonley
House, Riverside, Illinois, 1907.
Plan of furnishings and carpets.

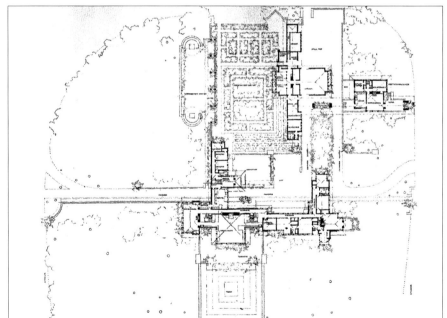

17.2
Frank Lloyd Wright, Coonley
House, Riverside, Illinois, 1907.
Plan of terraces and gardens.

therefore complete in itself." Accordingly, or analogously, architecture should have "the *repose* which only a sense of *completeness* can give [my italics]."[6] He argued these points a few years later under the title: "The Modern Home As a Work of Art," anticipating the totalizing authorship that was to become his practice in later years.

In 1896 another architect concerned with "the home as a work of art" left America after a three-year stay and returned to Vienna, having visited not only Chicago but also New York, Philadelphia, and St. Louis. Given this architect's great enthusiasm for America, it is important to stress that the *abendlaendischer kultur* to which he referred in the subtitle of his short-lived journal *Das Andere* was not the America of Frank Lloyd Wright, or that of "organic simplicity" diverging from the dining table to the hillside. For Adolf Loos, *abendlaendischer* meant not only the United States but also, and perhaps more largely, England. Loos infrequently mentioned architects in his writings; Wright's name is hardly prominent. Had he been discussed, he might well have been treated as a European, for his work clearly intended a domestic *gesamtkunstwerk*, the sort of compositional synthesis that became the object of Loos's stinging critique. Does this mean that Loos, and those who saw architecture similarly, disavowed the interconnection between the interior and exterior proposed in "organic design"?

"*Completeness*" is the central point of attack in Loos's "The Poor Little Rich Man."[7] Summarized briefly, the text presents a parable about total design, or the consequences of art governing the patterns and style of prosaic affairs. Loos describes a client whose talented architect "had forgotten nothing, absolutely nothing. Cigar ashtrays, cutlery, light switches—everything, everything was made by him." Expressed in all of these artifacts, and the house itself, was not some vague or generalized local, regional, or national characteristic of Austria or America, but the character and personality of the owner. This made it familiar, intimately, even psychologically so, but also complete, completely new, so much so the architect had to supervise the inhabitants during their first few weeks in the house in order to prevent the misplacement or substitution of an object by accident or illusion of convenience. The architect's visits were, however, inadequately preventative: "trouble" occurred when the hapless owner received and wanted to display a few birthday gifts. In reply to a request about their placement the architect thundered: "How do you come to allow yourself to be given gifts! Did I not design *everything* for you? Did I not consider *everything*? You don't need anything more. You are complete."[8] There were to be no more gifts for the poor little rich man, nor were there to be painters, artists, nor craftsmen; nor the desiring, striving, and developing that defines every individual's life. Thanks to the architect, the client was finished. *Complete.* That the individual could be identified with his surroundings was by this time a familiar conceit. Nineteenth-century writers in and outside architecture, such as César Daly and Edgar Allen Poe, had argued for this identification, and impressionist and symbolist painters had developed it into the principal subject matter of turn-of-the-century portraiture (Vuillard, Degas, or Sargent, for example). In Loos's parable the finality of the inventory of utensils was as important as its entirety; he ridiculed its once-and-for-all, unchanging, or atemporal character, for the unhappy client soon discovered what it was like "to go about life with one's own corpse." At risk in totalizing or complete design is not only spontaneity and choice but freedom.

Perhaps I have been unfair to Frank Lloyd Wright in directing Loos's irony and invective toward him. The designer whom Loos actually seems to have targeted was Josef Hoffmann. But alternatives could also include Joseph Maria Olbrich or Henry Van de Velde. Even architects from Britain, the pinnacle of *kultur* that was to "guide" Austria, can be seen as targets for Loos's critique. An obvious case would be Charles Rennie Mackintosh, whose works appeared in the eighth exhibition of the Wiener Secession in 1900 (the year of Loos's article), an exhibition that attracted about 25,000 visitors, of whom Loos was most certainly one. In praise of the exhibition, *Ver Sacrum* announced: "Those who have attained the heights of civilized refinement in their daily life, even if they have otherwise little time for art, make certain demands upon the things which serve them, upon their whole environment, demands which can only be satisfied with art."[9] Two years after the exhibition, in "Seemliness," Mackintosh repeated this conclusion in his call for "improvement in the design of everything . . . [proposing that] artistic intention [be] evident in the making or adornment of each article of everyday use or requirement, [assuming] a discriminating thoughtfulness in the selection of appropriate shape—decoration—design for everything no matter how trivial."[10] The Ladies' Luncheon Room in the Ingram Street Tea Rooms is a good example of this. From the large gesso panel on the back wall, to the screen wall below, the furniture, and the table setting, everything was designed by the architect or one of his collaborators—even the clothing of the waitresses (figure 17.3)—hence the uniformity and the complementarity of colors, the repetition of shapes and motifs, and the room's complete seemliness.

Given the irony of the "Poor Little Rich Man" text, it is hardly surprising to find Loos proposing just the reverse approach to residential furnishings: "I considered the design for a new dining room chair to be foolish, an utterly superfluous foolishness which entails a waste of time and effort. The dining room chair of the Chippendale period was perfect. It was the solution . . . just like our forks, swords, and screwdrivers."[11] Good solutions are inherited, tradition supplies the equipment of the domestic interior: "The best form is always already given and no one should be afraid to use it, even though it may come almost en-

17.3
C. R. Mackintosh, Ladies'
Luncheon Room, Ingram Street
Tea Rooms, 1900, reconstructed
by Glasgow Museum.

tirely from someone else."[12] The best way to invent new solutions is to neglect this inheritance as well as the practices through which it renews itself: "Those who have no table manners . . . find it easy to design new forks. This they do with artistic imagination." Does this sense of historical continuity isolate the interior from the exterior, insofar as the city, the modern metropolis, had in these years apparently dispensed with traditional patterns?

Loos's critique of artistic imagination weakens design, or at least reduces its scope and abbreviates its need to originate the forms that will "guide" modern life. It also problematizes the role of art in architecture, particularly in the typical settings of the house, their architectural (spatial) definition and their equipment. Yet even more important for me is the fact that this sense of the interior also redefines the relationships between different settings, both in and outside the building. Against the ideal of uninterrupted continuity, or formal sameness among the parts of an ensemble, Loos proposed differentiation and complementarity—not a "verging" but a reflexive or reciprocating spatiality. This was to be accomplished in several ways. First, differentiation was thought to be a matter of the physical body of the room, its materials: their "temperature," their dimension, and their situation within the extended topography. Loos's paper on the *bekleidung* principle explained that

different settings have different "effects." Each setting and associated effect is first envisaged by the architect and then realized through the selection, assembly, and finishing of materials. But the setting's temperature is not all that distinguishes it from others; equally important is its size. Presupposed in the *raumplan* configuration of settings is their dimensional differentiation: "Every room requires a specific height (the dining room needs one different from the larder) therefore ceilings must be arranged at different levels." But the *raumplan* also proposes the differentiation of volumes and their combination into one "unified" configuration.

Considering Loos's "distribution of volumes in space," many authors have described the *raumplan* as a way of treating the architectural interior as a world unto itself, a technique of structuring or ordering settings that are isolated from the public realm.[13] The usual support for this interpretation is an isolated phrase from Loos's essay *Heimatkunst*: "*Das haus sei nach aussen verschwiegen, im inneren offenbare es seinen ganzen reichtum*" [The house should be reticent on the outside and unveil its entire richness on the inside].[14] That his buildings were rich on the inside cannot be denied; this is apparent in their cladding materials and their sectional geometry. But if the sophistication of Loos's three-dimensional configurations cannot be denied, neither can their "integration" into the vicinity in which they were sited, for the "*miteinander verbinden*" (interlocking) of room to room in a "plan of volumes" was also a binding together of interior and exterior settings, even if large openings of the sort Wright proposed (window walls) are not in evidence. One cannot have reciprocity without distinct boundaries, without separation, between the corresponding parts.

Loos's argument about "reticence" or *Verschwiegenheit* concerned not only facades but also monuments and streets—those in old Vienna, as well as examples in German and Italian cities, with which Viennese examples could be compared. Critics of Loos's work have over stressed the "modernity" of his white walls; for Loos they were modern and historical. Worse still, the notion that Loos's reticent facades were without precedent in the vicinity of his buildings has encouraged neglect of the correspondences between the interiors they enclosed and their settings whether suburban or urban. In fact, the interiors and the facades were sited within a topography that tolerated both consonance and dissonance.

Hermann Czech and Wolfgang Mistelbauer have shown in their marvelous study of Loos's building on Michaelerplatz in Vienna that the building's site plan, section, and construction details were developed in dialogue with its ambient circumstances.[15] Loos himself prompted this interpretation, explaining, for example, that the limewash of the upper floors was a way of establishing continuity with Viennese street architecture: "*Wien eine kalkputzstadt ist*," he said. Czech and Mistelbauer have shown that spatial connections were also carefully structured. I believe the same reflexive relationships can be observed in Loos's other urban projects, the American Bar on Kärtner Strasse and the so-called Café Nihilismus, for example (figure 17.4). And I think his houses were conceived similarly. Considering the Moller or Rufer houses in Vienna or the Müller Villa in Prague (figure 17.5), one could reconstruct the distribution of settings inside their walls by considering carefully the opportunities for repetition and contrast latent in their sites, interpreting the vicinity as a set of "predispositions" within which a "plan of volumes" could be developed: entry at the front, service at the back, morning light from one side, quiet on another, and so on. One could develop such an interpretation because one knows through cultural experience how rooms of various types are typically oriented in typical sites, near to or far from this or that ambient quality. This is not to say that design in this sense involves the comprehensive duplication of models; instead, it develops systematic deviations from them, in recognition of or response to the exact particulars of the project, which devolve partly from its modernity. A reconstruction of the building's section from an interpretation of its vicinity, such as I am proposing, would not be error free, but it would not be impossible either. The *raumplan* is as much a function of the opportunities of the building's surrounds as it is of internal relationships and dependencies, the latter being insufficient in themselves to determine any configuration. More emphatically without the salient characteristics of the vicinity, Loos would have been at a loss to determine the most basic of topics such as window sizes and their location, the orientation and extent of a terrace, and the

17.5
Adolf Loos, Müller Villa, Prague, 1930. (Photo: Albertina, ALA 2472, no. 700/90)

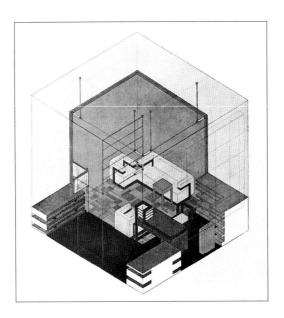

location of an entry. In other words, he would have been lacking exactly half of what it takes to establish a configuration of rooms in a way that would make them not only useful but significantly or "semantically" so. I do not mean to say the site, any more than the typical dining room, predetermines the solution, simply because it has been "received via tradition." Rather, both "inheritances" (the site and the program) serve as predispositions, pretexts, or first premises for design. Site and program or place and plot outline the basic limits of a possible configuration, against which topographical invention works itself out through modification, contrast, and differentiation, to the degree that design judgment determines is right. This decision making is where design technique (geometry) is guided by nontechnical and nonteachable forms of understanding, which in brief can be called practical or ethical understanding. The matrix of differently qualified settings that results from both kinds of understanding constitutes a legible terrain of affairs or topography that discloses the building's participation in a collective past through its modification of the forms in which that past had been known.

The aesthetic unity Loos criticized in "Poor Little Rich Man" was rejected by others in the period of early modern architecture, but on different grounds. The stylizing that typified late art nouveau or arts and crafts interiors was criticized by functionalist architects because it seemed to be insufficiently attentive to practical requirements. Moreover, from the functionalist point of view, Loos's work too was stylized—at least the Chippendale chairs that he installed into his houses, and the "tradition" to which he referred was bourgeois.

Thus, while it may seem sensible to challenge his work as the sort that uncritically affirms the status quo, it should be seen as the result of an attempt to modify or guide the status quo, as a conservative *and* progressive attempt. Nevertheless, in place of what they saw as stylized unity, functionalist architects seem to have substituted another form of compositional synthesis: images of functionality. As least that was the conclusion reached by one of Loos's near contemporaries in Vienna, Josef Frank. As with Loos's criticism of aesthetic unity, the problem Frank had with functionalist compositions was their finality:

> The mad desire for the uniformity of form, for the endless set, the basis of the antiquated idea of applied art as *a closed system* is unchanged [in functionalism] and it cannot understand how many-sided our lives have become, how everything that exists must be a part of it. Our era is the whole known of historical time. This idea alone can be the basis of modern architecture [my italics].[16]

More aggressively he wrote "I am of the opinion that anyone who has the desire to rest his posterior on a rectangle is in the depth of his soul filled with totalitarian tendencies."[17] German architects associated with the Werkbund or participant in the Weissenhof Siedlung—Mies van der Rohe and Walter Gropius—had these "tendencies." Perhaps an even more vivid example of this tendency is Gropius's office in the Bauhaus, drawn by Herbert Bayer (figure 17.6). Frank's rejection of any kind of synthesis—organic, aesthetic, or functional—is even more apparent in the assertions he made about domestic interiors in his late and very provocative paper "Accidentism": "The living room, where one can live and think freely, is neither attractive nor harmonic nor photogenic; it came about as the result of accidental events, which will never be finished, and by itself can absorb anything whatsoever to satisfy the owner's varying expectations."[18] This paper was written in Sweden, to which Frank had returned after his rather unsuccessful World War II years in the United States, a period that ended with an exhibition of his furniture in Edgar Kaufmann's department store in Pittsburgh, Pennsylvania, an exhibition that seems to have led to the arrival of one his chairs in Fallingwater, no doubt despite Wright's desire for organic unity.

Unlike Loos, Frank designed a great deal of furniture—over two thousand pieces, in fact. Nor did he advocate the use of forms "received via tradition" or not these only. Just as the rooms of a house were to be furnished over time, they could incorporate examples from different periods. His arguments against unified interiors led him to reject synthesis at the scale of the room and of the ensemble of elements: "Each [piece] must be independent of the rest, obstructing nothing and only giving the impression of belonging together as a 'group' in this particular context. We no longer need 'sets' consisting of two inseparable easy chairs, a couch, and a table."[19] Thus, pieces from different periods could be arranged together (figures 17.7a and 17.7b). Having been so arranged, each could, in time, be replaced by some other. An architect could propose such a change, as could someone living in the house. Pieces were chosen, placed, and preserved as long as they accommodated and represented a "set" of practical affairs, the "unity" of which was not formal but situational. If a fabric metaphor is useful, the craft of room construction was no longer weaving but stitching or sewing. It was the kind of assembly that brought together pieces that pre- and postdated the architect's project. This stance weakens the authority of the designer, or transforms architectural invention from the discovery of new shapes into the interpretation of recurring and contemporary dwelling situations.

The most striking aspect of Frank's arguments about such a fabric is that the adjustable synthesis proposed for the living room was also to be found in the street, as if the architect were to consider the environment like the interior, as if both were designed and "undesigned," which is to say interpreted and acknowledged: "The conditions valid for making living rooms comfortable are likewise valid for houses, streets, and cities whose present rigid forms are making their inhabitants homeless (*heimatlos*)."[20]

Josef Frank's doctoral dissertation examined the buildings and ideas of Leon Battista Alberti.[21] He focused on Alberti's churches—their motifs and typical forms. Apart from struggling with the "modernity" of Alberti's work, he drew comparisons between church and domestic architecture. This style of interpretation was not new to Frank; others had proposed these comparisons, and Alberti himself established analogies between different types, most famously between the house, the city, and the body, following ancient precedent. Frank's version of the analogy was set forth in a key article, "Das Haus als Weg und Platz."[22] He compared the center of the house to the piazza of the town, domestic passages to streets. These comparisons were not new, nor are they particularly significant, except insofar as all analogous forms—the living room, piazza, passage, and street—were understood as incomplete or always capable of being rethought and reformed. Frank observed that the rules for a good house never change in principle, yet he argued they must be "continually considered anew." Such consideration would question the way the garden is entered, the layout of the entry sequence, the opening of the entry door, the passage from the vestibule to the living room, the configuration of seating with respect to the door and window, and so on. Questions such as these, those of typical situations and practical affairs, must be asked anew because dwelling interests change, no matter whether one is considering the kitchen or boulevard. Asking and answering questions such as these is the basis for an architecture that would be "modern," and such architecture would be apparent both in and outside the house. Topography so conceived does not project settings that verge toward

17.7a–b
Josef Frank, Beer House,
Vienna, 1930.
a. Hall from above.
b. Hall from below.

and away from one another, as did Wright's, or the reciprocities envisaged by Loos. Instead, it is based on analogies and projects a field of similarly structured (and unstructured) practical situations. Such an ensemble is neither continuous nor discontinuous, concordant nor discordant; it is a field in which reiterations play against one another, each inviting choice and sustaining both historical memory and contemporaneity.

Another architect who came under Loos's influence in Vienna merits consideration because he introduced yet another sense of the relationship between the interior of a building and the environment, one that echoes Josef Frank's sense of unity devolving from the domestic *lebensraum,* but also recalls the aesthetic or compositional synthesis of Wright's work. After studying with Adolf Loos for one year, Rudolph Schindler left Vienna in 1914 for the United States, traveling from New York to Chicago, where he worked, but not in Wright's office until 1917. Work for Wright took him to California in 1920, where he eventually set up his own office, although he continued to work for Wright until 1923. But before then, while still in Chicago, he designed the Buena Shore Club (1916–1918), the only large building he completed. The building no longer stands and has been largely neglected in Schindler scholarship, but it indicates themes that were to preoccupy him throughout his career.[23]

In his own account of the design, Schindler emphasized topographical concerns: "Right at the sandy beach [of Lake Michigan]—below street grade, the planning Architect began to start his building, growing gradually to higher levels, as it is stepping back from the border of the water. The beach and the sea wall, the sunken garden with its banks and walls, the walls, the terraces and roofs—up to the street grade and still higher—up to four floors."[24] Both this passage and Schindler's perspectives describe a stepping or stratified spatiality that links together by sectional increment the watery origins of the site, the surrounding city, and the remote (because elevated) recesses of the building (the private rooms above those for card playing and billiards). Precedents for this stepped section and configuration of gardens, courts, interiors, and terraces can be found in much of Wright's work, particularly Midway Gardens of 1914. Wright's writings also seem to have anticipated Schindler's thinking. While still in Vienna, Schindler would have had access to Wright's Introduction to the 1908 Wasmuth publication of his projects, in which he advocated horizontal extension, sectional stepping, and the assimilation of the building into the "prairie" horizon.[25] But the comparison with Wright is not the only one that demonstrates Schindler's interests and background. Considering the three-dimensional relationships of the Buena Shore Club, those between the beach, the gardens, the dance hall, the "living room" above it, the porch/dining room/terrace, and the library, one can identify this configuration of volumes with the *raumplan* spatiality of Loos. Each setting has its own "temperature," dimensions, and sectional position (between the water, the street, and the roof), and they are interlocked with one another. The same concerns inform Schindler's design for the so-called Translucent House of 1927, a design of much more sophistication and subtlety than the Buena Shore Club, although he circumscribed its terrain by perimeter walls and dense planting.

Both *translucency* and *transparency* are indicative terms in Schindler's work. His usage invoked the customary sense of the words, meaning optical or visual conditions, the state of some material being impervious to or penetrable by light or air, allowing one to "see through" partially or completely. But transparency for him was also a quality of things that are familiar or habitually used, and this is an unusual sense of the word. Transparent figures were those that were unseen because they were inconspicuous or unobtrusively present in this or that setting. Within settings they are tacit, their significance latent. One is reminded of Loos's quip about the best-dressed man being the one least noticed in public. Schindler's usage, however, was developed in consideration of metal furniture. He wrote:

The few places which are necessarily moveable (chairs, etc.), become so in an accentuated degree. Moving, they are unfit to define the space conception and must therefore be eliminated architecturally for the sake of clarity. They are either folded up and stored away, or made transparent to become inconspicuous. This is the real meaning of the metal chair. Its essence is its transparency.[26]

This quality distinguished all deployable items from those that were built in or immovable, the permanent furniture used to "define" the "space conception." In fact, built-in furniture and architecture were thought to be inseparable, for the house, as Wright had insisted, is essentially a weave that includes walls and windows, beds and bookcases. Spatial ensembles are not stitched together but woven. This again repeats Wright, who had argued for the integration of furnishings into the permanent parts of the building. Wright also took up the issue of "unobtrusiveness" or "inconspicuousness." In the Wasmuth Introduction, he suggested that the several parts of an interior should be designed to "wear well" and have "absolute repose," by which he meant they should make "no especial claim upon attention." For Wright, repose was also a quality of the prairie landscape, and it assumed the completeness of an organic design. Schindler made similar but not identical arguments about a setting's background character: "It must be the basic principle of all interior decoration that nothing which is permanent in appearance should be chosen for its individual charm or sentimental associations, but only for its possible contribution to the room conceived as an organic entity, and as a *background for human activity* [my italics]."[27]

This last passage introduces an instructive contradiction: both movable and immovable furnishing were thought to serve as the "background for human activity," yet the first was to be "transparent" (unseen), and the second to be instrumental in the definition of the "space conception," definition that was surely meant as apparent, even prominent. In what way can both fixed and deployable furnishings be inconspicuous and yet define a room, especially if they are designed as "background," not to be noticed or to obtrude themselves into prominence? Can something built in be transparent, in the sense of being "seen through" and yet still be significant, "semantically" so? Schindler does not identify but certainly implies two kinds of "seeing": a lateral sort that apprehends configurations at the margins of a focused regard and a perspectival sort that concentrates attention. Paintings, not furnishings, are seen in this latter sense. By contrast, the equipment of domestic life does not obtrude itself into one's awareness continually or insistently. Yet somehow it can emerge (from the "transparent" fabric of practical affairs) in order to "define the space conception." Furnishings are sometimes figures, but most times they are background. Not only the "emergence" but the retreat of objects (the table or chair and the body they accommodate) into their vicinity is what needs to be considered and clarified as much as possible.

The relationship between the room and "world" outside it can help with these distinctions. Schindler's arguments about the interconnection between the building and its site

are similar to Wright's in their emphasis on horizontality, but they are not identical. While Wright referred repeatedly to the prairie as a symbolism of the American landscape—platforms "fitting in" with the terrain—Schindler emphasized changes in the ways people had come to understand and use their houses. Perhaps the best outline of his ideas is contained in a short text entitled "Shelter or Playground," the last of a series of articles on the "Care of the Body."[28]

Shelter and playground are alternative ways of seeing the house, each relevant to a historical epoch. In the past, when "the earth, the sky, and the neighbor," were "frightful," the house was envisaged as a shelter; "fear" dictated its form and spirit, hence the emphasis on safety, accomplished by and apparent in "heavy walls, small windows, ponderous grills, thick curtains, and dim light." In the first decades of the twentieth century this way of thinking about the house, and the anxiety implicit in it, regrettably was still common, despite the changes brought about by new construction technologies and new patterns of life. In the future, Schindler announced, the house will "cease being one of dens, some larger for social effect, and a few smaller (bedrooms) in which to herd the family. Each individual will want [and should be given] a private room to gain a *background* for his life. He will sleep in the open. A work-and-play room, together with the garden, will satisfy the group needs. The bathroom will develop into a gymnasium and will become a social center." The site and style of cooking were predicted to change too; they were to become another setting for "group play." This account provides a fairly precise description of the Schindler Chace House of 1921–1922 (figure 17.8).

The rooms in the house of the future will lose their autonomy, their compartmentalization, because they will merge or "melt" into a new "fluidity," as will the house itself, into the "flow" of the wider horizon, for situations previously located within the confines of the "shelter" will discover their furnishings and equipment in the garden, "in the open." I propose naming this lateral repositioning *displacement,* intending to contrast it with the verging, reciprocating, and analogous settings of Wright, Loos, and Frank, respectively.

In consideration of Schindler's arguments and buildings, one can infer that the framework for the displacement of settings and situations is a set of horizontal strata that extend from the recesses of the interior to the expanses of the building's vicinity. Three strata are prominent and recurrent: the horizon of the land, social encounter, and the sky. The emphasis on levels can be understood in contrast with earlier understandings of sectional topography: "The stereotyped form-sentence of the conventional designer: base, body, cornice, crown—has now lost its meaning. The contemporary form-sentence may move horizontally, around the corner, or even downwards . . . our time, with a more democratic scheme, has discovered the meaning of the neighbor and allows us to stretch our hands out horizontally."[29]

The origin of this lateral drift is not only social but postural, the traces of which are apparent in the furnishings we prefer. Schindler suggests but does not elaborate a history of postures. There was in these years, he said, a tendency to seek the horizontal as a more relaxed position. This was not so in the past; previously furniture had leaned against the wall. Now it "merges with the floor." The carpets, pillows, and low benches shown in all the views of Schindler living rooms (figure 17.9) are receptacles and signs of this horizontal inclination. The same is true for the articulations at the midlevel of the room, from sill and table to typical shelf height: "The imaginary horizon in the room has dropped from door to elbow height. This divides the room at a lower height and increases its spaciousness." Similarly, the concentric arrangement of furnishings had given way to linear configurations not bounded by the house's thermal barrier. Schindler invented storage "units" that could be deployed throughout the house. Like the house itself, they were low and wide, not intended for an upright position against the wall. When placed above one another, "they established

17.9
Rudolf M. Schindler, Schindler
Chace House, Los Angeles,
1921–1922. Living room.

several horizontal planes throughout the room, giving the furniture the character of floor terraces." The idea that a piece of furniture could be conceived as a terrace suggests its potential for relocation or displacement, so too for other "permanent" fixtures in the house.

Two of the most celebrated aspects of the Schindler Chace house are the exterior fireplaces and the rooftop "sleeping baskets." Both exemplify the displacement of settings that are typically thought to be "interior," and both demonstrate ways of interpreting the potentials of topographical strata. The floor slabs of the house comprise one level of the site section. Their use inside the house is obvious, but they are not confined to its limits, to those of the thermal barrier. As if to serve as the basic premises of an "encampment," the slabs extend into the garden court and serve as the surface on which open-air fires could be ignited. Overhangs above some of these slab extensions annexed into the holdings of the house other stretches of the surrounding gardens, insofar as they cut patches of shadow out of the sun's brightness and thereby marked thresholds between interiors and exteriors. Rooftop beds blanketed by canvas covers and the sky were displaced not laterally but vertically, defining levels within the sky horizon. Viewed in plan, the topography can be read as a mosaic of dwelling platforms, each providing no more than a pretext or premise for some practical purpose and preferred posture. Frequently they are not in typical positions. Nevertheless, the ensemble as a whole served as a "background for life," one that was meant to be unobtrusive in its presence and latent in its significance, marginally indicative of some situation.

Given Schindler's acceptance of the basic principles of much of Wright's built and written work, it is not surprising that he invoked the concept of the organic in explanation of his buildings. What is more, the outcome of organic composition was described as a unified ensemble, a synthesis. Having circled back to this ambition, after considering the counterarguments of Loos and Frank, it is now possible to turn to the problem of unity or wholeness itself in an attempt to indicate the ethical and philosophical implications of its different meanings.

At least two primary senses of unity can be discovered in the work of these architects, formal and practical unity. I propose this distinction even though much of the work I have considered resulted from efforts to make the first dependent on and expressive of the second. Wright's arguments in favor of plasticity and organic synthesis—verging spatiality— were based on his criticism of boxed-in enclosures. Schindler repeated this criticism and proposed a "fluid" alternative, in which settings could be freed from their traditional moorings and allowed a striking degree of leeward drift. In both cases, the "box" was a symbol for settings that were closed in on themselves, unified within perhaps, but isolated in their context—suffocatingly so. Both Loos and Frank also criticized closure—not in its spatial manifestation but for its effect on the inventory of domestic equipment, from the ashtray to the painting. Confined to surroundings in which everything has been designed, the life of the poor little rich man was not only "complete" (fully taken care of) but "finished" (over and done with). Josef Frank found the prejudice in favor of a "set" of "functional" furnishings evidence of totalitarian tendencies. Even more than Loos, he was against the atemporal or unchanging character of such a synthesis or "system"—hence, the assimilation of ages in his modernity and his acceptance of "the occasion" and "accident" as part of project making. The complete set, like the box within which it was shelved, contained and constrained existence against the practices it sought to perform—those present in one's memory and anticipation. Thus the alternative: instead of a formal synthesis, each of these architects proposed a unity that somehow reflected the pattern of typical situations, in both its spatial and temporal aspects. Yet Wright's articulation of this pattern also demonstrates his manner of stylizing, as did Schindler's to a lesser degree. Authorship was less in evidence in Loos and Frank, particularly the latter, whose sense of "accident" emphatically disavowed representational synthesis, even though he sometimes simulated chance encounters, particularly in the plans of his late houses.

I have called the architectural setting a *trace*. By this term I mean the sediment of some typical practice and its indication. But no trace of this kind can be placeless, even if the elements on which it is inscribed are movable; each one is located somewhere, each one typically here or there. While the settings that trace typical practices are always somewhere, they also always invite or suggest typical forms of appropriation, which means they are "there for that purpose." If elsewhere, their capacity is less, and less apparent. Nothing of this is lawful or fixed. At best one can say that preferred positions are probable within a given cultural context. Insight into likelihood can be gained in consideration of adjacent conditions. Where something is for a typical purpose depends on what it is nearby or what it is there *with:* the bookcase with the desk, the desk with the window, the window with the street—and in reverse. Each element traces aspects of typical situations that are dependent on others, no matter whether the dependency is approximate sameness or difference, gradation or contrast. The topographies of reversal, analogy, and displacement I have described enable and indicate the occurrence of similar and different situations, only some of which need to be constructed, resulting in the affirmation of all the others that have not been designed. The task of topography, which is not that of design, is to posit probable sequences through these relationships, some of which express sameness, others difference. The positive sense of difference is its evidence of the place's historicity. Disjunctions within the horizon of typicalities demonstrate how times have changed and how the inheritance has been recast in response to new interests.

Only in such a field can an event and its setting find a place. In design, architects are always concerned with bounded settings. Consequently we tend to see the field around them as a background, the darkness needed in the theater to show up our performances. Reflection on topography reorients design and thought to the world that is there independent of my knowledge and experience of it, let alone my action within it. This prioritizing of the (undesigned) world, this reaffirmation of the town, no doubt weakens design as originating authorship. Nevertheless, the real prospect for an architecture of our time is still to be found within the horizon of the city, that spatial and material trace of reciprocal interests. The reverse, however, is not true.

18

William W. Braham and Paul Emmons

Upright or Flexible? Exercising Posture in Modern Architecture

Modern functionalism in architecture is dead. Inasmuch as "function" was vestigial, with not even an examination of the Body Kingdom on which it rested, it failed and was exhausted in the Hygiene and Estheticism mystique (The Bauhaus, Corbusier's system, etc.). . . . I oppose the mysticism of Hygiene, which is the superstition of "Functional Architecture," [with] the realities of a Magic Architecture that takes root in the totality of the human being, and not in the blessed or cursed parts of that creature.[1]

I n 1934, Lewis Mumford saw in the demise of mechanistic thinking the possibility of a gentler, more "organic" modern architecture based on the new concepts of "form, pattern, configuration, organism, [and] ecological relationship."[2] A decade later Siegfried Giedion also recognized the "ending of mechanistic conceptions," citing evidence of new paradigms in quantum physics, Gestalt psychology, physiology, and the arts after cubism.[3] This chapter situates the elusive idea of organicism in its mature, late twentieth-century manifestation. Our intent is not to evaluate the fruition of these earlier predictions. Rather, we interrogate the idea of the organic outside the paradigm of historical progress offered by Mumford and Giedion. How does organic thought persist in architecture today, and what does it teach us about our own modern project?

We examine organic thought through the concept of posture, an ideal that is at once intimately corporeal and wholly abstract, referring broadly to corollary concepts of order, ideology, and form. Good physical posture, which requires training and close attention to stance and movement, offers a visible criterion by which the fit and the unfit can be distinguished. Mark Wigley has noted the parallels between the white buildings of the 1920s and the white-clad athletes of the same period.[4] Such parallels extend well beyond the stylistic boundaries of the historical avant-garde, and the criterion of fitness applies at some level to all modern buildings. As Matthew Nowicki observed in the early 1950s, the concept of function (and posture) is itself subject to change, conforming to the new virtue of organic systems and offering new standards for its evaluation: "The recent changes in modern architecture are perhaps as radical as those separating the 1920s from their predecessors. True, we share our vocabulary with this period of yesterday, but the same words now have a different and often basically opposite meaning. We still speak of functionalism, but while then it meant exactitude, now it means flexibility. Those are two opposite concepts."[5] Flexibility has become a central architectural virtue of the new paradigm: flexibility of form, configuration, use, appearance, even of identity.

In her book, *Flexible Bodies,* Emily Martin examined the many paths along which bodily identities have been reconfigured by these shifts.[6] The image of health as a fortress of hygiene repelling an invasion of disease germs that was established in the early twentieth century has been replaced by a more nuanced picture of an immune system that learns and adapts, is weakened or strengthened by other environmental factors, and is, in effect, a microcosm of the larger ecology it resembles. The decentering that has long been examined in psychoanalytical thought appears forcefully in this altered understanding of health and the body; the agencies of health are now multiple. The body-as-system exists in collaboration with its environment. As Mumford and Giedion both argued, we must expect that changed body image to modify our understanding of architecture or, rather, that aspects of the changing subjectivity will be discovered, explored, and demonstrated through building. The body-building connection is not limited, after all, to the visible identity between discrete monuments and unified, proportional bodies. If our bodies are increasingly conceived as dynamic interconnected systems, so too will our buildings be imagined and admired as flexible systems.

Our study focuses on examples for which the ideas of posture and flexibility are central. The first two are athletic facilities, whose role in the development of modern architecture has been largely unexplored. The second is a recent projects developed with advanced animation software. The Payne Whitney Gymnasium, built for Yale University by John Russell Pope in 1932, serves as an example of the earlier, mechanistic paradigm, a monument dedicated to the fitness of upright posture. The Bally Total Fitness chain of gymnasiums, which exploded into national awareness with a provocative ad campaign in 1996, exemplifies the vigorous and highly eroticized view of the flexible athletic body. Bally's building techniques follows a similar ethic. The complementary face of contemporary flexibility appears in the topological work of Greg Lynn, whose architectural designs are executed with software developed for movie animations. We make the unlikely pairing of those two animate figures, the jumping Bally patron with Lynn's moving architecture, to demonstrate the broad presence and appeal of flexibility in contemporary design thinking.

Topological Flexibility

The massive Payne Whitney building (figure 18.1) received an Olympic medal in 1932 for its contribution to athletics, though disputes at the time about the Gothic cladding of its steel frame overshadowed appreciation of its functional interiors.[7] The interiors resulted from years of research into athletic activities and the posture of the ideal athlete, which had

developed from the fresh air and sunshine ethic of the 1920s. Giedion traced that ethic to the marriage of science and medical therapeutics in the mid-nineteenth century and earlier to the revival of gymnastics in the late eighteenth.[8] There is a visible identity at Payne Whitney between the suspended student, correcting his posture by hanging, and the concealed frame of the building, each striving to achieve its ideal form. A further identity exists between the disciplined student's body and the elevated windows that provide light and air while excluding voyeuristic glimpses of the usually naked athletes. Only the therapeutic gaze of the posture camera was permitted.

Bally Total Fitness (figure 18.2) offers a radically different ideal of the bodies, buildings, the institutions that cultivate fitness, and even of design disciplines.[9] Concealed within the sweating figures of the familiar Bally advertisements lie Mumford's concept of organic system and Nowicki's flexible idea of function. The new biomechanical regimes exemplify those concepts, as does the new understanding of health as an extension of the body's immune "system," rather than as a simple defense against disease and germs. Bally's chain store organization, unified by a standardized media image, is a prime example of a flexible business practice and offers a visible departure from the fixed and institutional character of Payne Whitney. The individual Bally store incorporates a family of recognizable components and design themes—of which the most critical are the display window and mirror on the exercise floor—within vastly different sites, configurations, and layouts. Upright

18.2
Bally Total Fitness. Aerobics class.
(Photo: Bally Total Fitness)

posture, once a seemingly immutable ideal, has given way to the flexible virtues of the adaptive system.

In contrast to the virtues of upright posture or of market and component flexibility, Lynn's designs literally flex; they morph and throb on the screen. He describes them as "eco-systems" that "involve a structure that has a range of motion, mutation and flexibility." He continues: "What we used to call bodies have simply mutated and transformed into something else."[10] This "something else" is the flexible network of connections heralded by the simultaneous cultural dissemination of the ecological model of nature and the immunological model of health popularized during the second half of the twentieth century. Using the manipulation of formal parameters via computer modeling, the elements of Lynn's structures maintain dynamic connections to their environment and to one another or, more precisely, to abstracted forces and flows of that environment. The same conditions of change and flexibility discovered in ecosystems and the germ-scape are found in building sites previously viewed as static collections of durable artifacts and meanings. Understanding the urban environment as a system of traffic, activity, resources, and information makes it evident that buildings too exist only as a result of these flows and exchanges.

The comparison between Bally and Lynn's animations, however, is not simple. The operative flexibility of Bally Total Fitness concerns the corporation as a total system, while Lynn's animations provide conceptual adaptations within the process of design, allowing the building to reflect the flows of the site directly. Is this the same as the living flexibility of the mobile animal or of its T-cells? The flexible aspect of Lynn's projects occurs in the kinds of abstraction they achieve. Shrugging off the limitations of normative and static modes of architectural representation, they show, rather than explain, the results of dynamic and nonlinear influences. Those results then have to be translated to static configurations, leaving the animate flexibility behind on the screen. Conversely, the individual Bally's store is adaptable in a very few dimensions. It can accommodate shifts of corporate image and the specifics of new advertising campaigns, but its real flexibility lies in the interchangeability of the stores. Failing stores can be closed for the greater good of the chain, and new ones can be opened in what are thought to be more advantageous sites.

The polarity between chain store interchangeability and the dynamic design processes of the neo-avant-garde indicates the flexible state they both aspire to achieve: the readily changed, constantly adapting accommodation of human habits through construction. That condition can also be explained as the "Body without Organs," described by Deleuze and Guattari—the unique formal potential that arises without external direction from the specific conditions of contemporary life and building. [11] The rigidity of architectual forms impedes the speed at which such new building forms can develop, suggesting that the truly flexible building strives to become more like clothing or cosmetics and that its preferred means of adaptation would be its furnishings and the finishes of its visible surfaces. The sturdy and immobile wall is consigned to the role desribed in Semper's theory of dressing (*bekleidung*), the necessary framework on which the ever-changing finishes are hung.

Wall: Upright versus Supple

The stone wall of the Payne Whitney Gymnasium conforms to the pre-immunological understanding of the body that John Russell Pope would have encountered in the hygiene course required when he studied architecture at Columbia University.[12] The concepts of health, disease, and fitness formalized in such courses operate at many cultural levels, in both rational contexts and, perhaps more important, situations with inadequate information (decisions under uncertainty) or imaginative contexts that exceed rational dictates. The powerful image of the skin as a fortress wall protecting against dirt and disease initially slowed the acceptance of immunizations because the vaccinating needle had to puncture the thin barrier made important by the hygienic regime.[13] The scientific concept of the disease germ, widely accepted only at the end of the nineteenth century, and of fitness as

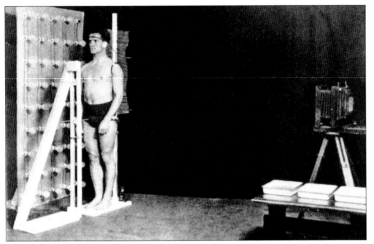

18.3
Posture camera and conformateur.
(Photo: After T. Cureton, Jr., 1941)

18.4
Conformateur. (Photo: After T.
Cureton, Jr., 1941)

upright posture both assume a body that is relatively passive, the boundaries of which are determined by a fixed and continuous skin. Flexibility was so rarely discussed that it had to be defined when mentioned in the hygiene literature and was generally considered an undesirable sign of weakness. The analogy also goes the other way. Yale's director of physical education, Robert Kiphuth, whose book *Posture Defects* appeared the year Payne Whitney opened, used the image of an eccentrically loaded column to explain the effect of poor posture.[14] In fact, it was Kiphuth who brought the phrase *body-building* into widespread use.[15]

Under Kiphuth's guidance, Yale's corrective posture training used the very walls of the body-building room of the gymnasium to "plumb and correct the student body."[16] Every freshman at Yale was required to undergo an "objective" posture exam, for which Payne Whitney was specially outfitted. In the posture analysis room, nude students were photographed beside a plumb line and the photos were then analyzed diagrammatically (figures 18.3 and 18.4). Over 80 percent of the students failed and were required to undergo "corrective" posture training provided by the specially equipped building.[17] Concepts from mechanics and statics were applied directly to student bodies, supported by widely quoted studies showing its benefits to mental and moral health.[18] Upright posture, the invisible plumb line of the body, revealed the Ivy League character, serving as well to exclude those judged inadequate. In a Browning poem chiseled around the lobby, "body and mind in balance" took on the precise meaning of measured control as the healthy body was defined by measurable statistical norms.[19]

In contrast, the immunological body wall is a porous system of flows and forces that undermines the significance of the rigid, impenetrable wall. While "flexibility" once im-

Bally Total Fitness. Window and mobile equipment. (Photo: Bally Total Fitness)

plied lack of moral fiber, it now connotes an adroit ability to adjust to changing conditions. This ecological view no longer presumes the primacy of the "right" angle eulogized by Le Corbusier and central to the French academic tradition out of which Payne Whitney emerged.[20] At Bally Total Fitness, where advertisements include the word flexible flashed across bodies in motion, the chain uses hot media rather than building form to propagate its corporate identity. Bally's energetic expansion program, supported by an annual $40 to $50 million media campaign, describes a form of contemporary practice in which monumental form has little place.[21] While the walls of Payne Whitney may still aspire to shape the posture of the Yale undergraduate, those of Bally Total Fitness recede behind the vigorous bodies, the view windows and mirrors, and the specialized equipment of the exercise floor (figure 18.5). The flexible wall of the chain store seeks only to accommodate the hotter changing images of its media identity.

The upright wall has not disappeared, of course, from either day-to-day life or the architectural imagination. It remains a touchstone in the search for architectural authority, offering a point of attack for architects seeking to challenge the concepts of authorship and authority. In an article on the premises of his animation techniques "Blobs (or Why Tectonics Is Square and Topology Is Groovy)" Greg Lynn assails those "tectonic practitioners" who argue "that humans have always structured themselves as 'standing upright' and by extension so should buildings." The negation of the upright wall is not merely an embrace of the nonvertical, but a rejection of the closed, static body in favor of the flexible one. Lynn finds that "the mobile, multiple, and mutable body, while not a new concept, presents a paradigm of perpetual novelty that is generative rather than reductive." The generative

18.6
Greg Lynn, *Blobs.*
Resultant *blob* model derived
from flexible intervention of five
independent modes of programmatic influence. Artist's space
installation, 1995.
(Photo: Princeton Architectural
Press, 1999)

properties of the new body are inspired by the development of "isomorphic polysurfaces," or what in the special effects and animation industry are referred to as "meta-clay," "meta-ball," or "blob' models," and whose adaptive characteristics would certainly have been lauded by Mumford (figure 18.6). Lynn explains, "In blob modeling, objects are defined by monad-like primitives with internal forces of attraction and mass. Unlike conventional geometric primitives such as a sphere, which has its own autonomous organization, a meta-ball is defined in relation to other objects. Its center, surface area, mass, and organization are determined by other fields of influence."[22]

In principle, dynamic modeling techniques allow building designs to adapt themselves to highly specific and local conditions, altering the nature of architectural authorship: "sites become not so much forms or contours but environments of gradated motions and forces," and the architect's task shifts to a role more closely resembling cooking or parenting, introducing "flexible prototypes" into "liquid digital environments," and then guiding their development.[23] This discourse emphasizes the flexible "reconciliation between building and ground," allowing the ground to remain continuous and shifting, while the wall or skeleton of the building adapts and is transformed.[24] Ernst Haeckel's first premise of ecology—that habitats and inhabitants mutually influence each other—transforms into a dream of the wholly supple wall.[25]

Equipment: Fixed versus Mobile

The careful calibration of the walls in Payne Whitney Gymnasium exemplifies the equipmental view for which authors from Jacques Ellul to Martin Heidegger have criticized mechanistic technologies. In the spirit of specialized function, Pope's office tailored each room to its particular sport or use, stacking rooms for boxing, fencing, body-building, and gymnastics, ingeniously fitting squash and handball courts into the deep steel trusses spanning the larger competition spaces of the symmetrically upright building. The building's most memorable unity of function, hygiene, and equipment would have to be the long, narrow corridor to the practice pool where (naked) bathers walked straddling a "crotch spray," which automatically activated as they proceeded to the pool. In room after room, exercise equipment or appliances were almost entirely built into the wall below the high windows. Mechanical exercisers used wall-mounted weights and pulleys to standardize their movements, eliminating "the uncertainty of the human hand."[26] Such wall-based appliances were so ubiquitous that their use was not even discussed in the literature, and they exemplified the permanence and durability expected of both the walls and the exercises built into them.

The appearance of portable equipment reportedly resulted from the demands of the ever-mobile military (whose changing tactics might also illustrate the new ethic of adaptive flexibility).[27] In a Bally gymnasium, freestanding equipment is now used for all forms of training. It can be easily reconfigured and is positioned relative not to walls but to the ubiquitous screens: mirror, window, television, and computer. The rate at which equipment changes far exceeds that of the walls, and the Bally image is largely expressed by secondary elements—banners, awnings, lighting, and signage—which are as easily changed as equipment. The monumental, wall-based equipment at Payne Whitney, conversely, has become a museum of mechanistic body posture, dedicated to the previous paradigm. Revisions have been studied since the 1950s, but, for example, the toilet rooms that were designated for women's use decades ago retain their built-in urinals.

Mobile exercise equipment goes in and out of fashion, like clothing and dietary trends, further reminding us that the state to which flexible bodies aspire consists as much of fleeting images and desires as of physical formations. The surgically and technically enhanced bodies in movies from *Blade Runner* to the Borg of *Star Trek* (including that ultimately flexible, "liquid metal" body in *Terminator II*) further suggest that the new paradigm of flexibility still largely operates as an enhancement to the mechanical body. Accessorized bodies and smart buildings are more clever and quicker to adapt; they learn through feedback and self-regulation. As Nowicki observed, the underlying ethic remains the same, organized according to the narrow concern with function. The examination of flexibility does not offer a simple choice between fixed and mobile, but a caution about the role of function. As Kiesler argued in his own critique of functionalism, "Form does not follow function. Function follows vision."[28]

Windows: Light and Air versus the Gaze

Windows most clearly reveal the dark shadow of flexibility, the aspects that are repressed or excluded from the ethics of agile posture. As the many hygiene handbooks of its time had explained, the operable windows at Payne Whitney were made large and placed high on the wall to maximize natural light and air. And while the building appeared massive on the exterior, its interior was deeply penetrated by six major lightwells, providing inner windows for the major activity spaces and carrying light and air down to the basement rowing tanks. At the summit of the tower sit aerial gymnasiums with three window walls, culminating in a Vita-glass solarium that transmitted the maximum amount of ultra-violet radiation.

High windows make views impossible. The building was originally designed for an all-male school, so women were excluded from all but the first floor. Exercises were largely conducted in the nude, following contemporary ideas of hygiene. Indeed, the clothing reform movement was closely related to the reforming spirit of modern architecture, especially in athletics, where appearance seems to coincide so closely with function.[29] The functional window lies at the center of the reforming, hygienic ethic, providing visible and measurable quantities of light and air.[30] The power of sunlight to kill microbes lent it an authority undiminished until it was discovered that those same ultra-violet rays maximized by Vita-glass also weakened the cells of the immune system. The mechanical view of light confronted its organic understanding. The contradiction between the two ethics is exemplified by the sunbathers of today, still prostrate before the sun but now protected by an invisible layer of sun block. The question of visibility, of the visible tan and the invisible coating, defines the poles of the current situation. And what about the emergence of physical desire in the windowless steam rooms at Payne Whitney, of the "Greek" friendships whose name could not then be spoken? These rooms were later closed in an attempt to regulate inappropriate postures. The techniques of hygiene derive from nothing so much as fear of pollution, whether by germs, ideas, or passions. Exercise might regulate the economies of such pollution, but it cannot eliminate them.[31]

The windows and mirrors of Bally Total Fitness are also its most important architectural feature. Unlike Payne Whitney, these fixed windows rely on mechanical "systems" to condition the air, removing the beads of sweat that are ever-present in the advertisements, and artificial lights provide the dramatic illumination. The "storefront" windows and mirrors function as picture windows of desire. *Advertising Age* described Bally's market segment as "people who want to be where the bodies are."[32] The gaze fixed on the windows and mirrors follows the images projected on television screens. But while its business structure and media campaign give Bally a decidedly successful form of flexibility, its windows and mirrors are bound to a rigid and frustrating heightening of desire. The limitations of voyeurism and the difference between the image of exercise and its actual practice bears out the lessons of Deleuze and Guattari's *Thousand Plateaus:* continually heightened flow of desire is most difficult to achieve (and it can be done wrong).[33] To the patrons walking on the treadmills or climbing the stair machines, the windows offer no more, and often less, than the athletic windows at Payne Whitney. As a an architectural contribution to the art of living and building well, Bally Total Fitness fails (though it may prosper, for a time, in market share and stock price).

The relationship to the video screen poses the critical question for Lynn's animated process of design. The use of animation to flexibly adapt buildings to their dynamic environments is among the most compelling design methods to emerge in recent architectural discourse, but the buildings ultimately become fixed and stable forms by translation, not from animate flexibility. The vigorous final form of the Lynn's Korean church, the first real demonstration of the new paradigm, results as much from the negotiation with construction managers and the limitations of contemporary construction as from the dynamic resolution of site and program. Critics like Michael Speaks have noted the apparent contradiction between the appealing dynamism of animate models and the inherently static nature of buildings. He locates the difficulty in the fixation of contemporary American practice with the relentless production of novel form, a practice generally defended by arguments for the aesthetic autonomy of architecture.[34] Speaks uses the critique of novel and autonomous form to ask for a more flexible form of practice, in effect opening design processes like Lynn's to the market fluidity of a Bally Total Fitness. But the opposition between building form and forms of practice, as insightful as it is, overlooks the traditional "other" of architectural form: matter.

Throughout the discussion of upright posture and flexibility, we receive glimpses of the long-standing opposition between matter and form, specifically the distrust of matter and its tendency to shift and change out of the forms into which it has been fitted. In this sense, buildings are always already animate and changeable. The valorization of flexible change appears provocative because the architectural discourse has for so long privileged the fixed, durable, and upright. The opposition between form and matter, or between fixed and changeable, in turn invokes the rest of the Aristotelian (or Pythagorean) contraries: straight versus curved, simple versus complex, and so forth. These additional associations partly explain the transgressive excitement of flexibility and the equally difficult problem of finding a place for it in the architectural discourse. David Summers has even argued that the disciplines of art and architectural history are so fully constituted around the analysis of form and the identification of authorship and authority, that they risk losing disciplinary identity when they are opened to questions of matter, change, and collaboration.[35]

The original sense of the word *project,* as the projection of a design into an uncertain future of construction and use, suggests not only that buildings have always adapted through the continued intervention of owners, architects, and builders, but that the idealization of architecture as autonomous form belongs to the effort of the profession to define and protect some independent class of work.

Mumford, Giedion, and Nowicki have identified flexibility as a correction to the mechanistic functionalism of early modernism; the urge toward architectural autonomy that characterizes the neo-avant-garde begins as a critique of the same formation. Greg Lynn's efforts to connect his explorations to an ecological understanding of contemporary life and cities promises a departure from that discourse. The comparison to Bally's is instructive, suggesting that in the current marketplace, the dream of endlessly responsive variation takes the form of a media outlet, of buildings as purveyors of signs. It also suggests that the blockages and frustrations of the dynamically flexible body, are not so different from those of the upright one, which suffers from the boredom of predictability and repetitiveness. Endless variation yields its own form of ennui.

Upright or Flexible?

The concept of fitness as an exactitude visible in upright posture seems a lost and somewhat rigid ideal when faced with the modern athlete or business enterprise. Anyone who participated in physical education classes as a child, however, readily understands how bodies are socialized in the locker room. They are not merely physical objects available for medical evaluation but culturally constituted images. The body-building paradigm did not end with either the Renaissance or the historical avant-garde; it continues on new routes with altered ideas of the body. This is not an argument against systems thought in architecture or against the admirable virtue of flexibility, but an effort to recall with Bataille that "the greatest myth of modern man is that he has no myths."[36] Despite the pervasiveness of the systems metaphor, this too is a cultural form subject to manipulation, whether through topological animation or adaptive business practices.

The comparisons of Payne Whitney's monumental presence, the chain store successes of Bally Total Fitness, and Greg Lynn's animate forms allow us to understand yet again the intimacy of bodies and buildings in imaginative constructions. That observation alerts us to historical changes in the quite concrete imaginative terrain we occupy, while permitting us to understand how new images of the body never wholly displace those that preceded them. The virtues of upright posture may be outdated, but the hopes and fears that underlie them persist. Even in the age of immune system training, the simple fear of disease germs and other bodily pollutions remains, transformed into the more ecological understanding of asthma and "sick building syndrome," albeit ready for the fresh air and sunshine provided by upright buildings.

Both the upright and the flexible body make visible the dream of buildings perfectly adapted to their conditions and uses. But more than a mere wish image, that state of ready adaptation constitutes the Body without Organs of contemporary architecture, the much-hoped-for condition of perfect mobility across which newly defined needs can be transmitted as soon as they are discovered. Deleuze and Guattari observed, "It is an inevitable exercise or experimentation, already accomplished the moment you undertake it," while cautioning that "you can botch" the construction of such a condition, "or it can be terrifying and lead you to your death."[37] The twinlike quality of those two appealingly fit figures suggests that the attainment of total flexibility should be delayed as long as possible, allowing each new situation, function, or desire to encounter the resistance of preexisting walls, fixtures, and finishes. Architecture exists only in that delay of flexibility; if it is not botched or terrifying, it can operate as a form of renewal, a body-building kind of exercise.

19

Kenneth Frampton

Corporeal Experience in the Architecture of Tadao Ando

The philosophical alienation of the body from the mind has resulted in the absence of embodied experience from almost all contemporary theories of meaning in architecture. The overemphasis on signification and reference in architectural theory has led to a construal of meaning as an entirely conceptual phenomenon. Experience, as it relates to understanding, seems reduced to a matter of the visual registration of coded messages—a function of the eye which might well rely on the printed page and dispense with the physical presence of architecture altogether. The body, if it figures into architectural theory at all, is often reduced to an aggregate of needs and constraints which are to be accommodated by methods of design grounded in behavioral and ergonomic analysis. Within this framework of thought, the body and its experience do not participate in the constitution and realization of architectural meaning.[1]

A particular concern for the role and presence of the corporeal in Tadao Ando's architecture makes itself manifest at a number of levels at once. In the first instance the austere mass form adopted by the architect, at once geometric and minimal, seems to display an uncanny capacity for revealing the latent characteristics of the site-for bringing these into focus, irrespective of whether the context is a natural landscape or the built-up fabric of a city. As far as the landscape is concerned, we may cite the initial phase of the stepped Rokko housing, terraced into a steep hillside site overlooking Kobe in 1983 (figure 19.1). For the city, we may point to the eight-story perforated concrete cube of the Festival shopping complex that he realized one year later in downtown Naha, on the island of Okinawa (figure 19.2). In both cases, an incisive, precisely structured form affects the site in such a way as to reveal its intrinsic character.

Apart from the catalytic presence of his primary concrete forms, Ando is particularly concerned with the experiencing subject that he characterizes through the term *shintai*, the Japanese word for *body*. This seemingly untranslatable concept, apparently more animate in its connotations than its English equivalent, acquires a particularly heightened significance in the architect's worldview inasmuch as it alludes to a receptive-reactive reflex that the building induces in the subject. Thus in his 1988 essay, "Shintai and Space," he wrote:

> When "I" perceive the concrete to be something cold and hard, "I" recognize the body as something warm and soft. In this way the body in its dynamic relationship with the world becomes the *shintai*. It is only the *shintai* in this sense that builds or understands architecture. The *shintai* is a sentient being that responds to the world. When one stands on a site which is still empty, one can sometimes hear the land voice a need for a building. The old anthropomorphic idea of the *genius loci* was a recognition of this phenomenon.

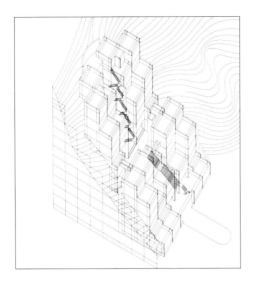

19.1
Tadao Ando, Rokko housing,
phase 1, 1983. Axonometric
showing the midpoint "plaza-
cum-*roji*."

What this voice is saying is actually "understandable" only to the *shintai*. (By under-standable I obviously do not mean comprehensible only through reasoning.) Architec-ture must also be understood through the senses of the *shintai*.[2]

Another way in which the body seems to be inscribed in Ando's architecture may be characterized as ritualistic to the extent that the subject's passage through his architecture invariably involves a carefully orchestrated spatial itinerary. While this last surely derives from Le Corbusier's concept of the *promenade architecturale,* as we find this in his purist villas of the second half of the 1920s, in Ando's case, this passage assumes a more phenom-enological character, as we may judge from his first house, the two-story Azuma residence realized in Sumiyoshi in 1976. This much is evident from the fact that one can pass from the ground floor living room to the dining room or from the dual diminutive living volumes at grade to the first-floor bedrooms only by traversing an open-air atrium, which neces-sarily entails being exposed to the elements for much of the year. Of such a seemingly afunctional arrangement, Ando has written:

I am interested in discovering what new life patterns can be extracted and developed from living under severe conditions. Furthermore I feel that order is necessary to give life dignity. Establishing order imposes restrictions, but I believe it cultivates extraordi-nary things in people.

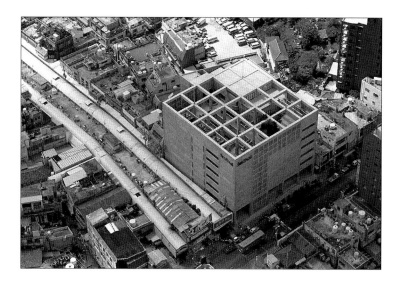

I believe in removing architecture from function after ensuring the observation of functional basics. In other words, I like to see how far architecture can pursue function and then, after the pursuit has been made, to see how far architecture can be removed from function. The significance of architecture is found in the distance between it and function.[3]

This drive toward some kind of phenomenological exposure, in part physical, in part metaphysical, is a constant presence in all of Ando's architecture, although the level and nature of its impetus varies considerably from one work to the next, and even among different sectors of the same work. Seen in this light, a courtyard becomes a space within which the ubiquitous void may be rendered perceivable, partly through changes of light and climate and partly through the changing percept of the space itself. This seems to be close to the idea of *yugen* in Japanese poetry, wherein the ineffable presence of living nature is sensed through such things as a faint drizzle or a sudden unexpected breeze, the onset of twilight or the premonition of dawn.[4]

Something similar is surely present in the prismatic, striated plan of the Koshino House in Ashiya above Kobe (1981), which is inscribed into the topography in such a way as to expose the principal rooms to the full trajectory of the sun. Sunlight enters precipitously into this house from above, through a narrow slot cut into the roof at its junction with a retaining wall. From this aperture, a single shaft of light descends to run its ever-changing

luminous course across the adjacent concrete wall that runs the full length of the living room (figure 19.3). The concrete surface of this plane seems to have been treated in such a way as to effect its dematerialization under the impact of sunlight, to illuminate, through the continual movement of the sun, the latex sheen of its subtly undulating surface. A similar light slot is let into the roof of the radial studio, added to the northern face of the house in 1984. In this instance, the pattern of the changing shaft of light is organic in shape as it falls onto a continuously curved wall.

The Koshino house features a totally different kind of luminosity within its interior, where a shadowy darkness of uncertain depth emanates from the concrete-lined corridor that links the living volume to the bedroom block. Here we are close to that traditional Japanese space of darkness, characterized by the novelist Jun'ichiro Tanizaki in his highly influential critique of Westernization, which first appeared in print in 1934 under the titles *In'ei raisan* (*In Praise of Shadows*). Tanizaki was to describe the symbiosis between Japanese secular and sacred light in terms that seems to parallel the varying levels of luminosity to be found in many of Ando's interiors:

Whenever I see the alcove of a tastefully built Japanese room, I marvel at our comprehension of the secrets of shadows, our sensitive use of shadow and light. For the beauty of the alcove is not the work of some clever device. An empty space is marked off with plain wood and plain walls, so that the light drawn into it forms dim shadows within emptiness. There is nothing more. . . . We are overcome with the feeling that in this small corner of the atmosphere there reigns complete and utter silence; that here in the darkness immutable tranquility holds sway. . . .

In temple architecture the main room stands at a considerable distance from the garden; so dilute is the light that no matter what the season, on fair days or cloudy, morning, midday or evening, the pale, white glow scarcely varies. And the shadows at the interstices of the ribs seem strangely immobile, as if dust collected in the corners had become a part of the paper itself. . . . The light from the pale white paper, powerless to dispel the heavy darkness of the alcove, is instead repelled by the darkness, creating a world of confusion where dark and light are indistinguishable. Have not you yourselves sensed a difference in the light that suffuses such a room, a rare tranquility, not found in ordinary light? Have you ever felt a sort of fear in the face of the ageless, a fear that in that room you might lose all consciousness of the passage of time, that untold years might pass and upon merging you should find you had grown old and gray?[5]

Tanazaki's hypersensitive awareness of an internal aura or atmosphere as this may be revealed through the mutual interplay of light and material is amplified in Ando's sensibility to include the more dynamic play of light and wind as it affects the body. As he put it in writing of his Koshino house in 1981, "I believe that the architectural materials do not end with wood and concrete that have tangible forms, but go beyond to include light and wind which appeal to the senses."[6]

Here, as Yuzura Tominaga pointed out, Ando seems to have been influenced by that archaic feeling for the natural environment, embodied in the Japanese word *fukei,* derived from the Chinese term for landscape, compounded of *fu* meaning wind, and *kei,* meaning sunlight, and thus implying a panorama continually animated by the play of wind and light. *Fukei* implies an artificial landscape, orchestrated by wind and light and not simply some primordial notion of nature as it is given in the raw.

Despite his stress on the volatile, somewhat intangible concept of *fukei,* Ando has not been consistently antithetical to the introduction of plant material, as one may judge from the first phase of his Rokko housing, where a diminutive plaza is introduced into the general pattern of movement. Thus, in ascending from the ground-floor garage to the upper seven floors of the ten-story, terraced complex, one is compelled to change elevators at the fifth floor and in so doing to cross an open-air plaza between one elevator and the next (figure 19.1). Apart from its challenging character as a hiatus, this is a hybrid provision in that it not only combines the occidental *piazza* with the oriental *roji,* or lane, but it also allows the concrete mass-form to be infiltrated by vegetation at its extremities. Of this he writes: "Here nature is allowed to penetrate the building to some extent. In a few years, the sur-

19.4
Tadao Ando, Mount Rokko Chapel,
Kobe 1985–1986.
(Photo: Mitsuo Matsuoka)

rounding vegetation should grow to the very edge of the building and enter into close relationship with the open space."[7]

In a 1986 interview, Ando remarked on the role to be played by continuity and discontinuity in the spatial organization of his work and on the way in which this relates to the Japanese concept *Ma,* the idea of an interval or a gap in the experience of the space. Thus we find him claiming, in seemingly contradictory terms, "I wish to introduce a discontinuous movement into the total organization of the rooms and spaces. One may have the impression that the rooms are separated but thanks to the discontinuity of *Ma* they are even more closely linked."[8]

The expressive role to be played by spatial discontinuities in his work assumes a particularly dramatic character in his ecclesiastical architecture, above all in the Mount Rokko Chapel overlooking Kobe (1985–1986) and in the Church-on-the-Water built in Tomamu, Hokkaido (1985–1988) (figures. 19.4 and 19.5). In each instance, an ingeniously constructed hiatus plays a prominent role in the *promenade architecturale.* In the Rokko Chapel, the subject enters through an arcade, covered on three sides with frosted glass, before abruptly descending and turning right into a concrete basilica. The ambient light and acoustic tone of these two spaces could hardly be more different, for where the arcade, flooded with crystalline light, resonates with every footfall, the basilica, illuminated by a large side window that opens onto an embankment covered with ivy, is a softly lit volume in which the acoustical tone, like the light, is subdued. The spatial void that separates the glazed arcade from the basilica entrance proffers at the end of the approach the emptiness

19.5
Tadao Ando. Church on the Water,
Tomamu, Hokkaido 1985–88.
Aerial view. Photo: Tadao Ando.

of the sky. There is no visual hint that this analogue for the traditional *torii*-lined temple approach will eventually end in a chapel. The steps that descend sharply at the limit of the arcade dramatize the effect, with figures disappearing below the horizon as they descend the rather precipitous stairway leading to the chapel.

An even more ritualistic approach, also engaging the sky-plane, occurs in the Church-on-the-Water where the promenade assumes a labyrinthine spiral character. One initially approaches the chapel through a short flight of stairs that lead to the highest level of a square viewing platform. Here one finds oneself in a roofless, half-cubic space. This virtual volume is bounded by four orthogonal steel frames, each subdivided by a mullion and a transom. This cruciform framing, repeated for each consecutive space, serve to support sixteen large plate glass panels. As opposed to the translucent arcaded approach to the Rokko Chapel, here the prerequisite wedding procession circumnavigates the interior of a four-sided transparent prism, passing between its glazed perimeter and four freestanding crosses in concrete that bound the empty center of the form. These square-sectioned crosses, almost touching at their corners, enclose a space that is open at its vertices but cannot be entered. This inaccessible roofless virtual cube rising from a translucent skylight framed with cruciform fenestration, over the concrete walled vestry beneath, enables the whole form to serve as a giant lantern at night when the core of the belvedere is flooded with light. The narrow causeway surrounding this core is interrupted on all four sides by short staircases, two ascending and two descending, so that the procession becomes momentarily elevated so as to overlook the landscape before it descends into the church, where the route completes itself by passing through a short radial corridor before entering the volume of the church. Inside, an enormous sliding glass wall framed in a cruciform of steel and covering the full width and height of the volume confronts the congregation. Both the distant landscape and the ornamental lake are framed by this opening, so that the prospect seems to be at once both panoramic and intimate. The congregation faces a steel cross set on the axis of the nave in the midst of an ornamental expanse of water that extends to the right beyond the confines of the chapel. This symbol seems to float above a glistening aqueous expanse that imperceptibly descends through a series of shallow weirs toward a horizontal datum lined with trees. The entire prospect, recalling the vision of Pantheistic, the Prussian painter Caspar David Friedrich (1774–1840), is bounded on one side by a flanking concrete plane that, with its return wall, establishes the *temenos* of the domain. The pool is in fact a horizontally stepped fountain, with the water slowly descending toward a gully on the horizon, before being pumped back to the podium of the church to begin its measured descent all over again.

The way in which the body is successively suspended in this work seems to be redolent with meaning. Thus, in the first instance, the wedding procession is momentarily poised before a panoramic prospect that is framed by the cruciform fenestration of a glass cage; in the second, the subject may glance back into the virtual cube contained by the concrete crosses. These last seem simultaneously to represent and deny the fundamental Christian symbol, for notwithstanding the conventional symbolism, these crucifixes seem to constitute through their repetition an abstract cosmogonic symbol that is inflected both inward and outward—inward toward a void, the floor of which is glazed, and outward toward the constantly changing prospect of the surrounding landscape. The containment and frontalization of this same view within the confines of the chapel, before a single cross, ultimately confirms the Christian character of the work, while at the same time opposing this image to the all-but-pagan character of the superstructure above. These cross-cultural alternations are elliptically alluded to in an essay by the architect, dating from 1989:

The Church-on-the-Water is on a plain in the middle of mountains north-east of the Yubari Range in Hokkaido. Covered with snow from December to April, the area becomes a beautiful white expanse of land. Water has been diverted from a nearby river, and a man-made pond 90 × 45 meters has been created. The depth of the pond was carefully set so that the surface of the water would be subtly affected by the wind, and even a slight breeze would cause ripples.

Two squares, one 10 meters to a side and the other 15 meters, overlap in plan and face the pond. Wrapped around them is a freestanding L-shaped wall in concrete. Walking along the outside of this long wall, one cannot see the pond. It is only on turning 180 de-grees at an opening cut out at the end of the wall that the pond is seen for the first time. With this in view, one climbs a gentle slope and reaches an approach area surrounded on four sides by glass. This is a box of light, and under the sky stand four separate crosses. The glass frames the blue sky and allows one to look up at the zenith. Natural light pervades the space, impressing on the visitor the solemnity of the occasion. From there one descends a curving, darkened stairway leading to the chapel. The pond is spread before one's eyes, and on the water is a cross. A single line divides earth and heaven, the profane and the sacred. The glazed side of the chapel facing the pond can be entirely opened, and one can come into direct contact with nature. Rustling leaves, the sound of water, and the song of birds can be heard. These natural sounds emphasize the general silence. Becoming integrated with nature one confronts oneself. The framed landscape changes in appearance from moment to moment.[9]

Two subsequent structures complete this sequence of sacred works: the Church of the Light of 1989, carefully inserted into an existing ecclesiastical compound in the Ibaraki dis-trict of Osaka (figures 19.6 and 19.7), and the so-called Water Temple, completed on Awaji Island overlooking Osaka Bay in 1991. The *shintai,* to return to Ando's terminology, expe-riences both works in a particularly intense way. In the first case, one enters the church through a triangular gap, or *roji,* created by a concrete wall cutting into the basic orthogo-nal prism of the basilica. Once inside, one finds oneself on a sloping timber floor, made up of roughly dressed planks, stained dark brown in contrast to the shadowy gray, shiny vol-ume of the concrete prism that comprises the main body of the church. The principal source of light enters this space through a cruciform slot cast into the altar wall for the full width and height of the prism. Once again, we have a configuration that both asserts and denies Christianity, for while it is indeed the sign of the cross, this cannot be read in an un-equivocal way by virtue of the fact that the continuous incision divides the altar wall into four dark rectangles. It is a figure-ground play where two different oscillating perceptions have an equal and opposite weight. This basic ambiguity is further activated and diffused by the constantly changing patterns of the sun's rays as these are cast through the cruciform aperture over the inner volume of cube. While entering this simple but deconstructed cam-era obscura, one becomes immediately aware of the resonance of the suspended timber floor. Thus, the space assumes a kinesthetic character not only because of the constantly changing pattern and intensity of the light, depending on the time of day and season of the year, but also because of the sound of one's footfall on the timber floor, together with the combined fragrance of cement and wood emanating from the chamber and the platform.

19.6
Tadao Ando. Church of the
Light, Ibaraki, Osaka 1989.
Interior. Photo: Mitsuo Matsuoka.

A totally different set of psycho aesthetic stimuli is active in the Water Temple at Awa-jishima, for here, after negotiating a screen-wall in concrete, one enters the temple via a narrow passarelle running along the short axis of a gigantic, elliptical lotus basin, this last being cast out of concrete and filled with water. Once again, the subject is made acutely aware of constantly changing natural phenomena; the transforming growth cycle of the lo-tuses as they cover the water together with the waxing and waning of their blossoms, agents being subject both to the seasonal cycle, as they modify the apparent viscosity of the pond. All of this is read at the level of the water as one commences an improbable, single-file de-scent via the concrete causeway and stair into the basin, passing beneath the water surface through a narrow passage, eventually to arrive in a concrete undercroft situated asymmet-rically beneath the surface of the pond (figure 19.8).

This partially subaqueous space is the heart of the institution. It is furnished with a tra-ditional Buddhist, timber-framed inner sanctum painted red, a somewhat compromised provision imposed by the monks since Ando had originally envisaged the space as a hy-postyle hall of red pillars, stopping short of the ceiling to enclose a simple, single statue of Buddha in the center. Irrespective of the final furnishing of the space and the different in-

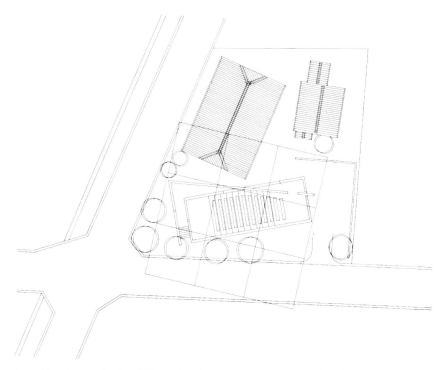

19.7
Tadao Ando. Church of the Light,
Ibaraki, Osaka 1989. Site plan.

tensity of the pigment both within and without the enter sanctum, the ultimate sensous effect is surely quite similar since low-angle sunlight entering from the west diffuses the red color of the timber structure throughout the volume of the undercroft.

In all of these religious buildings, the Corbusian *promenade architecturale* is transformed in such a way as to bring about an intense awareness of both earth and sky. Unlike the elevating *pilotis,* the double-height space, the layered planes, and the ramp rising up to the sky as in the transcendental modernity of the Villa Savoye, Ando's narrative space is compounded of somber bounding concrete walls anchored in the earth, enclosing atria, light slots, and translucent screens and equipped with stairs that seem to be forever descending downward into an undercroft of unspecified depth. Water first enters into Ando's telluric repertoire with his Times shops realized in Kyoto in 1984, where the canalized Takase River runs past the lower podium of the complex and out in a straight line, to terminate on a visibly distant horizon. Water again comes fully to fore as a cosmic element in his Chapel-on-the-Water of 1985, and henceforth it returns in his work with ever increasing frequency, in the Children's Museum in Hyogo (1989), the Museum of Literature in

19.8
Tadao Ando. Water Temple.
Awajishima, Osaka 1991. Lily pond.

Himeji (1991), and the Water Temple on Awaji Island of the same year. The cosmic significance of this element in his work has been well described by the architect himself:

> A stream called the Isuzu River flows through the compound of the Ise Shrine. I find the sight of its pure current very moving and beautiful. Revisiting the river brings back memories I had almost forgotten in the intervening years. Gazing at the long continuous wall that rises from the surface of the water to the level of the eye is strangely relaxing. Perhaps it is because that wall by the water endures even as nature undergoing change and time passes in a never-ending flow.
>
> Water has the strange power to stimulate the imagination and to make us aware of life's possibilities. Water is a monochromatic material, seemingly colored yet colorless. In fact, in that monochromatic world there are infinite shades of color. Then, too, water is a mirror. I believe there is a profound relationship between water and human spirit.[10]

For Ando, water and light are natural, elemental powers the transformations and fluctuations of which across time are the primary interlocutors of his architecture. Thus, the inert concrete planes that invariably embody his work come to be animated by the presence of nature in subtle and diverse ways, from the movement of the wind to the fluctuation of water, from the sensuous pressure of the subject to the constant modification of space under the impact of luminosity. Of this last we find him writing in terms that are reminiscent of Tanazaki:

Light, alone does not make light. There must be darkness for light to become *light*—resplendent with dignity and power. Darkness, which kindles the brilliance of light and reveals light's power, is innately a part of light. Yet, the richness and depth of darkness has disappeared from our consciousness, and the subtle nuances that light and darkness engender, their spatial resonances—these are almost forgotten. Today, when all is cast in homogeneous light, I am committed to pursuing the interrelationship of light and darkness. Light, whose beauty within darkness is as of jewels that one might cup in one's hands; light that, hollowing out darkness and piercing our bodies, blows life into "place."[11]

Finally in his essay on the *shintai*, we encounter a passage in which the body is seen to consummate space, while it, in turn, is conversely consummated by space:

Man articulates the world through his body. Since he has an asymmetrical physical structure with a top and a bottom, a left and a right, and a front and a back, the articulated world in turn naturally becomes a heterogeneous space. The articulation of the world by architecture is in reality the articulation of the world by the workings of mankind. Man is not a dualistic being in whom spirit and flesh are essentially distinct but a living, corporeal being active in the world. The "here and now" in which this distinct body is placed is the point of departure, and subsequently a "there" appears. Through a perception of that distance, or rather the living of that distance, the surrounding space becomes manifest as a thing endowed with various meanings and values. The world that appears to man's senses and the state of man's body become in this way interdependent. The world articulated by the body is a vivid, lived-in space.[12]

Here, Ando is insisting on the indissoluble unity of the mind and the body that in his view ensures the continued existence of culture. To the extent that we find ourselves compelled to differentiate between them in order to maximizes the processes of postindustrial production and consumption, Ando feels that we are exposed to erosive forces that threaten our very existence. Given that the traditional Japanese landscape is self-consciously articulated through subtle modifications of the earth's surface, it is hardly surprising that Ando should emphasize the ambulatory character of the subject. Thus, he envisages our experience of the world as being primarily dependent on our capacity to negotiate the ground:

> Since there has been life on earth it is our feet which reminds us we are alive. We know we exist when we feel it in the soles of our feet and all of us in infancy begin by learning to walk. No matter how computerized the world may become we will probably keep on walking and that will probably be the last thing we feel. If we finally lose all perception of reality our psychological disintegration will follow and in the midst of environmental catastrophe, famine and natural calamities, being alive will mean nothing any more. If the world is determined to destroy itself the only thing architects can do is make sure we don't lose our sense of touch.[13]

For Ando, the main hope for our survival resides in our tactile awareness rather than in the distanciation effected by the power of sight, our ocular senses having long since been overwhelmed by mediatic abstraction. For Ando, advanced technology can be neither denied nor celebrated, nor should it be a model or an instrument of liberation. For him it is merely the productive capacity of an epoch, a device with which to recalibrate the ground, and, above all, an agent with which to empower the subject as a spiritual being.

20

Vittorio Gregotti

Epilogue
Joseph Rykwert: An Anthropologist of Architectural History?

In attempting to define Joseph Rykwert as an anthropologist of architectural history, one runs the risk of falling victim to the modern compulsion for hastily derived labels so dear to contemporary architects. Yet although he may not describe himself this way, I believe it is a notion worth reflecting on. It is, of course, problematic to conflate the disciplines of art history and modern anthropology, the latter having undergone much recent change. Nevertheless, one readily recognizes in the art historical work of Rykwert a strong affinity for the synchronic inclinations of anthropological methodology wherein figurative evidence is used like historical wellsprings in the service of the reconstruction of the history of culture.

Defining Rykwert as an art historian does not adequately explain the particular nature of his work. Thinking of him as an anthropologist of architectural history, however, helps explicate what it is that makes his work so invaluable to us—we architects, in particular, who often use his conclusions as the raw material of our projects. His work always involves something more diverse, a complex but necessary path ending in subtle interpretations. In order to enter into this work, it is necessary to recognize Rykwert's attempt to operate outside the limits of either functionalism or structuralism—the poles between which much of modern anthropological debate has oscillated in recent years. A good example of this is found in his essay on the origin of the Corinthian order, wherein aesthetic judgment is clearly not the principal object of his investigation. Rykwert explains, "I hope to have established that the origin of these elements [of the column types] is not in formal fancy, but that it was a necessary, willed product of the feelings and ideas of the people who devised and used them."[1]

Beginning with the particular quality of a given artifact, Rykwert searches for the non-subjective motivations that precede its construction and from which the work has been produced. Recognizing that all works of art are constructed on the collective ground of time, he searches for the profound reasons and the historical chain of events on which the work rests. By valorizing the content of a given work, well distinguished from its subject, Rykwert operates in a Warburgian tradition more indebted to the cultural depth of Edgar Wind than to the iconology of Erwin Panofsky. Rykwert is similarly intent to discover and bring to light the complex threads that bind the great myths and ideologies of a specific time. Moreover, his gaze invariably focuses on the fabric of the interpersonal relationships that surround a work and influence its making. Biographies of the artists, liaisons, friendships, and intimacies great and powerful are less important to Rykwert, however, than are the great events with which they intersect. Indeed, he often seems to discover in the cross-currents generated by such obscure groups as the Templars, the Masons, or the Jesuits, the fulfillment, and at times the failure, of individual destinies.

In "The Idea of a Town," first published in 1963 as a special issue of Aldo van Eyck's Dutch review, *Forum,* Rykwert makes explicit his anthropological perspective.[2] Subtitled, "The Anthropology of Urban Form in Rome, Italy and the Ancient World," Rykwert examines the relation among spatial models, foundation rites, and religious and juridical associations in the making of a city. Among the books are other important themes: the collective psychology to which these ancient models respond, the motivation of the citizens responsible for choosing a site, the geometrical form of the city and the relational subdivision among its parts.

One of the central problems that weaves together the historical and anthropological perspectives in *The Idea of a Town* (1963) is Rykwert's underlying criticism of nineteenth-century writers on the city. These writers, Rykwert argues, contributed to the conceptual "poverty of much city discourse," due to their inability to represent the city symbolically.[3] But *The Idea of a Town* is certainly not the only book by Rykwert to have been written from an anthropological point of view. In *On Adams House in Paradise* (1972), no less densely interwoven with the histories of intellect, culture, religion, and art, Rykwert takes us on a backward journey that is at once a recollection and a promise.

In *The First Moderns* (1980), the contemporary implications of now-remote events are explored once again. Far more than a chronological history of seventeenth- and eighteenth-century architecture hierarchically arranged in descending order, it is also a point of reference for Rykwert's subsequent works. The intent of this extraordinary chronicle is to seek connections among the key questions of culture, religion, and power—including the manner in which they dialectically move between social groups and ideas, thereby restoring to the reasoning activity of the architect a more complex and profound picture. At the close of *The First Moderns,* Rykwert writes:

Seen from the vantage point of the 1970s and 1980s, Durand's positive dismissal of the problems which engaged and worried seventeenth- and eighteenth-century architects does not seem quite final. The nature of our responses to the world of artifacts, the way in which groups and communities appropriate space, occupies sociologists and anthropologists. . . . Yet their studies are, in the last reduction, almost inevitably about problems of form. This book recalls a time when the architect's business was just that.[4]

This problem of form, far from being an aesthetic problem, is for Rykwert a question of content and of meaning. Central to this is the problem that the same form is open to several interpretations by different social groups in varied situations. Rykwert concludes, "Perhaps, if there is to be a place for the architect's work within a future social fabric, he will have to learn how to deal with such problems again."[5]

But why is a working architect like myself so interested in these ideas? In essays such as "The Sitting Position—A Question of Method," "Learning from the Street," and, more recently, his book *The Dancing Column* (1996), Rykwert has confronted the issues of space and artifice in a manner that is manifestly anthropological.[6] While almost always speaking of the past, he is nonetheless able to influence the project of our own time significantly, helping to explicate some of its numerous difficulties. The best architectural critics of this century have been historians. Often with only a casual connection to the enterprise of architectural production, the expertise they offer is their ability to read a specific work in such a way that one is able to reconnect it to the motives and circumstances under which it was originally produced. Yet the critic is typically preoccupied with "the art in the work," often leading to a false point of departure for further inquiry. As a historian thoroughly grounded in anthropological methodology, Rykwert is preoccupied, conversely, with "the life in the work" and the fundamental motivations surrounding its formation.

All of this leads me to reflect on the many topics I have discussed with Joseph Rykwert and to ask what is, by now, an old question: whether it is possible for an architect such as myself to use a personal experience of history without betraying essential principles, without making history an instrument of consolation or justification, without making it a model for stylistic imitation. Just as it is not possible to imitate a painting or a novel directly, neither is it possible to imitate the history of architecture. Yet neither is it possible to elude history altogether without creating an inescapable emptiness—a useless void from which it is impossible to progress. It is useful for us therefore to reflect on the material that Rykwert has brought together in his writings. Through his independence and creative character, he provides invaluable material for contemplation relative to a specific project through the transposition of complex concepts, methods, and hypotheses of historical interpretation while maintaining a precise awareness of the metaphorical limits of these operations.

For us architects, history is a means of becoming aware of the nature of the ground on which we walk. It is not for architectural historians to teach us the art of walking, but Joseph Rykwert's anthropology of architectural history teaches us this, as revealed in his methodology, his reasoning and the intricacy of his conclusions. Rykwert's writings offer architects a valuable critical distance as we navigate the difficult waters of everyday practice. They provide us with a constant and lively reminder of the fullness and proximity of history that we should forget only at our peril.

The history that Rykwert writes is never nostalgic. It is derived from a connected web of reasoned facts and events grounded in the dialectical condition of contemporary culture on which and from which the artist operates and against which we draw the materials of our own work. At a time like the present, in which the aestheticization of the everyday subsumes one's engagement with material reality, architects seem content to float on the mutable surface of fashion. Within this vexing context, Rykwert continues to remind us of the importance of the ground on which we walk and that the systems of signification, derived from our work as architects, have an important moral dimension. The "mute eloquence" of forms, tacitly present in our work as architects, overcomes the barriers created by the languages of specialists.

Following in the tradition of Sigfried Giedeon (a master Rykwert acknowledges), Rykwert works in the marginal territories of architecture without being distracted by its trivialities. Always concerned with material culture, Rykwert is above all impassioned by the question of the origin of architecture and its place in the natural and celestial world. Fundamental to this enterprise are the rituals and ceremonies that societies have created to honor the world around them and the manner in which architecture is both influenced by these ceremonies and encourages them to emerge. Nothing could be more distant from the work of modernity, which appears to concentrate on instrumental questions regarding the suitable limits of action. Lost in the past fifty years is the utopian dimension of the avant-garde that once believed that art would be the salvation of humanity. Now the issues with which we struggle oscillate between productive pragmatism and, due to the impoverished teachings of functionalism, the acceptance of a purely decorative role for our art. The historical writings of Rykwert oppose both of these interpretations with considerable vigor.

Notes

Chapter 1

1. The phrase "a promise as well as a memory" appears in the last sentence of Rykwert's *On Adam's House in Paradise* and has also been employed as an implicit reference to Rykwert's own writings by Vittorio Gregotti that is included in this volume.

2. Canetti is the author of *Auto da Fé, Crowds and Power,* and a three-volume autobiography. He won the Nobel Prize for literature in 1981. Illich is the author of numerous texts that challenge the tenets of Enlightenment rationality, including *Celebration of Awareness, Deschooling Society, Tools for Conviviality, Shadow Work,* and *In the Mirror of the Past.*

3. Rykwert's students include Bryan Avery, Timothy Bell, Richard Bulleyne, Mario Carpo, Patrick Devanthéry, George Dodds, Robin Evans, Homa Fardjadi, John Farmer, Donald Genasci, Vaughan Hart, Desmond Cheuk-kuen Hui, Peter Kohane, Inèz Lamunière, David Leatherbarrow, Daniel Libeskind, John McArthur, Mohsen Mostafavi, Lawrence Nield, Simon Pepper, Alberto Pérez-Gómez, and Robert Tavernor. Although I was not one of his students, I spent much time in discussions with him during my postgraduate studies in London in the mid-1960s.

4. Rykwert 1982, 10.

5. Rykwert 1982, 91.

6. Rykwert 1982, 74.

7. Rykwert 1982, 75–76.

8. Rykwert 1982, 7.

9. Rykwert 1986, 82.

10. Rykwert 1986, 84.

11. Rykwert 1967, 465.

12. Evans 1997, 55.

13. MacIntyre is the author of many texts, including *Marxism and Christianity, Against the Self-Images of the Age,* and *After Virtue.*

14. Rykwert 1982, 23. "The Sitting Position: A Question of Method" was first published in Italian in *Edilizia Moderna* in 1964 and then in English in Jencks and Baird, 1969.

15. Rykwert 1963, 100.

16. Rykwert 1963, 112.

17. Editor's Introduction to Rykwert 1963, 98.

18. Editor's Introduction to Rykwert 1963, 99.

19. Rykwert 1972, 11.

20. Rykwert 1972, 105.

21. Gombrich 1973, 35.

22. Rykwert 1972, 14.

23. Rykwert 1980, 470.

24. At the end of my framing of this particular conclusion in respect to Rykwert's methods, especially his putatively lesser curiosity regarding the signature of the individual designer, it occurred to me to test my

hypothesis by rereading "Two Houses by Eileen Gray," in *The Necessity of Artifice*. Rykwert was one of the first contemporary critics to rediscover Gray, and his essay certainly acknowledges the distinctiveness of her design approach. But on my rereading, I found it intriguing how he emphasizes the way in which she has devised a "container for a carefully articulated way of life" rather than her "style." Indeed, he even laments what he calls her later "decline" to "what is now called Art Nouveau." In a provocative terminological choice, he also refers to her Roquebrune house as "one of the most remarkable 'ensembles' of the time." By choosing the word *ensemble* rather than the alternative *Gesamtkunstwerk*, Rykwert makes it clear that he sees Gray as operating in a quite different realm than, for example, Mies van der Rohe, to whose work he is famously averse. As he concluded, "Those of us familiar with latter-day proceedings, when an architect may think it in order to dictate the whole furnishing and even the details of the decoration to his client for fear that he might 'spoil' his building by use, may find some comfort in these proceedings. Eileen Gray built for herself; the houses were original, carefully considered, and matched to an open, relaxed way of life." Thus does Rykwert appropriate even such a stylist as Gray into his decisively anthropological conceptual framework for design.

Chapter 2

1. Diels and Kranz 1934, D.K. 82 B3 73.

2. Diels and Kranz 1934, D.K. 68 B 156.

3. Diels and Kranz 1934, D.K. 51.2 51.1.4.

4. Plato, *Timaeus*, 51.A–53.D. For a more detailed discussion see Gadamer 1980, 172–193.

5. The elementary conditions of the process are discussed in Plato, *Philebus*, 16D, and also in Gadamer 1980, 205.

6. Aristotle, *Gen. et Corr.*, 322 B26–323 A9.

7. Lucretius, *De Rerum Natura*, I, 11, 440–446.

8. Hahm 1977, 3–29.

9. There is a close affinity between "primary tradition" and "effective history" (*Wirkungsgeschichte*), a term used in current hermeneutics. See Gadamer 1985, 245–256, 267–274. In the domain of architecture, "primary tradition" refers to the concrete historical situation in which architecture is created. This includes studio and workshop practice, oral tradition, and the communicative space of culture as a whole. At a deeper level, the primary tradition coincides with the tradition of classical and Christian humanism. We are only beginning to understand its presence and role, and the following text is therefore no more than a contribution to such an understanding.

10. Plato, *Timaeus*, 44E.

11. Aristotle, *Physics*, 252B 26.

12. Gabirol ibn Solomon 1892, 1.2.

13. Ambrose, PL Vol. XIV, col. 265.

14. Chalcidius, in Mullach 1881, vol. 2, CC. cf. CCXXX.

15. Doctor 1898, 20.

16. Aristotle, *Physics*, 211 A30.

17. Aristotle, *Physics*, 212 A20.

18. I am not using here the term *human soul*, leaving the meaning of the soul open for a more general reading, which includes the notion of world soul as well as the contemporary understanding of the soul as an ontological movement of human existence. See Patocka 1995, 107–119.

19. Wittkower 1967, 29.

20. Federici-Vescovini 1965, 158–175.

21. Lomazzo 1973–1974, Cap. 35, 351.

22. Aristotle, *De Partibus Animalium*, 669B.

23. Aristotle, *De Motu Animalium*, 703A.

24. Merleau-Ponty 1974, 124.

25. The period of mannerism is particularly rich in the production of such texts (Paracelsus, Böhme, Cardanus, Campanella). In Jacob Böhme's *Aurora,* we find the following analogies: "The body cavity signifies the space between the stars, the arteries signify the courses of stars." Scheibler 1832, vol. II, p. 28.

26. Crooke 1615, 2–3.

27. The role of language in the understanding of proportion is well illustrated by the role that *trivium* (grammar, rhetoric, dialectics) played as a propaedeutics for the quadrivium (arithmetic, geometry, music, astronomy). See Wagner 1986.

28. Aristotle, *Post Analytics*, 78A.

29. Ricoeur 1978, 199.

30. The relation between geometrical proportion and metaphorical analogy is well illustrated in Plato, *Gorgias*, 508A.

31. Klein 1968, 79ff.

32. Gadamer 1980, 151.

33. Plato, *Phaedo*, 100A; *Meno* 86C; *Parmenides* 137B.

34. Plato, *Republic*, 526E.

35. Plato, *Republic*, 533C.

36. Magrini 1845, *Memorie Intorno A. Palladio*, Appendix, 12, in Wittkower 1967, 113.

37. Barbaro 1567, in *Proemio*, 8.

38. Barbaro 1567, 141.

39. Alberti 1988, 305.

40. Theon of Smyrna 1979, 70.

41. Plato, *Timaeus*, 31C.

42. The importance of mediation toward unity and of the continuity of proportion is demonstrated by the insertion of arithmetic and harmonic means in the intervals of primary structure of the soul articulated by geometrical proportion. The insertion of the harmonic (musical fourth) and arithmetic (musical fifth) means the scale completed in terms of perfect harmonic continuity.

43. In the articulation of the structure of the soul, Plato has taken into account all that is necessary for the dialectical understanding of reality—being, sameness, difference, and participation (*methexis*)—and "constructed a section of the diatonic scale whose range is fixed by considerations extraneous to music" (Cornford 1975, 72). One of the extraneous reasons was to attune the scale down to solid numbers. "Modern commentators seem not to have taken sufficient notice of the fact that this decision has nothing whatever to do with the theory of musical harmony" (Cornford 1975, 67).

44. Sextus Empiricus, *Against the Logicians*, 1, 98–101 (Loeb, 291).

45. Grosseteste 1978, 12.

46. Hedwig 1980, 177.

47. Shelby 1977, 83.

48. Wisdom of Solomon, 11, 20.

49. Bonaventure 1993, I, 11, 8.

50. Eco 1988, 67.

51. Alberti's criteria for *concinnitas* are rather revealing. Alberti's number, outline (*finitio*) and position (*collocatio*) seems to correspond closely with number, measure, and weight. Number has the same meaning in both cases; "Finitio of the building is the building's measure". *Collocatio* refers to the place of individual parts in the building as a whole (Gadol 1973, 110).

52. Coming to terms with the problem of identity, the equivalent of participation in the ultimate good, the unity of being, and the presence of the divine in human world dominated European history until the end of the seventeenth century. The problem of identity found its most explicit and most influential articulation in Proclus's *Elements of Theology* based on the hierarchy of once (*henads*) and in the metaphysics of light culminating in the multiplication of species (Bacon 1983).

Chapter 3

1. Kolb and Whishaw 1996, 418–424.

2. Blakemore and Mitchell 1973; Kolb and Whishaw 1996, 498–502.

3. Onians 1989.

4. Sappho 38, 1–3.

5. Homer, *Iliad*, XIII, 11, 130–133.

6. Homer, *Iliad*, XII, 1, 132.

7. Homer, *Iliad*, XIII, 11, 389–390.

8. Euripides, *Iphigenia in Tauris* 11, 50–57.

Chapter 4

1. Wagner 1988, 92.

2. *De Orat.*, III, 180.

3. Vitruvius, IV, 2, 2–3.

4. For an overview of the literature, see Weickenmeier 1985, Howe 1985.

5. For reasons of economy I will cite only essential or recent studies. Further references can be found in my companion article, Wilson Jones, forthcoming.

6. For comparative measurements, see Holland 1917, esp. 142ff. Cf. Hodge 1960.

7. Cook 1951, esp. 51; Roux 1992, esp. 155.

8. De Angelis D'Ossat 1941–1942; Stucchi 1974, esp. 114–117; Rykwert 1996, 187.

9. Vitruvius, IV, 2, 4; Washburn 1918, 1919; Demangel 1931, 1946, 1949; Roux 1992, esp. 159ff.; Peschken 1988.

10. Guadet 1909; Gullini 1974.

11. Zancani Montuoro 1940; Richard 1970; Beyer 1972.

12. Coulton 1988, 30ff., esp. 39.

13. Cook 1951, 1970; Howe 1985, esp. 370ff.

14. Corinth led the Greek world in the manufacture of roof tiles and stone construction, while Pindar (*Ol.* 13.21–22) seems to attribute her with the invention of the sculpted pediment. Cf. Cook 1951, 52; Cook 1970, 19; Rhodes 1987.

15. Vitruvius, IV, 1, 3.

16. Wesenberg 1971, 49ff.

17. Rykwert 1994, 11–21.

18. See Holland 1917, 12, for a list of examples. Cf. Bowen 1950.

19. Laum 1912; Cook 1951, 1970.

20. As argued by Viollet-le-Duc in his *Entretiens sur l'Architecture* (Paris 1863). The relevant section appears in English in *The Architectural Theory of Viollet-le-Duc. Readings*

and Commentary, M. F. Hearn (ed.), (Cambridge, Mass., 1990), 40–65.

21. Vitruvius, I, 3, 2.

22. Vitruvius, VI, 7, 7. My thanks to Indra McEwen for this observation.

23. Wilson Jones 2000, esp. 45.

24. Besides chapter 3 in this book, see also Onians 1988, 8; Onians 1999, 26–30.

25. Rykwert 1996, 182–185, 187.

26. For example, *Iliad,* I, 36–42.

27. Hersey 1988, 21ff., esp. 31. This specific idea echoes that of Sandro Stucchi, who likened the triglyphs on altars with Doric friezes to stylized bunches of thigh bones; see Stucchi 1974, 115, n. 150. On Greek sacrificial ritual, see Burkert 1983, 1985, 55–59; van Straten 1995, esp. 122–127, 141–144.

28. An undamaged example is a red figure bell krater, Agrigento, Archaeological Museum, inv. no. 4688; Froning 1971, pl. 16; van Straten 1995, fig. 30.

29. Black figure Panathenaic amphora, Rome, Villa Giulia, inv. no. 74957. An even more abstract example is shown on a black figure amphora in Munich, Antikensammlung 1379 (J 81); *LIMC* Kyknos I, 47. For a list of tripod shield devices, see Sakowski 1997, 335–348.

30. There follows a summary of the main points of a more extended formal analysis in a companion study: Wilson Jones forthcoming.

31. For Monrepos, see Schleif et al. 1939–1940, 75; Strøm 1988, 187ff.

32. On noncanonic archaic triglyphs, mostly from South Italy and Sicily, see Barletta 1983, Mertens 1993.

33. Athens, National Museum, inv. no. 17874; Haspels 1946; *LIMC s.v.* Hippokampos 9, Tritones 15.

34. For the Olympia griffin, see Hampe and Jantzen 1937, 90–92, Taf. 34–35; Verzone 1951, esp. fig. 2.

35. *Iliad*, 22, 443; 23, 40; *Odyssey*, 8, 434–437, 10, 359–361.

36. *Iliad*, 18, 344–348.

37. On the tripod-cauldron, see Rolley 1977 (with a useful summary of preceding research on pp. 15–23); Maass 1978, 1981; Strøm 1995.

38. *Iliad*, 8, 290; *Odyssey,* 4, 129; 13, 13.

39. *Iliad*, 8, 290; 19, 243.

40. *Iliad*, 24, 233.

41. *Iliad*, 9, 407; 11, 700; 23, 259–264; 23, 485; 23, 513; 23, 702–718.

42. For representations of tripods, see Benton 1934–1935; Sakowski 1997; Froning 1971.

43. von Bothmer 1977; Schefold 1992, 153–158; *LIMC s.v.* Herakles (2947–3066); Sakowski 1997, 113, 269–313.

44. Amyx 1944; Scheibler 1988.

45. Langdon 1987, 109. Cf. Morgan 1990; De Polignac 1994, esp. 11–12.

46. Hesiod, *Works and Days,* I, 657; cf. Pausanius IX, 31, 3.

47. Literary sources attesting to this practice include Herodotos, V, 59, 4; VIII, 27, 22; Pausanius, III, 18, 8. Cf. Snodgrass 1989–1990.

48. Herodotos, VIII, 82, 5; Pausanius, X, 13, 9; Thucydides, I, 132, 2.

49. Maass 1981, 19.

50. Iliad, 18, 373.

51. *Hymni Homerici in Mercurium,* 61.

52. The tripod-on-column may also reflect painterly preference, it being a favorite motif of the so-called Kadmos painter, for example; see Robertson 1992. For a selection of examples, see the Agrigento vase (see n. 28) and *LIMC s.v.* Apollon 303, Apollon 769 (foliate), Apollon 1040, Asklepios 1 (Ionic), Oreias 1.

53. On temple function see Coldstream 1985; Mazarakis Ainan 1988; Burkert 1988, 1996; Hollinshead 1999.

54. Kendrick-Pritchett 1971, 100. See also Burkert 1996, esp. 25.

55. Mazarakis-Ainan 1997, 383. For later periods, see Hollinshead 1999.

56. Burkert 1988, esp. 43–44; 1996, esp. 24–25. Cf. Fehr 1996, 165–191.

57. Vitruvius, IV, 1, 3.

58. Stafford 1999, esp. 48 and Pl. 12 for a painting with Ploutos advancing toward a choregic tripod.

59. Black figure amphora, Rome, Villa Giulia, inv. no. 8340; Amyx 1944, pl. 27f; Scheibler 1988, 311, pl. 88, 2–3; Sakowski 1997, SP-52.

60. Black figure loutrophon, Athens, Kerameikos, inv. no. 1682, ca. 550–540 B.C.; see Scheibler 1988, 312; Sakowski 1997, SP-47.

61. Black figure amphora, Munich, Antikensammlung inv. no. 1378; Scheibler 1988, pl. 89.4; Sakowski 1997, SP-54. Scheibler speculates that the tripod is the Delphic tripod and that the scene on the other side of the vase with a man and woman and tripod represents the rightful owners, Apollo and Pythia/Themis.

Chapter 5

1. *Optics* 1740, Quaestio XVIII.

2. As quoted in Voegelin 1948, 471.

3. See Rykwert 1996, 82; Wilson Jones 2000.

4. What follows has been developed from my Ph.D. thesis (Tavernor 1985), which was supervised by Joseph Rykwert.

5. Vitruvius 1960, 73.

6. They considered that these numbers display certain inherent qualities and characteristics: 6 is perfect as it is the sum of its factors (1 + 2 + 3) and, because in the context of bodily proportion architecture, the foot is one-sixth of a man's height; 10 is perfect because of our ten digits, five of which make a palm and four palms make a foot (and is the sum of 1 + 2 + 3 + 4). The numbers combine to generate the "most perfect" number of all, 16 (which is also the square of the first square, 2^4).

7. Vitruvius 1960, 73.

8. Augustine 1972, 1073–1074.

9. 1 Timothy 2, 5; Augustine 1972, 643.

10. Augustine 1972, 643.

11. Alberti 1988, 309.

12. This is the third book of Ficino's *De triplici vita* (On the Threefold Life, 1489). See Mebane 1989, 22–25.

13. Gombrich 1945, 31–81.

14. Alberti 1972, 97, who is citing Seneca, after Hesiod.

15. Tavernor 1998, 39–41.

16. Field 1997, 81.

17. Evans 1994, 151, 147–167.

18. Alberti 1972, 129–133; Evans 1994, 155–156; Tavernor 1998, 6–9.

19. Alberti 1972, 129–133.

20. Aiken 1980, passim.

21. According to the *Tabulae* the perfect numbers are distributed throughout the body. Consider an upright male figure in elevation: from the base of the pelvis and wrist to the navel; from the knee joint to the tip of

the hand; from the hips to the waist; and from the waist to the nipples are all one-tenth of the whole; and the foot, of course, is one-sixth of body height. Other proportions are fractional multiples of these numbers and are one-twentieth, one-fortieth, and one-sixtieth of the whole.

22. Including the main biblical characters of Christ and St. John in the *Baptism of Christ,* and bystanders, such as a group of women witnessing *The Proving of the True Cross.* See Baxandall 1972, 75; Gioseffi 1980; Evans 1994, 159–167.

23. Pacioli 1509, opposite p. 25.

24. Davis 1977; Tavernor 1998, 116.

25. Wittkower and Carter 1953, where a link is made with this measurement and a scale drawn by Luca Pacioli in his *Divina Proportione.* From my studies, the scale by Pacioli, like the height of Christ in the painting, appears to be derived from either the antique or quattrocento Roman "foot" that had a similar length. See Tavernor 1985, 187–189.

26. Uzielli 1899, 10–12. The Roman *pes,* or foot, is generally regarded as having been the equivalent of 0.296 meter in length: see, for example, Wilson Jones 2000, p. 104.

27. Ginzburg 1981–1982, 72–73. Initially, I was able to corroborate Ginzburg's observation only by using a 35-mm color transparency of the painting enlarged to full-size (Tavernor 1985). Researchers led by Joseph Rykwert and myself have since reconstructed the *Flagellation* on computer and can con-

firm the accuracy of these earlier findings. Our reconstruction was completed in 1994 under the auspices of the Alberti Group and presented at the Alberti Exhibition at Palazzo Te in Mantua, 1994. Carter stated that "the height of Christ measured on the picture is approximately 7.15"; 7.15 inches equals 18.16 centimeters (Wittkower and Carter 1953, 299, n. 1), not the 17.8 centimeters stated by Ginzburg; Lightbown states that Christ is 8¼ inches high, though as Christ's size is not a primary issue for Lightbown, I suggest it can be ignored as a gross approximation (Lightbown 1992, 60). Carter's dimension is also, he admits, "approximate," and the difference between his measurement of Christ and Ginzburg's is in any case less than 4 millimeters. There are also good philosophical reasons for believing that Ginzburg is correct, as I will argue below.

28. Wittkower and Carter 1953, 293, n. 4.

29. Unlike Ginzburg, in order to approximate life size, Wittkower and Carter scaled the height of the central foreground figure, not Christ in the painting, as 6 feet tall (Wittkower and Carter 1953, 300, n. 1). In their system, Christ scales as 11.4 modules, which did not suggest anything of significance to them.

30. These measurements result from a direct transposition of Wittkower and Carter's "grand unit" of 19 modules for 10 feet (1.9 modules equals 1 antique Roman foot). Ten feet is the combined height of the column and statue to which Christ is tied in the painting. The 50-foot distance of Christ from

the painter's eye comes from Wittkower and Carter's estimate, which equaled: $19 + 37^{1/2} + 38 = 94^{1/2}$ modules, or the equivalent of 49.74 feet ($94^{1/2} \div 1.9 = 49.74$). The slight discrepancy of a quarter of 1 foot is probably insignificant, because, as Carter observed, the painting lacks exact horizontals and verticals and also because the intersection of the picture plane and ground plane "must rest upon conjecture, the validity of which will depend upon the consistency and the probability of the resulting conclusions." Wittkower and Carter 1953, 297–298, n. 1. See also Tavernor 1985, 178–186; cf. Wittkower and Carter 1953, 293, n. 4.

31. On this light source, see Lavin 1972, 45–48; Bertelli 1992, 120; Lightbown 1992, 58–59.

32. Olivetti SpA of Italy sponsored the computer model as part of the Alberti Exhibition, held in Mantua in 1994, which Joseph Rykwert and I curated. Although our reconstruction of the painting appeared on a computer monitor in the exhibition, there is no account of it in the accompanying catalogue (Rykwert and Engel 1994). The reconstruction was made by Julie Cornish of the Alberti Group. See my interpretation of the painting based on Wittkower and Carter's abstract module described below (Tavernor 1985, appendix 10, 78–186). The computer model of the painting was built with the same vanishing and distance points that Piero used in this instance. Its accuracy was checked by superimposing the painted view of the scene onto the model and correcting any anomalies. One of the many advantages of the

computer model over a drawn or even solid model is the rigor demanded of the computer operator in its building. Cornish found, for example, that the ethereal light source lighting the coffered bay above Christ is not exactly in the position indicated by Lavin (Lavin 1972, 45–48, and figures 22 and 23; cf. Tavernor 1996, 15–19, figures 1–5). In the light source position indicated by Lavin, the bronze statue above Christ casts a shadow on the coffer and has to be adjusted in position to enable the angle of shadows cast by the down-stand of the coffered bay to match those in the painting. The computer model proves the degree of fine precision Piero employed in the perspectival construction of this painting (Tavernor 1996, 16, figures 1–5).

33. "The city herself stands in the center, like a guardian and master; towns surround her on the periphery [of the picture], each in its place. A poet might well speak of the moon surrounded by the stars; and the whole is very beautiful to behold. Just as on a round buckler, where one ring is laid around the other, the innermost ring loses itself in the central knob which is the middle of the entire buckler. Just so we here see the regions like rings surrounding and enclosing one another. Among them, the city is the first, like to the central knob, the center of the whole orbit. The city herself is ringed by walls and suburbs. Around the suburbs, in turn, lies a belt of rural mansions and estates, and around them the circle of towns; and this whole outermost region is enclosed in a still larger orbit and circle. Between the towns

there are castles, and towers reaching into the sky" (Baron 1966, 200).

34. Vagnetti 1974, 73–110; Orlandi 1974a, 1974b.

35. For a discussion of the *radium* and *orizon* in the context of *Descriptio urbis Romae*, see Vagnetti 1974, 80. Its form is derived from the contemporary astronomical astrolabe, divided around its circumference into 24 hours and 360 degrees.

36. In the same chapter of *De re aedificatoria* that Alberti referred to the surveyor's horizon, he mentions Eratosthenes of Cyrene's ancient calculation of the earth's circumference. See Alberti 1988, 335–341, 336. According to Eratosthenes, this is 252,000 Greek stadia (or 31.5 million Roman paces), though this figure is absent from all but one of the manuscripts of *De re aedificatoria*. See Alberti 1988, 413, n. 90. See also Tavernor 1998, 208–209, n. 4, for the following account and the Latin original of the text.

In the first English translation of *De re aedificatoria* Leoni attempted to clarify Alberti's statement by adding that 252,000 furlongs/stadia equaled 31,500 miles (Alberti 1955, 221). He has Alberti write: "Eratosthenes tells us, that the compass of this great globe is two hundred and fifty-two thousand furlongs, or about thirty-one thousand five hundred miles." An interpretation after Vitruvius, who wrote that the earth's circumference was 252,000 stadia, that is, 31,500,000 paces: Vitruvius 1960, 27–28. In Orlandi's Italian edition (Alberti 1966, 918–919), the earth's circumference is left blank because the figure of 252,000 stadia in the manuscript Orlandi was referring to appears to be a later inclusion. However, 252,000 stadia is undoubtedly the correct figure because it relates directly to Vitruvius's figure of 31.5 million paces:

1 pace	= 5 *pedes*
1 stadium	= 625 *pedes*
252,000 × 625 ÷ 5	= 31,500,000

The lacuna is curious, as it was straightforward enough for Alberti to look up Erastothenes, or Vitruvius, for the figure (Vitruvius 1960, 27–28). Indeed, he could calculate the circumference using the long-established formula $2\pi r$. Although Alberti is nowhere explicit about the value to be used for pi, he does describe the diameter of a circle and its circumference in his *Ludi rerum mathematicarum* (c. 1450), where it can be deduced as equivalent to the fraction 22/7, or 3 1/7. On Alberti's use of pi, see Alberti 1568, 239. This value for pi was commonly used throughout the Middle Ages too. The range for pi had been set in antiquity by Archimedes as between 3 1/7 and 3 1/8. See Pottage 1968, 190–197. Wittkower and Carter 1953, 301, n. 3, 4, conjectured (after Cantor) that Piero may have used a value for pi of 3 3/20, or 3.15. However, more precision was sought during the first half of the fifteenth century, and Nicholas of Cusa, with whom Alberti (and probably

Piero) was familiar, used the more precise ratio of 3 3/20: Wittkower and Carter 1953, 302. With this value for pi and Eratosthenes' circumference of 31.5 million paces, then the earth has a diameter of exactly 10 million paces, or 50 million feet. The earth has a circumference of 31.5 million paces as Vitruvius related it; thus, $2\pi r = 31.5$ million paces. If pi is set at 3.15 it is an exact fraction of the earth's circumference measured in paces: 31,500,000/3.15, and the earth has a radius (r) of $31,500,000 \div 2 \times 3.15 = 5,000,000$ paces. So its diameter (2r) equals 10,000,000 paces.

In the Roman system of measures, 1 pace (*passus*) equals 5 feet (*pedes*); thus, 10 million paces equals 50 million feet. Eratosthenes' calculation is only 1 percent in error according to modern calculations. See Vitruvius 1999, 167.

37. Bertelli 1992, 118–120.

38. Bertelli 1992, 118–122, n. 21.

39. Wittkower and Carter 1953, 293, 297. The precise intersection of the picture plane cannot be calculated, but if the painter's eye is 50 feet from Christ and the picture plan about one-third of that distance from the "eye," 50 divided by 3 = 16.66 feet.

40. Furthermore, the two rods in the painting—the one held by the golden statue on top of the flagellation column and the other by Pilate—have scaled measures of 1 "foot," and 1 ⅔ "feet," respectively, the "perfect" ratio of 6:10.

41. Kuhn 1990, 117ff., 130, n. 60.

42. Wittkower and Carter 1953, 294, n. 3; after Vasari, 1965, 196.

43. A similar method was used by subsequent artists with the *camera obscura*, which itself derives from Alberti's "demonstrations" using a "show box," better known as the *camera ottica*, or optical chamber (Alberti 1972, 69; Tavernor 1998, 90–91).

44. This term having been coined by Alberti in *De pictura*: Alberti 1972, 103.

45. For example, see summaries in Bertelli 1992, 184; Dal Poggetto 1992, 118–121, 452–455; Lightbown 1992, 49–69, 283.

46. It is first listed in an inventory compiled by P. Ubaldo Tosi in the first half of the eighteenth century and located in the sacristy of Urbino Cathedral. It was moved to the ducal palace in 1916. See Bertelli 1992, 182. Lavin 1972, 81–83, suggests that it was originally intended for a private chapel in the ducal palace, the Capella del Perdono.

47. Tavernor 1998, 11–12, 125–127, 189–192.

48. It was to Guidobaldo, as the young duke of Urbino, that Piero dedicated his treatise on the five regular solids, *De quinque corporibus regularibus.*

49. Bertelli 1992, 218–224; Lightbown 1992, 229–243.

50. Baxandall (1972) has summarized the appreciation of fifteenth-century paintings: "Renaissance people were . . . on their mettle before a picture, because of the expectation

that cultivated people should be able to make discriminations about the interest of pictures. These very often took the form of a preoccupation with the painter's skill, [which] was something firmly anchored in certain economic and intellectual conventions and assumptions. . . . At some fairly high level of consciousness the Renaissance man was one who matched concepts with pictorial style." Baxandall 1972, 36.

51. Rather perversely, Lightbown (1992, 58–59) suggests that the geometry under Christ is of an oval, not a circle, and the coffers above rectangular. This can easily be disproved geometrically when reconstructing the perspective of the composition by drawing a line through the diagonal of the far right coffer in the bay of the Praetorium nearest the viewer and continuing that line through adjacent coffers, as in Wittkower and Carter (1953, 298–299, and figure 4) and as confirmed by our own computer reconstruction.

52. Vitruvius 1960, 252. A square of 6 units has a diagonal of 8½, which forms the side of a square with a diagonal of 12, and so results in the number sequence 6, 8½, 12, 17, 24, 34, 48, etc.

53. Bertelli 1992, 119.

54. Lavin 1972, 76–79.

55. Vitruvius 1960, 15; Rykwert 1996.

56. Alberti 1988, 309.

57. The meditation process might then continue as follows: As Christ is 6 feet tall, per-

haps the circle beneath him, like the circle bounding the Vitruvian man—or as a symbol of the earth—has a diameter equivalent to 8½ feet. The square within which the circle is placed is divided into 64 plain square tiles elsewhere in the painting, eight to each side. If the circle beneath Christ has a diameter of 8½ feet, then the square by which it is contained has sides of 8½ feet and a diagonal of 12 feet (8 cubits), so the eight tiles on the diagonal each have a diagonal of 1½ feet (or 1 cubit). The Praetorium ceiling appears to have coffers the same size as the tiles, separated by ribs one-sixth their width. (See Wittkower and Carter 1953, 45, figure A.) Also, if the Praetorium has been set out on a 10-foot grid and contains a tiled terra-cotta flooring arranged in 8½-foot squares, then the white marble strips surrounding the tiles must be 3 feet wide ($10 - 8\frac{1}{2} = 1\frac{1}{2}$ to the grid $\times 2 = 3$ for the strip width), and so too the bases of the columns. The geometrical construction of the black and white decorative Praetorium floor cannot be contemplated so straightforwardly. See Tavernor 1985, 183–186.

58. The quotation was first recorded by Passavant in the early nineteenth century, who read it on the painting beside the figures in the foreground (Passavant 1839), though it was no longer visible by 1864 (Brandi 1954–1955, 91). It has been argued that it was never part of the painting but was an inscription on the frame that was subsequently removed during restoration (Bombe 1909, 470). This line was taken by Bertelli (1992, 182) but dismissed by Lightbown (1992, 65) who has re-

verted to Passavant's initial claim that it was an integral part of the painting. The only text still visible in the painting is positioned on the edge of Pilate's throne, and it identifies Piero as the artist of the painting, and reads as "OPVS PETRI DEBVRGO S[AN]C[T]I SEPVLCRI."

59. Lavin 1972, 78, renders this, "They come together;" Lightbown 1992, 65, prefers the more colloquial translation, "They met together." And see my argument below.

60. Lavin 1972, 78; Lightbown 1992, 65.

61. See in particular Lavin 1972, and more recent summaries in Bertelli 1992; Dal Poggetto 1992; and Lightbown 1992.

62. For example, consider a recent interpretation by Ronald Lightbown, who has reasoned that the lost quotation pointed most obviously to the fall of Constantinople in 1453 and the perceived threat to Western Christendom by Muslim Turks. The painting, he believes, was made about this time. He identifies the well-dressed figure on the right of the foreground trio as Francesco Sforza and the orientally garbed figure across from him as an unidentified emissary from Byzantium. Between them is an angel intercessor. Lightbown links the painting with the Congress of Mantua in 1459, which had been called by Pope Pius II as an alliance of Christian princes against the Turks—Francesco Sforza's wife, Bianca Maria Visconti, having personally paid for 100 troops to fight the infidels (Lightbown 1992, 65–69). Earlier interpretations include the notion that the foreground group represent figures from a famous political plot in Urbino; a tragic trio connected to Mantua; and a range of philosophers and churchmen. Pope Hennessy (1986) has even identified the figure being scourged as St. Jerome, not Christ. The problem of identities is compounded since the date of the painting is uncertain. The earliest date for it is 1448, though it may as plausibly date from as late as 1470—before and well after the fall of Constantinople and Pope Pius II's papacy (see summaries in Bertelli 1992, 184; Dal Poggetto 1992, 118–121, 452–455; Lightbown 1992, 49–69, 283).

63. Bertelli 1992, 122.

64. After the Resurrection, Jesus urges his followers to disseminate his divine power: "All power is given unto me in heaven and in earth. Go ye therefore, and teach all nations" (Matthew 28, 18–19).

65. My reading differs from Lavin, who argues that the phrase "Convenerunt in unum" has been "lifted out of context and set down in isolation to emphasize the face value of the words," though she interprets it as meaning that "the two groups come together" in the painting—"one from life [the trio in the foreground] and one from the Gospel [the flagellation scene]" (Lavin 1972, 78). My belief is that this phrase relates to the fundamental organization of the painting, not the groups of figures who are subordinate to Christ compositionally, their positions relating proportionally to the column of Christ. They achieve unity—a coming together—

only through the perfection represented by his body. The primary structure of the painting is therefore overlaid with groups of figures whose bodies articulate the numerical and dimensional qualities of the painting. Their identities (about which there can be no certainty, and are not the focus of this study) are a secondary consideration.

66. Tavernor 1998.

Chapter 6

I am grateful for the support of the Graham Foundation in preparing this chapter.

1. Payne 1999, 1–10.

2. Palladio 1980, 276: "Io ho posto de' tabernacoli con statue, come per le ruine *pare che vi fossero.*"

3. Palladio 1980, 277.

4. Palladio 1980, 523, n. 5. Alberti mentions the story too (VII, 16). Alberti 1988, 240.

5. Alberti 1988; Francesco Di Giorgio 1967; Scamozzi 1964; Serlio 1964; Vignola 1985.

6. Vasari 1986. Vasari's 1568 edition of the *Vite* shows the same bias.

7. Payne 1999.

8. Alberti *Faksimile*, VII, 16, 134.

9. Spini 1980, 30–201.

10. Spini 1980, 179.

11. See especially Günther 1988.

12. Puppi 1990.

13. Palladio (1988, 18) comments on the Arch of Constantine in his *L'antichita di Roma* when he reviews the triumphal arches in Rome; it is the only arch that receives such an accolade. For Palladio's use of arches as authority to justify his use of bas-reliefs on the facade of San Petronio see Palladio 1988, 133. Palladio specifically praises the *intagli* of the Arch of Titus as an example of "edifici che furono fatti ai buoni tempi" unlike the Temple of Peace (Basilica of Maxentius) that he illustrates: Palladio 1980, 262.

14. Alberti 1988, 266.

15. Serlio 1619, 109v. For his criticism, see, for example, comments on the Arco dei Argentieri, which shows members that are *vitiose, confusione,* same profiles one on top of the other (100–101r); on the Arch of Constantine, which has *mensole e dentelli* and *confusione di intagli* (106v); and on the Arch at Benevento, which has too many *intagli* and caters to the *piacere del vulgo* (104v).

16. Rowland 1994, 104; Frommel 1989, 39–49.

17. The seminal text that best illustrates this position is without a doubt Adolf Loos's "Ornament und Verbrechen." Although traditionally dated 1908, more recent research shows that Loos wrote it as a lecture in late 1909 or 1910 (Rukschcio 1985, 57–68). Le Corbusier published the essay in 1920 in *L'Esprit Nouveau.* His own *L'Art decoratif d'aujourd'hui* (1925) and *Après le cubisme* (1918, with Amedee Ozenfant) constituted equally influential (if somewhat differently oriented)

statements on the subject. On the larger issue of imbrication between architectural history writing and contemporary discourse, see Payne 1994, 322–342.

18. The tectonics discussion owed much to Friedrich Schinkel, whose well-known position ("Architektur ist eine Fortsetzung der Natur in ihrer konstruktiven Tätigkeit") was developed by Bötticher 1852 and others. On Schinkel, see Börsch-Soupan 1976, 161. The discussion, focused on materials and building technique as determinants for architectural form initiated by Gottfried Semper, found an enthusiastic reception in the written work of Otto Wagner. See his influential *Moderne Architektur* (Vienna 1896, 1898, 1902). For the abstraction-empathy lineage of the ornament discussion, see especially Riegl, *Stilfragen* (1893) and Worringer, *Formprobleme der Gotik* (1910) and *Abstraktion und Einfühlung* (1907).

19. Burckhardt 1987.

20. Burckhardt 1987, 192.

21. Burckhardt 1987, 191.

22. See, for example, the 1893 article on Adolf von Hildebrand: Wölfflin 1946a, 84–106.

23. "Das Ornament ist Ausdruck überschüssiger Formkraft. Die schwere Masse treibt keine Blüten"; "die Schwere ist überwunden, der Überschuss der strebenden Kraft erscheint in der Hebung des Giebels und feiert den höchsten Triumph in den plastischen Figuren, die, dem Druck en-

thoben, hier frei sich entfalten können." Wölfflin 1946b, 41.

24. Geoffrey Scott, the champion of Einfühlung for the English-speaking world, also ignored the place of figural ornament in classical architecture and, like Wölfflin, concentrated on the orders, proportion, mass, and space. Scott 1965.

25. Wittkower 1949. The tradition leading up to Wittkower included Willich and Zucker's influential *Baukunst der Renaissance in Italien* (1914–1926). Following in the steps of Schmarsow, they focused on the spatial characteristics of Renaissance architecture and described ornament as "devoid of content" and "the architectural furnishing of the facade as unimportant." Willich and Zucker 1914, vol. 1, 1926, 2: 257, 266.

26. Alberti 1988, 312.

27. Lotz defines Alessi's treatment of the Villa Cambiaso as a case of "ornament drowning structure" and his style more generally as "pictorial." Heydenreich and Lotz 1974, 290–291. On the association of *malerisch* (pictorial) with ornament in modernist architectural criticism and theory, see Payne 2001. On structure/ornament, see Sankovitch 1998, 686–717.

28. von Bode 1902; Summers 1981.

29. See Paoletti 1897–1898.

30. See, for example, Boucher 1991; Howard 1975; Kiene 1995.

31. See Lotz 1977, 140–151. Among exceptions, see also Wolters 1992–1993, 102–110; Del Turco and Salvi 1995; Shell and Castelfranchi 1993; and Brandt 1994.

32. Vitruvius I, 1; II, 1, 7; 1983, 9–21 and 85.

33. Vitruvius VII, 5, 5; 1983, 107.

34. Vitruvius distinguishes the *ornamenta* from the columns and uses the term for the elements above the column that he discusses separately under this rubric. See Vitruvius, I, 1, 6 and IV, 2, 1.

35. Vitruvius, IV, 3.

36. Alberti 1988, VI, 13. Thoenes and Günther 1985, 261–271.

37. Vitruvius, IX, praef.

38. "*Decor* demands the faultless ensemble of a work composed, in accordance with precedent, of approved details. [*Décor autem est emendatus operis aspectus probatis rebus conpositi cum auctoritate.*] It obeys convention (*statio*), which in Greek is called *thematismos*, or custom (*consuetudo*) or nature (*natura*)." Vitruvius, I, 2, 5.

39. On the aesthetic implications of *décor* and its reception in the Renaissance see Payne 1999, chaps. 1, 3; on its implications for the representation of a socioeconomic hierarchy through architectural means, see Onians 1988.

40. On the impact of literary theory on architecture, see Payne 1999.

41. On Spini's contribution to the theory of architecture, see Payne 2000b, 143–156.

42. Spini 1980, 68. For similar categories used in poetics, see Minturno 1563.

43. Spini 1980, 68.

44. Spini 1980, 68–69.

45. See Aristotle 1982, III, 4: "Speaking generally, poetry seems to owe its origin to two particular causes, both natural. From childhood men have an instinct for representation, and in this respect man differs from the other animals that he is far more imitative and learns his first lessons by representations. What happens in actual experience proves this, for we enjoy looking at accurate likenesses of things which are themselves painful to see, obscene beasts, for instance, and corpses. The reason is this. Learning things gives great pleasure not only to philosophers but also in the same way to all other men, though they share this pleasure only to a small degree. The reason why we enjoy seeing likenesses is that, as we look, we learn and infer what each is, for instance, that is so and so.'" On the tradition of imbrication between the literary and figural arts, the seminal work remains Rensselaer W. Lee, *Ut pictura poesis: The Humanistic Theory of Painting* (New York: Norton, 1967).

46. On the relationship between the debates on language and architectural ornament, see Payne 2000c.

47. Barbaro 1567, 115.

48. Lenzoni 1556, 129.

49. Scamozzi 1615, II, 140.

50. For the archaeological and exegetical program of the academy, see especially Tolomei 1985, 31–61.

51. Howard 1975, 27.

52. On Cornaro's relationships with Ruzzante and Falconetto, see Fiocco 1965; *Alvise Cornaro e il suo tempo,* ed. L. Puppi (Padova: Commune di Padova and Assessorato ai Beni Culturali, 1980).

53. Coffin 1964, 191–211; Gallaccini MS, f. 78v.

54. Burns and Tafuri 1998.

55. Perino del Vaga's drawing of a project for the facade of the palace of Andrea Doria in Genoa (Amsterdam, Rijksmuseum, 1948/133) shows similar devices and may suggest another possible filiation. See Burns and Tafuri 1989, 1998, 307.

56. Vasari 1986, 901.

57. Alberti 1988, IX, 8, 312.

58. Benjamin 1968, 217–252.

59. See, for example, Vasari's criticism of the Gothic manner, in particular of the "maledizzione" of agglomerated sculptural incident in his introduction to architecture. Vasari 1986, 35.

60. The trend toward increased sculpturalization in Palladio's work has been noted and variously assessed; see Ackerman 1977. Puppi finds the late work problematic for this reason and describes his manner as "exaggerated pictorialism"; see Puppi 1986, 236. In an earlier article, Wolters (who focuses mostly on interior decoration but also assesses the Loggia del Capitaniato) also sees Palladio's "decorated" style as attributable to outside factors (whims of the client or professional *stuccatori* to whom he would have given no design guidance). Wolters 1968, 255–267.

61. On Palladio's tectonics, see Payne 1999, chap. 8.

62. Palladio 1980, 67.

63. Palladio 1980, 67.

64. Alberti 1988, 385.

65. Francesco di Giorgio Martini 1967, II, 385.

66. Spini 1980, 84.

67. "In an *istoria* I like to see someone who admonishes and points out to us what is happening there; or beckons with his hand to see; or menaces with an angry face and with flashing eyes, so that no one should come near; or shows some danger or marvellous thing there; or invites us to weep or to laugh together with them." Alberti 1966, 78.

Chapter 7

1. Francesco's approach was that of an expert and experienced fortress builder as well as an architectural theorist, and it is this double qualification that distinguishes his claim to primacy against those of Filarete and

Alberti, neither of whom could claim specialist expertise in military engineering. However, Filarete worked on the sculptural decorations and possibly some aspects of the construction of the gateworks of the Sforza castle in Milan between 1451 and 1453 (Lazaroni and Munoz 1908, 163–165, updating Beltrami 1894, 47–58) and on some aspects of the fortifications at Bellinzona in 1457 (Sciolla 1975, 70). Whether fortification should be regarded as part of the history of engineering or of mainstream "architecture" is still debated. Ruskin (not surprisingly in view of his antipathetic attitude to the classical world and its intellectual heirs) finds the Renaissance bastion to be mere building, save where it is decorated by moldings—when it becomes architecture for him. That this was not a universally held nineteenth-century view is shown by Viollet-le-Duc's very different treatment of the subject. Modernists generally have less difficulty with the functional aspects of Renaissance fortification. As one distinguished critic put it: "To our own generation . . . which has learned to appreciate simple, utilitarian forms and clearly planned buildings, so long as their proportions are good, Leonardo's fortifications seem beautiful the more because of their exquisite simplicity and their proportions." Heydenreich 1954, 1:83. Hale adopted Heydenreich's position on engineering's potential as art, calling for artistic judgment to be applied to "some of the Renaissance's finest works." Hale 1977, 59; see also Bury 1980, 7–20. If a definitive contemporary ruling on the centrality of fortification to Renaissance architecture is sought, one has to look no further than the preface to Alberti's *Ten Books,* where, in a lengthy passage adapted from Vitruvius, he spells out the important contribution of architects to the design of "Engines and Machines of War, Fortresses, and the like inventions necessary to the Defending the Liberty of our Country" and proceeds to assert (more strongly than I would care to defend) that the "Enemy was oftener overcome and conquered by the Architect's Wit without the Captain's Arms, than by the Captain's Arms without the Architect's Wit" (Alberti 1955, x).

2. Papini 1946, is still fundamental. For Francesco's fortifications see Dezzi Bardeschi 1968, 97–138; Fiore 1978, 1987, 197–208; Volpe 1982; Dechert 1990, 161–180; and Adams 1993, 126–163.

3. Hersey 1988.

4. "Siccome Denocrate manifestamente ad Alessandro in figura mostrò, el quale sentendo Alessandro desideroso nuova città edificare, lui allora Aton monte a guisa d'omo formò, el quale nella mano sinistra teneva una tazza che tutte le vene del corpo in essa corrivano, e nella mano destra le circulate mura della nuova città." Francesco di Giorgio Martini 1967, I, 3. The figure with the bowl in one hand and the model of city walls in the other is taken from the codex Magliabechiano II, I, 141 and appears in the same form in the Codex Senese S. IV, 4. The body surrounded by walls and towers with a castle as crown appears in the Codex *Torinese*

Saluzziano, 148. The story of Denocrates and Mount Athos was probably taken from Vitruvius, but Plutarch's "Life of Alexander" gives another version in which the architect attracts Alexander's attention by clothing himself in a lion's skin, with a wreath of poplar on his head, and bearing a club like the one carried by Hercules. Filarete uses the same example. Spencer 1965, 18–19.

5. Francesco di Giorgio 1967, 3–4.

6. For Florentines and their subjects, tropes on the Medici were commonplace, but even the Sienese, when they petitioned Charles V to postpone his plans for a citadel in their city, begged the emperor not to use "so sharp a *medicine* that it destroys the body and consumes life." Pepper and Adams 1986, 61.

7. Von Moos 1978. See also Woods-Marsden 1985, 2: 553–568; Woods-Marsden 1989, 396; Forster 1971, 65–104; Pepper 1973, 22–27, and a much more detailed study of the role of fortresses in the ritual theater of tournaments, state entries, and other formal events in Pepper 2000b.

8. Hale 1977, 41–43.

9. Boxer and de Azvedo 1960.

10. Marconi 1973, 79, and figure 83.

11. In the face of increasingly effective and mobile siege guns, the tall towers and slender curtains of traditional medieval fortresses and city walls proved both vulnerable and poorly adapted to accommodate defensive artillery. Thus was set in motion an evolutionary process that supplanted these potent symbols of the premodern world and replaced them with low, squat bastions and ramparts, set in deep ditches, and, ideally, almost invisible from ground level. The literature is extensive, but the key recent English-language sources on the Italian origins of the new fortifications are to be found in De la Croix 1960, 263–290; De la Croix 1963, 30–50; Hale 1965, 466–494; and Pepper and Adams 1986. The wider military implications of this development are central to the thesis of Parker 1988, and the debate Parker stimulated is the subject of an interesting collection edited by Rogers 1995.

12. For the rebuilding history of the Castelnuovo, see Filangieri 1929, 49–73; 1936, 251–323, 1937, 267–333, 1938, 258–342. See also Hersey 1973.

13. Pepper 1995, 263–294.

14. Hersey 1969, 90, argues for an attribution to Francesco. His involvement in some of the 1490s works is secure. Certainly he was in Naples before, during, and after the sieges of 1495 and is identified as "Un messere Francisco, senese, tavolario della Maistà del sig. re Alfonso et mastro zufficiente de adificie" by the contemporary Ferraiolo, *Una Cronaca figurata del Quattrocento* (ed. Filangieri 1956), 112. Whether any of his designs posthumously formed part of the scheme of enlargement carried out by others from 1509 remains speculative.

15. The self-consciously old-fashioned *merlatura* features in the sketch made in 1539 or 1540 by Francesco de Holanda, now con-

served in the library of the Escorial (28.1.20, f.53v.) and reproduced most recently in the catalogue by Fiore and Tafuri 1993, 292, exhibit XV.1.3. Here, Nicholas Adams points out quite correctly that the *merlatura* itself is nothing like any of the upper works in Francesco di Giorgio's built or drawn oeuvre. For Holanda, see Bury 1979, 163–202.

16. The decoration on the Florentine Fortezza da Basso (see below) is perhaps the closest equivalent. This was the work praised by Vasari as "fa bellissimo vedere" (Milanesi, 1: 129). The deeply rusticated masonry of the Federician gate at Capua, also mentioned below, and that of mid-fifteenth-century *torrioni* flanking the city-facing facade of the Castello Sforzesco in Milan are also notable but probably were unknown to Vasari.

17. More explicit examples include Dürer's multipaneled woodcut of a triumphal arch designed for the Emperor Maximilian and the earlier series of cartoons on the theme of the Triumph of Caesar, painted by Mantegna for the Gonzaga of Mantua c. 1486 and now in Hampton Court. See Martindale 1979 and, more generally, Caradente 1963. Petrarch's *Trionfi* were illustrated using classical conventions in the early printed publications of the poet's work, while Titian employed the same devices for his *Triumph of the Faith* woodcut. The genre is obviously related closely to the formal entries and pageants that were such an important aspect of late-medieval and Renaissance court ceremonial.

18. Hersey 1973, 13–16.

19. Abulafia 1988, 285. See also Shearer 1935 and Kantorowicz 1957.

20. Abulafia 1988, 281.

21. Pepper 1973, 22–27, and Porada 1967, I, 11–12, and note 27 below.

22. Surveying, cartography, and the drawn images of geometrical fortress systems also clearly played an important part in Renaissance and baroque Europe's perception of military architecture. See Bennett and Johnston 1996 and Pollack 1991, 1998, 109–124.

23. Belluzzi (or Bellucci), *Nuova inventione di fabricar fortezze di varie forme* (Venice, 1598) quoted by De la Croix 1960, 275.

24. Scully 1952, 38–45.

25. Hale 1977, 42.

26. Quoted by Wittkower 1949, 14.

27. Frugoni 1991, 13, who also quotes Muller 1961, 53: "Jerusalem remains, on medieval world maps, a circle at the centre of the world, and is defined as 'umbilicus terrarum . . . in orbis medio posita' by Urban II when preaching the first crusade, in an expression attributed to him by Robert of Reims in 1095." See also Ehrenberger Katz 1969, 1–27; Lavedan 1954; and Deonna 1940, 119–212.

28. The qualification, postmedieval, is important here because geometry as well as a whole range of iconographic references may well have played a part in the design of medieval fortresses. Witness the many theories

surrounding the building program of Frederick II.

29. Firpo 1987, 287–230.

30. Averlino 1965: text associated with the illustrations on folios 11v, 13v, 33r, 35r, and 43r. Spencer's edition has the best illustrations, taken from the codex dedicated to Piero de' Medici and now in the BNF Magliabecchianus II, IV, 140.

31. Lang 1952, 95. See also Lang 1972, 391–397, discussing the source for Sforzinda and the possible role of Francesco Filelfo (a fellow Florentine émigré in Milan) as Filarete's collaborator. Onians 1972, 96–114, makes further connections.

32. Doukas 1975, chap. 45, 11.

33. For the walls, see Van Millingen 1899, and for the ancient and modern components, Gabriel 1934, 85–114.

34. Necipoglu 1991, 3–13, for the main Ottoman imperial projects after 1453.

35. Högg 1932.

36. Du Fresne-Canaye 1897, 285, and Dapper 1703, 488. Dapper was originally published in Flemish in 1688.

37. Restle 1981, 361–367; see also Raby 1982, 3–8.

38. For the view, figure 30 in De Seta 1989, 11–57.

39. For the Henrician fortresses, see Saunders 1989, chap. 2, and figure on p. 37.

40. Necipoglu 1991, 10.

41. Babinger 1978, 504–507. Marconi 1973, 66, turns it around when he suggests that the 1457 Ottoman work at Yedikule could have been known to Filarete, who frequented both Venice and Milan (the latter enjoying close links with Constantinople after 1453).

42. A detailed description of these and other early Ottoman fortifications is in Pepper 2000a.

43. Maggi and Castriotto 1564, f. 52r.

44. Hale 1968, 501–532, for the full story of this seminal urban fortress. For the quote, see Segni 1830, 2: 400.

45. Adams and Pepper 1994, 61–74. For the drawings, see the catalogue section, 303.

Chapter 8

Much of the research here was carried out at the National Gallery in Washington, D.C., working on behalf of the Mark J. Millard Architectural Collection, in preparing the book *Northern European Books: Sixteenth to Early Nineteenth Centuries*. I thank the National Gallery, and in particular Katherine Whann, for sending me the illustrations for this chapter. Nearly all of the books discussed here are contained within the Millard Collection.

1. In northern practice, classical motifs are first seen in the Fugger Chapel in the Augsburg church of St. Anna (1509–1518), but here, as with most other examples from the first half of the century, Renaissance forms

are restricted to a few decorative details applied to unclassical fabrics. The only significant exception to this rule is the Renaissance design of the Johann-Friedrich-Bau of Schloss Hartenfels at Torgau (1533–1536), a work of Konrad Krebs. Even after 1550, classical forms are rarely found in the North. The most prominent example in Germany was the court facade of the Ottheinrichsbau at Heidelberg, started in 1556; the most distinguished classical work in the Netherlands is the Antwerp Town Hall (1561–1565). The reason for the North's slow acceptance of classicism in the sixteenth century was undoubtedly the social turmoil induced by the Reformation. Not only did religious strife greatly curtail building activity, but Protestantism's antipathy toward Rome also led many areas of the North to reject Italian artistic models. Lutheranism, in particular, sought a return to Gothic ways in its building forms.

The honor of being the first Renaissance theorist of architecture in the North belongs to Walther Hermann Ryff (b. 1500), also known by his Latin name of Gualtherus Rivius. In 1543 Ryff published a Latin version of the ten books of Vitruvius in Nuremberg. In 1547 he composed the first Germanic treatise on classical architectural theory, *Der fürnembsten, notwendigsten, der gantzen Architectur angehörigen Mathematischen und Mechanischen Künst, eygentlicher bericht.* In the next year there appeared his famed *Vitruvius Teutsch,* a German translation of Vitruvius. Classical theory got a slightly earlier start in the Netherlands, when Pieter Coecke van Aelst in Antwerp, the largest town in the North and the leading center of classical ideas, published a Flemish translation of the fourth book of Sebastiano Serlio's proposed treatise in 1539, a French and German translation of this same book in 1542. The first Germanic column book to be inspired by Serlio was produced in Latin by the Swiss Hans Blum in 1550. His German translation, *Von den fünff Seülen,* was issued in Zurich five years later and itself became a much emulated model.

2. Hitchcock 1978.

3. Dietterlin 1598, Preface.

4. Baer 1913, 270–271.

5. Dietterlin 1598, Preface.

6. Blunt 1977, 613–614.

7. Blunt 1977, 614–618.

8. Rubens 1622, Preface.

9. Ryckemans had recently worked for Rubens on the engraving of *Christ and the Twelve Apostles,* a painting that Rubens had executed in Spain.

10. The only significant northern publications appearing during the Thirty Years War were Joseph Furttenbach's numerous publications, chiefly his *Architectura civilis* (1628), *Architectura navalis* (1629), and *Architectura martialis* (1630).

11. Eric Jönsson Dahlberg, *Suecia antiqua et Hodernia*, 3 vols. (Stockholm, c. 1716); Lauritz de Thurah, *Den danske Vitruvius*, 2 vols. (Copenhagen, Ernst Henrich Berling, 1746–1749). Dahlberg's impressive topographic study of Sweden and its cities and architecture was inspired by Merian's topographic ventures published in Frankfurt. Thurah's trilingual work was more properly a monograph and aimed to inform the European reader that Denmark too possessed many examples of "beauty and magnificence in the art of architecture."

12. See Andrea Pozzo, *Perspectivae pictorum atque architectorum,* 2 vols. (1st German edition Augsburg, Jeremias Wolff, 1706–1709); Ferdinando Galli-Bibiena, *L'Architecttura civile* (Parma: Paolo Monti, 1711); Giuseppe Galli-Bibiena, *Architectture e Prospettive* (Augsburg, Andreas Pfeffel, 1740). All three artists had direct connections with the Habsburg court.

Chapter 9

The spelling in quotations (excepting titles) has been modernized, and the dates are new style. Before 1752 the convention of the "historical year" was used, in which the year was deemed to begin on March 25.

1. Wotton 1624, 17.

2. The columns' characteristics were also emphasized in the English "Lomazzo." Lomazzo 1598, 84–85.

3. Wotton 1624, 33–34.

4. Inigo Jones's 1567 copy of the Barbaro *Vitruvius* (III.i), against Vitruvius, 109 ln. 40, against Vitruvius, 111 ln. 38.

5. See Peacock 1990, 154–179.

6. Jonson 1965–1970b, lns. 340–345.

7. Marcelline 1625, 18–19.

8. Marcelline 1625, 19.

9. See Kantorowicz 1957; Weston and Greenberg 1981, 11, 47.

10. Kantorowicz 1957, 141.

11. James I 1610, "B." James here echoes Jean Bodin on the theory of divine right. See Herndl 1970, 81; Levack 1990, 35. The date is new style, adjusted from the published date of 1609.

12. Shute 1563, sig.Aijr.

13. Cesare Cesariano in his edition of *Vitruvius* of 1521 represented the Vitruvian man (in a square) as a crucified figure, thereby "Christianizing" Vitruvius through the adaptation of Leonardo's celebrated drawing. In the English *Lomazzo,* Haydocke's plates are after Dürer, but the first plate, of Adam and Eve, is only loosely based on Dürer's engraving of 1504. On the "Christianization" of the Vitruvian figure, see Sgarbi 1993.

14. Dee 1570, sig.ijr.; Wotton 1624, 12.

15. Jones 1655, 33.

16. Puttenham 1589, 80.

17. Jonson 1965–1970c,43–45.

18. King 1620, 34, 37.

19. See Kantorowicz 1957, 87–192; Palme 1957.

20. See Sharpe 1992.

21. See Cowell 1607, "Qq. I"; Levack 1990, 29–44.

22. See Herndl 1970, 77–78; Weston and Greenberg 1981, 1–7.

23. Jonson 1965–1970a, lns. 25–26.

24. Strong and Orgell 1973, 257 lns. 116–118.

25. Strong and Orgell 1973, 51–52, 63–66, 71–72.

26. Jones 1655, 54.

27. See Hart 1994, 140–150.

28. The law (whether canon, common, or Roman) and Roman architecture clearly share traditions and concepts. Renaissance legal and architectural treatises, for example, in the composition of their "argument" or their "design," shared references to the rules of rhetoric, nature and its "laws," and indeed the body as the ultimate "measure of all things." See Herndl 1970, esp. 77, 303 n. 75; Kelly 1966, 184–199; Kelly 1970, 174–194; Kelly 1979, 777–794; Kelly 1990, 31–34. The common practices and the published codes of law and architecture drew from precedents and customs recorded over time at one extreme and universal Platonic ideals at the other. See Kelly 1976, 267–279; Kelly 1988, 84–102; Kelly 1990, 180–183. On a practical level, the law was certainly not foreign to a Renaissance architect's concerns. Vitruvius had included law among subjects in which the architect should be well experienced; see Vitruvius, I, i, 3, and I, i, 10 (the first passage was quoted by Jones, in Jones 1655, 4). Following Alberti's study of canon law at Bologna University, he wrote the legal treatises *De Jure* and *Pontifex* (both 1437), which are thought to have influenced his urban thinking. See Saura 1988.

29. The *Oxford English Dictionary* (*OED*) defines *ordonnance* or *ordinance* as "systematic arrangement, architectural parts or features, an order of architecture" and "in reference to France and other continental countries: An ordinance, decree, law, or by-law, under the monarchy, a decree of the King or the regent." The former sense is found in Shute's reference to "whole ordonnances" (Shute 1563, sig.viii*v*), and both readings are contained in Claude Perrault's *Ordonnance des cinq espèces de colonnes selon la méthode des Anciens* (Paris, 1683). A *norma* is defined in the *OED* as "carpenter's or mason's square: hence pattern, rule, law."

30. The architectural orders were also compared to the established medieval art form of heraldry. See Hart 1993.

31. Dee 1570, sig.aj*r-v*. See Sherman 1995, 135–136; Yates 1969, 109, 146.

32. See Shapiro 1983, 163–193; Kelly 1988, 99–101.

33. See Hart 1994, 130–131.

34. See Johnson 1987, 170.

35. Wotton 1624, 92.

36. James I 1615, 1619.

37. The *Dictionary of National Biography* entry for Jones states, "Before the close of 1630 Jones was made a Justice of the Peace for Westminster."

38. See Gotch 1928, 118.

39. Marcelline 1610, 31.

40. Thornborough 1641, 221–222.

41. Thornborough 1641, 222, 234.

42. See Hart 1994, 42–44; Hart 1995a.

43. See Hudson n.d., Sharpe 1992, 665–683.

44. Strong and Orgell 1973, 457 lns. 338–343.

45. See Dugdale 1658, 115.

46. See Hart 1995b.

Chapter 10

This chapter develops a number of ideas found in my recent book (Harries 1987, especially 137–138, 228–235). It has its more immediate origin in remarks made on the occasion of Joseph Rykwert's seventieth birthday. Of course, given his thorough discussion of Vitruvius's account of the origins of architecture and of the many ways subsequent theorizing remained indebted to Vitruvius, to honor him in that way was a bit like carrying owls to Athens.

1. Vitruvius, 38.

2. Vitruvius, 40.

3. Vitruvius, 37.

4. Poppe 1909, 9.

5. Heidegger 1953, 48–49.

6. Alciatus 1542, 122.

7. Cf. Blumenberg 1986.

8. Macdonald 1982, 120–121.

9. Villari 1990, 17.

10. For a discussion of the connection between the balloon, French Revolution, and hopes for a liberated humanity, see Reinicke 1988.

11. Reinicke 1988, 76–77.

12. Vidler, 314.

13. Cf. Sennett 1996, 292.

14. Boullée 1976, 86.

15. Boullée 1976, 107.

16. Boullée 1976, 107.

17. Boullée 1976, 107.

18. Boullée 1976, 107.

19. Conrads 1975, 79.

20. van Doesburg in *De Stijl*, Jaffé 1967, 206.

21. van Doesburg in *De Stijl*, Jaffé 1967, 206–207.

22. Conrads 1975, 79.

23. van Doesburg in the final number of *De Stijl*, Jaffé 1967, 240.

24. Plato, *Philebus* 51c–d, trans. B. Jowett.

25. Boullée 1976, 88.

26. Boullée 1976, 86.

27. Vitruvius, 116.

28. Colvin 1991, 7.

Chapter 11

The topic of this chapter was first presented in the Geske Lecture Series at the University of Nebraska, Lincoln.

1. This praise appears in *L'Homme du monde éclairé par les arts* and in his *Discours*.

2. Szambien 1986, 177.

3. Briseux 1743, 1: 25.

4. This argument had been made earlier in the century. The preface to Briseux's book is almost identical to an earlier, similar work, published anonymously in 1728 with the title, *Architecture Moderne ou l'Art de Bien Bâtir* that has often been also attributed to Briseux (1728 and 1764), also attributed to Tiercelet.

5. In his *Essai*, Laugier (1755) stated that it was not enough to concern oneself with proportions or the classical orders. "In arts that are not merely mechanical," he wrote, "it is not enough to know how to work, we must first learn to think. Real principles are required, and the practical interest of earlier theories (including Vitruvius) has clouded our capacity to understand them." Thus, he criticized Briseux's attempt to refute Perrault, for this was a futile exercise. It was obvious, Laugier thought, that Perrault had not meant what he wrote. Yet in his book, *Observations sur l'Architecture*, Laugier (1765) proposed a truly prescriptive theory of proportions, much more specific than Briseux's, based on the rationality of vision and associated to expressive intentions.

6. Laugier 1755, II, 115ff.

7. Laugier 1755, 115.

8. Laugier 1755, 153.

9. Laugier 1755, 156.

10. Arendt 1958.

11. Pérez-Gómez 1977.

12. Pérez-Gómez 1983, 57–60.

13. Briseux 1752, 1.

14. Briseux 1752, 4. Perrault had associated proportions with "arbitrary beauty," a beauty derived from convention, but he insisted that architects had to know such proportions in order to practice well. This "arbitrary beauty" was, according to Perrault, associated with "positive beauty" by the public, creating the impression of beauty based in proportions.

15. Briseux 1752, 2.

16. Briseux 1752, 1.

17. Briseux 1752, 2.

18. Briseux 1752, 3.

19. Briseux 1752, "Avant-propos," 4–11.

20. Pérez-Gómez 1997, 57.

21. Briseux 1752, 7–8.

22. Briseux 1752, 43.

23. Rameau's theory, first published in 1722 in his *Traité de l'Harmonie Reduite à ses Principes naturels,* changed somewhat throughout the century and was reiterated in various writings with increasing epistemological and metaphysical ambition. By mid-century his position had become highly contentious, and Rameau became involved in an important debate with Rousseau, D'Alembert and Diderot that would rage from about 1750 to 1764.

24. Rameau 1752, 49–50.

25. Rameau 1752, 49.

26. Rameau 1752, 50.

27. Rameau 1752, 2–3.

28. Rameau 1762, 91–101. See also Lescat 1987.

29. Rameau 1754, xv–xvi.

30. Rameau 1762.

31. Kepler 1619, quoted by Hallyn 1993, 232.

32. Hallyn 1993, 233.

33. Hallyn 1993, 234.

34. Hallyn 1993, 236.

35. The issue was the expression of human emotions through the personal volition or imagination of the composer. The reconciliation of this mode of musical significance with the aspirations of music as a language or communicative practice has remained an issue ever since. There are fascinating parallels between music and architecture in this regard.

36. Verba 1993, 38.

37. Soufflot 1961. See Pérez-Gómez and Pelletier 1997, 71.

38. Verba 1993, 53.

39. Rousseau 1969, 236–237.

40. Rousseau 1969, 475.

41. Rousseau 1969, 496.

42. In a letter to La Motte Houdar (1727), he said that musicians working for the theater (like himself) should "study nature before painting it, thus becoming capable of applying their science to the judicious choice of colours and nuances, perceived [by reason and taste] as appropriate to the needs of expression." Rameau to La Motte Houdar, October 15, 1727, quoted by Baridon 1987, 449.

43. Briseux 1752, chaps. 1, 14.

44. Briseux 1752.

45. Briseux 1752, 21.

46. Briseux 1752, 34–36.

47. Briseux 1752, 51–53.

48. Briseux 1752, 53.

49. Briseux 1752, 6.

50. Briseux 1752. Rameau, for his part, accused Newton of simple-mindedness for having merely applied a "diatonic" scale to his theory of color. Rameau argued that Newton could have identified a base or gen-

erating color from which "harmonic" groupings of colors might have emerged. See Rameau 1752, 63–64.

51. Briseux 1752, 45.

52. Briseux 1752, 46.

53. For this issue, see Pérez-Gómez 1994, Introduction.

54. Pérez-Gómez 1994, 51.

55. Pérez-Gómez 1994.

56. Rameau 1752, 62. This argument is the well-known cornerstone of Condillac's *théorie des sensations*, but I have not come across direct references to this work, by either the architect or the composer.

57. Briseux 1752, chap. 3, 39.

58. Briseux 1752, 39.

59. Briseux 1752, 43.

60. Briseux 1752, 44.

61. Briseux 1752, 74–75.

62. Briseux 1752, 79.

63. Briseux 1752, 91–96.

64. Perrault 1684, 12, n. 14.

65. Perrault 1684, 12, n. 13.

66. Briseux 1752, 101.

67. Briseux 1752, 56–57.

68. Briseux 1752, 58.

69. Briseux 1752, 58–59.

70. Briseux 1752, 105.

71. Briseux 1752, 106.

72. Briseux 1752, 63.

73. Briseux 1752.

74. Briseux 1752, 64.

75. Briseux 1752, 69.

76. Briseux 1752, 72–73.

77. Briseux 1752; vol. 2 is usually bound together with vol. 1, but with new pagination. The first thirty pages concern the history of architecture, followed by the orders according to Vignola, Palladio, Scamozzi, and himself.

78. Briseux 1752, 2: 11.

79. Fréart de Chambray 1650.

80. Briseux 1752, 2: 168.

81. For example, in Le Camus de Mezières 1780.

82. Briseux 1752, 2, 7.

83. See Pérez-Gómez and Pelletier 1997, 89–104.

84. Briseux 1752, 2, 177.

85. Briseux 1752, 181.

86. Le Corbusier 1987, 114.

Chapter 12

1. Cf. Simmel, "The Stranger."

2. Sophocles 1954, 55; (original, *Oedipus Tyraneus*, Loeb, 1030–1035).

3. Sophocles 1954, 73 (*Oedipus Tyraneus*, 1453).

4. Sophocles xxx, 607–620.

5. In the following four sentences, I have taken the liberty of paraphrasing myself. They appear in Chapter 3 of Sennett, 1994.

6. Cox 1966, 49.

7. Translated and quoted in Pelikan 1985, 49–50.

8. Augustine 1958, 325.

9. Berlin 1976, xxiii.

10. Berlin 1976, 197–198.

11. See Sennett 1993, 154–173, 224–236.

12. de Feir 1882, 23. For a full list of contemporary criticisms of this painting, see Clark 1986, 310–311, n. 65. Although my analysis of this painting is radically at odds with Clark's, I wish to acknowledge the ever-provoking analysis of my ever Marxizing colleague.

13. Jules Compte, quoted and translated by Clark 1986, 240.

14. Houssaye 1883, 242. I have used Clark's translation, though the diction of the French original is much more emphatic. See Clark 1986, 243.

15. Stern 1894, 6: 353.

16. Stern 1894, 6: 359.

17. Stern 1894, 6: 466.

18. Herzen 1974, 3: 1024.

19. Herzen 1974, 3: 1024.

20. Herzen 1974, 3: 1025.

21. Herzen 1974, 3: 1399.

22. Herzen 1974, 3: 1399.

23. Herzen 1974, 3: 1386.

24. Herzen 1974, 3: 686.

25. Herzen 1974, 3: 655.

Chapter 13

This chapter could not have been completed without the inspiration and assistance of many colleagues. In particular, I am grateful for the help and advice of Yvonne Sherratt, who has already made the argument for a link between narcissism, mimesis, and the death instinct (see M. Phil. thesis, University of Cambridge). I am also grateful to Matt Connell and Darren Deane, with whom I first discussed the ideas for this chapter.

1. Wittkower 1962.

2. Plato 1973, 50–57.

3. Gadamer 1986.

4. Vitruvius 1960, 73.

5. See, for example, the comments of John Dee in Hart 1994, 69–71.

6. On this, see Battisti 1981, 42. For a detailed elaboration of this subject, see Casazza and Boddi 1978, 207–212.

7. Vitruvius 1990, 7.

8. *Spandere* is a contraction of *expandere*. See s.v., Thesaurus Linguae Latinae (Leipzig: Teubner, 1931), 5, 1599: "porrigere; de Christianis qui orantes bracchia in crucis formam extendunt" (cf. Tert. Orat. 29, 200.9; Paul. Med., Vita Ambr., 47).

9. Marcuse 1969, 29–30.

10. Marcuse 1969, 29.

11. Freud 1984, 329.

12. Marcuse 1969, 164.

13. Marcuse 1969, 164.

14. Freud 1984, 84.

15. Marcuse 1969, 170.

16. Marcuse 1969, 168.

17. Marcuse 1969, 194.

18. Adorno 1979, 34.

19. Adorno 1984, 80. Here we might recognize a distinction between the treatment of the concept of mimesis in Benjamin and Adorno. For Adorno, mimesis is nonconceptual and relates to a sensuous correspondence with the world. For Benjamin, it is conceptual and relates to a nonsensuous correspondence.

20. "I believe that if ideational mimetics are followed up, they may be as useful in other branches of aesthetics" (Freud 1960, 193). For further reading on mimesis, see Auerbach 1953, Taussig 1993, Gebauer and Wulf 1995.

21. Benjamin 1978, 336. On this, see Derrida 1987, 255ff. Mimesis also can be seen to share the same epistemological fragility of hermeneutics, in that its only source of validation is that of the interpreting agent.

22. Benjamin 1969, 217.

23. Hansen 1993, 53.

24. Adorno and Horkheimer 1979, 180.

25. Adorno 1978, 222.

26. Adorno 1984, 81.

27. For Adorno, mimesis refers to a sensuous correspondence with the world. On this see note 5 above.

28. Lévi-Strauss 1966, 225.

29. For example, the myth of Master Manole at the monastery of Arges. On this, see Eliade 1970, 164–190.

30. On this see Lechte 1990, 215–219.

31. All this begins to hint at a theory of visual pleasure for architecture. Such a theory might subscribe to the same processes of narcissistic identification outlined by Laura Mulvey in her theory of visual pleasure for film. Yet it would extend beyond the straightforward identification with human beings to include identification with the built environment itself. This is not to reduce architecture to mere visual pleasure. Architecture should also offer the possibility of a meaningful engagement with the world. Architecture, like art, should exceed the empty gratification of beautiful illusion. Art, for Adorno, should never be easy. It has to be engaged with in a process that evokes the *durcharbeiten*—the

working through—of psychoanalytic theory. See Mulvey 1975, 16–18.

Chapter 14

I acknowledge George Dodds's insightful editing, as well as comments by Joseph Rykwert, Marco Frascari, and David Leatherbarrow during the research from which this chapter was derived.

1. Rykwert 1982, 44.

2. Bayer, Gropius, and Gropius 1938, 15, 20, 32.

3. Rykwert joins other critics who have addressed this aspect of the early Bauhaus. Lang (1965, 29, 73) identified this time as the Bauhaus's first phase, a "romantic" phase, with Itten's mystical-philosophical approach to design education. Francisono's (1971) noteworthy work on Bauhaus educational foundations, as well as Greenberg's (1979, 58) work on the affinities between the Bauhaus and dada and Wick's book on Bauhaus pedagogy (1982, 101–104), add to our knowledge of the various factions at the school. Paul Citroen's student recollections of the Mazdaznans and Itten, published as early as 1964 (Greenberg 1979, 102, n. 42), noted Itten's demonic quality (Citroen 1970, 46), while Kröll (1974, 46–51) brought to the light dilemmas and misunderstandings between the "Itten-Group" and Gropius. Magdalena Droste's work (1993), drawn extensively from the Bauhaus Archiv, expands and revises the Bauhaus history. Droste as well as other critics, such as Forgács (1995) and Baumhoff

(1994), provide alternative perspectives that amend and alter our knowledge of this design school. See also Feuerstein 1997, nn. 1, 2.

4. Forgács 1995, 51; Bayer, Gropius, and Gropius 1972, 14.

5. Bayer, Gropius, and Gropius 1972, 20.

6. Gay 1970, 78.

7. Wingler 1986, 112.

8. Forgács 1995, 51.

9. Wingler 1986, 372.

10. Franciscono 1971, 120.

11. Schmid 1964, 503.

12. Jackson 1926, 12. "Zarathustra" is translated as "Righteous Descendant of White."

13. Schlemmer 1990, 111.

14. Schlemmer 1990, 114.

15. Schlemmer 1990, 110.

16. Bayer, Gropius, and Gropius 1972, 25.

17. Feuerstein 1997, 48.

18. Nehamas 1985, 46.

19. Heilke 1990, 7.

20. Voegelin 1998, 3–25; Heilke 1990, 22.

21. Schlemmer 1961, 17.

22. In 1924, Schlemmer elucidated his theory of costume design. He wrote, "Costume can be developed out of the inner organism, which is the body, and thus visibly express the invisible—the metaphysical anatomy; or

it can be derived from the external appearance of the body's configuration and its individual characteristics and, by refining the accidental and elevating it to the typical. . . . Costume can also be designed following the principles of space, and—space in space itself become a spatial structure. Or it can be derived from and developed according to movement—the elements of movement of either the biological-organic world or the technical-mechanical world. Costume design can be based on one set of these principles as well as on some combination or synthesis of several. After all, these are nothing more than a complex of variations of different principles and fundamentals that form the basis for design." Scheper 1985, 13.

23. Schlemmer 1961, 26.

24. Schlemmer 1961, 26.

25. Schlemmer 1961, 27.

26. Schlemmer 1961, 27.

27. Hollander 1993, 250.

28. Schlemmer's costume types (as well as Voegelin's theory of archetype) share many characteristics of eurythmia, an interpretation of harmony in movement, discussed in Pollitt 1974, 169, and as evinced at Emile Dalcroze's School of Eurythmia in Hellerau, an educational institution contemporary with the Bauhaus. Schlemmer was aware of Dalcroze's work (Feuerstein 1998, 134.)

29. Scheper 1988, 8, 23.

30. George Muche's design for the first international Bauhaus exhibit of 1923 in Weimar was similar to an earlier proposal by Itten. Itten's project was a cubelike object placed in the open. The internal organization of Itten's design is unknown, although its massing suggests small interior spaces gathered around a larger central interior space. Analogous to Itten's design, Muche's project was object-like, surrounded by an open lawn and organized into a cube, the outer edge of which was filled by cells. The inner space was empty. The central void in both Itten's and Muche's projects implies an inner sanctum for the domestic interior that turned away from the community and toward the private central space, presumably filled by the family. It is noteworthy that Itten named his own design "the house of the White Man."

31. Maur 1993, 47.

32. Feuerstein 1998, 162–164.

33. Herzogenrath and Maur discuss the content of this sketch, although neither identifies its implications as a design for the Bauhaus exhibition house of 1923 (Herzogenrath 1998, Maur 1993).

34. Schlemmer's essay, dated 1922 (Maur 1979, 357), makes reference to Frank Lloyd Wright's design at Fallingwater. This is curious. Fallingwater was built between 1936 and 1938. Schlemmer may have revised or updated the essay after Wright's project was published in Germany, or the essay's title may have influenced this dating.

35. Maur 1979, 357.

36. Schlemmer submitted this drawing for an exhibit at the Essen Folkwang Museum. The similarity between this drawing and Gropius's design of the Bauhaus masters' houses at Dessau is striking, as noted by Maur 1993, 46.

37. Schlemmer's initial sketch, similar to a later photograph of families and masters standing and lounging on the masters' houses at the Bauhaus, introduces speculation about the relationship of Schlemmer's sketch to Gropius's design of these houses.

Chapter 15

The following individuals and institutions assisted in the production of this chapter: Guido Pietropoli, Rovigo; Domenico Luciani, Director, Fondazione Benetton studi richerche, Treviso; Sergio Los, Bassano del Grappa; Arrigo Rudi, Verona; Aldo Businaro, Monselice; Adriano Cornaldi (IuaV), Venice; Ida Frigo, Fondazione Benetton studi richerche, Treviso. Tony Cutler, Giorgio Galletti, Jori Erdman, John Dixon Hunt, Elizabeth Meyer, and my coeditor Robert Tavernor read and corrected drafts of this chapter, which began as a joint research project with Marco Frascari, to whom I am much indebted for his direction and generosity (Dodds and Frascari 1998). I express particular gratitude to Caroline B. Constant for her multiple readings, edits, and guidance. Two Delmas Foundation research grants and a Salvatori Award from the Center for Italian Studies at the University of Pennsylvania provided partial funding for this research. Completion of this chapter was made possible by a 1998–1999 Junior Fellowship at Harvard University's Dumbarton Oaks, Washington, D.C.

All translations are by the author unless otherwise noted.

1. *Hypernotomachia Poliphili*, Francesco Colonna, adapted from the Lorna Maher translation. See Stewering 1998, 6 (emphasis added). Also see Colonna 1968, 233–234.

2. Dodds 2000.

3. "Desire" for Scarpa was a concept and not simply a state of being. As a concept it was closely aligned with and influenced by surrealism and the erotic.

4. Rogers 1958a, 304.

5. Numerous tombs bear the name Brion in the public cemetery of San Vito di Altivole, attesting to the family's longstanding ties to this rural region. Brion was the founder of the Brion-Vega electronics company, a leading Italian postwar producer of consumer goods made to modern industrial design standards.

6. Scarpa's and Ennio Brion's stories regarding the acquisition of the site differ (Scarpa 1989, 17; Brion 1997, 151).

7. Scarpa 1989, 17–18.

8. Scarpa claimed that allocating the cypress grove as a burial ground for local clergy was a way of assuaging the local criticism of

the immodest scale of the private burial site (Scarpa 1989, 20). No local clergy have ever been interred there. For the symbolic use of plants in the garden, see Seddon 1991. Roses in particular had a special significance for Scarpa and were used in a number of locations, including in the "floating" labyrinth in the reflecting pool (Pietropoli interview, May 1997). The significance of the rose is associated with "the garden of Eros and the Paradise of Dante" (Cirlot 1962, 263). A drawing of roses in the "floating" planter is one of the last sketches Scarpa made before leaving for Japan in November 1978 (Pietropoli interview, Rovigo, May 1997).

9. Scarpa's use of "borrowed views" was largely influenced by his study of Chinese classical gardens. Scarpa owned numerous books on oriental gardens, including a copy of Sirén's (1949) book on Chinese gardens. Sirén included a number of English translations of extracts from *Yüan Yeh*, the treatise on gardening from the Ming period in which the idea of "borrowed views" was introduced to Chinese garden literature.

10. Mazzariol and Barbieri 1984, 10.

11. Across its open and tree-lined space, one could see from the loggia a framed view of rural fields through a small break in the line of buildings that edge the slow-moving water of the canalized Fiume Bacchiglione.

12. Scarpa 1972.

13. "Ci vorrebbe . . . neppure un Dio inventerebbe una base Attica Greca, perché solo

quella è bella. Tutto il resto sono diventate scorie, perfino quelle di Andrea Palladio!" (Scarpa 1978).

14. The landscape dimension of Scarpa's architectural production is beyond the scope of this chapter (Dodds 2000).

15. Brendel 1944; Focillon 1963, 108.

16. Brendel 1944.

17. Pozza 1976, 216–217.

18. Cirlot 1962, 194; Graves 1966, 120; Jung 1968, 160; Keightley 1877, 467. In the sixteenth century, it was far easier to see the Dolomites from Venice than it is today due to the manufactured haze of agriculture and industry. John Ruskin reportedly ended each day in Venice with a walk to the Fondamenta Nuove, from which he watched the Dolomites reflect the last day's light. Scarpa owned a number of Ruskin's works, including *The Stones of Venice*, and he often quoted Ruskin's romantic observations of the city (Pietropoli interview, May 1997).

19. Scarpa 1972.

20. "Viewing body," is a term coined by Jonathan Crary to describe the mechanization of vision that occurred during the nineteenth century in Western Europe (Crary 1990, 73). Scarpa's intention was the inverse of this: to engage the sentient body through both the construction of views and the manipulation of the body of the viewer.

21. "No, non è vero, non è vero, io stesso mi confesso, continuo a insistere dicendo che

avrei sufficiente. . . . . la mia vita, un critico eventuale, uno studioso sul mio lavoro scoprisse le intenzioni che io ho sempre avuto: un'enorme volontà di essere dentro la tradizione, ma senza fare i capitelli e le colonne!" (Scarpa 1978).

22. Spengler 1926, 271.

23. Wilde 1974.

24. Muir 1981, 119–134. Also complicit in this is the longstanding tradition of gendering both nature and Venice as feminine (Soper 1985; Tanner 1992).

25. Wilde 1974, 77. Giorgione and Titian used female models who were ostensibly courtesans, underscoring the confluence of a feminized landscape and erotic desire (Soper 1995).

26. Clark 1976.

27. Also see Reynolds 1997, 120–126.

28. Schor 1987, 11–22.

29. Boullée, 1976, 88.

30. Schor 1987, 4.

31. In the manner of the great connoisseur of painting, Giovanni Morelli, Scarpa understood that to appreciate the authenticity of a work fully, it was necessary to study its details intensely. Morelli, a native of Verona, was a physician and anatomist who owned a collection of paintings in Bergamo, his adopted home (Wind 1964, 32–51). Morelli's work as an adjudicator of the authenticity and attribution of paintings would have been well known to Scarpa, if for no other reason than it was Morelli who attributed the *Sleeping Venus* to Giorgione. Prior to this, it had been catalogued in the Dresden gallery as a copy of a (lost) painting by Titian executed by Sassoferrato (Wind, 1964, 38). Edgar Wind discusses this in *Art and Anarchy* (1964), an Italian translation of which Scarpa owned.

32. Lagerlöf 1990, 7. Bembo's poem was yet another textual source for Giorgione's and Titian's landscapes (Lagerlöf 1990, 7).

33. Arrigo Rudi, interview, Verona, May 1997. Perhaps the first painting that Scarpa saw from the Venetian school in which mandorla-shaped mountains dominate the background was Bartolomeo Montagna's *La Vergine in trono con il Bambino e i Santi Giovanni, Bartolomeo, Fabiano e Sebastiano*. Scarpa may have known the painting as a young boy in Vicenza but certainly knew it later in life. The painting, formerly installed above the altar of the church of San Bartolomeo, is now in the Museo Civico, Vicenza.

34. See "Carlo Scarpa," 1958. A photograph on page 11 shows the framed view of the *rocca* at Asolo that is no longer visible.

35. Although he often tried, Scarpa was never able to find another apartment in Asolo, due largely to the city's popularity with wealthy expatriates, a tradition started by the British in the late nineteenth century.

36. Brusatin 1984b.

37. Aldo Businaro kept a separate apartment on the top floor of his villa for the use of the Scarpas. The vista from the balcony includes an unobstructed view of Monselice's Monte Ricco (Businaro interview, April 1997).

38. Pietropoli, May 1997.

39. Scarpa 1978. This text has been transcribed (and translated) directly from the recording of the lecture (Pietropoli collection, 1997). I thank Giorgio Galletti for assistance in the transcription.

40. Rosand 1982, 18; Brusatin 1983.

41. Scarpa owned French (Roussel 1965) and Italian language-editions of *Locus Solus.* Implied references to *Locus Solus* appear throughout the Brion project, such as Scarpa's desire to create a pool of water beneath the arcosolium so that the sarcophagi would seem to float in the liquid (Saito 1997, 152–153). Scarpa settled for covering the underside of the "bridge" with tiles in varying hues of blue, green, and yellow that simulate the effect of the reflection of water on the bridge's underside. Other elements in the garden that refer to the playful aspect of Roussel's garden are the glass door and the musical steps that lead to what was to have been the water-filled arcosolium (Duboy 1975, Frascari 1985). Frascari reports that Scarpa wrote "locus solus" on a number of his design studies for the Brion project and confided that he often identified with the story's protagonist (Frascari interview, via internet, January 2000).

42. De Amicis 1896, 92–93, 99.

43. Ranalli 1984, 7.

44. Scarpa 1977. The Brion family paid for 200 copies of the monograph. It was printed by Stamperia Valdonega, known for its publication of fine art books, catalogues, and such works of literature as their reprint of the *Hypnerotomachia Poliphili,* a copy of which Scarpa owned.

45. "MONVMENTI IN MEMORIAM IOSEPHI BRION AB HONORINA VXORE FILIISQVE FACTI HIS CARTIS CONTINENTVR IMAGINES" (Scarpa 1977).

46. The photograph was taken by Guido Pietropoli (Pietropoli interview February 1999).

47. The other entrance to the sanctuary, from the northwest, is coded as secondary, largely serving the enclave's funeral program.

48. In the *Hypernotomachia Poliphili,* Francesco Colonna describes a garden as a "lovely body." See Stewering 1998, p. 6.

49. Seddon 1991, 149. This cedar is one of the most tangible signs of Scarpa's collaboration on this project with Italy's most important landscape architect of his generation, Pietro Porcinai (Matteini, 1991, 214).

50. Scarpa 1979, 50.

51. ACS 70 129 102, 70 129 105.

52. ACS 70 129 300.

53. Pietropoli 1990, 95.

54. Marginal drawings were, for Scarpa, a way of rethinking issues, indicating their importance and at times their lack of resolve.

55. ACS 70 129 300.

56. Brusatin 1984a, Pietropoli 1990.

57. Gimbutas 1989, 169–173.

58. Comito, 1978; Daley 1986; Matter 1990, xxiv–xxv, Stewart 1966.

59. Cirlot 1962, 194.

60. Hertz 1973, 20.

61. Frascari (1987) suggests that when Scarpa places himself in a drawing, he signifies the importance of the location.

62. In *Mimesis as Make-Believe,* Kendall Walton (1990) explains that objects or views that act as "prompters" encourage one to "see" things that otherwise one would not have imagined (21–28). A number of key design elements code the Brion garden as Venetian. Beyond the combination of walling and *prato,* the grillwork in the northeast corner is a typically Venetian device that is both decorative and permits air movement in the enclosure, something that is crucial to an enclosed garden in Venice. On a number of occasions, Scarpa implicitly underscored the metaphorical association of the Brion enclave with the idea of Venice as a garden in the midst of the sea (Hunt 1981), variously referring to the surrounding fields as "*un mare*" and "a great plane of water" (Pietropoli interview 1997; Scarpa 1979, 50).

63. Frascari 1991a.

64. Scarpa expressly used 11 (the sum of the number of characters in his name) and 5.5 as a proportional numbering system in the design of the Brion sanctuary as well as in other projects (Scarpa 1978, Frascari 1991a, Frampton 1995, 312–314). Jung (1968, 160) implicitly connects mountains and the mandorla shape with the union of 1 and 1 (11) and the alchemical tradition of the Jewish Maria Prophetissa in which upper and lower worlds unite.

65. Battisti 1972, 5; Scarpa 1979, 53.

66. Scarpa 1979, 53.

67. Scarpa 1979, 50, 53.

68. Pietropoli reports in an interview in 2001 that the last drawings Scarpa made before leaving Vicenza for Japan in 1978 were a series of studies of additions to the reflecting pool. These additional elements were primarily located beneath the water surface, further explaining the function of the *involucrum* in directing the visitor's vision both downward to the immediate foreground and to the garden and landscape beyond.

69. Albertini and Bagnoli 1988, 220.

70. Scarpa's drawings and the manner in which he clad the underside of the arch in tiles whose color simulate the reflective effects of water indicate that in Scarpa's mind, the arcosolium was a water element. This explains why the source of the water for the reflecting pool emanates from the arcosolium.

71. Pietropoli interview 1997.

72. Saito 1997, 152

73. Rosand 1992, 162.

74. Pignatti 1994, 248.

75. Saito 1997, 152.

76. Ponti 1957, 157–158.

Chapter 16

1. Seneca, 1965, 3: 3.

2. Sacks 1987.

3. Schilder 1950.

4. Phantom limbs are a necessary presence following leg or arm amputation. For instance, a phantom appears when a leg is surgically removed, and the individual vividly feels the presence of leg, to the point that he or she may forget the amputation and fall down.

5. Alberti 1966. "What is a happy life? It is peace of mind and lasting tranquility." The wise man reaches happiness by "order, measure, and fitness," which produce "greatness of soul" and "steadfastness that resolutely clings to a good judgment just reached." Seneca *Epistulae* 92.3, 1965.

6. Ruzante presents the most crafted and radical form for the notion of *vita beata* in a dialogue entitled "Dialogo facetissimo et Ridicolissimo," 1525, originally written as home entertainment for Alvise Cornaro. Mostly known for his treatise on the sober life, Cornaro himself was interested in an architecture for a *vita beata* that he theorized in his two drafts for a treatise and in his project for the basin of San Marco in Venice. For Ruzante Cornaro and Falconetto, see Fiocco 1968, and for *vita beata*, see Fino 1988, 39–51.

7. Filarete 1972, 2: 532–535.

8. Filarete 1972, 1: 42.

9. *Madonna Sofrosina* is a personification of Aristotle's virtue of temperance that is present in many Venetian stories. Francesco Colonna's *Hypnerotomachia Poliphili*, 1980, 1: 359, is the most famous among architectural literature.

10. *Counterpoid* is a term invented by Jean Louis Barrault as part of his general theory of mime. The original family name of Barrault was Barrautti, a typical Veneto family name. See Barrault 1951, Mignon 1999.

11. Pastor graduated from the IUAV in 1955. During the earliest part of his professional practice, he worked on several Scarpa projects, beginning with the redesign of the Aula Magna at the Ca' Foscari (1955–1956), and he was active until the design proposal for the new offices of the Regione Veneto within the Procuratie Nuove in Venice (1975–1976). Pastor worked on a few of Scarpa's seminal designs, such as the renovation and reorganization of the Gallerie dell' Accademia (c. 1955), the design of the Venice Biennale Venezuelan Pavilion (1954–1956), and the extension of the Gipsoteca canoviana in Possagno (1955–1957). Pastor became director of the IUAV (1979–1982), four years after Scarpa had resigned from that post (1975).

12. Pastor 1989, 46–47.

13. Dorcy 1961, 34.

14. Dorcy 1961, 35.

15. The body images of Pastor are Venetian, as are the body images of women used by Scarpa. To understand the regional nature of Scarpa's nudes, see the section on the Venetian painting tradition in Clark 1956.

16. This connection is acknowledged in Pastor 1989, 48–51.

17. Cacciari and Pastor 1989, 200.

18. The *Modulor* man has the same characteristic of the corporeal mime of the Etienne Decroux school: naked, the face covered with a piece of canvas, and the solar plexus used as a locus for irradiating action.

19. For the concept of conterpoids, a representation in the muscle movement of outside nonpresent forces, see Barrault 1951, Mignon 1999.

Chapter 17

1. Rykwert 1982, 9–16. For an elaboration of parts of this article, see in the same book "The Sitting Position," 23–32.

2. Rykwert 1982, 16.

3. Wright 1954, 38.

4. Wright 1954, 28.

5. Wright 1954, 29, 43.

6. Wright 1992, 31–32.

7. Loos 1981, 198–203. Similar observations on both Loos and organic architecture are made in Baird 1995, chaps. 2, 6.

8. Loos 1981, 202: "Wie kommen sie dazu, sich etwas schenken zu lassen! Habe ich ihnen nicht alles gezeichnet? Habe ich nicht auf alles rücksicht genommen? Sie brauchen nichts mehr. Sie sind komplett!"

9. *Ver Sacrum* 1900, 343.

10. Mackintosh 1990, 220–225.

11. Loos 1982, 216: "Josef Veillich."

12. Loos 1982, 130: "Heimatkunst."

13. Representative examples, in chronological order, are Gravagnuolo 1982, 50–51; Colomina 1994, ch. 6, esp. 233–282; and Heynen 1999, 75–94.

14. Loos 1982, 129: "Heimatkunst."

15. Czech and Mistelbauer 1984, esp. chap. 5.

16. Frank 1981, 166.

17. Frank 1981, 215.

18. Frank 1981, 236–240.

19. Frank 1923, 338.

20. Frank 1981, 236.

21. Frank 1910.

22. Frank 1981, 36–39.

23. The building has been recently studied at some length in Giella 1995, 38–47.

24. R. M. Schindler, letter of April 21, 1921, quoted in Giella 1995, 41.

25. Wright 1992, 101–115.

26. Schindler 1996, 49–56.

27. Schindler 1996, 39–41.

28. Schindler 1988, 46.

29. Schindler 1996, 50.

Chapter 18

1. Kiesler 1970, 151–153.

2. Mumford 1934, 370.

3. Giedion 1948, 712.

4. Wigley 1995.

5. Nowicki 1951, 273–279.

6. Martin 1994.

7. *Architectural Record* 1933.

8. Giedion 1948, 651–675.

9. The best reference for information on Bally Total Fitness is its ever-changing and extremely flexible web site: http://www.ballyfitness.com.

10. Lynn 1997, 171–172.

11. Deleuze and Guattari 1987, 149–166; De Landa 1997, 257–274.

12. McLeod Bedford 1994, 1998.

13. Stevenson 1995, 17.

14. Kiphuth and Phelps 1932, 50.

15. Kiphuth and Wickens 1937, 38–48.

16. Kiphuth and Wickens 1937. Also MacEwan, Charlottea, and Howe 1932, 144–157.

17. Cook 1922.

18. Klein and Thomas 1931.

19. Browning 1869, lines 400–406.

20. Lahiji and Friedman 1997, 35–61.

21. *Advertising Age* 1993, 2.

22. Lynn 1996, 58–61.

23. Lynn 1997, 54–61.

24. Robinson 1993.

25. Haeckel 1902; Bramwell 1989.

26. Tait McKenzie 1923, 363.

27. Tait McKenzie 1923, 369.

28. Kiesler 1949, 733–742.

29. For the relationship between the historical avant-garde and clothing reform, see McLeod 1994, 148–269; Giedion 1948, 671–677; Wigley 1995.

30. Boumphrey 1935, 126.

31. Douglas 1966.

32. *Advertising Age* 1990, 39.

33. Deleuze and Guattari 1987, 149.

34. Kipnis 1993, 40–49; Speaks 1998, 26–31.

35. Summers 1993, 243–271. A revised version is located in Summers 1994. Also see Summers 1989, 372–406.

36. Bataille 1994.

37. Deleuze and Guattari 1987, 149.

Chapter 19

1. Gartner 1990. Gartner's argument is heavily influenced by Johnson 1987.

2. Ando 1988.

3. Ando 1980, 45–46.

4. Rimer 1981.

5. Tanizaki 1977, 20–22.

6. Tominaga 1995, 510.

7. Ando 1986, 11.

8. Ando 1987, 46.

9. Ando 1995a, 455.

10. Ando 1995b, 462.

11. Ando 1995c, 471.

12. Ando 1995d.

13. Maruyama 1995, 480.

Chapter 20

This chapter was translated from Italian into English by George Dodds and Robert Tavernor.

1. From "The Corinthian Order," in Rykwert 1982, 41.

2. Published in expanded book form, with the same title, in 1976.

3. Extract quoted from the book version of *The Idea of a Town*, Rykwert 1976, 24.

4. Rykwert 1980, 470.

5. Rykwert 1980, 470.

6. These essays have been collected in Rykwert 1982, 23–32, and 103–114, respectively. *The Dancing Column* was first published in 1996; see Rykwert 1996.

References

Chapter 1

For the main texts by Joseph Rykwert referred to, see the Bibliography of Joseph Rykwert.

Calasso, R. 1994. *The Ruin of Kasch.* Cambridge, MA.

Canetti, E. 1962. *Crowds and Power.* London.

———. 1979. *Auto da Fé.* New York.

Evans, R. 1997. "Figures, Doors, Passages." In *Translations from Drawing to Building and Other Essays.* Cambridge, MA.

Jencks, C., and G. Baird (eds.). 1969. *Meaning in Architecture.* London.

Rykwert, J. 1954. "Sigfried Giedion and the Notion of Style." *Burlington Magazine* 96 (April), 123–124.

———. 1967. "Giedion: The Discovery of Space." *Listener,* October 12, 463–466.

Wittkower, R. 1949. *Architectural Principles in the Age of Humanism.* London.

Chapter 2

Alberti, L. B. 1988. *On the Art of Building in Ten Books.* Trans. J. Rykwert, N. Leach, and R. Tavernor. Cambridge, MA.

Ambrose, St. 4th c *Hexaemeron* VI, IX, 55, Migne, Pat. Lat., XIV.

Bacon, R. 1983. De Multiplicatione specierum transl. Lindberg D.C. Oxford.

Barbaro, D. 1567. *I dieci libri dell'architettura.* Venice.

Bonaventure, St. 1993. *The Soul's Journey into God.* New York.

Cornford, F. 1975. *Plato's Cosmology.* Indianapolis.

Crooke, H. 1615. *Microcosmographia.* London.

Diels, H., and W. Kranz. 1934–1938. *Fragmente der Vorsokratiker,* 5th ed. Berlin.

Doctor, M. 1898. *Die Philosophie des Josef Ibn Zaddik in Beitrage zur Gesch. der Philos. des Mittelalters.* Munster.

Eco, U. 1988. *The Aesthetics of Thomas Aquinas,* trans. H. Bredin. London.

Federici-Vescovini, G. 1965. *Studi sulla prospettiva Medievale.* Turin.

Gabirol ibn Solomon. 1892. Lat. Trans. Gundissalinus, ed. C. Baeumker in *Beiträge zur Gesch. der Philos. des Mittelalters.* Munster.

Gadamer, H. G. 1980. *Dialogue and Dialectics.* New Haven, CT.

———. 1985. "The Rehabilitation of Authority and Tradition," and "The Principle of Effective History," in *Truth and Method.* London.

Gadol, J. 1973. *L. B. Alberti, Universal Man of the Renaissance.* Chicago.

Grosseteste, R. 1978. *On Light,* trans. C. Riedel. Milwaukee, WI.

Hahm, D. E. 1977. *The Origins of Stoic Cosmology.* Newark, OH.

Hedwig, K. 1980. *Sphaera Lucis. Studien zur Intelligibilität des Seienden in Kontext der Mittelalterlichen Lichtspekulation.* Münster.

Klein, J. 1968. *Greek Mathematical Thought and the Origin of Algebra.* Cambridge, MA.

Lomazzo, G. P. 1973–1974. *Italia Scritti sulle Arti,* ed. R. Ciardi. Florence.

Merleau-Ponty, M. 1974. *The Phenomenology of Perception.* London.

Patocka, J. 1995. *Body, Society, Movement, World.* Prague.

Mullach, F. 1881. *Fragmenta Philosophorum Graecorum.* Paris.

Ricoeur, P. 1978. *The Rule of Metaphor.* London.

Scheibler, K., ed. 1832. *J. Böhme.* Leipzig.

Sextus Empiricus. *Against Mathematicians.*

Shelby, L. 1977. *Gothic Design Techniques.* Carbondale, IL.

Theon of Smyrna. 1979. *Mathematics Useful for Understanding Plato.* San Diego.

Wagner, D. L. (ed.). 1986. *The Seven Liberal Arts in the Middle Ages.* Bloomington, IN.

Wittkower, R. 1967. *Architectural Principles in the Age of Humanism.* London.

Chapter 3

Blakemore, C., and D. E. Mitchell. 1973. "Environmental Modification of the Visual Cortex and the Neural Basis of Learning and Memory." *Nature, 241,* 467–468.

Kolb, B., and I. Q. Whishaw. 1996. *Fundamentals of Human Neuropsychology,* 4th ed. New York.

Onians, J. 1989. "War, Mathematics and Art in Classical Greece." *Journal of the History of the Human Sciences,* Spring, 39–62.

Onians, J. 1999. *Classical Art and the Cultures of Greece and Rome.* New Haven, CT.

Rykwert, J. 1996. *The Dancing Column.* Cambridge, MA.

Chapter 4

Abbreviations: *LIMC,* Lexicon Iconographicum Mythologiae Classicae. Note that *FRGV* is used in captions, with the full equivalent given there.

Amyx, D. A. 1944. "An Amphora with a Price Inscription in the Hearst Collection of San Simeon." *University of California Publications in Classical Archaeology, 1,* 179–205.

Barletta, B. A. 1990. "An 'Ionian Sea' Style in Archaic Doric Architecutre." *American Journal of Archaeology, 94,* 45–72.

Benton, S. 1934–1935. "The Evolution of the Tripod-Lebes." *Annual of the British School at Athens, 35,* 74–130.

Beyer, I. 1972. "Der Triglyphenfries von Thermos C." *Archäologischer Anzeiger,* 197–226.

Bowen, M. L. 1950. "Some Observations on the Origin of Triglyphs." *Annual of the British School at Athens, 45,* 113–125.

Burkert, W. 1983. *Homo Necans: The Anthropology of Ancient Greek Sacrificial Ritual and Myth.* Berkeley, CA.

———. 1985. *Greek Religion: Archaic and Classical.* Trans. from 1977 German ed. Oxford.

———. 1988. "The Meaning and Function of the Temple in Classical Greece," in *Temple in Society*, ed. M. V. Fox. Winona Lake, MN.

———. 1996. "Greek Temple-Builders: Who, Where and Why?" in *The Role of Religion in the Early Greek Polis, Proceedings of the Third International Seminar of Ancient Greek Cult, Swedish Institute in Athens*, ed. R. Hägg, 21–29. Stockholm.

Coldstream, J. N. 1985. "Greek Temples: Why and Where?" In *Greek Religion and Society*, ed. P. E. Easterling and J. V. Muir, 67–97. Cambridge.

Cook, R. M. 1951. "A Note on the Origin of the Triglyph." *Annual of the British School at Athens*, *46*, 50–52.

———. 1970. "The Archetypal Doric Temple." *Annual of the British School at Athens*, *65*, 17–20.

Coulton, J. J. 1988. *Ancient Greek Architects at Work*. London.

De Angelis D'Ossat, G. 1941–1942. "L'origine del triglifo." *Atti della Pontificia accademia romana di archeologia. Rendiconti*, *18*, 117–133.

Demangel, R. 1931. "Fenestrarum Imagines." *Bulletin de Correspondance Hellénique*, *55*, 117–163.

———. 1946. "Fenestrarum Imagines, bis." *Bulletin de Correspondance Hellénique*, *70*, 132–147.

———. 1949. "Retour offensif des théories vitruviennes sur la frise dorique." *Bulletin de Correspondance Hellénique*, *73*, 476–482.

De Polignac, F. 1994. "Mediation, Competition, and Sovereignty: The Evolution of Rural Sanctuaries in Geometric Greece," in *Placing the Gods: Sanctuaries and Sacred Space in Ancient Greece*, ed. S. E. Alcock and R. Osborne, 3–18. Oxford.

Fehr, B. 1996. "The Greek Temple in the Early Archaic Period: Meaning, Use and Social Context." *Hephaistos*, *14*, 165–191.

Froning, H. 1971. *Dithyrambos und Vasenmalerei in Athen*. Würzburg.

Guadet, J. 1909. *Eléments et Théorie de l'Architecture*. Paris.

Gullini, G. 1974. *Sull'origine del fregio dorico. Memorie dell'Accademia delle Scienze di Torino. Classe di Scienze morali, storiche e filologiche*. 31. Turin.

Hampe, R., and U. Jantzen. 1937. "Die Grabung im Frühjahr 1937." Bericht über die Ausgrabungen in Olympia, *1*, 25–94.

Haspels, C. H. E. 1946. "Trépieds archaïques de Thasos." *Bulletin de Correspondance Hellénique*, *70*, 233–237.

Hersey, G. 1988. *The Lost Meaning of Classical Architecture*. Cambridge, MA.

Hodge, A. T. 1960. *The Woodwork of Greek Roofs*. Cambridge.

Holland, L. B. 1917. "The Origin of the Doric Entablature." *American Journal of Archaeology*, *21*, 117–158.

Hollinshead, M. B. 1999. "'Adyton,' 'Opisthodomos,' and the Inner Room of the Greek Temple." *Hesperia*, *68*, 189–218.

Howe, T. N. 1985. "The Invention of the Doric Order." Ph.D. dissertation, Harvard University.

Kendrick-Pritchett, W. 1971. *Ancient Greek Military Practices*. Berkeley, CA.

Langdon, S. 1987. "Gift Exchange in the Geometric Sanctuaries," in *Gifts to the Gods = Boreas* 15, ed. T. Linders, G. Nordquist, Uppsala.

Laum, B. 1912. "Die Entwicklung das griechischen Metopenbilder." *Neue Jahrbücher für das klassische Altertum, Geschichte, deutsche Literatur und Pädagogik, 29*, 612–644.

Maass, M. 1978. *Die geometrischen Dreifüsse von Olympia—Olympische Forschungen*, 10 Berlin.

———. 1981. "Die geometrische Dreifusse von Olympia." *Antike Kunst, 24*, 6–20.

Mazarakis Ainan, A. 1988. "Early Greek Temples: Their Origin and Function," in *Early Greek Cult Practice*, ed. R. Hägg et al., 105–119. Göteborg.

———. 1997. *From Rulers' Dwellings to Temples: Architecture, Religion and Society in Early Iron Age Greece, 1100–700 B.C.* Jonsered, Denmark.

Mertens, D. 1993. *Der alte Heratempel in Paestum und die archäische Baukunst im Unteritalien*. Mainz.

Morgan, C. 1990. *Athletes and Oracles: The Transformation of Olympia and Delphi in the Eighth Century B.C.* Cambridge.

Onians, J. 1988. *Bearers of Meaning: The Classical Orders in Antiquity, the Middle Ages, and the Renaissance*. Princeton, NJ.

———. 1999. *Classical Art and the Cultures of Greece and Rome*, New Haven, CT.

Peschken, G. 1988. "The Original Significance of the Model for the Doric Pteron and Triglyph, Canon." *Princeton Journal for Thematic Studies in Architecture, 3*, 11–33.

Rhodes, R. F. 1987. "Early Corinthian Architecture and the Origins of the Doric Order." *American Journal of Archaeology, 91*, 477–480.

Richard, H. 1970. *Vom Ursprung des dorischen Tempels*. Bonn.

Robertson, M. 1992. "Europa and Others: Nostalgia in Late Fifth Century Athenian Vase-Painting," in *Kotinos. Festschrift für Erika Simon*, ed. H. Froning, 237–240. Mainz.

Rolley, C. 1977. *Les trépieds à cuve clouée: Fouilles de Delphes*. Paris.

Roux, G. 1992. "La Tholos de Sicyone à Delphes et les origines d'entablement dorique," in *Centenaire de la "Grande Fouille" réalisée par l'Ecole Française d'Athènes, 1892–1903*, ed. J.-F. Bommelaer. Leiden.

Rykwert, J. 1994. "On the Palmette." *Res. Anthropology and Aesthetics, 26*, 11–21.

———. 1996. *The Dancing Column: On Order in Architecture*. Cambridge, MA.

Sakowski, A. 1997. *Darstellungen von Dreifusskesseln in der griechischen Kunst bis zum Beginn der klassischen Zeit*. Frankfurt.

Schefold, K. 1992. *Gods and Heroes in Late Archaic Greek Art*. Cambridge.

Scheibler, I. 1988. "Dreifussträger. *Kanon. Festschrift Ernst Berger, Antike Kunst,* suppl. 15, 310–316.

Schleif, H. et al. 1939–1940. *Der Artemistempel. Architektur, Dachterrakotten, Inschriften, Korkyra. Archäische Bauten und Bildwerke*, ed. G. Rodenwaldt. Berlin.

Snodgrass, A. M. 1989–1990. "The Economics of Dedication at Greek Sanctuaries." *Scienze dell'antichità*, 3–4, 287–294.

Stafford, E. J. 1999. "Masculine Values, Feminine Forms: On the Gender of Personified Abstractions," in *Thinking Men: Masculinity and Its Self-Representation in the Classical Tradition*. London.

Strøm, I. 1988. "The Early Sanctuary of the Argive Heraion and Its External Relations (8th–6th Cent. BC): The Monumental Architecture." *Acta Archaeologica* (Copenhagen), 59, 173–203.

———. 1995. "The Early Sanctuary of the Argive Heraion and Its External Relations (8th. to Early 6th. century BC): The Greek Geometric Bronzes." *Proceedings of the Danish Institute at Athens*, 1, 37–127.

Stucchi, S. 1974. "Questioni relative al tempio A di Prinias ed il formarsi degli ordini dorico e ionico," in *Antichità cretesi, Studi in onore di D. Levi*. Palermo.

van Straten, F. T. 1995. *Hierà Kalá: Images of Animal Sacrifice in Archaic and Classical Greece*. Leiden.

Verzone, P. 1951. "Il bronzo nella genesi del tempio greco," in *Studies Presented to David M. Robinson*, ed. G. E. Mylonas. St. Louis.

von Bothmer, D. 1977. "The Struggle for the Tripod," in *Festschrift für Frank Brommer*, ed. U. Höckmann and A. Krug. Mainz.

Wagner, O. 1988. *Modern Architecture*, trans. H. F. Mallgrave. Santa Monica, CA.

Washburn, O. 1918. "Iphigenia Taurica 113 as a Document in the History of Architecture." *American Journal of Archaeology*, 22, 434–437.

———. 1919. "The Origin of the Triglyph Frieze." *American Journal of Archaeology*, 23, 33–49.

Weickenmeier, N. 1985. "Theoriebildung zur Genese des Triglyphon, Versuch einer Bestandsaufnahme." Ph.D. dissertation, University of Darmstadt.

Wesenberg, B. 1971. *Kapitelle und Basen: Beobachtungen zur Entstehung der griechischen Säulenformen*. Dusseldorf.

Wilson Jones, M. 2000. *Principles of Roman Architecture*. New Haven, CT.

———. forthcoming. "The Origins and Iconography of the Doric Frieze." Submitted for publication.

Zancani Montuoro, P. 1940. "La struttura del fregio dorico." *Palladio*, 23, 49–64.

Chapter 5

Aiken, J. A. 1980. "Leon Battista Alberti's System of Human Proportions." *Journal of the Warburg and Courtauld Institutes*, 43, 68–96.

Alberti, L. B. 1568. *Opuscoli morali di Leon Battista Alberti, Gentil'huomo Fiorentino,* ed. C. Bartoli. Venice.

———. 1954. *Opuscoli inediti di Leon Battista Alberti,* ed. C. Grayson. Florence.

———. 1955. *Leon Battista Alberti: Ten Books on Architecture,* trans. J. Leoni.

———. 1966. *Leon Battista Alberti, L'Architettura,* ed. and trans. G. Orlandi. Milan.

———. 1972. *L. B. Alberti: On Painting and On Sculpture: The Latin Texts of De Pictura and De Statua,* ed. and trans. C. Grayson. London.

———. 1986. *Leon Battista Alberti: Momo o Del Principe,* ed. and trans. R. Consolo. Genoa.

———. 1988. *Leon Battista Alberti: On the Art of Building in Ten Books,* ed. and trans. J. Rykwert, N. Leach, and R. Tavernor. Cambridge, MA.

Augustine, St. 1972. *The City of God,* trans. H. Bettenson. Harmondsworth.

Baron, H. 1966. *The Crisis of the Early Italian Renaissance.* Rev. ed. Princeton, NJ.

Battisti, E. 1973. *Piero della Francesca.* Milan.

Baxandall, M. 1972. *Painting and Experience in Fifteenth Century Italy.* Oxford.

Bertelli, C. 1992. *Piero della Francesca.* New Haven, CT.

Bombe, W. 1909. "Zur Genesis des Auferstehungsfreskos von Piero della Francesca." In *Repertorium für Kunstwissenschaft.* Berlin.

Brandi, C. 1954–1955. "Restauri a Piero della Francesca." *Bollettino d'Arte, 39,* 241–258.

Dal Poggetto, P. 1992. *Piero e Urbino, Piero e le Corti rinascimentali.* Venice.

Davis, M. D. 1977. *Piero della Francesca's Mathematical Treatises.* Ravenna.

Evans, R. 1994. *The Projective Cast: Architecture and Its Three Geometries.* Cambridge, MA.

Field, J. V. 1997. "Alberti, the Abacus and Piero della Francesca's Proof of Perspective." *Renaissance Studies, 11,* 61–88.

Ginzburg, C. 1981–1982. *Indagini su Piero.* Turin.

Gioseffi, D. 1980. "Introduzione all'arte, introduzione a Piero." *Arte in Friuli, Arte a Trieste, 4,* 9–25.

Gombrich, E. H. 1945. "Botticelli's Mythologies: A Study in the Neoplatonic Symbolism of His Circle." *Journal of the Warburg and Courtauld Institutes, 8,* 7–60.

Kuhn, J. R. 1990. "Measured Appearances: Documentation and Design in Early Perspective Drawing." *Journal of the Warburg and Courtauld Institutes, 53,* 114–132.

Lavin, M. A. 1972. *Piero della Francesca: The Flagellation.* New York.

Lightbown, R. W. 1992. *Piero della Francesca.* New York.

Newton, I. 1740. *Optics.* London.

Mebane, J. S. 1989. *Renaissance Magic and the Return of the Golden Age.* Lincoln, NE.

Orlandi, G. 1974a. "Testo latino della 'Descriptio Urbis Romae' e traduzione italiana di G. Orlandi," in *Convegno Internazionale indetto nel V Centenario di Leon Battista Alberti (Roma-Mantova-Firenze, 25–29 April 1972), Accademia Nazionale dei Lincei, 371,* 112–127.

———. 1974b. "Nota sul Testo," in *Convegno Internazionale indetto nel V Centenario di Leon Battista Alberti (Roma-Mantova-Firenze, 25–29 April 1972)*, Accademia Nazionale dei Lincei, *371*, 129–137.

Pacioli, L. 1509. *De divina proportione.* Venice.

Passavant, J. D. 1839. *Rafael von Urbino und sein Vater Giovanni Santi.* Leipzig.

Pope Hennessy, J. 1986. "Whose Flagellation?" *Apollo,* September, 162–163.

Pottage, J. 1968. "The Vitruvian Value of Pi." *Isis, 59,* 190–197.

Rykwert, J. 1996. *The Dancing Column: On Order in Architecture.* Cambridge, MA.

Rykwert, J., and A. Engel. 1994. *Leon Battista Alberti,* exhibition catalogue, Palazzo Te, Mantua. Milan.

Tavernor, R. 1985. "Concinnitas in the Architectural Theory and Practice of Leon Battista Alberti." Ph.D. dissertation, University of Cambridge.

———. 1996. "Casting New Light on 'The Flagellation' by Piero della Francesca." *Computers and the History of Art, 6,* 13–19.

———. 1998. *On Alberti and the Art of Building.* New Haven, CT.

Ubaldo Tosi, P. 1744. *Miscellanea.* Urbino, Biblioteca Universitaria, Fondo del Comune, Ms.93, c.224r.

Uzielli, G. 1899. *Le Misure Lineari Mediovale e l'Effigie di Cristo.* Florence.

Vagnetti, L. 1974. "Lo Studio di Romanegli Scritti Albertiani," in *Convegno Internazionale indetto nel V Centenario di Leon Battista Alberti (Roma-Mantova-Firenze, 25–29 April 1972)*, Accademia Nazionale dei Lincei, *371,* 73–110.

Vasari, G. 1965. *Giorgio Varsari: The Lives of the Artists,* trans. G. Bull. Harmondsworth.

———. 1973. *Le Vite de'più eccellenti pittori, scultori e architettori, (nelle redazioni del 1550 e 1568),* ed. G. Milanesi. Rev. ed. Florence.

Vitruvius 1960. *Marcus Vitruvius Pollio: The Ten Books on Architecture,* trans. M. H. Morgan. New York.

Vitruvius 1999. *Vitruvius: The Ten Books on Architecture,* trans. I. D. Rowland, with T. N. Howe. Cambridge.

Voegelin, E. 1948. "The Origins of Scientism." *Social Research, 15,* 462–494.

Wilson Jones, M. 2000. "Doric Measure and Architectural Design 1: The Evidence of the Relief from Salamis." *American Journal of Archaeology, 104,* 1–23.

Wittkower, R., and B. A. R. Carter. 1953. "The Perspective of Piero della Francesca's 'Flagellation.'" *Journal of the Warburg and Courtauld Institutes, 16,* 292–302.

Chapter 6

Ackerman, J. S. 1977. *Palladio.* Harmondsworth.

Alberti, L. B. 1966. *On Painting,* trans. J. Spencer. New Haven, CT.

———. 1988. *On the Art of Building,* ed. and trans. J. Rykwert, N. Leach, and R. Tavernor. Cambridge, MA.

Alberti Index. [1975]. *Leon Battista Alberti. De re aedificatoria. Florenz 1485. Index verborum und Faksimile,* ed. H.-K. Lücke. Munich.

Aristotle. 1982. *The Poetics,* ed. and trans. W. Hamilton Fyfe. London.

Barbaro, D. 1567. *I dieci libri dell'architettura di M. Vitruvio tradotti et commentati da Mons. Daniel Barbaro eletto Patriarca d'Aquileia da lui riveduti et ampliati.* Venice.

Benjamin, W. 1968. "The Work of Art in the Age of Mechanical Reproduction," in W. Benjamin, *Illuminations.* New York.

Bode, W. von. 1902. *Florentiner Bildhauer der Renaissance.* Berlin.

Börsch-Soupan, E. 1976. "Der Renaissance Begriff der Berliner Schule im Vergleich zu Semper," in *Gottfried Semper und die Mitte des 19. Jahrhunderts,* ed. E. Börsch-Soupan. Basel.

Boucher, B. 1991. *The Sculpture of Jacopo Sansovino.* New Haven, CT.

Garris Brandt, K. W. 1994. "The Relation of Sculpture and Architecture in the Renaissance," in *From Brunelleschi to Michelangelo: The Representation of Architecture. Palazzo Grassi, April–November 1994,* ed. H. Millon and V. Lampugnani. Milan.

Burckhardt, J. 1987. *Architecture of the Italian Renaissance.* Chicago, 1st ed. Stuttgart, 1867.

Burns, H., and M. Tafuri. 1998. "From Serlio to the Escorial." *Giulio Romano.*

Coffin, D. 1964. "Pirro Ligorio and the Nobility of the Arts." *Journal of the Warburg and Courtauld Institutes, 27,* 191–211.

Coulton, J. J. 1977. *Ancient Greek Architects at Work: Problems of Structure and Design.* Ithaca, NY.

Del Turco, N. R., and F. Salvi. 1995. *Bartolomeo Ammannati. Scultore ed architetto, 1511–1592.* Florence.

Fiocco, G. 1965. *Alvise Cornaro; il suo tempo e le sue opere.* Vicenza.

Francesco Di Giorgio Martini. 1967. *Francesco di Giorgio Martini. Trattati di architettura ingegneria e arte militare,* ed. C. Maltese and L. Degrassi Maltese. Milan.

Frommel, C. L. 1989. "Serlio e la scuola Romana," in *Sebastiano Serlio,* ed. C. Thoenes, 39–49. Milan.

Gallaccini, T. (n.d.). [*Trattato sopra gli errori degli architetti*], Ms. King's 281, British Library, London.

Günther, H. 1988. *Das Studium der antiken Architektur in den Zeichnungen der Hochrenaissance.* Tübingen.

Heydenreich, L. H., and W. Lotz. 1974. *Architecture in Italy, 1400–1600.* Harmondsworth.

Howard, D. 1975. *Jacopo Sansovino. Architecture and Patronage in Renaissance Venice.* New Haven, CT.

Kiene, M. 1995. *Bartolomeo Ammannati.* Milan.

Lee, R. W. 1967. *Ut pictura poesis: The Humanistic Theory of Painting.* New York.

Lenzoni, C. 1556. *In difesa della lingua fiorentina et di Dante.* Florence.

Lotz, W. 1977. "The Roman Legacy in Sansovino's Venetian Buildings," in W. Lotz, *Studies in Italian Architecture,* 140–151. Cambridge, MA.

Minturno, A. 1563. *L'arte poetica.* Venice.

Onians, J. 1988. *Bearers of Meaning.* Princeton, NJ.

Palladio, A. 1980. *I quattro libri dell'architettura,* ed. L. Magagnato and P. Marini. Milan.

———. 1988. *Andrea Palladio. Scritti sull'architettura (1554–1579),* ed. L. Puppi. Vicenza.

Paoletti, P. 1897–1898. *L'architecture et la Sculpture de la Renaissance à Venise.* Venice.

Payne, A. 1994. "Rudolf Wittkower and Architectural Principles in the Age of Modernism." *Journal of the Society of Architectural Historians, 53,* 322–342.

———. 1999. *The Architectural Treatise in the Italian Renaissance.* New York.

———. 2001. "Architecture, Ornament and Pictorialism: Notes on the History of an Idea," in *Architecture and Painting,* ed. K. Koehler. London.

———. 2000a. "*Ut poesis architectura:* Poetics and Tectonics in Architectural Criticism c. 1570," in *Antiquity and Its Interpreters,* ed. A. Payne et al. 143–156. New York.

———. 2000b. "Architects and Academies: Architectural Theories of *Imitatio* and the Literary Debates on Language and Style," in *Architecture and Language,* ed. G. Clarke and D. Crossley. New York.

Puppi, L. (ed.). 1980. *Alvise Cornaro e il suo tempo.* Padua.

———. 1986. *Andrea Palladio: The Complete Works.* New York.

———. 1990. *Palladio Drawings.* New York.

Rowland, I. 1994. "Raphael, Colocci and the Orders." *Art Bulletin, 76.*

Rukschcio, B. 1985. "Ornament und Mythos," in *Ornament und Askese im Zeitgeist des Wien der Jahrhundertwende,* ed. A. Pfabigan, 57–68. Vienna.

Scamozzi, V. 1615. *L'idea della architettura universale.* Ridgewood, NJ. 1964; facs. ed., Venice: by the author.

Schmarsow, A. 1903. *Unser Verhältnis zu den bildenden Künsten.* Leipzig.

Scott, G. 1965. *The Architecture of Humanism.* Gloucester, MA.

Serlio, S. 1619. *Tutte l'opere d'architettura et prospettiva di Sebastiano Serlio Bolognese.* Ridgewood, NJ. 1964; facs. ed. Venice: Giacomo de Franceschi.

Shell, J., and L. Castelfranchi (eds.). 1993. *Giovanni Antonio Amadeo. Scultura e architettura del suo tempo.* Milan.

Spini, G. (n.d.). [Degli'ornamenti dell'architettura di Gherardo Spini]. Ms. It., IV, 38 Biblioteca Nazionale Marciana, Venice.

———. 1980. "I tre primi libri sopra l'istituzioni intorno agl'ornamenti," in *Il disegno interotto. Trattati medicei d'architettura,* ed. F. Borsi et al., 30–201. Florence.

Summers, D. 1981. *Michelangelo and the Language of Art.* Princeton, NJ.

Thoenes, C., and H. Günther. 1985. "Gli ordini architettonici: rinascitá o invenzione?" in *Roma e l'antico nell'arte e nella cultura del Cinquecento*, ed. M. Fagiolo, 261–271. Rome.

Tolomei, C. 1985. "Lettera al conte Agostino Landi," in *Trattati. Con l'agiunta degli scritti di architettura di Alvise Cornaro, Francesco Giorgi, Claudio Tolomei, Giangiorgio Trissino, Giorgio Vasari*, ed. E. Bassi and M. Walcher Casotti, 31–61. Milan.

Vasari, G. 1986. *Le vite de' piu eccellenti architetti, pittori, et scultori italiani, da Cimabue insino a' tempi nostri. Nell'edizione per i tipi di Lorenzo Torrentino Firenze 1550*, ed. L. Bellosi and A. Rossi. Turin.

Vignola, G. B. da. 1985. "La regola delli cinque ordini," in Pietro Cattaneo and Giacomo Barozzi da Vignola, *Trattati. Con l'agiunta degli scritti di architettura di Alvise Cornaro, Francesco Giorgi, Claudio Tolomei, Giangiorgio Trissino, Giorgio Vasari*, ed. E. Bassi and M. Walcher Casotti. Milan.

Vitruvius, M. P. 1983. *De architectura. On Architecture*, ed. and trans. F. Granger. London.

Willich, H., and P. Zucker. 1914–1926. *Baukunst der Renaissance in Italien*. Wildpark-Potsdam.

Wittkomer, R. 1949. *Architectural Principles in the Age of Humanism*. London.

Wölfflin, H. 1946a. "Ein Künstler über Kunst," in *Kleine Schriften*, ed. J. Gantner, 84–106. Basel.

———. 1946b. "Prologomena zu einer Psychologie der Architektur," in *Kleine Schriften*, ed. J. Gantner, 13–47. Basel.

Wolters, W. 1968. "Andrea Palladio e la decorazione dei suoi edifici." *Bollettino del centro internazionale di studi Andrea Palladio*, 10, 255–267.

———. 1992–1993. "Architettura e decorazione nel cinquecento veneto." *Annali di architettura*, 4–5, 102–110.

Chapter 7

Abulafia, D. 1988. *Frederick II, a Medieval Emperor*. London.

Adams, N. 1993. "L'architettura militare di Francesco di Giorgio," in *Francesco di Giorgio Architetto*, ed. M. Tafuri and F. P. Fiore. Milan.

Adams, N., and S. Pepper. 1994. "The Fortification Drawings," in *The Architectural Drawings of Antonio da Sangallo the Younger and his Circle*, ed. C. L. Frommel and N. Adams. Cambridge, MA.

Alberti, L. B. 1955. *Ten Books on Architecture*, trans. J. Leoni, ed. J. Rykwert. London.

Averlino, A. (called Filarete). 1965. *Trattato dell'Architettura*, trans. with intro. and notes J. R. Spencer. New Haven, CT.

Babinger, F. 1978. *Mehmed the Conqueror*. Princeton, NJ.

Belluzzi, G. B. (or Bellucci). 1598. *Nuova inventione di fabricar fortezze di varie forme*. Venice.

Beltrami, L. 1894. *Il castello di Milano all'epoca degli Sforza*. Milan.

Bennett, J., and S. Johnston. 1996. *The Geometry of War, 1500–1750*. Oxford.

Boxer, C. R., and C. de Azvedo. 1960. *Fort Jesus and the Portuguese in Mombasa*. London.

Bury, J. 1979. "Francisco de Holanda: A Little Known Source for the History of Fortification in the Sixteenth Century." *Arquivos do Centro Cultural Portugues, 14*, 163–202.

———. 1980. "Are Renaissance Fortifications Beautiful?" *Fort, 8*, 7–20.

Caradente, G. 1963. *I Triomfi nel primo rinascimento*. Turin.

Dapper, O. 1703. *Description exacte des iles de l'Archipel*. Amsterdam.

De la Croix, H. 1960. "Military Architecture and the Radial City Plan in Sixteenth Century Italy." *Art Bulletin, 42*, 263–290.

———. 1963. "The Literature on Fortification in Renaissance Italy." *Technology and Culture, 6*, 30–50.

De Seta, C. 1989. "Le mura simbolo della città," in *La città e le mura*, ed. C. De Seta and J. Le Goff. Rome.

Dechert, M. S. A. 1990. "The Military Architecture of Francesco di Giorgio in Southern Italy." *Journal of the Society of Architectural Historians, 49*, 161–180.

Deonna, W. 1940. "Histoire d'un emblème: La couronne murale des villes et pays personnifiés." *Genava, 18*, 119–212.

Dezzi Bardeschi, M. 1968. "Le rocche di Francesco di Giorgio nel Ducato di Urbino." *Castellum, 8*, 97–138.

Doukas (sometimes, Ducas). 1975. *Decline and Fall of Byzantium to the Ottoman Turks*, trans. H. J. Magoulias. Detroit, MI.

Du Fresne-Canaye, P. 1897. *Le Voyage du Levant de Philippe du Fresne-Canaye (1573)*. Paris.

Ehrenberger Katz, J. 1969. "Les répresentations de villes fortifiées dans l'art paléochrétien et leurs dérivées byzantines." *Cahiers Archéologiques, 19*, 1–27.

Filangieri, R. 1929. "La cittadella Aragonese e il recinto bastionate di Castel Nuovo." *Atti della Accademia Pontaniana, 59*, 49–73.

———. "Rassegna critica delle fonti per la storia di Castel Nuovo: Parte Prima, il castello angioino." *Archivio storico di provincie napoletane, 61*, 251–323.

———. 1937. "Rassegna critica . . . Parte Seconda: Il castello aragonese." *Archivio storico di provincie napoletane, 62*, 267–333.

———. 1938. "Rassegna critica . . . Parte Terza: Opere di compimento e di restauro durante il periodo aragonese." *Archivio storico di provincie napoletane, 63*, 258–342.

Fiore, F. P. 1978. *Città e macchine del '400 nei disegni di Francesco di Giorgio Martini*. Florence.

———. 1987. "Francesco di Giorgio e il rivellino 'acuto' di Costacciaro." *Quaderni dell'Istituto di Storia dell'Architettura*, n.s. 1–10, 197–208.

Fiore, F. P., and M. Tafuri (eds.). 1993. *Francesco di Giorgio Architetto*. Milan.

Firpo, L. 1987. "Leonardo as Urban Planner," in *Leonardo da Vinci, Engineer and Architect*, ed. P. Galluzzi. Montreal.

Forster, K. 1971. "Metaphors of Rule: Political Ideology and History in the Portraits of Cosimo I de' Medici." *Mitteilungen des Kunsthistorischen Institutes in Florenz, 15*, 65–104.

Francesco di Giorgio Martini. 1967. *Trattati di architettura, ingegneria e arte militare*, ed. C. Maltese and L. Maltese Degrassi. Milan.

Frugoni, C. 1991. *A Distant City: Images of Urban Experience in the Medieval World*, trans. W. McCuaig. Princeton, NJ.

Gabriel, A. 1934. *Châteaux turcs du Bosphore*. Paris.

Hale, J. R. 1965. "The Early Development of the Bastion: An Italian Chronology c. 1450–c. 1534," in *Europe in the Late Middle Ages*, ed. J. R. Hale, J. R. L. Highfield, and B. Smalley, 466–494.

———. 1968. "The End of Florentine Liberty: The Fortezza da Basso," in *Florentine Studies: Politics and Society in Renaissance Florence*, ed. N. Rubinstein. London.

———. 1977. *Renaissance Fortification: Art or Engineering?* London.

Hersey, G. 1969. *Alfonso II and the Artistic Renewal of Naples, 1485–1495*. New Haven, CT.

———. 1973. *The Aragonese Arch at Naples*. New Haven, CT.

———. 1988. *The Lost Meaning of Classical Architecture*. Cambridge, MA.

Heydenreich, L. 1954. *Leonardo da Vinci*. New York.

Högg, H. 1932. *Türkenburgen an Bosporus und Hellespont*. Dresden.

Kantorowicz, E. 1957. *The King's Two Bodies*. Princeton, NJ.

Lang, S. 1952. "The Ideal City from Plato to Howard." *Architectural Review*, August.

———. 1972. "Sforzinda, Filarete and Filelfo." *Journal of the Warburg and Courtauld Institutes, 35*, 391–397.

Lavedan, P. 1954. *Representations des Villes dans l'Art du Moyen Age*. Paris.

Lazaroni, M., and A. Munoz. 1908. *Filarete scultore e architetto del secolo XV*. Rome.

Maggi, G., and J. Fusto Castriotto. 1564. *Della fortificatione delle città . . . Libri III*. Venice.

Marconi, P. (ed.). 1973. *La città come forma simbolica: studi sulla teoria dell'architettura nel rinascimento*. Rome.

Martindale, A. 1979. *The Triumphs of Caesar*. London.

Müller, W. 1961. *Die Heilige Stadt, Roma Quadrata, himmlisches Jerusalem und die Mythe von Weltnabel*. Stuttgart.

Necipoglu, G. 1991. *Architecture, Ceremonial and Power: The Topkapi Palace in the Fifteenth and Sixteenth Centuries*. Cambridge, MA.

Onians, J. 1972. "Alberti and Filarete." *Journal of the Warburg and Courtauld Institutes, 34*, 96–114.

Papini, R. 1946. *Francesco di Giorgio Martini, Architetto*. Florence.

Parker, G. 1988. *The Military Revolution: Military Innovation and the Rise of the West, 1500–1800*. Cambridge.

Pepper, S. 1973. "The Meaning of the Renaissance Fortress." *Architectural Association Quarterly*, 5, 22–27.

———. 1995. "Castles and Cannon in the Naples Campaign of 1494–95," in *The French Descent into Renaissance Italy 1494–95,* ed. D. Abulafia. Variorum.

———. 2000a. "Ottoman Military Architecture in the Early Gunpowder Era: A Reassessment," in *City Walls: The Urban Enceinte in Global Perspective,* ed. J. D. Tracy, 282–316. Cambridge.

———. 2000b. "Siege Law, Siege Ritual and the Symbolism of Renaissance City Walls." In *City Walls: The Urban Enceinte in Global Perspective,* ed. J. D. Tracy, 573–604. Cambridge.

Pepper, S., and N. Adams. 1986. *Firearms and Fortifications: Military Architecture and Siege Warfare in Sixteenth Century Siena.* Chicago.

Pollack, M. 1991. *Military Architecture, Cartography and the Representation of the Early Modern European City: A Checklist of Treatises on Fortification in the Newberry Library.* Chicago.

———. 1998. "Military Architecture and Cartography in the Design of the Early Modern City," in *Envisioning the City: Six Studies in Urban Cartography,* ed. D. Buisseret. Chicago.

Porada, E. 1967. "Battlements in the Military Architecture and Symbolism of the Ancient Near East," in *Essays in the History of Architecture presented to Rudolf Wittkower,* ed. D. Frazer et al. London.

Raby, J. 1982. "A Sultan of Paradox: Mehmed the Conqueror as a Patron of the Arts." *Oxford Art Journal,* 1.

Restle, M. 1981. "Bauplanung und Baugesinnung unter Mehmed II Fatih." *Pantheon,* 39, 4.

Rogers, C. 1995. *The Military Revolution Debate: Readings on the Military Transformation of Early Modern Europe.* Boulder, CO.

Saunders, A. 1989. *Fortress Britain: Artillery Fortification in the British Isles and Ireland.* Liphook, U.K.

Sciolla, G. C. (ed). 1975. *La città ideale nel Rinascimento.* Turin.

Scully, V. 1952. "Michelangelo's Fortification Drawings: A Study in the Reflex Diagonal." *Perspecta,* 1, 38–45.

Segni, B. 1830. *Storie fiorentine.* Livorno.

Shearer, C. 1935. *The Renaissance of Architecture in Southern Italy: A Study of Frederick II of Hohenstaufen and the Capua Triumphtor Archway and Towers.* Cambridge.

Van Millingen, A. 1899. *Byzantine Constantinople: The Walls of the City and Adjoining Historical Sites.* London.

Vasari, G. 1973. *Le vite de' più eccellenti pittori, scultori ed architettori (nelle redazioni del 1550 e 1568),* ed. G. Milanesi, Florence, 1906; rev. ed., 7 vols, Florence.

Volpe, G. 1982. *Rocche e fortificazioni del Ducato di Urbino.* Urbino.

Von Moos, S. 1978. *Turm und Bollwerk: Beiträge zu einer politischen ikonographie der italienischen Renaissance-Architektur.* Zurich.

Wittkower, R. 1949. *The Architecture of Humanism.* London.

Woods-Marsden, J. 1985. "Pictorial Legitimation of Territorial Gains in Emilia: The Iconography of the *camera peregrina aurea* in the Castle of Torchiara," in *Renaissance Studies in Honor of Craig Hugh Smyth.* Florence.

———. 1989. "How Quattrocento Princes Used Art: Sigismondo Pandolfo Malatesta of Rimini and *cose militari.*" *Renaissance Studies,* 3.

Chapter 8

Becker, L. 1913. *Allgemeine Lexikon der bildenden Künstler,* ed. U. Thieme. Leipzig.

Blunt, A. 1977. "Rubens and Architecture." *Burlington Magazine,* September.

Dietterlin, W. 1598. *Architectura von Ausstheilung, Symmetria und Proportion der fünff Seulen.* Nuremberg.

Hitchcock, H.-R. 1978. *Netherlandish Scrolled Gables of the Sixteenth and Early Seventeenth Centuries.* New York.

Rubens, P. P. 1622. *Palazzi di Genova.* Antwerp.

Chapter 9

Cowell, J. 1607. *The Interpreter, or Booke Containing the Signification of Words . . . as Are Mentioned in the Lawe Writers, or Statutes of This Victorious and Renowned Kingdome.* Cambridge.

Dee, J. 1570. Preface to H. Billingsley, *Euclid.* London.

Dugdale, W. 1658. *The History of St. Paul's Cathedral in London.* London.

Gotch, J. A. 1928. *Inigo Jones.* London.

Hart, V. 1993. "Heraldry and the Architectural Orders as Joint Emblems of British Chivalry." *Res,* 23, 52–66.

———. 1994. *Art and Magic in the Court of the Stuarts.* London.

———. 1995a. "Imperial Seat or Ecumenical Temple? On Inigo Jones' Use of Decorum at St. Paul's Cathedral." *Architectura,* 25, 194–213.

———. 1995b. *St. Paul's Cathedral: Sir Christopher Wren.* London.

Herndl, G. C. 1970. *The High Design: English Renaissance Tragedy and the Natural Law.* Lexington, KY.

Hudson, W. (n.d.). "A Treatise of the Court of Star Chamber." Manuscript, Cambridge University Library Add. 3106, in *Collectanea Juridica,* ed. F. Hargrave, (1792), London.

James I. 1610. *The Kings Majesties Speach to the Lords and Commons . . . Wednesday the xxi of March.* London.

———. 1615. *By the King: A Proclamation for Building.* London.

———. 1619. *By the King: A Proclamation Declaring His Majesties Further Pleasure for Matter of Buildings.* London.

Johnson, A. W. 1987. "Angles, Squares or Roundes: Studies in Jonson's Vitruvianism," D. Phil. dissertation, Oxford University.

Jones, I. 1655. *Stone-heng . . . Restored.* London.

Jonson, B. 1965–1970a. *A Panegyre, on the Happie Entrance of James, Our Soveraigne, to His First Sesion of Parliament,* in *Ben Jonson: Works,* ed. C. Herford and P. Simpson. Oxford.

———. 1965–1970b. *Newes from the New World Discover'd in the Moone,* in *Ben Jonson: Works,* ed. C. Herford and P. Simpson. Oxford.

———. 1965–1970c. *A Tale of the Tub,* in *Ben Jonson: Works,* ed. C. Herford and P. Simpson. Oxford.

Kantorowicz, E. 1957. *The King's Two Bodies.* Princeton, NJ.

Kelly, D. R. 1966. "Legal Humanism and the Sense of History." *Studies in the Renaissance, 13,* 184–199.

———. 1970. "The Rise of Legal History in the Renaissance." *History and Theory, 9,* 174–194.

———. 1976. "Vera Philosophia: The Philosophical Significance of Renaissance Jurisprudence." *Journal of the History of Philosophy, 14,* 267–279.

———. 1979. "Civil Science in the Renaissance: Jurisprudence Italian Style." *Historical Journal, 22,* 777–794.

———. 1988. "Jurisconsultus Perfectus: The Lawyer as Renaissance Man." *Journal of the Warburg and Courtauld Institutes, 51,* 84–102.

———. 1990. *The Human Measure: Social Thought in the Western Legal Tradition.* Cambridge, MA.

King, J. 1620. *A Sermon at Paules Crosse, on Behalfe of Paules Church.* London.

Levack, B. P. 1990. "The Civil Law, Theories of Absolutism, and Political Conflict in Late Sixteenth- and Early Seventeenth-Century England," in *Law, Literature, and the Settlement of Regimes,* ed. G. J. Schochet. Washington, D.C.

Lomazzo, G. 1598. Trans. Richard Haydocke as: *A Tracte Containing the Artes of Curious Paintinge, Carving and Buildinge.* Oxford.

Marcelline, G. 1610. *The Triumphs of King James the First.* London.

———. 1625. *Epithalamium, Gallo-Britannicum.* London.

Palme, P. 1957. *The Triumph of Peace: A Study of the Whitehall Banqueting House.* London.

Peacock, J. 1990. "Inigo Jones as a Figurative Artist," in *Renaissance Bodies: The Human Figure in English Culture c. 1540–1660,* ed. L. Gent and N. Llewellyn. London.

Perrault, C. 1683. *Ordonnance des cinq espèces de colonnes selon la méthode des Anciens.* Paris.

Puttenham, G. 1589. *The Arte of English Poesie.* London.

Saura, M. 1988. "Architecture and the Law in Early Renaissance Urban Life: Leon Battista Alberti's 'De Re Aedificatoria.'" Ph.D. dissertation, University of California.

Sgarbi, C. 1993. "A Newly Discovered Corpus of Vitruvian Images." *Res*, 23, 31–51.

Shapiro, J. 1983. *Probability and Certainty in Seventeenth-Century England: A Study of the Relationships Between Natural Science, Religion, History, Law, and Literature.* Princeton, NJ.

Sharpe, K. 1992. *The Personal Rule of Charles I.* New Haven, CT.

Sherman, W. H. 1995. *John Dee: The Politics of Reading and Writing in the English Renaissance.* Amherst, MA.

Shute, J. 1563. *The First and Chief Groundes of Architecture.* London.

Strong, R., and S. Orgell. 1973. *Inigo Jones: The Theatre of the Stuart Court.* London.

Thornborough, J. 1641. *A Discourse, Showing the Great Happinesse, That Hath, and May Still Accrue to His Majesties Kingdomes of England and Scotland, by Re-uniting Them into One Great Britain.* London.

Vitruvius, 1556. *I dieci libri dell'architettura di M. Vitruvio tradotti e commentati da Monsig. Daniele Barbaro.* Venice.

——. 1931. *De architectura*, trans. F. Granger. Cambridge, MA.

Weston, C. C., and J. R. Greenberg. 1981. *Subjects and Sovereigns: The Grand Controversy over Legal Sovereignty in Stuart England.* Cambridge.

Wotton, H. 1624. *The Elements of Architecture.* London.

Yates, F. 1969. *Theatre of the World.* London.

Chapter 10

Alciatus, A. 1542. *Emblematum Libellus.* Paris.

Blumenberg, H. 1986. *Lebenszeit und Weltzeit.* Frankfurt am Main.

Boullée, E.-L. 1976. *Boullée and Visionary Architecture*, trans. H. Rosenau. New York.

Collins, C. 1971. *Changing Ideals in Modern Architecture.* London.

Colvin, H. 1991. *Architecture and the After-Life.* New Haven, CT.

Conrads, U. (ed.). 1975. *Programs and Manifestoes on 20th-Century Architecture*, trans. M. Bullock. Cambridge, MA.

Harries, K. 1997. *The Ethical Function of Architecture.* Cambridge, MA.

Hegel, G. W. F. 1937. *Vorlesungen über die Aesthetik, Jubiläumsausgabe*, ed. H. Glockner. Stuttgart.

Heidegger, M. 1953. *Sein und Zeit*, 7th ed. Tübingen.

Jaffé, H. L. C. 1967. *De Stijl.* New York.

Macdonald, W. L. 1982. *The Architecture of the Roman Empire: An Introductory Study*, rev. ed. New Haven, CT.

Poppe, W. 1909. "Vitruvs Quellen zum zweiten Buche "de architectura," Ph.D. dissertation, University of Kiel.

Reinicke, H. 1988. *Aufstieg und Revolution. Über die Beförderung irdischer Freiheitsneigungen durch Ballonfahrt und Luftschwimmkunst.* Berlin.

Sennett, R. 1996. *Flesh and Stone: The Body and the City in Western Civilization.* New York.

Vidler, A. 1990. *Claude-Nicolas Ledoux: Architecture and Social Reform at the End of the Ancien Régime.* Cambridge, MA.

Villari, S. 1990. *J. N. L. Durand (1760–1834),* trans. E. Gottlieb. New York.

Chapter 11

Anon. (attrib. Briseux, C.-E.). 1728 and 1764. *Architecture Moderne ou l'Art de Bien Bâtir.* Paris.

Arendt, H. 1958. *The Human Condition.* Chicago.

Baridon, M. 1987. "Le Concept de la Nature dans l'Esthéthique de Rameau." *Jean-Philippe Rameau: Colloque International,* 441–453.

Blondel, J.-F. 1774. *L'Homme du monde éclairé par les arts.* Amsterdam.

———. 1752. *Discours sur la Nécessité de l'Etude de l'Architecture.* Paris.

Briseux, C.-E. 1743. *L'Art de Bâtir des Maisons de Campagne où l'on traite de leur distribution, de leur construction et de leur Décoration.* Paris.

———. 1752. *Traité du Beau Essentiel dans les Arts.* Paris.

Fréart de Chambray, R. 1650. *Parallèle de l'Architecture Antique et de la Moderne.* Paris.

Hallyn, F. 1993. *The Poetic Structure of the World.* New York.

Kepler, J. 1619. *Harmonices Mundi.* Linz.

Laugier, 1755. *Essai sur L'Architecture.* Paris.

———. 1765. *Observations sur l'Architecture.* Paris.

Le Camus de Mezières, N. 1780. *Le Génie de l'Architecture.* Paris.

Le Corbusier (Charles Édouard Jeanneret). 1987. *The Decorative Art of Today.* Trans. J. I. Dunnett. Cambridge, MA.

Lescat, P. 1987. "Conclusion sur l'origine des sciences. Un texte méconnu de Jean-Philippe Rameau," in *Jean-Philippe Rameau: Colloque International organisé par la Société Rameau.* Paris.

Pérez-Gómez, A. 1977. "The Use of Geometry and Number in Architectural Theory, 1680–1820." Ph.D. dissertation, University of Essex.

———. 1983. *Architecture and the Crisis of Modern Science.* Cambridge, MA.

———. 1994. *Polyphilo or the Dark Forest Revisited.* Cambridge, MA.

Pérez-Gómez, A., and L. Pelletier, 1997. *Architectural Representation and the Perspective Hinge.* Cambridge, MA.

Perrault, C. 1684. *Les Dix Livres d'Architecture de Vitruve.* Paris.

Rameau, J.-P. 1722. *Traité de l'Harmonie Reduite à ses Principes naturels.* Paris.

———. 1752. *Nouvelles Réflexions sur sa démonstration du Principe de l'Harmonie.* Paris.

———. 1754. *Observations sur notre instinct pour la musique.* Paris.

———. 1762a. "Conclusions sur l'origine des sciences." *Journal Encyclopédique,* 5, 91–101.

Rameau, J.-P. 1762b. "Lettre de M. Rameau aux philosophes," in *Journal de Trévoux,* Paris.

Rousseau, J.-J. 1969. *Dictionnaire de musique.* Paris.

Soufflot, J.-G. 1961. "Mémoire sur les proportions d'architecture," in M. Petzet, *Soufflots Sainte-Geneviève.* Berlin.

Szambien, W. 1986. *Symétrie, Goût, Caractère.* Paris.

Verba, C. 1993. *Music and the French Enlightenment.* New York.

Chapter 12

Augustine, St. 1958. *The City of God,* trans. G. Gerald et al. New York.

Berlin, I. 1976. *Vico and Herder: Two Studies in the History of Ideas.* London.

Clark, T. J. 1986. *The Painting of Modern Life: Paris in the Art of Manet and his Followers.* Princeton, NJ.

Cox, H. 1966. *The Secular City,* rev. ed. New York.

de Feir, C. 1882. *Guide du Salon de Paris 1882.* Paris.

Herzen, A. 1974. *My Past and Thoughts.* New York.

Houssaye, A. 1883. "Le Salon de 1882," in *L'Art français depuis dix ans.* Paris.

Pelikan, J. 1985. *Jesus through the Centuries.* New Haven, CT.

Sennett, R. 1993. *The Fall of Public Man.* New York.

———. 1994. *Flesh and Stone: The Body and the City in Western Civilization.* New York.

Simmel, G. 1979. "The Stranger," in *The Sociology of Georg Simmel,* ed. K. Wolff. Chicago.

Sophocles. 1954. *Oedipus the King,* trans. D. Greene. Chicago. (Original, *Oedipus Tyraneus,* Loeb, 1030–1035).

Sophocles. *Oedipus Coloneus.* Cambridge, MA.

Stern, D. 1894. *Oeuvres,* vol. 6. Paris.

Chapter 13

Adorno, T. W. 1978. *Minima Moralia: Reflections from Damaged Life,* trans. E. F. Jephcott. London.

———. 1979. "Functionalism Today." *Oppositions,* 17.

———. 1984. *Aesthetic Theory,* ed. and trans. C. Lenhardt, G. Adorno, and R. Tiederman. London.

Adorno, T., and M. Horkheimer. 1979. *Dialectic of Enlightenment,* trans. John Cumming. London.

Auerbach, E. 1953. *Mimesis,* trans. W. Trask. Princeton, NJ.

Battisti, E. 1981. *Brunelleschi: The Complete Works.* London.

Benjamin, W. 1969. "The Work of Art in the Age of Mechanical Reproduction," in *Illuminations,* ed. H. Arendt, trans. H. Zohn. New York.

———. 1978. "Mimetic Faculty," in *Reflections,* trans. E. Jephcott. New York.

Casazza, O., and R. Boddi. 1978. 'Il Crocitisso ligneo di Filippo Brunelleschi' *La Critica Arte* 43, (July–December), 209–212.

Derrida, J. 1987. "Restitutions of the Truth in Painting," in *The Truth in Painting,* trans. G. Bennington and I. McLeod. Chicago.

Eliade, M. 1970. *Zalmoxis: The Vanishing God.* Chicago.

Freud, S. 1960. *Jokes and Their Relation to the Unconscious* (1905), trans. J. Strachey. London.

———. 1984. *On Metapsychology: The Theory of Psychoanalysis,* trans. J. Strachey. London.

Gadamer, H.-G. 1986. *The Relevance of the Beautiful and Other Essays,* trans. N. Walker. Cambridge.

Gebauer, G., and C. Wulf. 1995. *Mimesis,* trans. D. Reneau. Berkeley, CA.

Hansen, M. 1993. "Mass Culture as Hieroglyphic Writing: Adorno, Derrida, Kracauer." *Critical Enquiry* 39.

Hart, V. 1994. *Art and Magic in the Court of the Stuarts.* London.

Lechte, J. 1990. *Julia Kristeva.* London.

Lévi-Strauss, C. 1966. *The Savage Mind.* London.

Marcuse, H. 1969. *Eros and Civilisation.* London.

Mulvey, L. 1975. "Visual Pleasure and Narrative Cinema." *Screen* 16.

Plato. 1973. *Phaedrus and Letters VII and VIII,* trans. W. Hamilton. London.

Taussig, M. 1993. *Mimesis and Alterity.* London.

Vitruvius. 1960. *The Ten Books on Architecture,* trans. M. H. Morgan. New York.

———. 1990. *De L'Architecture,* trans. P. Gros. Paris.

Wittkower, R. 1962. *Architectural Principles in the Age of Humanism.* London.

Chapter 14

Baumhoff, A. 1994. *Gender, Art, and Handicraft at the Bauhaus.* Baltimore.

Bayer, H., W. Gropius, and I. Gropius. 1972. *Bauhaus, 1919–1928.* New York.

Citroen, P. 1970. "Mazdaznan at the Bauhaus," in *Bauhaus and Bauhaus People,* ed. E. Neumann, trans. E. Richter and A. Lorman. New York.

Droste, M., and the Bauhaus Archive. 1993. *Bauhaus 1919–1933.* Berlin.

Feuerstein, M. F. 1997. "The Absent Woman." *Intersight, 4*, 48–56.

———. 1998. *Oskar Schlemmer's Vordruck*. Philadelphia.

Forgács, É. 1995. *The Bauhaus Idea and Bauhaus Politics*, trans. J. Bátki. Budapest.

Franciscono, M. 1971. *Walter Gropius and the Creation of the Bauhaus in Weimar*. Urbana, IL.

Gay, P. 1970. *Weimar Culture: The Outsider as Insider*. New York.

Greenberg, A. C. 1979. *Artists and Revolution. Dada and the Bauhaus, 1917–1925*. Ann Arbor, MI.

Heidegger, M. 1971. "Building Dwelling Thinking," in *Poetry, Language, Thought*. Trans. A. Hofstadter. New York.

Heilke, T. W. 1990. *Voegelin on the Idea of Race*. Baton Rouge, LA.

Herzogenrath, W. 1988. "Die junmännische Bewegung unserer Zeit—Die Themenentfaltung der Wandbilder Oskar Schlemmers für den Brunnensaal des Museums Folkwang Essen, 1928," in *Oskar Schlemmer Wand—Bild Bild—Wand*, Mannheim.

Hollander, A. 1993. *Seeing Through Clothes*. Berkeley, CA.

Williams Jackson, A. V. 1926. *Zoroaster: The Prophet of Ancient Iran*. New York.

Kröll, F. 1974. *Bauhaus, 1919–1933*. Düsseldorf.

Lang, L. 1965. *Das Bauhaus 1919–1933. Idee und Wirklichkeit*. Berlin.

Maur, K. von. 1979. *Oskar Schlemmer. Monographie und Œuvrekatalog der Gemälde. Aquarelle, Pastelle und Plastiken. Band 1: Monographie*. Munich.

———. 1993. *Oskar Schlemmer Der Folkwang-Zyklus Malerei um 1930*. Stuttgart.

Nehamas, A. 1985. *Nietzsche: Life as Literature*. Cambridge, MA.

Pollitt, J. J. 1974. *The Ancient View of Greek Art: Criticism, History, and Terminology*. New Haven, CT.

Rykwert, J. 1982. "The Dark Side of the Bauhaus," in *The Necessity of Artifice*. New York.

Scheper, D. 1988. *Das Triadische Ballett und die Bauhausbühne*. Berlin.

Schlemmer, O. 1961. "Man and Art Figure," in *The Theater of the Bauhaus*, ed. W. Gropius and A. S. Wensinger. Middletown, CT.

———. 1985. *Oskar Schlemmer—The Triadic Ballet*, trans. L. Ickstadt. Berlin.

———. 1990. *The Letters and Diaries of Oskar Schlemmer*, trans. K. Winston. Evanston, IL.

Schmid, O. Y. 1964. "Zend Folk," in *Schaff-Herzog Encyclopedia of Religious Knowledge*, ed. S. Macauly Jackson. Grand Rapids, MI.

Voegelin, E. 1998. *The History of the Race Idea from Ray to Carus*, ed. K. Vondung, trans. R. Hein. Baton Rouge, LA.

Wick, R. 1982. *Bauhaus Pädagogik*. Cologne.

Wingler, H. 1986. *Bauhaus*. Cambridge, MA.

Chapter 15

Albertini, B., and S. Bagnoli. 1988. *Carlo Scarpa: Architecture in Details,* trans. D. Mills. Cambridge, MA.

Battisti, E. 1972. "Natura Artificiosa to Natura Artificialis," in *The Italian Garden,* ed. D. R. Coffin. Washington, D.C.

Boulée, E.-L. "Architecture, essai sur l'art," in *Bouleé and Visionary Architecture,* trans. S. de Vallée. London.

Brendel, O. 1944. "Origin and Meaning of the Mandorla." *Gazette des Beaux-Arts* (January), 5–24.

Brion, E. 1997. "We Needed a Poet. An Interview with Ennio Brion," in *Carlo Scarpa.* Tokyo.

Brusatin, M. 1983. *Storia dei colori.* Turin.

———. 1984a. "I minimi sistemi dell'architetto Carlo Scarpa," in *Carlo Scarpa: Il progetto per Santa Caterina a Treviso,* ed. M. Boccato et al., trans. S. Curl. Treviso.

———. 1984b. "La casa dell'architetto," in *Carlo Scarpa, Opera completa,* Milan.

"Carlo Scarpa, *Ampliamento della Gipsoteca Canoviana a Possagno* (1956–1957)." 1958. *Casabella continuità,* no. 22, 9–14.

Cirlot, J. E. 1962. *A Dictionary of Symbols,* trans. J. Sage. New York.

Clark, K. 1976. *Landscape into Art.* London.

Comito, T. 1978. *The Idea of the Garden in the Renaissance.* New Brunswick, NJ.

Colonna, F. 1968. *Hypernotomachia Poliphili,* ed. G. Pozzi and L. A. Ciapponi. Padua.

Crary, J. 1990. *Techniques of the Observer: On Vision and Modernity in the Nineteenth Century.* Cambridge, MA.

Dal Co, F. and G. Mazzariol. 1984. *Carlo Scarpa, Opera completa.* Milan.

Daley, B. E. 1986. "The 'Closed Garden' and the 'Sealed Fountain: Song of Songs 4:12, in the Late Medieval Iconography of Mary," in *Medieval Gardens,* ed. E. B. Macdougall. Washington, D.C.

De Amicis, E. 1896. *Contantinople,* trans. M. H. Lansdale. Philadelphia.

Dodds, G. 2000. "Landscape and Garden in the Work of Carlo Scarpa." Ph.D. dissertation, University of Pennsylvania.

Dodds, G., and M. Frascari. 1998. "Miming a Manner of Building: Drawing as Story in the Work of Valeriano Pastor and Carlo Scarpa," in *Constructing Identity.* Washington, D.C.

Duboy, P. 1975. "Locus Solus, Carlo Scarpa et le cimetière de San Vito d'Altivole (1969–75)." *L'Architecture d'Aujourd'hui* 181 (September–October).

Focillon, H. 1963. *The Art of the West in the Middle Ages,* ed. Bony, trans. D. King. London.

Frampton, K. 1995. *Studies in Tectonic Culture: The Poetics of Construction in Nineteenth and Twentieth Century Architecture.* Cambridge, MA.

Frascari, M. 1985. "Carlo Scarpa in Magna Graecia: the Abatellis Palace in Palermo." *AA Files* 9, 3–9.

———. 1987. "The Body and Architecture in the Drawings of Carlo Scarpa." *Res* 14, 123–142.

———. 1991a. "A Deciphering of a Wonderful Cipher: Eleven in the Architecture of Carlo Scarpa." *OZ* 13, 36–41.

———. 1991b. *Monsters of Architecture: Anthropomorphism in Architectural Theory.* Savage, MD.

Gimbutas, M. 1989. *The Language of the Goddess.* San Francisco.

Goldscheider, L. (ed.). 1952. *Leonardo da Vinci, Landscapes and Plants.* London.

Graves, R. 1966. *The White Goddess.* New York.

Hertz, R. 1973. "The Pre-eminence of the Right Hand: A Study in Religious Polarity," in *Right and Left: Essays on Dual Symbolic Classification.* Chicago.

Hunt, J. D. 1981. "L'idea di un giardino del bel mezzo del mare." *Rassegna* 8, 56–65.

Jung, C. G. 1968. *Psychology and Alchemy,* trans. R. F. C. Hull. Princeton, NJ.

Keightley, T. 1877. *The Mythology of Ancient Greece and Italy.* London.

Lagerlöf, M. R. 1990. *Ideal Landscape: Annibale Carracci, Nicholas Poussin and Claude Lorrain.* New Haven, CT.

Matteini, M. 1991. *Pietro Porcinai: architetto del giardino e del paesaggio.* Milan.

Matter, E. A. 1990. *The Voice of My Beloved.* Philadelphia.

Mazzariol, G., and G. Barbieri. 1984. "Vita di Carlo Scarpa," in *Carlo Scarpa, Opera completa,* ed. F. Dal Co and G. Mazzariol. Milan.

Muir, E. 1981. *Civic Ritual in Renaissance Venice.* Princeton, NJ.

Pietropoli, G. 1990. "L'invitation au voyage." *Spazio e Società* 50 (April–June), 90–97.

Pignatti, T. 1994. "Giorgione and the Veneto Landscape," in *La terra di Giorgione,* ed. F. Rigon, T. Pignatti and F. Valconover, trans. J. Benison. Cittadella.

Ponti, G. 1957. *Amate l'architettura.* Genoa.

Pozza, N. 1976. *Tiziano.* Milan.

Ranalli, G. (ed.). 1984. *Carlo Scarpa: Drawings for the Brion Family Cemetery.* New Haven, CT.

Reynolds, J. 1997. *Discourses on Art,* ed. R. R. Wark. New Haven, CT. (Originally published 1997)

Rogers, E. N. 1958a. *Esperienza dell'architettura.* Turin.

———. 1958b. "Ampliamento della Gipsoteca Canoviana a Possagno (1956–57)." *Casabella continuità* 222.

Rosand, D. 1982. *Painting in Cinquecento Venice: Titian, Veronese, Tintoretto.* New Haven, CT.

———. 1992. "Pastoral Topoi: On the Construction of Meaning in Landscape," in *The Pastoral Landscape,* ed. J. D. Hunt. Washington, D.C.

Roussel, R. 1965. *Locus Solus.* Paris.

Saito, Yutaka. 1997. *Carlo Scarpa.* Tokyo.

Scarpa, C. c. 1972. "Una ora con Carlo Scarpa," *Incontri, Radio Televisione Italiana (RAI) television series,* ed. G. Favero. Video recording.

———. 1977. *Memoria Causa.* Verona.

———. 1978. Madrid Lecture, sound recording, Pietropoli Collection, Rovigo.

———. 1979. "Carlo Scarpa: Une Façon d'Enseigner, and La tombe de Monsieur Brion: Kann Architektur Poesie Sein?" trans. and anno. F. Semi, *Architecture Mouvement Continuité* 50, December, 21–27, 49–54.

———. 1981. "Volevo Ritagliare l'assurro del cielo." *Rassegna,* 7, 82–85.

———. 1985. "A Thousand Cypresses," in *Carlo Scarpa: The Complete Works,* ed. F. Dal Co and G. Mazzariol and trans. R. Sadleir. New York.

———. 1989. "Can Architecture Be Poetry?" in *The Other City: Carlo Scarpa,* ed. J. Wieninger and R. Haslinger. Berlin.

Schor, N. 1987. *Reading in Detail: Aesthetics and the Feminine.* New York.

Seddon, G. 1991. "The Brion Cemetery, S. Vito, Italy 1970–72." *Landscape Australia* 2, 146–147.

Sirén, O. 1949. *The Gardens of China.* New York.

Soper, K. 1995. *What Is Nature? Culture, Politics and the Non-Human.* Oxford.

Spengler, O. 1926. *The Decline of the West.* New York.

Stewart, S. 1966. *The Enclosed Garden: The Tradition and the Image in Seventeenth-Century Poetry.* Madison, WI.

Stewering, R. "The Relationship between World, Landscape, and Polia in the *Hypernotomachia Poliphili,*" trans. L. Maher. *Word and Image,* 14, nos. 1 & 2.

Tanner, T. 1992. *Venice Desired.* Cambridge, MA.

Walton, K. L. 1990. *Mimesis as Make-Believe: On the Foundations of the Representational Arts.* Cambridge, MA.

Wilde, J. 1974. *Venetian Art from Bellini to Titian.* Oxford.

Wind, E. 1964. *Art and Anarchy.* New York.

Chapter 16

Alberti, L. B. 1966. "De Iarchia," in *Opere Volgari,* ed. C. Grayson. Bari.

Barrault, J. Lo. 1951. *Reflections on the Theatre.* London.

Cacciari, M., and V. Pastor. 1989. "Composition Between Differentiation: Dialogue Between Valeriano Pastor and Massimo Cacciari." *Anfione Zeto,* 1, 194–202.

Clark, K. 1956. *The Nude: A Study in Ideal Form.* New York.

Colonna, F. 1980. *Hypnerotomachia Poliphili,* ed. G. Pozzi et al. Padua.

Dorcy, J. 1961. *The Mime.* New York.

Filarete (Antonio Averlino). 1972. *Trattato.* Milan.

Fino, F. 1988. *Il Paradiso dei Buoni Compagni.* Padua.

Fiocco, G. 1968. *Alvise Cornaro.* Vicenza.

Mignon, P.-L. 1999. *Jean-Louis Barrault. Le théâtre total.* Monaco.

Pastor, V. 1989. "Alcuni motivi del progetto." *Anfione Zeto* 1, 1989, 46–47.

Ruzzante (Angelo Beolco). 1967. *Teatro,* trans. and ed. L. Zorzi. Turin.

Sacks, O. 1987. *The Man Who Mistook His Wife for a Hat and Other Clinical Tales.* New York.

Schilder, P. 1950. *The Image and Appearance of the Human Body.* New York.

Seneca, Lucius Annaeus. 1965. "De vita beata," in *Moral Essays,* trans. J. W. Basore. Cambridge, MA.

Chapter 17

Baird, G. 1995. *The Space of Appearance.* Cambridge, MA.

Colomina, B. 1994. *Privacy and Publicity.* Cambridge, MA.

Czech, H., and W. Mistelbauer. 1984. *Das Looshaus.* Vienna.

Frank, J. 1910. "Über die ursprüngliche Gestalt der kirchlichen Bauten des Leone Battista Alberti." Ph.D. dissertation, Technischen Hochschule, Wien.

———. 1923. "Einselmöbel und Kunsthandwerk." *Innen-Dekoration* 34.

———. 1981. "Die Rolle der Architektur," in *Josef Frank 1885–1967,* ed. J. Spalt and H. Czech. Vienna.

Giella, B. 1995. "Buena Shore Club," in *R. M. Schindler Composition and Construction,* ed. L. March and J. Sheine. London.

Gravagnuolo, B. 1982. *Adolf Loos: Theory and Works.* Milan.

Heynen, H. 1999. *Architecture and Modernity.* Cambridge, MA.

Loos, A. 1981. "Von einem armen, reichen Manne," in *Ins Leere Gesprochen.* Vienna.

———. 1982. *Trotzdem.* Vienna.

Mackintosh, C. R. 1990. "Seemliness," in *Charles Rennie Mackintosh. The Architectural Papers,* ed. P. Robertson. Cambridge, MA.

Rykwert, J. 1982. *The Necessity of Artifice.* London.

Schindler, R. M. 1988. "Shelter or Playground," in A. Sarnitz, *R. M. Schindler Architect.* New York.

———. 1996. *The Furniture of R. M. Schindler,* ed. M. C. Berns. Santa Barbara, CA.

Ver Sacrum. 1900.

Wright, F. L. 1992. "Architect, Architecture, and the Client," [1896], in *Frank Lloyd Wright: Collected Writings,* vol. 1, ed. B. B. Pfeiffer. New York.

Wright, F. L. 1954. *The Natural House.* New York.

Wright, F. L. 1992. *Ausgeführte Bauten und Entwürfe von Frank Lloyd Wright,* in *Frank Lloyd Wright: Collected Writings,* vol. 1, ed. B. B. Pfeiffer. New York.

Chapter 18

Advertising Age, 1990. 61, December 3.

———. 1993. 64, March 29.

Architectural Record. 1993. "The Payne Whitney Gymnasium and Ray Tompkins House at Yale University, John Russell Pope, Architect." 73 (February).

Bataille, G. 1994. *The Absence of Myth: Writings on Surrealism.* London.

Boumphrey, G. 1935. "Façade and Function." *Architectural Review,* 77.

Bramwell, A. 1989. *Ecology in the 20th Century: A History.* New Haven, CT.

Browning, R. 1869. *The Ring and the Book.* London.

Cook, R. J. 1922. "Report of the Orthopedic Examination of 1393 Freshmen at Yale University." *Journal of Bone and Joint Surgery* 4 (April).

De Landa, M. 1997. *A Thousand Years of Non-Linear History.* New York.

Deleuze, G., and F. Guattari. 1987. *A Thousand Plateaus: Capitalism and Schizophrenia.* Minneapolis.

Douglas, M. 1966. *Purity and Danger: An Analysis of Concepts of Pollution and Taboo.* New York.

Giedion, S. 1948. *Mechanization Takes Command: A Contribution to Anonymous History.* New York.

Haeckel, E. 1902. *The Riddle of the Universe.* New York.

Kiesler, F. 1949. "Pseudo-Functionalism." *Partisan Review* 16 (July).

———. 1970. "The Magic Architecture of the Hall of Superstition," in *Surrealists on Art,* ed. L. R. Lippard. Englewood Cliffs, NJ.

Kipnis, J. 1993. "Towards a New Architecture," in *Architectural Design Profile No. 102: Folding in Architecture.* London.

Kiphuth, R., and W. Phelps. 1932. *The Diagnosis and Treatment of Postural Defects.* Baltimore.

Kiphuth, R., and S. J. Wickens. 1937. "The Body Mechanics Analysis of Yale University Freshmen." *Research Quarterly of the American Physical Education Association* 8 (December).

Klein, A., and L. Thomas. 1931. *Posture and Physical Fitness.* Washington, D.C.

Lahiji, N., and D. S. Friedman. 1997. "At the Sink: Architecture in Abjection," in *Plumbing: Sounding Modern Architecture.* New York.

Lynn, G. 1996. "Blobs (or Why Tectonics Is Square and Topology Is Groovy)." *ANY* 14.

Lynn, G. 1997. "An Advanced Form of Movement," *After Geometry, Architectural Design Profile No. 127.* London.

———. 1997. "From Body to Blob," in *Anybody,* ed. C. Davidson. New York.

Martin, E. 1994. *Flexible Bodies: Tracking Immunity in American Culture—From the Days of Polio to the Age of AIDS.* Boston.

MacEwan, C., and E. Howe. 1932. "An Objective Method of Grading Posture." *Research Quarterly of the American Physical Education Association* 3.

McLeod Bedford, S. 1994. "The Architectural Career of John Russell Pope." Ph.D. dissertation, Columbia University.

———. 1998. *John Russell Pope: Architect of Empire.* New York.

McLeod, M. 1994. "Undressing Architecture: Fashion, Gender, and Modernity," in *Architecture: In Fashion,* ed. D. Fausch et al. Princeton, NJ.

Mumford, L. 1934. *Technics and Civilization.* New York.

Nowicki, M. 1951. "Origins and Trends in Modern Architecture." *Magazine of Art.*

Robinson, C. 1993. "The Material Fold: Towards a Variable Narrative of Anomolous Topologies," in *Folding in Architecture, Architectural Design Profile No. 102.* London.

Speaks, M. 1998. "It's out There . . . the Formal Limits of the American Avant-Garde," in *Architectural Design Profile No. 133: Hypersurface Architecture.* London.

Stevenson, L. 1995. "Science down the Drain: On the Hostility of Certain Sanitarians to Animal Experimentation, Bacteriology, and Immunology." *Bulletin of the History of Medicine* 29.

Summers, D. 1989. "'Form,' Nineteenth-Century Metaphysics and the Problem of Art Historical Description." *Critical Inquiry* 15 (Winter).

———. 1993. "Form and Gender." *New Literary History* 24 (Spring).

———. 1994. *Visual Culture: Images and Interpretations.* Middletown, CT.

Tait McKenzie, R. 1923. *Exercise in Education and Medicine.* Philadelphia.

Wigley, M. 1995. *White Walls, Designer Dresses: The Fashioning of Modern Architecture.* Cambridge, MA.

Chapter 19

Ando, T. 1980. "The Emotionally Made Architectural Spaces of Tadao Ando." *Japan Architect* 276 (April).

———. 1986. "Tadao Ando: Rokko Housing," in *Quaderni di Casabella.* Milan.

———. 1987. "Ce que le terrain nous raconte." *AMC* 250, 46.

———. 1988. "Shintai and Space," in *Architecture and Body.* New York.

———. 1995a. "From the Church on the Water to the Church of the Light," in *Tadao Ando, Complete Works,* ed. F. Dal Co. London.

———. 1995b. "From the Periphery of Architecture," in *Tadao Ando, Complete Works,* ed. F. Dal Co. London.

———. 1995c. "Light," in *Tadao Ando, Complete Works,* ed. F. Dal Co. London.

———. 1995d. "Shintai and Space," in *Tadao Ando, Complete Works,* ed. F. Dal Co. London.

Gartner, S. 1990. "The Corporeal Imagination: The Body as the Medium of Expression and Understanding in Architecture," in *The Architecture of the In-Between: The Proceedings of the 1990 ACSA Annual Conference.* San Francisco.

Johnson, M. 1987. *The Body in the Mind.* Chicago.

Maruyama, H. 1995. "Interview with Tadao Ando," in *Tadao Ando, Complete Works,* ed. F. Dal Co. London.

Rimer, T. 1981. Introduction to *From the Country of Eight Islands,* ed. and trans. H. Sato and B. Watson. Seattle, WA.

Tanizaki, J. 1977. *In Praise of Shadows,* trans. T. J. Harper and E. Seidensticker. New Haven, CT.

Tominaga, Y. 1995. "Reflections on the Architecture of Tadao Ando," in *Tadao Ando: Complete Works,* ed. F. Dal Co. London.

Aerial view of a design project
for a new museum adjacent
to Salisbury Cathedral, England.
2000 © Daniel Libeskind

A list of principal publications
compiled by Anne Engel

Bibliography of Joseph Rykwert

Books

The Golden House, Froshaug, Penzance, 1947.

The Idea of a Town, C. van Saane, "Lectura Architectonica," Hilversum, 1963; second edition, Faber & Faber, London, and Princeton University Press, 1976; Einaudi, Turin 1981, Blume Madrid 1985; third edition, MIT Press, Cambridge, MA, 1988; Misuzu Shobo, Tokyo 1991. Second Italian edition, Adelphi, Milan 2002.

Church Building, Burns & Oates, London 1966.

On Adam's House in Paradise, Museum of Modern Art, New York 1972; Adelphi, Milan 1972; Gili, Barcelona 1975 and 2000; Seuil, Paris 1976; Second edition, Mondadori, Milan 1977, MIT Press, Cambridge, MA 1982; third edition, Adelphi, Milan 1991; Kajima, Tokyo, 1994; Chinese, German, and Brazilian forthcoming.

The First Moderns: The Architects of the Eighteenth Century, MIT Press 1980 and 1984; Gili, Barcelona 1982; Mondadori, Milan 1986, Hazan, Paris 1991.

The Necessity of Artifice, Academy Editions, London 1982 and Rizzoli, New York 1982; Dumont Buchverlag, Cologne 1983; second edition, Mondadori, Milan 1989.

James and Robert Adam; the Men, the Style (with Anne Rykwert), Electa Editrice, Milan 1984; Rizzoli International, New York, and William Collins, London 1985; Deutsche Verlags-Anstalt, Frankfurt 1987.

L'Architettura e le Altre Arti, Jaca Books, Milan 1993.

The Dancing Column: On Order in Architecture, MIT Press, Cambridge, MA, 1996 and Adelphi, Milan 2005.

The Seduction of Place: The City in the Twenty-first Century, Pantheon Books, New York, and Weidenfeld & Nicolson, London 2000.

Translations and Editions

The Ten Books on Architecture by L. B. Alberti, edited by J. Rykwert, A. Tiranti, London 1955.

Parole nel Vuoto, by Adolf Loos, Adelphi, Milan 1972.

On the Art of Building in Ten Books of L. B. Alberti: a new translation and commentary (with Neil Leach and Robert Tavernor), MIT Press, Cambridge, MA, 1988 and 1991.

Leon Battista Alberti, ed. (with Anne Engel), catalogue to accompany the exhibition held at the Palazzo Te, Mantua, September–December 1994.

Longer Essays Contributed to Books and Exhibition Catalogues

"Modern Times," in *Art, Artists and Thinkers,* Longmans, London 1958.

"Passé Récent et Problèmes Actuels de l'Art Sacré," in *Le Catholicisme Anglais,* Editions du Cerf, Paris 1958.

"Meaning and Building," in *Meaning in Architecture,* ed. G. Baird and C. Jencks, Barrie & Rockliff, London 1969; in French as *Le Sens de la Ville,* Seuil, Paris 1972; in Spanish by G. Gili, Barcelona 1976.

"Letters on Rhetoric" (with George Baird and Gui Bonsiepe), *Konzept 2,* Wasmuth, Tübingen 1976.

"Gottfried Semper on Style," in *Gottfried Semper und die Mitte des 19. Jahrhunderts,* edited Adolf Max Vogt et al, Birkhäuser, Zürich 1976.

"Learning from the Street," in *Streets as Elements of Urban Structure,* ed. Stanford Anderson, MIT Press, Cambridge, MA 1977.

"On Strata in the Kitchen," in *The Anthropologist's Cookbook,* ed. Jessica Kuper, Routledge & Kegan Paul, London 1977; reprinted London 1999; French as *La Cuisine des Ethnologues,* Berger-Levrault, Paris 1981.

"Aktuelle Positionen in der Architektur," in *Opposition zur Moderne,* Fr. Vieweg & Sohn, Braunschweig 1980.

"In the Nature of Materials: A Rational Theory of Architecture," in *Solitary Travelers,* Cooper Union School of Architecture, New York 1980.

"A Healthy Mind in a Healthy Body," in *History in, of and for Architecture,* Cincinnati 1981.

"The Ecole des Beaux-Arts and the Classical Tradition," in *The Ecole des Beaux-Arts and Nineteenth Century French Architecture,* ed. R. Middleton, Cambridge, MA, and London 1982.

"Jean-Nicolas-Louis Durand and the Perils of Eclectic Indifference," in *Giuseppe Jappelli e il suo Tempo,* ed. Giuliana Mazzi, Liviana Editrice, Padua 1982.

"Het Idee van een Stad," in *Het Idee van de Stad,* ed. Jan Brand and Han Janselijn, Arnhem, Netherlands 1983.

"Rituale e Isteria," in *Segni Erratici,* ed. Norma Lupi, Rome 1984.

"Die Stadt unter dem Strich: eine Bilanz," in *Modelle für eine Stadt,* Siedler Verlag, Berlin 1984.

"Organisch, Mechanisch, Funktionell—Terminologie oder Ideologie?" in *Das Abenteuer der Ideen, Architektur und Philosophie seit der Industriellen Revolution,* ed. Vittorio Magnago Lampugnani, IBA Berlin 1984, in Italian as *L'Avventura delle Idee,* XVII Triennale, Milan 1985.

"Construction du Corps et Souvenir de la Ville," in *Ville et Projets,* Mardaga, Brussels 1986.

"Cities," in *World Encyclopedia of Religion,* ed. M. Eliade. Macmillan, New York 1987.

Preface, *Gio Ponti: Cento Lettere,* R. Archinto, Milan 1987.

"Repenser la Rue," in *La Ville Inquiète,* Ed. Gallimard, Paris 1987.

"On the Oral Transmission of Architectural Theory," in *Les Traités d'Architecture de la Renaissance,* ed. Jean Guillaume, Picard, Paris 1988.

"Architecture," Vol. 9, Since the Second World War, Cambridge, 1988; Introduction, Vol. 4: The Seventeenth Century, 1989, *The Cambridge Guide to the Arts in Britain,* ed. Boris Ford.

"Sigfried Giedion, Der Entwurf einer modernen Tradition," in *Die Ewige Gegenwart,* Ammann Verlag, Zürich 1989.

"Gottfried Semper: Architect and Historian," in *Gottfried Semper: The Four Elements of Architecture,* ed. Harry Mallgrave, Cambridge University Press, 1989.

"Body and Mind," in *Storia delle Idee, Problemi e Prospettive,* ed. Massimo L. Bianchi, Edizioni dell' Ateneo, Rome 1989.

"Mécanique et Organique," in *Composer le Paysage,* ed. Odile Marcel, Collection Milieux, Champ Vallon, Paris 1989.

Preface to *Arquitectura Española Contemporánea,* Ed. Gustavo Gili S. A., Barcelona 1990.

"Für die Stadt—Argumente für ihre Zukunft," in *Die Welt der Stadt,* ed. Tilo Schabert, Piper, Munich 1991.

"Off Limits: City Pattern and City Texture," in *Constancy and Change in Architecture,* ed. M. Quantrill and B. Webb, Texas A&M, 1991.

"When Diogenes . . . ," *Radical Scavengers,* ed. Richard Francis, Museum of Contemporary Art, Chicago, February 1994.

El Museo, *Museos y arquitectura, nuevas perspectivas,* ed. Martha Thorne, Circulo de Bellas Artes, Madrid, May 1994.

"Windows and Architects," in *The Architecture of the Window,* ed. V. M. Lampugnani, Tokyo, 1995.

"Landscapes and Ecology: City and Countryside," edited Paul Bairoch, *Einaudi History of Europe,* Vol. V, Turin 1997.

"Il Concetto di 'organico' e la Critica dell'Architettura in Mumford," *Alle Radici della Città Contemporanea, Il Pensiero di Lewis Mumford,* ed. Francesco Ventura, Milan 1997.

"Theory as Rhetoric: Leon Battista Alberti in Theory and in Practice," *Paper Palaces,* ed. Vaughan Hart and Peter Hicks, Yale University Press, New Haven, CT 1998.

Preface to *The Palladian Ideal,* Rizzoli, New York 1999.

"Second Thoughts," *Visionary Clients for New Architecture,* ed. P. Noever, Vienna 2000.

Preface to *The Villa,* Abrams, New York 2000.

Preface to *Louis Kahn,* Abrams, New York 2001.

Published Verse

Images of Tomorrow (Anthology, ed. J. Heath-Stubbs) SCM Press, London 1953.

Points, Paris 1951.

Time and Tide, London.

Art International, Lugano, Summer 1973.

Articles and Reviews in

Abitare

A + U (Architecture and Urbanism)

A + V (Arquitectura y Vivienda)

Architect's Journal

Architectural Association Files

Architectural Association Quarterly

Architectural Design

Architectural Digest

Architectural Forum

Architectural Record

Architectural Review

Architecture and Building

Arquitecturas Bis

Art in America

Art Monthly

Burlington Magazine

Casabella

Connaissance des Arts

Critique

Daidalos

Design Book Review

Diogène

Domus

Eighteenth-Century Studies

Faces

FMR

Freibeuter

Harpers and Queens

House and Garden

The Independent

Journal of the Society of Architectural Historians

The Listener

Los Angeles Times

Lotus

New Republic

New Society

New York Review of Books
Nuovi Argomenti
October
Oppositions
Perspecta
Preuves
Quinzaine Littéraire
Religion
RES
RIBA Journal
Sciences, Paris
Social Research
Spazio e Societa
The Spectator
The Sunday Correspondent
The Tablet
Time and Tide
The Times Literary Supplement
Trace
Umriss
Universities Quarterly

Contributors

George Baird

William Braham

George Dodds

Paul Emmons

Marcia F. Feuerstein

Kenneth Frampton

Marco Frascari

Vittorio Gregotti

Karsten Harries

Vaughan Hart

Neil Leach

David Leatherbarrow

Harry Francis Mallgrave

John Onians

Alina Payne

Simon Pepper

Alberto Pérez-Gómez

Richard Sennett

Robert Tavernor

Dalibor Vesely

Mark Wilson Jones

George Baird is G. Ware Travelstead Professor of Architecture at the Graduate School of Design at Harvard University and partner in Baird Sampson Neuert Architects Inc. of Toronto, Canada. Baird Sampson Neuert and its predecessor firm won Canadian Architect Awards of Excellence in 1984, 1985, and 1994 and the Governor-General's Medal for Architecture in 1996. The firm's recent Cloud Gardens park has been published in *Canadian Architect, Architecture Magazine,* and *The Architectural Review.* Baird was awarded the 1992 Architecture and Design Award of the Toronto Arts Foundation. He is the coeditor (with Charles Jencks) of *Meaning in Architecture* (1969) and author of *Alvar Aalto* (1970) and *The Space of Appearance* (1995). He is currently working on *A New Theory of Public Space.*

William Braham is a member of the architecture faculty at the University of Pennsylvania. He has worked as an architect, lighting designer, planner, and solar energy consultant, investigating the much-contested boundary between architecture and technology. His recent research addresses the many facets of the environmental technologies, including lighting, daylighting, color, and sustainability. He has recently completed a book titled *Modern Color/Modern Architecture* and is currently working on a study of Reyner Banham, called *Not Quite Architecture.*

George Dodds earned his master's degrees in theory and design and his Ph.D. in Architecture from the University of Pennsylvania. His dissertation was *Landscape and Garden in the Work of Carlo Scarpa*. He has taught and lectured in Europe and the United States and is on the editorial board of the *Journal of Architectural Education* (2002–2005). He is currently an Assistant Professor and the coordinator of history and theory for the College of Architecture and Design at the University of Tennessee.

Paul Emmons is an architect and assistant professor of architecture at the Washington Alexandria Architecture Center of Virginia Tech and is currently completing a Ph.D. at the University of Pennsylvania. He writes, designs, and produces artwork about issues of representation in architecture.

Marcia F. Feuerstein is assistant professor of architecture at Virginia Polytechnic and State University. She is chair of the International Archive of Women in Architecture and editor of its annual newsletter, and is on the board of directors of the Blue Ridge Chapter of the AIA. She received the bachelor of science from Tufts University, the master in architecture from the State University of New York at Buffalo, and both the master of science and the Ph.D. in architecture from the University of Pennsylvania. Her publications include *Changing Places: ReMaking Institutional Buildings* (1992) and *Hands On Architecture—Design Guide* (1986).

Kenneth Frampton is the Ware Professor of Architecture at Columbia University. He studied architecture at the AA in London, and has worked as an architect in England, Israel, and the United States. He has written extensively and contributed to numerous journals. His publications include: *Modern Architecture: A Critical History*; *Modern Architecture 1851 to 1945*; *American Masterworks* (1995); and *Studies in Tectonic Culture* (1995).

Marco Frascari is the G. T. Ward Professor of Architecture and the Coordinator of Architectural Representation and Education study option at the Alexandria Campus of the College of Architecture and Urban Studies, Environmental Design and Planning Ph.D. Program, Virginia Polytechnic Institute and State University. He is the author of *Monsters of Architecture: Anthropomorphism in Architectural Theory* (1991).

Vittorio Gregotti graduated in architecture from Milan Polytechnic and practiced in Novara from 1954 to 1967 and then in Milan (first at Architetti Associati and since 1974 Gregotti Associati). He has designed many buildings in Italy, France, Germany, Spain, and

Portugal and has also worked in the Middle East and North Africa. Having won the competition for the Bicocca quarter of Milan in 1985, he has become the planner-architect of a new town. Gregotti has been professor of architecture in Venice since 1976 and director of visual arts at the Venice Biennale. He has written several books and edited *Casabella* from 1982 until 1997 and *Rassegna* since its foundation. He has taught at most major architectural schools.

Karsten Harries is professor of philosophy at Yale University. Born in Jena, Germany, he has published and lectured widely on Heidegger, early modern philosophy, and the philosophy of art and architecture. He has coedited with Christoph Jamme *Martin Heidegger: Kunst, Politik, Technik* (1992), which appeared in an English version as *Martin Heidegger: Politics, Art, and Technology* (1994). He is the author of more than 140 articles and reviews and of five books: *The Meaning of Modern Art* (1968), *The Bavarian Rococo Church: Between Faith and Aestheticism* (1983), *The Broken Frame: Three Lectures* (1990), and *The Ethical Function of Architecture* (1997), and *Infinity and Perspective* 2001. The American Institute of Architects awarded him the 8th Annual International Architecture Book Award for Criticism for *The Ethical Function of Architecture.*

Vaughan Hart is reader in architectural history at the University of Bath. He directs the Centre for Advanced Studies in Architecture at Bath. His books include *Art and Magic in the Court of the Stuarts* (1994), *St. Paul's Cathedral: Sir Christopher Wren* (1995), *Sebastiano Serlio on Architecture* (with Peter Hicks, 1996), and *Paper Palaces: The Rise of the Renaissance Architectural Treatise* (with Peter Hicks, 1998).

Neil Leach is professor of architectural theory at the University of Bath and course master at the Architectural Association. He is cotranslator (with Robert Tavernor and Joseph Rykwert) of *Leon Battista Alberti: On the Art of Building in Ten Books* (1988) and the author of *Millennium Culture* (1999) and *The Anaesthetics of Architecture* (1999). He is the editor of *Rethinking Architecture: A Reader in Cultural Theory* (1997), *Architecture and Revolution: Contemporary Perspectives on Central and Eastern Europe* (1999), *The Hieroglyphics of Space* (2002) and *E-Futures* (2002).

David Leatherbarrow is professor of architecture and chairman of the Ph.D. program at the University of Pennsylvania, where he has taught architectural design and theory since 1984. He studied architecture at the University of Kentucky and completed his Ph.D. at the University of Essex. In his scholarly work he has published most recently *Ground:*

Architecture, Technology and Topography (2000); *Surface Architecture,* with Mohsen Mosta-favi (forthcoming 2002); *The Roots of Architectural Invention: Site, Enclosure and Materials* and *On Weathering: The Life of Buildings in Time,* with Mohsen Mostafavi, which won the 1995 International Book Award in architectural theory from the American Institute of Architects. His awards include a Visiting Scholars Fellowship at the Centre Canadien d'Architecture, the Cass Gilbert Distinguished Professorship at the University of Minnesota, and a Fulbright Hays scholarship for study in Great Britain.

Harry Francis Mallgrave received his doctorate from the University of Pennsylvania in 1983. Since 1986 he has served as editor of architecture and aesthetics of the Texts and Documents series for the Getty Research Institute for the History of Art and the Humanities. He has authored and translated various works related to German architectural theory and aesthetics. His most recent book, *Gottfried Semper: Architect of the Nineteenth Century,* won the 1997 Alice Davis Hitchcock Award of the Society of Architectural Historians.

John Onians was trained as a classical archaeologist at the University of Cambridge and as an art historian at the Courtauld and Warburg Institutes, London. He was the founding editor of the journal *Art History.* Among his books are *Art and Thought in the Hellenistic Age* (1979), *Bearers of Meaning: The Classical Orders in Antiquity, the Middle Ages and the Renaissance* (1988), and *Classical Art and the Cultures of Greece and Rome* (1999). He is editing *Atlas of World Art* and writing *A Natural History of Art,* an account of the biological origins of artistic activity. He has taught at institutions in the Czech Republic, France, India, Italy, the Netherlands, and the United States and is currently director of the World Art Research Program in the School of World Art Studies at the University of East Anglia, Norwich, England, and consultative chair, Research and Academic Programs, Clark Art Institute.

Alina Payne is professor of architectural history in the Department of Fine Art, University of Toronto. She is the author of *The Architectural Treatise in the Italian Renaissance. Architectural Invention, Ornament and Literary Culture* (1999), coeditor of *Antiquity and Its Interpreters* (2000), and author of numerous articles on Renaissance and modern architecture.

Simon Pepper is a professor of architecture at the University of Liverpool. He received his Ph.D. from the University of Essex and held a scholarship at the British School at Rome for his early research on Renaissance military architecture. He has published (with Nicholas Adams) *Firearms and Fortifications: Military Architecture and Siege Warfare in Sixteenth*

Century Siena (1986) and (also with Nicholas Adams) contributed to the *Architectural Drawings of Antonio da Sangallo the Younger and His Circle* (1993), in addition to numerous articles and books on twentieth-century social housing.

Alberto Pérez-Gómez is director of the graduate program in the history and theory of architecture at McGill University. He obtained his undergraduate degree in architecture and engineering in Mexico City, did postgraduate work at Cornell University, and was awarded an M.A. and a Ph.D. by the University of Essex in England. He was appointed director of the Carleton University School of Architecture from 1983 to 1986 and in 1987 Saidye Rosner Bronfman Professor of the History of Architecture at McGill University. Between 1990 and 1993 he was also the director of the Institut de recherche en histoire de l'architecture, a research institute cosponsored by the Canadian Centre for Architecture, the Université de Montréal, and McGill University. Pérez-Gómez is the author of *Architecture and the Crisis of Modern Science* (1983), which won the Alice Davis Hitchcock Award in 1984, and *Polyphilo or The Dark Forest Revisited* (1992); coauthor of *Architectural Representation and the Perspective Hinge* (1997); and coeditor of the new series *Chora: Intervals in the Philosophy of Architecture*. He has also published two books of poetry in Spanish.

Richard Sennett is Centennial Professor of Sociology at the London School of Economics and Political Science, where he teaches on "The Cities Programme." His recent books include *The Conscience of the Eye* (1990) and *Flesh and Stone: The Body and the City in Western Civilization* (1994).

Robert Tavernor is professor and chair of architecture at the University of Bath. He studied architecture in London, the British School at Rome, and Cambridge University, where he graduated with a Ph.D. and as a registered architect. He was appointed Forbes Professor of Architecture at the University of Edinburgh (1992–1995) and in 1998 was Visiting Professor at the Center for Medieval and Renaissance Studies, UCLA. With Joseph Rykwert he curated the international exhibition "Leon Battista Alberti," for Olivetti of Italy (Mantua, Italy, September 1994). As an academic writer, he cotranslated and edited the fifteenth-century Latin treatise on architecture by Leon Battista Alberti, published as *On the Art of Building, in Ten Books* (1988), and the sixteenth-century Italian treatise by Andrea Palladio, published as *Andrea Palladio: The Four Books on Architecture* (1997). He is the author of *Palladio and Palladianism* (1991) and *On Alberti and the Art of Building* (1998).

Dalibor Vesely studied architecture, history of art, and philosophy in Prague and Munich. He has worked and taught in the United Kingdom from 1968 at the Architecture Association, and the University of Essex. He has held a lectureship at the University of Cambridge since 1978 and has taught and codirected the master of philosophy program in the history and philosophy of architecture since 1985. He has held visiting professorships at Princeton, Harvard, and the Central European University in Prague. He is a member of the Advisory Committee of the Czech Academy of Sciences. The work on which he lectures and writes is focused on the phenomenology of architecture—more specifically, on the role of the sciences and humanities in current architecture, the problem of representation, the nature and role of fragment as a critical dimension of modernity, and creativity in the age of production. He is the author of a forthcoming book, *Architecture and Divided Representation* (MIT Press).

Mark Wilson Jones received his first degree in architecture at Cambridge University and a diploma in architecture from the Polytechnic of Central London (now University of Westminster), completing his education with the award of a two-year tenure of the Rome Prize in Architecture at the British School at Rome. This experience inspired an archaeological dimension to his historical research, bearing fruit in a series of articles in leading archaeological journals and the book *Principles of Roman Architecture* (2000). He was the 1997–1998 Kress lecturer for the Archaeological Institute of America and has been visiting professor at the School of Architecture of the University of Virginia and at the University of Rome La Sapienza. He has designed or built architectural, urban, and interior design projects in England and elsewhere in Europe and teaches at the University of Bath.

Index